Forgetting Jack

By Julie Finn

Julie Finn lives and works in West Lancashire with her family. She runs her own floristry business together with her husband. She has spent time teaching floristry in colleges in the North West.

All the characters in this publication are fictitious and any resemblance to real persons either living or dead is purely coincidental.

ISBN 1484141091

Copyright ©Julie Finn 2013

This book is dedicated to:

My Husband Maurice for putting up with me on a daily basis.

My children Matt and Maisie for forgiving me when I miss events and weekends due to work.

My Mother Marion, for having the desire to be a florist in the first place and being a strong role model.

All my family and friends, who have been supportive in my endeavour to write, you know who you are.

The Recent Past.

Annie Pickering opened the back doors of the florist's van wide, to reveal the beautiful and elegant floral tribute. The fragrance from the white oriental lilies, white avalanche roses and eucalyptus foliage that had been contained within, dissipated as it hit the air. Annie walked up the ramp on the outside of the building and made her way to the back door of 'Whittaker's Funeral Home'. She had been here many times before, always on someone else's behalf, for a husband, wife, brother, sister, son or daughter who was devastated by the loss of a loved one. For Annie, flowers were an important part of the funeral ceremony, symbolising the temporary beauty of life and its fragility. At work, Annie would listen intently as fragments of the deceased person's life story would be shared by their relative or friend, and then she would suggest a suitable and fitting tribute to be designed and delivered just as she was doing now, but this time it had been created and designed to her own specifications, it was for someone she had lost. This tribute was for her Husband - Nick.

Annie walked through the foyer with walls covered in pastel peach shades, the undertaker Stephen came from behind a closed door to meet her. A vase of fresh spray carnations and wax flower sat on a small coffee table. There were two chairs; one positioned either side of the table. In the countless times that Annie had delivered to Whittaker's, she had never seen anyone sit in them; still, they had to fill the space with something.

The aroma in this funeral parlour was the same as every other she had ever been in. She wondered if they all bought the same fragrance from the supply catalogue showing the latest casket designs. 'Eau de parlour' was her pet name for it, the only thing she could liken it to was an old lady's smell – a mix of rose water, talc, lavender and bleach, certainly distinctive, not necessarily pleasant.

Stephen greeted her with the necessary formality associated with such occasions.

'Annie – How are you today? Have you come to see Nick?' he enquired looking at her with well-rehearsed sympathetic eyes.

'Yes.' she sighed, 'I've brought the flowers for tomorrow. They're in the van.'

'Nick's through here.' Said Stephen leading her through to the Chapel of rest. Stephen stood back indicating that Annie should go in alone. Her eyes settled on the curtains at the frosted glass window, which were made of heavy blue velvet, she wondered if they were obligatory for funeral parlours too.

'I'll leave you two alone for a little while whilst I get the flowers.' said Stephen before pulling the door closed behind him as he left the room.

She re-focused her eyes on to the scratched foot of an old brown dining chair that stood to her right, the kind with a sagging leather seat in the middle that should have been put out to retirement after the Second World War. It was obviously intended for those who were too over come to stand at the side of the coffin or for those who were there for the long haul. Annie concentrated on anything available to avoid looking into the casket. It wasn't the fact that she had never seen a dead body that stopped her from looking – in her line of work it was hard to avoid. She had seen several people toe tagged, waiting to be pampered and dressed in their 'Sunday Best' or 'Angel Gabriel's' smock. It was the fear of the reality about to hit her that she was trying to delay. Her world of numbness and disbelief was about to be shattered. The moment she looked at his still lifeless form, she would have to admit that he was gone, their life together had gone and it was never going to be the same again. The tape that kept running inside her head shouting *'No, No it can't be true!'* was going to tear and break.

Eventually she drew all the strength she had inside together and slowly moved her eyes upwards from the floor, on to the coffin and ultimately she forced herself to look at Nick for the very last time. The body in the coffin didn't look like Nick to Annie. There was no essence of vitality, even his facial features looked different - unrecognisable. He did look peaceful and for that she was grateful. Seeing him without that twinkle in his eyes that he had always had, in some ways made it easier to bear. She didn't feel as if the was burying Nick – where he was she didn't know, but he wasn't here now, in this box. The body in this box was merely his shell.

Annie had opted to hold the funeral at the earliest convenience of the undertakers. She wanted the whole event over with as soon as possible, for her daughter Violets' sake as much as her own. They had already had to wait for the body to be released, which she was assured normal procedure after an accident, but living in 'limbo land' was not something Annie could do easily. The days were endless, as were the nights. Sleep was fitful, sporadic and scarce. She hated waiting for other people to arrange things. She was far too practical herself. Nick was always mocking her- had always mocked her, she corrected herself. He had tried to encourage her light-hearted side by suggesting things like midnight walks, splashing in puddles, dancing in the middle of the shopping centre to the piped music on a Saturday afternoon – silly senseless things, but her practicality always came out on top and won, squashing his sense of fun and telling him to 'grow up'. Annie had never been able to lose herself in the moment; she did that once as a teenager and had spent her whole life living with the consequences. All she could think about was how she would ultimately end up wet and cold or someone she knew would see her, any reason she could grasp – now she wished she'd given in. She would have those extra memories to keep her company in the dark days she was living now and those that were bound to be ahead – but it was too late now for spontaneity.

Chapter 1

Violet stood at the window watching the rain making random patterns on the glass. Annie studied her daughter; she knew she was watching and waiting for the arrival of the hearse. It broke Annie's heart to see her young, beautiful child without her father. At fifteen Violet was just about to get started on 'life', now Nick wouldn't be there to help direct her. No 'soft touch' to even up the 'tough love' that Annie was so good at dishing out. Violet was the original 'Daddy's girl' – she always had been. Sometimes Annie felt superfluous to requirements, the bond between them seemed impenetrable. Any problems Violet had with school or homework, she always took them to her father. Annie had never known why Violet found it hard to confide in her, for no particular reason it had always been that way. Now Annie was going to have work hard to make Violet think differently. Violet would certainly need to have someone to talk to and Annie needed it to be her.

Violet slowly turned away from the window. 'They're here.' She whispered looking at her mother with pleading eyes as if to say, *'Please tell me this is a great big hoax and we don't have to go through with this?'* The hearse pulled to a standstill in front of the house. Annie could see Stephen getting out of the car, preparing to come and get them. Annie moved across to Violet and put her arm around her shoulders.

'We can do this Violet – let's do it together for dad.' She said giving her a loving squeeze. They hugged spontaneously with force, willing strength to be carried from one to the other through osmosis. Violet looked at her mother, trying to fight back the tears.

'Do you think he felt anything – when it happened?' Violet asked, pulling back slightly in order to see her mother's true response. She didn't want to be lied to, just so she would feel better, she had to know the truth. Please God, she hoped he hadn't suffered.

'Darling, you were there when the police told us - that he wouldn't have known anything. He didn't suffer. I promise you.' It's just the people that are left who suffer thought Annie silently. Violet accepted the answer she was given, to dispute it would have been unbearable to live with.

The awaited knock was placed on the front door. 'Will you stay close to me?' said Violet eventually releasing her mother from their hug and taking her hand.

'Just you try and stop me.' Said Annie placing a kiss on Violets forehead.

The small group of friends and family had moved from inside to out and gathered under dark umbrellas. There was silence as Annie and Violet walked out of the house. Annie paused by the hearse before getting in to the large black Mercedes. Stephen, the undertaker held an umbrella over their heads to keep the worst of the rain off them, but with the wind driving the rain, it was futile. From the back seat of the car, Annie's eyes were drawn to the flowers on the top of the coffin which had been made with such love the day before. There were several smaller tributes from family, friends and work colleagues. There would be time enough later to look at them and collect the cards. At least the hearse was full of flowers. Nick was loved and people cared. Making the floral tribute was the last thing she could do for Nick. All her years of floristry training were not in vain. The flowers had to be special for him – and they were.

At the same time in Australia.

On the other side of the world Jack Parrish was helping his mother sort through his Father's belongings. Jack had flown back immediately from America, to be with his mother, when the news had reached him of his father's death. His Father had suffered a clot on his brain, which had caused his instant death. Jack felt numb when he heard the news; he had been unable to show any emotion so far, to say that the relationship between them was strained was an understatement. His mother was sure he was still in shock, Jack knew otherwise. The relationship between father and Son had never been close. It was no use pretending now. It wasn't that he had no love for his father, but a strained relationship over many years had caused Jack to build tall, strong barriers, for self-preservation. The grieving process for his father had taken place a long time ago. Jack felt as if he were at the funeral of an old acquaintance, someone he knew once, but hadn't seen in years. The only reason he attended the funeral was for his mother's sake. Jack personally didn't care much one way or the other.

The church and the crematorium had been full of unfamiliar faces, all claiming to be great friends with his father. Jack had no idea if any of these statements were true or not. Jack and his mother, Marcia, were the only family at the service. They ploughed through the day mumbling words of thanks in exchange for words of sorrow from the strangers. The list of platitudes grew with each person Jack spoke to. None of the expressions of sympathy had any meaning for Jack; the words weren't a true reflection of the man Jack knew. John Parrish had been a popular member of the business community and golf clubs around Sydney, but not the most popular member of his family. No one from England, not even his Sister had bothered to make the long journey to see him depart this mortal earth. Part of Jack felt pity for his father and the life he had led, but that was because Jack was a very different kind of person to his father. John Parrish would have shown no remorse or sorrow at having so few family members present at his funeral - if he could have commented. He was more concerned about how he was regarded in the wider world, especially his business colleagues. To John Parrish the people at work were his family.

On the day after the funeral Jack began to tackle the mountainous job of sorting his father's financial affairs. John Parrish's office at home was everything you would expect of a business man. It contained a large desk with a black leather chair, which had been designed especially for him. The walls were painted in a masculine, bold shade of 'Warrior Red', a few pieces of art and sculpture to show any visitors that he was a man of knowledge and refinement, then the room was finished with various trophies and certificates, especially from his beloved golf, all to showcase his achievements. A few photographs had been carefully selected and displayed on the walls. Jack looked at each one in detail hoping that at least one of them would hold a surprise, showing a side of his father he hadn't known or that Jack had forgotten existed – but there was nothing. All the pictures were of business colleagues or winning trophies. Not one contained a photo of Jack or Marcia – The photo's said it all.

The task of sorting through his father's affairs was an undertaking Jack could have well done without, but his mother was absolutely clueless when it came to the financial side of running the house. This was mainly due to his Father's insistence on being in control of all areas. His mother was going to find it difficult to adapt. In all of her married life, she had never had to pay a bill, but she would have to learn. Jack was sat in his father's chair, going through all the papers trying to put in place a simple system for his mother to use in paying the household expenses. Marcia was showing no interest in finding out what she needed to do, but to be fair, Jack realised she had just buried her husband and paperwork was the last thing on her mind. He made an executive decision to find all the main day to day bills and see that they were paid. This would at least buy her a little time to come to terms with the new role she had acquired. He also made the decision to put as many of the bills on-line as possible, that way, if she was struggling, he could take control no matter where he was in the world. He would sort anything else as the need arose. He had made a start on clearing his father's desk yesterday, after the funeral. He chatted to the numerous strangers for as long as he could tolerate, then he quietly slipped away to his father's office. Once there, it seemed natural to start organising things for his mother. There was one document he was looking for specifically, that his mother had not been able to locate, his father's life insurance policy, it was eluding him. He had tried the shelves, the desk and all the drawers, but it was not to be found. Eventually fatigue set in and when he was sure all the guests had departed he made his way to his old bedroom and to sleep.

Jack had resumed his search early in the morning, starting in the filing cabinet. He searched through each document in detail. By the time he had reached the bottom drawer, he was beginning to believe he would never find it. He pulled the draw open and heaved the contents on to the desk. He went through each document in turn, but the life insurance policy was nowhere to be found. He was about to put everything back in the cabinet and try his luck in the sideboard, when out of the corner of his eye he noticed a pile of letters tied together with an elastic band, they had been pushed to the back of the filing cabinet, behind the draw, almost as if they were being concealed on purpose. He reached in and pulled them out. Jack recognised the handwriting immediately, although it had been many years since he had seen it. Suddenly he went cold. He sat back in the chair holding the bundle of letters - he was very confused. Why did his father have a collection of letters from Annie in his filing cabinet? He slid the letters out of the elastic band and took each one out and read it carefully, line by line, word by word. The bottom half of the pile, he discovered were the letters he had written to Annie, all of them without a post mark. Dis-belief swallowed him. As he read Annie's letters he constantly shook his head unbelieving the words on the paper in front of him. The contents of these timeworn letters were life changing. His breathing became deep and strong, his nostrils flared and his pupils dilated. Anger reigned within him; all other emotions had been blocked. The veins in his temples stood out from his forehead announcing his fury. They started to pulsate. In a rage of temper he swung his arm out to the front and knocked his father's desk lamp hurtling to the floor, hoping to disperse some of the anger rampaging through his body. His mother came rushing in to see what had caused the commotion.

'Did you know about this!? Tell me! Did you know!' he demanded of his mother. He was on his feet now, waving the letters under her nose.

'Know about what?' she asked unsure of what was happening. 'I don't know what you're talking about Jack – What letters?'

'These letters! Old letters – Hidden away in the back of his filling cabinet! – They're from….' He almost couldn't speak her name; it had been so long '….. There from Annie! Tell me! - Did you know about them?' He was shouting. Marcia had never seen Jack so furious. She was a little afraid of what he was capable of doing. She had suffered John Parrish's rages often and knew to keep her distance. She had never seen Jack lash out in anger; she anticipated it was a trait he had managed to dis-inherit.

'No. I don't know anything about any letters?' She stated adamantly. As much as it agitated him, he believed her. His father was very capable of being deceitful, without any help or encouragement from his mother. He sat down, needing to catch his breath before explaining the contents of the letters to his mother.

'Annie was pregnant Mum! She wrote to me for help!' Marcia stood her ground, absorbing the information. She was surprised by the contents of the letters and the news that her late husband had concealed them, but she had to admit to herself that, had she known about the letters, she would have been complicit in the deception.

'These letters were addressed to me Mum, but he took them! I never got them! - I never got them!' Jack was shouting again. 'Annie must have thought I didn't care! Or want her and our baby! That bastard has ruined my life! He knew how upset I was that Annie hadn't written to me and my two faced lying shit of a father just left me to suffer not knowing…. and Annie, God!! Poor Annie, going through everything alone!' Marcia opened her mouth with the intention of trying to find some words to defend her dead husband and then she stopped herself. Jack was in no mood to hear them. Jack passed the letters to his mother. She read each letter with the same incredulity as Jack had, but not the anger. John Parrish had done something wicked and appalling. She was slightly ashamed to discover she would have done the same. If he had gone to Annie, it would have ruined his life and his career. Marcia was in agreement; her husband took the correct course of action. It was too late to change whatever history these hidden letters had created. She had no idea if she was a grandmother or if Jack was a father. The dilemmas in the letters would have found their resolution by now. It was no use crying over milk that had been spilt many years ago.

Jack pushed the chair back and rose to his feet. 'I have to leave here now. I can't stay in his house a moment longer. I feel suffocated, manipulated and nauseous!' He stated with disgust.

'But where are you going Jack?' His mother moved towards him with the intention of stopping him from leaving the room, but he was too quick. In a flash he was past her and out of the door.

'What are you going to do?' Marcia shouted after him, fearful of her Son's

reaction.

'Let see?' Jack paused for a moment. 'I would have throttled my father had he been alive! At least God did it for me!'

'Jack! How dare you speak of the dead in such a way?'

'Mother don't you dare defend him! My whole life has been based on lies – his lies. Annie was – is the only person I have ever truly loved and he drove her away and now she's married to someone else when she should be married to me. Well he's not going to control me anymore now he's dead! I'm going to find out the truth!'

'Aren't you forgetting that you are already a married man? What difference does the past make now, unless you are going to abandon Cassie and run off on a wild goose chase? You can't just forget your Wife and run away to Annie?' Marcia reminded him. 'And the last you knew, Annie was married to that friend of yours from college?' Jack grimaced at the thought of being classed as a friend of Nick's.

'Nick was never a friend of mine and since this is a day for the truth to come out Mother, Cassie and I got divorced last year. That's the real reason why she didn't come to the funeral, not because she's working as I said. - I didn't tell you, because I didn't want a lecture on being a disappointment from my Father. It was what we both wanted - I never really loved her and I think she always knew it. Anyway last year she met someone else who made her happy and she asked me for a divorce. I was going to tell you, but it never seemed the right time and I know Dad would have a called me a failure – but now - I don't care!'

'But you don't have to leave Jack? You have no flight booked and nowhere to stay tonight?' It dawned on Marcia that she may never see her son again if she let him leave now.

'It doesn't matter mother, but ultimately I'm going back to England to find Annie.' He was calm now. He had made the decision in his head and no one or nothing would dissuade him. He couldn't live the rest of his life if he didn't look for Annie and the child that may or may not have been given the chance of life. If Annie was still married to Nick, well, it was her life and there was nothing he could do about that, but the matter of Annie's pregnancy was different. He had the right to know if he was a father - or not.

Jack spent the night in the airport hotel whilst he waited for the first available flight to Manchester. He was too hyped up to sleep. Every possible scenario of outcomes played out inside his head. He kept replaying the last time he had seen Annie, when he had finished university and the small child she was holding in her arms. He assumed that Nick was the Father – maybe he was wrong.

He emptied the contents of the mini bar in an attempt to lose consciousness and get some sleep. It didn't work; it just meant that he was sitting on the plane with one of the worst hangovers he could ever remember. Before he boarded the plane he rang his secretary and told her he was taking some annual leave to deal with some personal matters. Everyone understood, after all his father had just died. He told them he would be in England tying up some loose ends regarding his fathers' estate, in truth he was going to search for Annie and possibly his child.

Chapter 2

Sixteen years earlier.

Annie waited impatiently by the gates at the edge of the college grounds. She had left the exam room twenty minutes before the end of her last English exam, confident that she could do no more to secure a pass at the very least. It was one of those rare early summer days when the sun was shining and the sky, the colour of pale azure blue. She was hot and in a hurry to get home to cool off, but Jack had a nasty habit of keeping her waiting. She considered walking home on her own, but she knew she would wait for him, as she always did.

Nick Pickering beamed broadly as he came out of the same exam as Annie; he spotted her trying to dodge the sun by looking for some shade from a tall willow tree nearby. He made his way towards her, without thinking. She was a magnet and he was always pulled in her direction. It was rare to see her in college without her shadow – Jack Parrish. Nick had been trying to gain Annie's attention since they had met in their first week of college. That was almost two years ago, but he could never get anywhere near her, she was never alone. He had been trying to find an opportunity to ask her out for months, but either Jack's presence or Nick's nerves had stopped this event from taking place. Now he had the perfect opportunity - he wasn't going to waste it. Soon they would all be leaving college, and then it would be too late. He strolled over as casually as he could; trying not to look as if he was walking her way on purpose, he failed miserably.

'Hi Annie – How did the exam go?' *Talk about sweeping her off her feet*. He internally chastised himself for being such a 'nerd'. 'Do you think you did okay in the exam?' Again he had shown her what a prize plank he was. Annie smiled at Nick - He melted and forgot that he was embarrassed.

'I think it went okay, but you can't tell, have to wait and see. How about you?' she asked with genuine interest, but at the same time looking past him seeing if Jack was on his way and knowing he wouldn't be.

'Could have done better, but I hope I've done enough to scrape through.' Nick hopped from one foot to the other as he was speaking. This was a nervous twitch from childhood he still hadn't managed to control. Whilst talking to was trying to decide if now was the right time to ask Annie if she would go to the 'Leavers Ball' with him. It was a case of should he take the knock back now - or later? He decided to chance his arm. Besides they only had a couple of weeks to go and there was no guarantee he would catch her on her own again before it was too late. They were only going in to the college for exams, if he left it, he may miss her completely. He coughed slightly to clear his throat.

'Anne are you going to the 'Leavers' Ball'? Because I was wondering if you would like to go with me?' His grey eyes were open wide and staring expectantly at Annie. It wasn't until this moment that she realised how attractive his eyes were. They were alive and dancing, reflecting his feelings. It was plain to see that he was sweet on her, but it wasn't enough to make her say 'yes', even though she didn't have a date to the dance. She was hoping that Jack would ask her to go with him, but waiting for Jack to make a decision was like waiting for a moth to change into a butterfly. You know it's going to happen at some point, but it may be gobbled up by another insect first. Nick seemed to read her mind in the minute pause. 'Or are you going with Jack?' Nick had to ask, as he knew this was a strong possibility. He had already thrown himself into the shark infested water, he might as well find out what was going on between them - if anything. Annie pushed her shoulder length, silky, straight brown hair behind her ears trying to buy some time before answering, hoping that a miracle would happen and that she wouldn't have to let Nick down – but it didn't. There was hesitancy in her answer.

'Well I haven't decided if I'm definitely going.' - She decided honesty was the best policy. 'I don't know if I'll be going with Jack' she paused slightly 'He hasn't asked me yet. 'She looked into Nick's deep grey eyes, hoping he would realise that she wanted Jack to ask her. Nick nodded silently accepting the situation. 'I understand' he said in a soft voice.

'I am pleased that you asked me.' Added Annie blushing slightly, trying to say something, anything, to let him down more gently, 'I'm sorry Nick.'

'It's okay, don't worry. God loves a trier.' Then he turned to continue out of the college grounds. Annie felt mean; Nick was a perfectly nice guy. If Jack didn't exist, there would be no reason to refuse going to the dance with him – but Jack did exist. After a couple of steps Nick turned back to face her, 'Well if he doesn't ask - and you want to go, it would be my pleasure to take you.' He threw his killer smile. If that didn't get her nothing would he thought to himself as he walked out of the tall Victorian gates. Annie laughed, as she often did in his company. He could have easily told her to get stuffed, but he didn't. Nick wasn't aware, but he had managed to crack Annie's armour - just a little.

Twenty minutes after the exam had finished and there was still no sign of Jack. Annie was still leaning on the gates waiting. Thankfully the coldness of the iron and the shade from the willow tree was keeping her cool. She wished for a moment that she had chosen a best friend with better time keeping skills, but if truth be told it was Jack that had chosen her. They had known each other since primary school. Mrs Kingsley sat them together on their first day and they had followed each other around everywhere ever since. It was a mutual agreement. She couldn't actually remember a time when she hadn't known Jack. He was just always there. He saved her when she was being chased by mean Georgie

Howarth and his pet frog 'Bulldog', also when Susan Sherringham and Clare Copthorne spent all lunch time telling the Teachers and welfare staff that Annie and Jack were kissing on the sports field – which they never did. She was there for him too when the boys tried to beat Jack up for letting her play football. You know how mean kids can be. Jack and Annie were inseparable all the way through the school system.

A large group of students exited the exam hall. She searched the huddle of bodies coming towards her, relief on all of their faces as one more exam hit the dust. She knew Jack was in there somewhere even though she couldn't yet see him. It was instinct, just something that happened. She was like a wild animal that could smell its prey from two miles away. She couldn't explain it, but she always knew when he was around. Then the crowd parted a little and he was there in front of her. Dark blond hair dripping over his eyes, as was the fashion. A gold stud in one ear and the deepest blue eyes she had ever seen. As usual the group surrounding him were all females vying for his attentions. He spotted Annie and her peevish look through a gap in the crowd and waved. Six pairs of eyes turned and scowled at her. She didn't know why, it wasn't as if she and Jack were 'going out'. They were only friends; good friends, but it was all they would ever be. She had resigned herself to that before they left high school. She had spent many nights crying over him and the fact that he only ever saw her as a friend or sister figure. No matter what she did he never showed any interest in her as a girl. He was gender blind. She had given him plenty of opportunities to make a move at the school disco's and parties over the years – but he never did .It was if he couldn't see the fact that she was a girl, to him she was just Annie. It appeared impossible to jump the huge ravine between friendship and going out together. Besides which – he wasn't *that* good looking and he was *very* unreliable, but still it was as if there was an invisible connection between them, maybe she knew him from a past life, but she knew neither of them wanted to sever it. Jack might not want to be her boyfriend, but he always made sure she was somewhere around in the background should she be needed. Shelley, Annie's arch nemesis linked arms with Jack and smiled with sickly sweetness for Annie's benefit. It was wasted; Annie and Jack's friendship was far beyond anything that could be touched by jealousy. Annie just smiled back knowing Jack liked all the attention, but that was all – she hoped.

Jack and his entourage passed her and went out through the gates like royalty on a walk about. Annie tagged along behind as usual waiting for the big hair and lip gloss posse to leave and catch their respective buses. All of the girls left eventually, except for Shelley who lived in the same direction as Jack and Annie. Every few steps Shelley turned round and smiled '*that*' smile at Annie. You know the one that says 'he might be your friend, but I'm going to make sure I'm his girlfriend very soon' sort of smile – smug. *'Stupid slapper'* thought Annie. It was then that Shelley stuck the knife in Annie's heart and turned it sharply.

'Guess who's taking me to the 'Leaver's Ball?' the question was directed at Annie. She tried to hide the desperate fear that was growing in her mind. The look on Shelley's face told her everything she needed to know. Annie shrugged her shoulders. She didn't trust herself to speak without a string of expletives.

'Well 'Jackie' of course!' she exclaimed delighting in the pain she knew she was causing. Annie flashed a glance at Jack to see if it was true. He didn't flinch; he was too occupied with his portable CD player and trying to change the track. All Annie could muster was 'oh'. The disappointment in Annie's voice pulled Jack back into the conversation.

'Well there's a group of us going together.' butted in *'Jackie'*. 'You'll be there as well' he added as if she should already know she was invited, even without being asked. He automatically smiled at Annie.

'She'll have to make her own way there!!' retorted Shelley. 'We can't fit her in - it's going to be a tight squeeze as it is!' Shelley stopped *'Jackie'* dead in the street by grabbing the collar on his jacket and pulling him into her personal space. Annie had no time to re-direct her feet and barely managed to get past them without walking into them. It was all a stage show for Annie's benefit – she knew that, but she didn't want to let Jack see just how upset she was feeling. Not at Shelley's behaviour, Annie was disappointed that he didn't ask her to go to the leaver's ball with him alone. Annie carried on walking, leaving them stood in a half embrace in the street. Annie had seen enough.

'Actually I've got a date for the 'Leaver's Ball', so I won't need to tag along with you – got to rush!' Annie started running up the street before anyone could stop her. She didn't turn around, so she didn't see the look of disappointment on both of their faces. Shelley's plans had back fired. She was hoping Annie would be so annoyed that she would refuse to go to the ball at all. Jack was deflated because he couldn't believe Annie would not be at his side with all his friends on their leaving night, besides which Annie didn't do boyfriends – who was she going with? He wanted to know.

Annie only stopped running when she was sure she was out of sight. She shook her head in an effort to stop the tears from coming- it didn't work. She brushed them away with the back of her hand as quickly as they were appearing. How could he be so insensitive? She already knew the answer. He just saw her as a friend, so in his own eyes he was doing nothing wrong. It was Annie that had the problem – not him. She turned on to Garstang road, still keeping a steady pace. She didn't see or hear Jack running behind her, making ground. The noise of the traffic disguised his footsteps, when he was close enough; he grabbed her shoulder to make her jump.

'Jesus Christ!' Shouted Annie, hoping that he couldn't tell she'd been crying.

'Whatcha!' he smiled innocently 'Why didn't you wait for me?'

'I didn't want to cramp your style!' she answered with a liberal dressing of sarcasm.

'You mean Shelley?' he was confused for a second. 'She's just a friend – there's nothing going on between us.'

'You don't have to explain to me – I'm only a friend too remember – no one special just one of the gang!' She wondered why he was so thick when it came to women. Couldn't he see that Shelley would do anything to be with him and as much as Annie didn't want to admit it – so would she? Annie tried to calm her sharp tongue. She realised that she was taking her frustrations out on Jack who didn't have a clue what he had done to upset her. He couldn't help being ignorant of her feelings if she didn't have the balls to tell him. It was Shelley she wanted to flatten, not Jack. She took a deep breath and recovered herself. If she didn't pull herself together she would turn into one of those whining girls in the lip-gloss posse that she wholeheartedly despised. Jack passed her one of his ear phones for his CD player and they walked in silence listening to the music.

Jack was completely confused by Annie's reaction he truly had no idea why Annie was getting so uppity. It wasn't as if he had said she couldn't go with them. He wanted her to be there. He wondered if women were always going to be a mystery to him or if one day in his future the fog would lift and everything would become clear. This sort of sullen nonsense he came to expect from most of the girls he knew, but Annie was different, this wasn't her usual style of behaviour, he hoped it was a hormonal blip, but he knew better than to ask her. He was also intrigued to find out who she was going to the ball with, but now was not the time to ask her. He decided to try and lift the tension and change the subject.

'Are you coming over to mine to do some revision later?' he questioned moving towards her, slinging his arm around her shoulders in an attempt to diffuse the situation. At least she didn't dig him in the ribs. 'My last maths exam tomorrow, he continued, 'I could do with going over it with you?' he got no flicker of a response. Annie picked the leaves off the privet hedges as they passed along the road side. 'What's your next exam?' Jack was starting to find it all hard work. He might have to resort to tickling her.

'English lit on Thursday' She answered eventually.

'So you coming over?' he encouraged, squeezing her shoulder.

'Suppose.' said Annie begrudgingly. She let him chat happily until they reached the corner of Annie's street. He was so absorbed in his own conversation; he failed to notice that Annie was quiet. They both came to a natural stand still at the corner where they usually parted. He released her shoulder, much to Annie's disappointment. Annie placed the borrowed earphone into Jack's hand.

'Call for me about six?' He instructed, flashing his best smile and starting to walk away. 'Oh no - make it seven. Mum and Dad want to 'talk' to me.' He made invisible inverted commas in the air. 'It's too late for a pep talk about the exams now, but that won't stop them. Don't forget if they're still on at me when you arrive you're on my side!' He shouted running off down the road towards his home.

As she walked past the familiar semi-detached houses in her street Annie started to think about their future. In two weeks and they would have left college for good - next step university. Annie had been accepted at Manchester University for a course in Art and Design. Annie wasn't sure which direction she wanted to go in, but it was a good place to start they were both subjects she excelled in. She thought about the possibility of teaching if nothing else came to fruition. She could have studied at Preston, but the course in Manchester had a very good reputation and the night life was known to be excellent. She had been to the clubs in her home town of Preston a few times, but always with the watchful and curtailing eyes of her parents, she was looking forward to living a little – a lot. Jack, on the other hand knew exactly where his life was heading. He was off to Edinburgh to take a degree in Business Management. He had everything mapped out - or rather his parents did. They knew exactly where he was going and how he was going to get there. His parents were not the sort of people used to hearing the word 'No' and anything less than excellent was not acceptable. Jack was given no other option in life than to succeed. Annie found it hard to think about life without Jack. It could be done – she was sure of that, but it was going to be so alien not having him around, her sounding board – her crutch? She dismissed all the thoughts of separation. She would deal with it when it happened. She had exams to get through first and then the long summer holidays to spend with Jack.

Jack's mother and father were sat in the garden waiting for him. The sun was still shining, making Jack wish that the summer break was already here. He couldn't wait to get his last exam over with. His mother, who hated being too hot sat in the shade of the willow tree that hugged their garden, his father on the other hand, sat in a reclining chair on the patio enjoying the full strength of the sun – without sunblock.

'Hello darling.' his mother smiled in adoration the moment her eyes saw him. He was the bee's knees, the sunshine in her life and the only reason she had to get up in the morning. Marcia had been a stay at home mother, on the insistence of his Father. She hadn't minded when Jack was young as her days were busy enough, going out to lunch with the other mum's, looking after Jack and her husband's needs, but now he was older he didn't need her anywhere near as much - more was the pity and the time she managed to spend with him was rare and precious. Too often their cosy chats were interrupted by the arrival of Annie. Then Jack would up and disappear without a second thought for her. Many of the other mum's had gradually gained their own independence, finding jobs to fit in with school holidays and then many taking the plunge and going full-time. This was not a path that had been open to Marcia. Gradually her circle of friends had become smaller and smaller, leaving her in an isolated time warp. John Parrish's wife was not allowed to go out to work.

'There is a Tub of ice on the table and a can of your favourite 'tooth rotter' cooling in it for you.' She pointed at the table.

'Unum, you know how to make it sound so appealing Mum.' Said Jack sarcastically. He moved over to the table and helped himself to a can of coke, his father, who had until this moment ignored Jack's entrance folded his newspaper and rested his gaze upon Jack. Jack knew this was the sign for the pep talk to begin. He slid into the nearest chair, which also happened to be the furthest away from his father.

'Now Jack, there's something we need to discuss.' His father was looking directly at him and smiling, which was a bad sign – this was going to be serious.

Chapter 3.

Jack didn't remember leaving his house. He just got up from his chair and started to run. He had a vague recollection of his father and mother shouting after him, but he couldn't stop. He had to get away from the words his father was spouting at him. He ran down the street as fast as his legs would carry him. Eventually found himself in the park, passing people walking dogs, small children on the swings with their parents, school children playing football, smiling, laughing, and having fun. To all intent and purposes the world seemed normal, but Jacks' world had just turned upside down – literally.

When his legs wouldn't carry him any further, he threw himself on the grass, panting like a thoroughbred after a long race. It took time for his breathing to return to normal. He had managed to put distance between himself and his parents, but it didn't stop his father's words constantly repeating inside his head. He picked himself up from the grass and started walking, trying to put more distance between himself and the words. He had no conscious direction in mind, but half an hour later he found himself stood at Annie's front door, pressing the doorbell. Annie came to the door.

'Wasn't I supposed to be coming to you?' She started to say as she opened the door, but when she saw the look on his face she stopped. 'Are you alright? You look upset?' The look in his eyes confirmed that something was very wrong.

'Come with me and I'll tell you' He said taking her hand and gently pulling her out of the door. 'I don't want to explain in front of your Mum and Dad.' Annie shouted to her parents that she was going out with Jack and pulled the front door closed behind her. Jack took them back in the direction of the park, they walked in silence. Annie knew that something major had happened, she knew he would tell her when he was ready. He was still holding her hand, gripping it for dear life. After walking to the far end of the park he finally he settled on a remote spot overlooking the river, with few passers-by who would notice that he was upset. They sat on the grass looking out over the view.

'Whatever's happened?' Annie asked with true concern. His distress was almost tangible; he took a deep breath and then started to explain.

Jack's father had been offered a large promotion and he was going to take it. This meant that the family would have to relocate - to Sydney – Australia - permanently. It was all finalized. No consultation, no options. A new home had been found on the outskirts of Sydney and it was only a short train or bus ride to the university that Jack's father had chosen for him. A place was already waiting for him. His father's firm had pulled some strings, a donation towards a new wing and Jack's place was guaranteed- even without an interview.

Annie's jaw dropped. She didn't know what to say. What could she say? The bottom had just fallen out of her world too. She wanted to burst into tears and rant and rave with Jack, but that wouldn't help him. He needed her to be strong and calm. If in doubt – hug. This was one of her mottos. She moved closer to him and wrapped him in her arms. His body was rigid and unyielding. She didn't give up, she just held on.

'And it gets worse!' Said Jack shaking his head in his own disbelief. Tears rolled involuntarily down his cheeks. His emotion was so raw it consumed Annie too, she couldn't help herself, and she started to cry. He turned to face her 'They want to move in three weeks!!' He wiped the tears with the back of his hand but they were replaced immediately. 'Three weeks Annie!! They want me to leave my whole life behind.' She pulled him closer, if it was possible. At this point he relaxed into her a little, placing his arms around Annie and reciprocating the hug. They sobbed inconsolably into each other's arms for what felt like hours, until they could cry no more.

'Do you have to go with them?' Asked Annie searching for a solution.

'That's what I said to the knob! He said mum wants us all to be together. She doesn't want me in a different country!'

'Can't you just put your foot down and say 'No'?' Asked Annie already knowing the answer.

'They won't fund me to go to University in Edinburgh if I don't go with them. I'll have nowhere to live and no money! He's got me by the fucking balls! He as good as said that if I don't go he'll disown me. Leave me to fend for myself. Can you believe that he could be such a devious, selfish bastard?' Annie's brain couldn't comprehend what she was hearing.

'But what about your Mother, didn't she have anything to say about everything? Surely she wouldn't abandon you?'

'She said plenty! She backed him all the way and she can't even stand the sun, even today she was sat in the shade because it was too hot! - She said that they had to do what was right for the whole family, that I would love it over there once I gave it a chance. There was no reason for me to stay here and my prospects would be far greater over there….. The only concession they did make was that if I didn't want to stay in Australia after my three year course, they'd consider funding my move back to England – providing that I pass all elements of my degree of course!'.

'Bastards' Muttered Annie under her breath. She had never once bad mouthed them in all the time she had known them, but to do this, to make such important decisions for Jack without even consulting him? She tried to imagine how she would feel if her parents had sprung such news on her - she couldn't. The thought that in two or three weeks he would be starting a whole new life with new friends – no wonder Jack was blowing a fuse if not the whole fuse box. Jack threw himself backwards on the grass, using his hands as a pillow behind his head.

'I'm just not going and that's an end to it! I can get a job in Edinburgh to support myself, something in the evenings and Saturdays when there are no lectures. Other people manage to do it? So I'm going to do it!' Annie reflected on his last statement. They were brave words, but she knew him better than he knew himself. He would give in sooner or later, his father always got his own way – no one crossed John Parrish and survived.

It took a full week of Jack's constant emotional pleading, coupled with his father's temper and unreasonable behaviour before Jack finally caved in. He accepted that his chances of successfully completing a degree were greater if he had his father's backing. He would be able to concentrate on his studies instead of trying to find work, feed himself and put a roof over his own head. Besides which, he intended to come back to England as soon as university was finished. Then he would be able to get a job and join the work force. He wouldn't need his father – or his money.

One thing did start to trouble him, at first it was hardly noticeable, but as the days moved on and the reality of moving took hold it became stronger and it was related to Annie. After all the years of taking her for granted he was beginning to imagine what life without her was going to be like. Before the mention of Australia, he assumed they would get together on weekends. He would travel to Manchester and she could come up to Edinburgh, so the thought of living without her had never entered his head – until now. He realised that he was going to miss Annie more than he could ever have imagined and to complicate things, now she had told him that she was going to the ball with Nick. In truth he wanted to take Annie, without the lipstick posse and make it a special night to remember for the both of them, before he left. He thought about asking Annie to change her mind, but he knew her well enough to know she didn't go back on her word, besides which, he knew Annie was furious when Shelley had proclaimed her plans for the ball which excluded Annie. Jack had known nothing about any of these arrangements until Shelley spoke. They had spoken in general about all getting together before the Ball, but Shelley had taken it upon herself to arrange the fine detail without consulting Jack – and certainly not Annie. The last and most unwelcome complication was Nick. Jack had suspected that Nick had a secret crush on Annie for a long time. Jack never thought for one moment that Annie felt the same, so why was she choosing to go with him to the ball? He never did understand girls.

The following ten days went by in a haze for Annie and Jack. One exam followed another. The news that Jack was leaving for Australia had become common knowledge and every corner Annie turned round at college, she found Jack explaining what was happening or someone asked her how she felt about it. In truth she didn't know how she felt about it. Was she entitled to an opinion? After all they were only friends, she had no hold on him, her opinion didn't matter and it wouldn't change anything. Her life would still move on in its own direction. Maybe they had out grown each other? Maybe this was the only way for them to move on from each other independently? If they were only a few miles apart they would soon get into the same old habit of getting together at weekends and holidays, besides she didn't know how long she could carry on being in love with someone who plainly didn't feel the same way. She hated to admit it but maybe it was for the best?

Chapter 4

Nick was perfectly on time to pick Annie up for the ball. The white starched collar on his hired dinner suit strangled him. He ran his index finger in the inside of the collar trying to stretch it, whilst ringing the doorbell with the other hand. It made no difference. He wouldn't breathe again properly until the night was over and the shirt sent back to the hire shop. He had been so surprised and delighted when Annie came up to him after the English Literature exam and said she would like to go to the ball with him. Nick's surprise was evident. He didn't know what had changed her mind – he didn't care, she had decided to go with him – not Jack. She had stated that it was as friends and not romantically, but Nick didn't care. Nick accepted her terms; he was just delighted Annie had changed her mind. It would give him a chance to spend time with her and maybe win her over – as long as Jack didn't mess things up for them.

Nick caught his breath as Annie opened the door. She looked wonderful. He had never been so nervous in his life and the sight of her made that constricting collar even tighter. Annie was wearing a long soft, pale blue dress, with a small amount of Crystal detailing around the neck line. There was a deep 'V' cut at the front exposing a little flesh, but not too much, her small neat breasts safely hidden. The straps were halter neck, leaving her back bare and exposed. Her hair was pinned in soft curls revealing the nape of the neck; soft loose ringlets framed her face. Annie and her mother, *taken by force*, had agonised for weeks on what colour and cut the dress should be and it had taken three shopping trips and many shops until they found 'the one'. Annie was pleased with the way she looked, even if she did say so herself. It was the first time she had dressed with the intention of trying to be 'attractive'. She usually left all that nonsense to the lipstick posse and made do with jeans and a 'T' shirt, but tonight she had to feel and look special for her own peace of mind.

'You look wonderful! Enthused Nick with genuine admiration. He still couldn't quite believe how different she looked. He had always known she had a great personality and that she was attractive, but her body was always hidden behind clothes that were three sizes too big. Now he could see the outline of her body, the difference was remarkable.

'Are you sure I look okay?' She asked needing more than her Mother's confirmation – Mother's sometimes lie.

'Far beyond okay!!' He said escorting her to his dad's car. 'You look amazing!' Annie smiled and grew an inch taller with confidence.

The ball was being held at a large local hotel on the A6 road out of Preston. It was definitely the most sophisticated event Annie and Nick had ever been to – excluding family weddings and even they weren't very sophisticated.

A long line of Cars drew up outside the front doors of the hotel, all driven by parents. The occupants alighted in haste and the cars and drivers were ushered away by teenagers not wanting to be seen with their parents for a moment longer than absolutely necessary. Nick and Annie were no exception.

'Thanks Dad.' Said Nick with one hand on the car and the other on the door handle after helping Annie out., waiting for the first opportunity to slam it and send him on his way.

'Remember not to come 'til one o'clock or you'll just be waiting out here - and don't come in for us – we'll come out.' With that instruction Nick slammed the car door shut and waved his father away. Annie didn't get chance to thank Nick's dad for the lift, she hoped he didn't think she was ungrateful. At least she would be able to thank him on the way back.

'Are you ready?' Nick said offering Annie his hand.

'As I'll ever be?' Smiled Annie and placed her warm hand in his. He gave it a gentle squeeze to reassure her. She was glad Nick was at her side. He was funny, attentive and sweet, if she had been with Jack; she would have had to spend all evening in the background watching as the lip gloss posse tried to vie for Jack's attention. Nick made her feel like the main event, not some side show and tonight that was what she needed. Besides, Jack was leaving in a few days she had to start creating a life for herself that didn't include him.

Signs in the main entrance pointed them in the direction of the ball. The reception area was crowded. A throng of adolescents had congregated, waiting for friends to arrive. Everyone was laughing and in high spirits. The girls, mainly with big hair and revealing dresses tried to look sophisticated, whilst the boys with ill-fitting suits fidgeted as they waited impatiently. Annie and Nick turned to smile at each other, thinking the same thought and having the ability to laugh at themselves. It took a couple of minutes for a path to clear and the crowd to disperse through the doors. Once inside the full power of the music and lights hit them. There were small groups of friends dotted everywhere, meeting and greeting, commenting on each other's outfits. The dance floor was empty; it was far too early for anyone to think about dancing.

'You wait here. I'll go and get us a drink.' Said Nick ushering Annie to the side of the room, where she wouldn't get trampled by the new arrivals. It took Annie one visual sweep of the room to locate Jack. He was stood at the far end of the room near the bar, as expected; he was surrounded by the lip gloss posse. He didn't notice her arrival. He was pre-occupied with Shelley, who had managed to drape half of her body across him. Even from this great distance Annie could see Shelley's hand moving up and down Jack's back stroking and caressing as it moved. Jack seemed relaxed. He wasn't trying to manoeuvre out of her reach, but neither was he encouraging her. Shelley's dress as expected left little to the imagination, her ample bosom was barely encased in the two pieces of bunting trying to pass themselves off as the top of her dress. Annie felt nauseous inside. She had walked in feeling like a swan, but compared to Shelley, she had turned back into the ugly duckling. Annie didn't want to watch, yet she couldn't take her eyes off them. She knew that by the end of the evening Shelley would be his girlfriend and her friendship with Jack would be obliterated, Shelley would see to that. Eventually she looked away, casting her eyes down, focusing on the shimmering crystals attached to her blue dress. She suddenly felt foolish for trying to dress as something she wasn't. She would never be flirty, frothy and frivolous like Shelley, it wasn't in her nature and then she realised that she didn't want to be. Shelley was a jumped up tart that cared nothing for anyone else's feelings and if that was what Jack wanted to was welcome to her. Annie smiled to herself, pleased at the fact that she'd had the decency to use more bunting on the top of her dress.

Nick returned with a white wine spritzer and a pint of large. 'I've just spotted some friends from our English group at a table around the corner, do you want to go and sit with them?' He asked tentatively. She looked around. There was no one else she wanted to sit with. She didn't want to be alone with Nick all night and give him false hope and she had no intention of joining Jack and the lipstick posse.

'Yes that's fine! I don't think my feet can stand in these heels all night, a seat would be good.' Said Annie following Nick across the room. She glanced across at Jack; he was oblivious to her and obviously enjoying himself. She decided she would choose a seat with her back to him. Watching Jack would just make her miserable. The less she saw of Jack and Shelley the better. Nick didn't mention Jack, he was a taboo subject, but she noticed him looking over as they passed. She was aware that Nick felt somewhat jealous of her friendship with Jack, though she had assured him on several occasions that they were just friends. She didn't however tell Nick that she was in love with Jack and wished with all her heart that things were different – especially the fact that she wished she was with him tonight.

Jack observed Annie, as she crossed the room with Nick. She stood out like a glowing beacon of beauty. She looked so different in her flowing blue gown, high heels and soft curls in her hair. He wondered why he hadn't noticed how beautiful she was before. The ache in his heart grew stronger; he was beginning to understand what it meant. For all the time he had spent with her, this was the first time he was seeing her as a young woman, not the child he had played with.

Maybe it was the thought of leaving for Australia that made him see her differently or was it the fact that she was there with another man. He wasn't sure. He just knew he had to be with her tonight. It mattered more than ever, now he was leaving England.

Jack's patience finally snapped with Shelley, she was still trying to glue herself to him. Up until the point of seeing Annie, he hadn't paid much attention to her. She was always all over him, she meant nothing to him. Occasionally they would have a drunken kiss and a fumble at a party, but nothing more had ever happened, he had no intention of making her his girlfriend, even though she made it perfectly clear that was what she wanted. It had always been out of the question. Shelley was not the type of woman he wanted to spend quality time with and this evening was no exception. Suddenly he couldn't bear her touch any longer. He grabbed her arms without warning and scrapped them away from his body. He needed to get far away from her, he excused himself saying he needed the gents - it was a lie.

After about an hour of small talk and drinking fast the DJ announced that the buffet was ready to be served. The students couldn't afford the price of the three course sit down meal, so the college council came to an arrangement with the hotel for something that was more fitting to their very shallow pockets. The buffet was everything you would expect for their ages and price bracket; there were sausages on sticks, bread sticks, cheese sandwiches, pork pies and vol-au-vents. There was no politeness about waiting for food in turn; subsequently the queue circled the dance floor as impatient teenagers jostled for their place in line. The scene was more like a school dinner queue than a ball. Nick and the other friends on the table were bragging about the different universities and the nightlife they expected to experience on arrival. Annie was only half listening to their conversations, adding the odd 'oh' and 'yes' where she hoped was appropriate. She was itching to turn around and see what Jack was up to, but her pride was keeping her in line and facing forwards.

When the main buffet queue had dispersed and only a small cluster remained, Annie decided she needed some food to soak up the wine Nick was buying so frequently. The wine was easy to drink and as she was sat with a group of people she had no common interest with, other than attending the same college, the distraction of drink was welcomed. It also helped to take her mind off Jack.

'Would anyone else like some food?' asked Annie to the surrounding group, most of whom had already been for food and were busy feeding their faces, trying not to spill on their hired suits and best dresses.

'I'll go and get something for you' Offered Nick rising from his seat.

'No I'm fine.' said Annie touching his arm, gently pushing him back into his seat. 'I could do to stretch my legs - if you intend to get me dancing later that is?' Annie glided down a short set of stairs with ease, the soft flowing fabric of the dress trailing behind her. The alcohol was probably something to do with the floaty feeling she was experiencing. She could see Jack watching her, following her with his eyes from the other side of the room. Annie threw her shoulders back and her chest out and purposefully looked the other way. Shelley was still with him, although, he had managed to remove her from his body. Annie didn't want to give him the satisfaction of acknowledging him whilst he was with one of the lipstick posse. She concentrated on crossing the dance floor effortlessly in her high heels and joined the short queue of people waiting impatiently for the buffet. By the time Annie had reached the front of the queue there was little left to choose from. A few curled sandwiches, sausage rolls and a bowl of crisps. Annie decided to pass, but further along the table she could see a platter of desserts that had not been demolished yet. It didn't take her long to choose what she would like, as there were only two choices. Annie picked up a cake slice and had just helped herself to a piece of black forest gateaux, when she felt two hands swiftly and deftly slide around her waist; she jumped in surprise and spun around, nearly toppling over in her heels. It was Jack; he caught her and stopped her falling. His eyes were fixed on hers, his hands still holding firmly on to her waist. He had no intention of letting go. She felt her skin tingle from where his fingertips were touching her. She didn't know if it was the sheerness of the fabric accentuating the feeling, but she felt like a bowl of ice-cream out in full summer heat – she was melting.

'Annie you look amazing.' he almost whispered it, his eyes penetrating deep into her soul, well that's how she felt when he looked at her that way, as if he could read her mind and know all her secrets. There was nowhere to hide. Annie stood frozen to the spot, holding the plate of black forest gateaux. She didn't dare move in case he let her go. She wanted to stay just as they were for ever – well as long as she could possibly make it last. She could feel the pressure of his fingers and the warmth of his hand against her skin through the fabric. He moved his head towards hers. She had never seen him looking so handsome. The cut of his suit and the bright white of his shirt made his shoulders look even broader than normal. The smell of his fresh aftershave overwhelmed her, she felt like she was drowning in a sea of fragrance. For a moment she thought he was going to kiss her – *'God damn it'* she wanted him to kiss her. As if on command to spoil the moment, Shelley appeared out of the blue, pushing Jack sideways and knocking the plate of cake flying into the air before it smashed on tiled floor. A great cheer erupted from the guests, as the sound of smashed crockery evaporated into the music.

'Oh my God, I'm so sorry Annie.' lied Shelley whilst at the same time giving Annie a look warning her to back off. Annie couldn't even bring herself to speak or answer Shelley. The loathing she felt was so intense. It wasn't in her nature to hate, but at that moment she could have quite easily killed Shelley. She imagined taking a plate of cake from the buffet and squashing it firmly into Shelley's fake, flawless face, then smashing the plate over her head for good measure.

The moment subsided and Annie bent down to pick up the pieces of broken plate and cake as any good citizen would do. Jack caught hold of her arm to stop her.

'Don't! I'll do it.' He said already starting to pick up the pieces. 'You might get cake or cream on your dress.' Shelley mimicked Jack behind his back sarcastically. It didn't go unnoticed, but Jack ignored her.

'I don't know why you're bothering?' Whined Shelley, 'The waiters will come and sort it out. It's what they're paid for!' Jack didn't speak; he just continued to pick the debris up from the floor. When he had finished, he turned his attention to Shelley. 'Why don't you go and find the others and I'll be along in a minute.' Shelley was surprised to find that she was being dismissed by 'Jackie'.

'But I …..' Shelley started to object.

'Don't argue! – just go.' He threw her a look confirming he was not going to change his mind. She threw Annie another filthy look, Annie simply smiled sweetly, knowing it would have a greater effect than mimicking her behaviour.

'Well, if you think I'm going to wait around for you all night whilst you clean up after your 'shadow' you're wrong!' she threatened, '…. And if you don't come with me now you can spend the rest of the night without me!' Jack continued with the clearing up whilst at the same time making eye contact with Shelley. The message was clear. She huffed and puffed, then turned on her heels and marched away blazing with fury. Annie couldn't have wished for a happier ending. She was about to thank Jack for helping her when Nick appeared out of the crowd that had gathered to witness the commotion.

'Are you okay Annie?' He looked both concerned and annoyed to find Annie ankle deep in cake - and with Jack.

'Yes I'm fine – I just dropped my plate, Jack's helping me – that's all.' Annie could feel Nick's irritation.

'What was Shelley saying to you?' He wanted the inside story.

'Nothing of global importance. You know Shelley. She can make a scene when she's on her own in a room! It was nothing – Everything is fine - honestly.'

'And what's he got to do with it?' Nick was referring to Jack.

'Jack happened to be here and helped me when I spilled the cake. Nick, it's no big deal.' But it was to Nick. He could see the way Jack was looking at Annie and the familiar way in which he touched her. Nick couldn't stand the fact that Jack was closer emotionally to his date than he was.

'I'll look after Annie now.' Nick's words were directed to Jack. 'Thanks for helping her, but I'll take it from here.' Nick started to usher Annie back to their table.

'Don't you think that's for Annie to decide? She does have a mind of her own!' Jack was not in the mood to be dismissed in the same way he had just dealt with Shelley and he certainly wasn't going to be kept away from Annie by Nick. Jack took a step closer to Nick.

'Annie and I go way, way back Nick, so I'll always make sure she's okay - whether she's with you or anyone else.' Nick and Jack stood chest to chest like a pair of peacocks in a territorial war. Annie could feel the tension rising. 'Stop it you two! I am capable of looking after myself and speaking for myself! Stop making a scene! It's only some spilt cake! I don't need either of you interfering – especially if you are both going to behave like this!' A scene was the last thing Annie wanted as a memento of the ball.

'You heard the lady!' Nick's voice was raised now. The contempt Nick felt for Jack, fuelled with alcohol wasn't a good mix. Nick had downed several pints and she knew he didn't usually drink. 'She doesn't need you 'Jackie boy'! Now go away and leave her alone! She's with me tonight and I'll look after her!' Nick was poking Jack in the chest with his index finger. Annie covered her face with her hands dreading what might happen next.

'I'll leave when I'm good and ready mate! And if you'd actually listened to her, she doesn't need you either!' Jack squared up to Nick. He didn't like fighting, but he wasn't scared of Nick. Jack glanced across at Annie; he could see the misery and embarrassment the situation was causing her. Jack knew Annie was mortified and for her sake Jack decided to back down. The last thing he wanted to do was ruin the night for her. If he was honest with himself, he wanted to be with her, to hold her, dance with her, to tell her how much he was going to miss her and tell her how wonderful she was, but she had gone to the Ball with Nick. He only had himself to blame for being an 'arse' and letting Shelley take control. Jack Looked at Annie, who was still peeping from behind her hands. He smiled at her then turned and walked away from the situation.

'The sooner you leave for Australia 'Jackie boy' - the better!' Nick shouted loudly, and then added, 'for all of us! Especially Annie! She can't wait for you to go!' Jack turned back momentarily. Annie could see the hurt in his eyes. It was the last thing Annie wanted, for Jack to move away. Jack didn't reply to the comment, he just continued to walk away, picking his way through the throng of bodies on the dance floor. Annie glared at Nick. She was shaking with rage.

'How dare you Nick Pickering! - How dare you tell Jack that I want him to go! Have you any idea how upset he is at having to leave his home and all his friends to go to another country against his will... How can you be so cruel? Besides which, you have no idea what is good or bad for me. You don't even know me!' Annie turned and followed Jack. 'Wait!' Nick shouted 'you came with me!' Annie spun round to face him.

'I came with you, but I'll die before I leave with you! You are immature and spiteful! Now go away and leave me alone!' A moment later she had been swallowed up by the dance floor. Nick in anger punched his fist on to a nearby table sending an array of dis-guarded drinks in several directions. There was no way he was staying around to suffer more humiliation at the hands of Jack. He pushed and jostled his way to the exit. Annie could whistle for a lift home. She had made her choice. Nick started to walk in the direction of home. The fresh air would do him good, maybe it would calm his anger, either way, he was through chasing Annie – Jack was welcome to her.

Annie went to the ladies first, mainly to collect her thoughts. She felt bad about Nick, but he was in the wrong. There was no way she would stand by and watch someone treat her best friend the way Nick had and for no good reason. When Annie came out of the cubicle to wash her hands, Shelley was waiting for her. Annie decided to take the same line as Jack and walked past her without a word. Shelly on the other hand couldn't resist. She had been waiting for a moment to get Annie on her own for a long time.

'Look everyone, Jackie's shadow is all dressed up, trying to look like a girl today! She's even invested in a box of tissues to give her some tits.' Shelley poked her in the chest. 'He may like you today Cinderella, but when you turn back into your normal daggy clothes and personality, he'll soon be back with me, 'cause I know what he likes- do you know what I mean? And let's face it, she wouldn't know what to do to a man to make him happy – would you? Jackie told me Annie.... that you've never done 'it'... so that's why he'll come back to me - 'Little Miss Mousy Tits'.....when he's tired of waiting for you to put out and let's face it, he won't wait long!' Annie crumbled inside, her face instantly turned crimson, but she wasn't going to give her the satisfaction of seeing her upset or validating her words by replying. She didn't know if Jack had told Shelley she was a virgin or if it was just a lucky guess, either way she was right. Annie left without a backwards glance; at least she wasn't going to end up a single mother, which in all probability was Shelley's future.

Jack was easy to find. He was propped on a stool at the bar nursing a glass of J.D.

and coke. Annie sat on the stool next to him. He took a moment to realise it was Annie, not Shelley or any other member of the lipstick posse that had come to disturb him. Jack ignored her. He was still smarting from his exchange with Nick and the lies that had been told. Annie caught the eye of the bar man.

'I'll have what he's having please and he's paying for it.' Jack looked at her with surprise. She had caught his attention.

'Isn't Nick buying your drinks tonight? He is your date after all?' Jack wasn't happy.

'He's gone home in a huff and I don't know where my bag is, so I thought I'd sponge off you for the rest of the night. You can make up for all those bars of chocolate you stole from my lunch boxes over the years!' Jack smiled despite himself.

'They weren't stolen – just liberated.' He added.

'I'm sorry for the things Nick said to you.' Annie touched his shoulder to show her sincerity. 'He wasn't speaking for me. Don't take any notice of him.' Jack sighed deeply, shaking his head into his glass.

'Thing is, I don't think he is wrong.' Jack turned to face her, at the same time reaching up and taking her hand from his shoulder, he cupped it in his own hands. 'I haven't been a great friend to you this last couple of years. I took you for granted, thinking you'd always be there - and you probably would have been if things had turned out as we planned.' Jack kissed the back of Annie's hand. 'They say you don't know what you've got till it's gone Annie, and I'm just realising what I'm losing in you.' He said staring into her soul again. Annie became tearful, stunned by his sentimental words, especially after the verbal thrashing she had undergone from Shelley. She tried to brush his words aside.

'Don't be so daft. You are and have been a great friend and you won't lose me! I wouldn't change anything we've done together – except when you fed me dog chocolate as an experiment in primary school!' Annie tried to laugh away the tears. The intense moment was gone and the mood lifted. 'Come and dance with me. This is supposed to be a celebration of our leaving college not a wake!' she pulled him off his bar stool.

'God Annie! You know I hate 'Wham' don't make me dance to this crap!'

'Go on, just for me? You know you have a look of George Michael – in the dark, with the light off – I've heard the lipstick posse say so! And they're always right about everything.' Jack gave in. It was worth putting up with the dancing, just to be with her, but not before he pulled faces at her first. He always did have trouble saying 'no' to her and there were worse things she'd made him dance to in the past, he didn't care what the song was, Annie was with him here and now. He was going to savour their last few memories together, even if he did have to suffer 'Wham'. They both threw themselves into the dancing, not caring if they looked cool or not. They had no one to impress, as they both knew and understood each other perfectly. The more outrageous the dancing the better as far as they were concerned. They danced continuously until the D.J. decided to slow things down. Annie out of habit started to head off from the dance floor, as they always did when the 'Smoochies' came on. Jack gently pulled her back towards him.

'Dance with me?' he mouthed. Annie was stunned for a second, not believing that after all the years of knowing him he was actually asking her to 'slow' dance. This was the first time she would dance with him cheek to cheek and body to body. He slipped his arm slowly and purposefully around her waist, still maintaining eye contact. Annie stifled a nervous giggle that was threatening to escape. She placed her hand on his shoulder. It felt strange yet familiar both at the same time. He gently gripped her free hand and held it in the traditional dance position. Annie could feel a slight tremble in Jacks hand. She put it down to the fact he was still mad at Nick. It didn't occur to her that he was nervous about dancing with her. They both started to move rhythmically, but neither of them heard the music or the song, just the base beat signalling when to move. Annie was in heaven. She looked over Jack's shoulder to see if the world had stopped to watch them, but they were just another couple on the dance floor, everyone was ignorant of their momentous event. As they settled into the rhythm, Jack pulled Annie as closer. He took her hand and placed it on his other shoulder, abandoning the traditional dance hold. His free hand glided around the other side of her waist. Although they had hugged many times before, they had never been this close or for so long. She could feel the contours of his taught body through his thin cotton shirt. Every time his hips moved to the rhythm of the music her body responded pulsating desire to every inch of her body. She was sure her cheeks were flushed.

It felt natural to Jack to be holding Annie in his arms. As the dance progressed he felt her relax against his body. He could feel her breasts move as she breathed in and out. The hardness of her nipples through the sheer fabric teased him every time their bodies connected; he was starting to feel aroused. Why had she never had this effect on him before? He could smell the sweet yet slightly alcoholic mix of Charlie perfume, shampoo and hair spray. He could feel her hand on the back of his neck, her soft fingers and sharp nails gently gliding through his short, styled hair sending his whole body into red alert. Dancing with a girl had never felt this good – but this wasn't a girl……. it was Annie. Jack decided he couldn't wait any longer. If he didn't do it now he never would. He bent down and placed the softest of kisses on her lips. Her response was immediate and yielding. She kissed him back with a depth of passion he hadn't expected. It was like nothing either of them had ever experienced before. It felt like home.

Shelley witnessed everything from the side of the dance floor. This wasn't in her plan. Tonight he was supposed to be hers. Her body shook with anger. She couldn't understand what he saw in Annie, she wasn't even pretty and never made the best of herself with clothes and make up. Shelley resigned herself to the loss and took comfort in the knowledge that Annie would also be losing Jack when he moved to Australia. Annie hadn't won.

Shelley caught the eye of one of the other boys in her year. She knew he wanted her; he walked over to her on her command, not knowing that tonight was his lucky night, thanks to Jack.

Chapter 5

The summer night air was warm as they made their way towards home. They sauntered along hand in hand neither in any hurry to be separated. Jack offered to call for a taxi, but Annie didn't want the night to end and suggested they walked. The air was refreshing after being surrounded by people at the Ball. Annie's shoes were crippling her, but it was worth it, to be with Jack after 'that' kiss. Neither one of them spoke. It was enough to be walking along side each other. Annie shivered as the night air became colder. Jack in true style removed his jacket and placed it around her shoulders. Annie had questions that needed to be answered.

'Why tonight?' Annie asked Jack whilst they were walking, 'Why after all our years of friendship did we break the rules tonight?'

'I don't know?' said Jack truthfully 'Maybe it was the drink? Maybe it was the mood? Maybe it's because I'm going away and I realised tonight what you mean to me?' He glanced over and met her gaze, unsure of how she would respond to his words. Annie couldn't resist the question.

'What do I mean to you?' Jack hesitated for a moment. If he told her the truth she might run a mile, on the other hand he was running out of time. He had nothing to lose. He took a deep breath. 'I think I'm in love with you – and I only realised it fully tonight...... When you walked in with Nick, looking so beautiful.'

'Yes, he did look beautiful!' Mocked Annie.

'Stop it. I'm trying to be honest with you! I was as mad as a wasp when I saw you. Not because he was with you, but because I wasn't.' Annie couldn't believe what she was hearing. She had spent years wishing and dreaming of having Jack say such things to her, but she never expected it to actually happen.

'I'd have worn a ball gown to school if I'd have known I'd get that sort of reaction!'

'Does that mean you feel the same?' Jack asked, daring to hope.

'I've got some bad news for you Jack.' she said putting a sad face on. Jack wondered if he had made the wrong decision in being honest with her. Maybe he was frightening her off? Maybe she did have feelings for Nick? 'Go on?' he said 'tell me. I can take it whatever it is?'

'I don't think I'm in love with you.' She continued, '– I *know* I'm in love you –and have been for a long time.' then she smiled wickedly.

He stopped her from walking. 'Do you though, really? – do you love me? You didn't ever say anything?'

If it had been daylight, he would have seen that she was blushing. 'I didn't say anything because you only ever saw me as a friend and I couldn't bear to say anything in case it made you feel uncomfortable and not want to be with me. Of course I love you! – Do you think I would have put up with the lip-gloss posse if I didn't?' He had to agree they had made life difficult for Annie, she had put up with a lot.

'But you didn't even give me any clues?' He pushed her for more information.

'No Jack, you're just dense when it comes to women! I didn't think you felt the same way. As you said yourself, you, only realised how you felt tonight? And Shelley certainly gives me the impression that you are her boyfriend – she's always trying to get rid of me when I'm around, but most of all I didn't want things to become weird between us. I didn't want to lose your friendship. I couldn't risk saying anything...until I was sure you might feel the same.' This time she didn't wait for Jack to lead the way; she leant forward and kissed him with all the pent up passion she had been cherishing over the last few years. Jacks' youthful body responded as any healthy young man's body would. Jack wrapped his arms tightly around Annie. He felt torture and pleasure all rolled into one, with that kiss she released him from the role of 'friend'. His sexual desire for her was almost un-containable. He wanted to pull her to the ground right there and then and make love to her – but he didn't, he wanted more for her. Eventually Annie released his lips. Jack felt like he had been hit by a stun gun.

'Ohh – my - God Annie! I thought you were a good girl!' He reeled back on his heels away from her.

'I am!' she smirked, 'A very good girl.'

'You never told me you could kiss like that!' He chastised her.

'You never asked me! In case you didn't notice - I grew up.' She dropped her eyes to the level of his trousers. '- just like you did.' His arousal hadn't gone un-noticed.

'If I didn't know before tonight, I certainly do now!' Jack put his arm around Annie's shoulder and they continued walking. Jack desired Annie in every sense of the word. It felt even more important that he should be with her, with Australia looming. He knew what he wanted, he didn't know if Annie wanted the same thing. There was only one way to find out. It was a risk, but it was one he was prepared to take.

'Stay the night with me?' His voice trembled at the thought of her rejection, 'The house is empty. Mum and Dad are away saying goodbye to relatives and….'

'Do you mean just somewhere to crash?' She had to get it clear in her head just what he was asking of her. He shook his head, afraid he had offended her, after all, there was no good reason why she would jump into bed with him. She knew all his faults and shortcomings. Somewhere he found the courage to explain what he wanted.

'No I mean with me. I wish we had more time and then we could take it slowly, but you know I haven't got that. I don't want to waste the little time we have left. I want to hold you and kiss you and make love to you and….' Annie pressed her fingers too his lips to silence him. There was something she needed to clarify with him.

'You do know that I've never done this before?' She was slightly embarrassed, but she figured he would most likely already know, especially after her conversation with Shelley. She thought about asking him if he'd told her, but Annie didn't want to spoil the moment by reminding him of the delectable Shelley, besides which, in her heart she knew it wasn't a conversation he would have had with her.

'I thought it might be your first time and if you don't want to that's fine, we could just be together. More than anything I just want to be with you tonight and if it's just holding you in my arms, well that's fine?'

'I do want to be with you. My answer is 'Yes'.' Annie didn't need to think about it. It was what her body and soul had been aching for, for years. This may be their only opportunity. She wasn't going to lose it by pretending she was prudish and pure. She wanted him, just like he wanted her; she couldn't think of anyone she would rather give her virginity to than Jack.

Jack opened the back door of his parents' house and led Annie into the kitchen. He pulled two glasses from the cupboard and an opened bottle of his Dad's wine from the fridge.

'Ah Mr Lover Lover, Looks like you've done this before' said Annie teasing him.

'Every other day at least. You're one in a long line of girls as you well know. You're lucky I have time to fit you in!! But the next one's not due for another hour, so I've got plenty of time. Just make sure you leave by the other exit!' He was joking she knew, but he was more experienced than her, she started to lose confidence in her own ability to be a woman, to be as sexy as Shelley. She didn't want to disappoint him. Annie knew Shelley won that contest hands down.

He passed her the bottle to carry, then took her hand and led her up the deep mahogany staircase to his bedroom. She had made this journey a thousand times before, but this time it was different. He paused on the stairs and turned to her, as if reading her mind.

'You know,' he said 'I may not be completely innocent when it comes to girls –but I've never done this before - brought someone back here to seduce them and I know Shelley gives you the impression that we are together, we're not, I've never slept with her. I don't want her, I never have. I want you.'

'And I thought you were a good Catholic boy Jack Parrish!'

'I am,' he said, 'a very '*good* boy'.'

'Touché.' Replied Annie with a wicked smile.

Jack closed his bedroom door behind them. A small angled spot light over his desk gave the only light to the room. He pushed the top towards the wall to take the brightness away; the dimness seemed to make it less clinical. Annie stood in the centre of his room, not sure what she should do next. He poured them both a drink from the bottle of wine – God knows they both needed it to steady their nerves.

Jack was not a virgin, but this wasn't some drunken liaison. This was Annie he was about to make love to. She had a special place in his heart; he didn't want to ruin it for her. His couple of drunken experiences with lustful girls at party's had been unimportant. They were girls who had chased him for months, letting him know in no uncertain terms what they would like to do for him. He had read enough of his mother's Marie Claire magazine's to know that girls set a lot of store by their 'first time'. He didn't want to put her off sex for life, especially as he wanted that life to be with him.

'Are you sure you want to do this?' He asked her again as he led her to his bed. Annie took a long sip of the wine and then placed the glass on the bedside unit. This was the moment she hoped for but had never dared to dream of. She knew she would never regret it, at this moment she knew it was the right thing to do.

'I've never been surer of anything.' She said leaning in and kissing him again. She ran her hand along his shirt and up to his tie pulling it loose. The buttons on his shirt popped easily one by one releasing his smooth tanned chest, his body not yet mature enough for chest hair.

'Are you sure you haven't done this before?' He questioned. She slapped his arm in a gesture to bring him back under her control. With his encouragement and assistance, she easily freed him from his clothes until he was almost naked. He pulled her into his arms and kissed the back of her neck at the same time as unzipping the blue ball grown. Moments later it fell to her feet revealing her youthful beauty. He gazed at her perfectly formed pert breasts. He gently ran his finger down the centre of her breast bone, stopping momentarily to cup and caress each one of the small breasts. His touch was sensuous and tender; her skin fizzed with every sensation arousing her desire. She had never been this intimate with another human being. It was such a complex feeling, so alien to have someone touching you intimately, but at the same time so utterly fantastic that it was addictive. Of all the things she had heard from other girls and read about 'it', she never thought 'it' could be as wonderful as she was now experiencing.

Jack lingered, taking his time, if he had to go to Australia he was going to savour every moment that he had left with Annie. He was no great lothario, he wasn't even that experienced, but he was in love with the girl he was caressing and she was in love with him. There was no better feeling in the world. He kissed her slowly at first on the mouth, eager to explore her soft lips. Smoothly, he manoeuvred her onto the bed, his lips traced his way down to her breasts. His mouth and lips teased each nipple into surrender in turn. He could hear her breathing change into short sharp rasps, studded with small sighs of delight escaping from her lips. His arousal was becoming too intense. He couldn't wait much longer. He gently eased her legs apart, stroking the inside of her thigh.

'Are you sure?' He asked, praying that she wouldn't say no. 'I'm sure Jack Parrish – don't you dare stop.' she whispered with delight.

Eventually the fury of their passion subsided and they lay contentedly entangled in each other's embrace. Annie still couldn't believe what they had just done and how amazing she felt. 'You know I said I *think* I love you.' Jack whispered in her ear, 'Well I *know* now for sure – I do.' In the faint glow of the light Jack could see Annie grinning like the proverbial Cheshire cat. His face was not dis-similar.

Annie glanced over at Jack's football alarm clock, the one she bought him for his eleventh birthday. The time flashed up as 4.30am. Jack had given in to unconsciousness, but he still held on to her tightly in the single bed. This must be what heaven is like she thought. She felt peaceful, warm, safe and loved. Her body was relaxed and sleep was coming for her. She flexed her eyes, trying to stop them from closing. Jack would be leaving the country soon. She had no idea what the next day would bring. If this was to be her only memory of their intimacy, she was going to make sure was awake for every minute; she wanted to consume it all. Slowly and deliberately she took a mental picture of Jack's room. The posters on the wall of Preston North End football team, the dart board surrounded by multiple holes in the plaster on the wall – many of which had been caused by Annie's missed shots over the years. The 'Best friend' mug that she had bought for him the Christmas before last, sat on the shelf, filled with pens, near to a framed photo of them both in the school play. Her surroundings were only part of the event she wanted to commit to memory, more important than any of these things; she would remember the feeling of lying naked in his arms, the smoothness of his breathing and the warm air being expelled softly on to her cheek. She felt wonderfully alive, even if still a little drunk. Life couldn't get any better than this moment. She had everything she had ever wanted, but it was only temporary, it wasn't going to last. That's why she had to remember everything. There was no time for sleep.

Outside, Annie could hear the birds starting their morning chorus. Jack twitched and re-positioned himself in the bed, Annie hoped he would free her arm that had lost all feeling ages ago – he didn't. It was no good; she needed to moved, besides which she needed to pee. Reluctantly she disentangled herself from Jack and made her way to the bathroom. She looked closely at her reflection in the bathroom mirror. Her eyes were smudged; big dark rings of mascara accentuated the lack of sleep. Her hair curls were all tangled and dishevelled. Cinderella had returned home from the ball and was back to sweeping cinders. The reality of their actions started to hit home. They had crossed the line between friends and lovers. They couldn't turn back time. What if it was just drink talking with Jack? What if in the cold light of day he thought being with Annie was all a great big mistake? She mentally calmed herself and decided that no matter what happened in the future, she still had this moment and she would treasure it. She made her way back into the bedroom and Jack's arms, holding him as close as she dare without waking him. What she felt, what they did together, it wasn't wrong - it couldn't ever be wrong. In the corner of the shelf she noticed the small statue of Our Lady that his parents gave him on his first Holy Communion. Annie closed her eyes and prayed as she drifted off to sleep, *'Our Lady, please let him feel the same way. Please don't let them take him away.'*

Chapter 6

Annie and Jack stood on the vast Victorian platform at Preston train station hugging as if their life depended upon it. Jack's Mother and Father were sat a short distance away as a small metal bistro table drinking coffee, which had spent the last hour in a tea pot on top of a warm hob trying to keep its contents luke warm against all odds.

To Annie it was both Heaven and Hell waiting for the arrival of Jack's train to Manchester Airport and ultimately the other side of the world. It was 'Heaven' that Jack was still in her arms and 'Hell' because then he would be gone, without the knowledge of when he would return for her to feel him in her arms again. Jack pulled her slightly to one side to make sure he was out of ear shot from his parents.

'Annie, It's not too late?' He begged 'I can still stay. I don't have to go!' These were the words she longed to hear, but she knew he had to go. She had promised herself and Jack's Mother- (*Annie had been cornered*) that she wouldn't interfere in Jack's education. His mother promised that if Annie encouraged Jack to go, she wouldn't stand in his way of coming back to England after his education had been completed. What Marcia was really saying was if you interfere with the decision to go I'll make sure I break up your relationship for good. Annie knew Marcia Parish well enough to understand she had the power to make things very difficult for her and Jack and that was the last thing she wanted. Annie looked deeply and imploringly into his eyes.

'We've been through this a hundred times.' She reaffirmed 'You can't stay for me. You have your own life to lead. You have to do what's right for you.' She touched the side of his face tenderly with her fingertips. 'It won't be for long - and when you finish your degree and I finish mine - well let's see what happens? I may come out there or you might come back here? There's no point putting pressure on ourselves now? We can do this Jack, Can't we?' Jack nodded, but without the conviction needed to believe him. What was going to happen? She really had no idea. They may both feel completely different in three years' time. There was no way of seeing the future; they just had to live it day by day, even though she was encouraging him to go, she wanted to make it clear that she would wait for him. Her heart was his; no amount of distance would change that.

'Like we agreed Jack I'm going to get a part-time job and save up. Maybe next year I can come over to see you or you could come and see me?' She choked on the words as they exited her mouth, tears were streaming down her face.' You don't get rid of me that easily Annie!! We've been friends since I can remember; I'm not going to let a little thing like moving across the other side of the world stop that!' He said trying to make light of the situation. Jack tenderly wiped her tears away with his the corner of his jacket. She took a deep breath trying to pull her-self together. She wanted to leave him with a wonderful lasting memory until their next meeting, not the vision of her snotty nose and blotchy, puffy eyes. She looked up at him. Jack's face was ashen. His eyes were brimming with tears, but having his father in his line of vision was stopping him expressing fully what he was feeling. His father had been less than sympathetic when Jack had pleaded his case for staying with Annie; he had no comprehension of why Jack would want to stay, with all the opportunities that were waiting for him. Jack's Mother and Father were shocked to say the least, when he told them about Annie. They had engaged in several private conversations debating the foolishness of his actions and putting them down to a knee jerk reaction to going. Never once did the possibility of his feelings being true enter into the conversation. John Parrish was convinced Jack was trying to make things more complicated on purpose.

Jack glanced across at his father, his disapproval rolled across the empty space between them on the platform, destroying any possibility of intimacy in their final moments together. Any Public shows of emotion where not acceptable to John parrish. The tannoy system jerked in to life - *'The next train to arrive at platform two is the ten twenty to Manchester Airport, calling at Chorley, Bolton and Salford'.* Jack could see his father leaping to his feet and gathering their bags. There was no possibility of missing the train through miss -management of time! John and Marcia Parrish walked towards Jack and Annie.

'Better make it a swift goodbye Jack we don't want to miss the train.' John Parrish turned his attentions to Annie. 'Annie take care of yourself and study hard when you get to university. Good luck with the rest of your life.' Typical thought Annie, he obviously doesn't think he'll see me again, but it was usual for him to show as much sensitivity as a lion in the gladiators ring. He couldn't have been more transparent if he tried. Marcia hugged Annie with little affection, but more gratitude that a scene had been avoided and they were going to manage to get Jack on to the train without bringing attention to themselves.

'It's been a pleasure having you round at our house over the years Annie - We'll give you two a minute to say your goodbyes, but remember the train will leave a couple of minutes after it arrives.' Marcia guided John Parrish by his arm and against his will to their platform to await the train.

Almost as Marcia finished her words the rattle of the train engine could be heard making its way up the track way before it came into sight. Annie reached into her bag and pulled out a small parcel that had been perfectly wrapped in red and grey paper.

'This is for you.' She said placing it carefully into his hands. 'Don't open it now – do it later, on the train.' Jack nodded and placed the parcel in his pocket. Then he pulled her back into his arms for the last time until, well he didn't know when.

'I love you Annie - No matter how far apart we are or for how long remember that will never change. I'm sorry Annie, but – one day we will be together.' Tears were flowing down both of their cheeks. Annie nodded, she couldn't speak, for if she did, she knew she would shout the words *'don't go'* and she couldn't stop him going- not now. For a while at least they would have to lead their lives separately. She took his face in her hands feeling every crease and contour committing it to her eternal memory. She kissed the tears from his eyes, and then silenced his stifled sobs with a tender kiss on his lips. 'I love you too' she whispered' and remember Jack Parrish I've not finished with you yet so you'd better come back!'

On the train Jack's Mother and Father sat together, whilst Jack sat behind, watching his life disappear behind him with every mile of track. He took the parcel Annie had given to him out of his pocket. He opened it slowly and carefully, there was no rush, it would take them at least three quarters of an hour before they would reach the airport. Inside the parcel he found a delicate silver picture frame containing a photo of Annie, dressed in her Ball gown. Tucked into the corner of the frame was a small folded piece of paper. He opened it and read 'To Jack, my one true love, yours forever, Annie xx' Jack turned his face towards the window trying to make sure none of the other passengers or his father could see his tears that he now allowed to flow freely. He had approximately half an hour to fall apart and pull himself back together before reaching the airport.

Chapter 7

Three weeks later Annie was alone in the house for the first time in days. She went upstairs and into the bathroom, locking the door behind her. She didn't want to take any chances, even though her mum and dad were out doing the weekly shop, blissfully oblivious to the trauma Annie was experiencing. She sat on the side of the bath trying to mentally prepare herself for what might happen next. She gave herself a good talking to, trying to calm herself down. She was probably panicking for nothing, but she had to find out one way or the other. She slipped the pregnancy test out of its box and read the instructions carefully. She had only ever seen one of these in the adverts on television or in magazines. She had been careful not to buy it at her local chemist, she didn't want any of the neighbours to see her and report back to her parents.

'God the shame', if this was positive. She had no idea what she would say to her parents. The 'God Catholic girl' had gone bad. She could try pleading the 'Immaculate Conception', but she had a feeling they wouldn't buy it. With all the fuss and commotion of getting everything ready for university she hadn't realised that her period was late. It was only when she opened her dressing table draw to start her packing that she came across the box of tampons and realised something was wrong – it was still full and she knew she had bought it when she was still at college. Something was definitely amiss. She stood up and looked into the bathroom mirror. She pulled her 'T' shirt tautly over her chest. Had her breasts got bigger? Or was it just her imagination running wild. For a split second she allowed herself to believe that all was well and it was going to be some hormone imbalance that had stopped her period or the shock of Jack leaving for Australia, but she also knew that she had never been so much as even a day late since the day her periods started. She followed the instructions on the box carefully. It wasn't the easiest thing to pee on a stick, but she managed it. She placed the stick on the corner of the bath and waited. The temptation to peak at the results took hold of her, but her need to have a correct reading was greater. *'Please, please let it be a false alarm'* she silently pleaded with her own body. It was true, that on the night of the ball Jack and Annie did have unprotected sex, but surely she wouldn't get caught the first time – would she? She couldn't be that unlucky? She ran every possible scenario through her head in the time she was waiting. Three minutes seemed like three hours. The egg timer that she had taken into the bathroom eventually pinged. Annie picked the pregnancy test up and stared at it trying to make her brain register the reading and respond, but all she could do was sit and stare – *shame of all shames* -it was positive. The 'good Catholic girl' was pregnant. It was at least twenty minutes later before Annie opened the bathroom door. Her eyes red and cheeks stained with tears. She had no idea what she was going to do next. It was all such a great big mess. A million questions raced through her head. What will Jack say? Should she even tell Jack? – What help could he offer from such a great distance? He could do nothing to

help from Australia, could he? How were her parents going to react – especially her father? Would they throw her out? What was she going to do about college? How would she cope with caring for a baby – and then the question she didn't even dare admit to herself? Should she even go through with the pregnancy and have the baby or should she commit the mortal sin of taking her unborn babies life? She had been taught from a young age that to do this would be wrong – in the churches eyes, but in reality it wasn't the church or her local priest who would be giving up his future and his life, but that wasn't what worried her. It was coping with it alone that frightened her. It was all just too much to cope with and the one person she would normally confide in was half way around the other side of the world and virtually unable to be contacted. She went in to her bedroom and lay down on her bed, whispering in between sobs into the thin air surrounding her over and over again 'Jack I need you', but it did no good, her whispers were lost in the air before ever finding their way out of the bedroom - she was still alone – and pregnant.

Annie kept well clear of her parents when they returned from their shopping trip. She wasn't sure if she could put on a brave face and pretend nothing was wrong, when what she really wanted to do was to run to her parents and tell them everything and wait for them to assure her that everything would turn out well in the end. So she opted to got to town and then to the cinema, anything to take her mind off the situation. She told her parents she was going with friends from college, but she went on her own. She didn't want to subject anyone to suffering the mood she was in.

Annie could see the lights on in the front room as she neared her house. Once inside she stuck her head a round the living room door, just to say she was tired and going to bed. She made the encounter as short and sweet as possible. Her mum and dad never questioned her actions; they were still blissfully oblivious to Annie's dilemma and the pain she was going through.

Annie looked across at the alarm clock; it flashed three a.m., she still hadn't managed to switch her brain off long enough to get any sleep. She had kept the news of her pregnancy to herself, the fewer people who knew the better. She didn't want anyone to slip up and be put into the position of being forced to tell her parents before her own mind was set. She wanted a little time to think and decide what she should do.

She needed to speak to Jack, but she couldn't risk asking to use the phone at home, she'd be forced into explaining to her mum and dad, what was so important that she needed to ring if she was found out. She slid out of bed and dressed in her jeans and sweatshirt, then made her way out of the house as quietly as possible, taking a handful of change from the jar in her bedroom. She walked briskly to the phone box at the corner of the park and dialled Jack's number. No reply, just an answer machine. That was not the way she wanted Jack to find out. She hung up. She would have to find another way to contact him.

No one had noticed her absence. Annie crept back into the house without detection. Once back in her bedroom she put the bedside light on and pulled a pad of paper from her shelf. She stared at it hoping that a letter would write itself, as she had no idea how to break the news to Jack that he was potentially going to be a father. It would be the last thing he was expecting in one of her letters. It took Annie some time and a dozen false starts, before she found the words and began to write.

Dear Jack,

I am sorry to have to write this letter to you and worry you at such a difficult time, but you are my best friend and this concerns you. I felt it was only fair to let you know what is happening.

Please understand that I am not asking you to do anything. I just want to tell you and to know what you think. Please forgive me for sending the news in this way, but I have no choice. I'm pregnant – yes I'm shocked too. I only found out yesterday and you should be the first to know. I want you to know that I don't regret anything that we did. The night of the ball was and will always be the most special day of my life - whatever the outcome please know I will love you always. Please don't worry. I'm fine and well. I just need to know what you think and feel before I decide what to do next. Please write as fast as you can or ring if your parents will let you as I should leave for Manchester in a little over two weeks and need to make some decisions. I haven't told my parents yet, but it's only a matter of time before they find out.

I'm sorry Jack, but I didn't know who else to turn too.

My love always,

Annie X

Annie read and re-read the letter before sealing it into the envelope. She didn't want to sound too needy or depressed. The last thing she wanted to do was upset and worry Jack, when she knew there was little he could do from such a great distance. If she allowed herself to daydream, she imagined him flying in, sweeping her off her feet and telling her that it was wonderful news about the baby. In reality she knew was going to be very different.

Annie took the letter to the main post office first thing the following morning. She asked the Post Office Assistant to send it the fastest way possible – whatever the expense. She handed the letter over to the post master with a silent wish attached, hoping he would contact her soon. As the letter left her hands, she knew there was nothing else she could do now except to wait.

John Parrish announced his entrance to the empty house as he unlocked the door. There was no reply, he was home alone. He had chosen a large gated house in the small town of Katoomba, in the Blue Mountains, on the outskirts of Sydney.

'Anyone at home?' He called again. Jack was probably at University which was a thirty minute train ride away. Jack had barely had time to unpack before he was due to enrol, as the term times were different. He was already miles behind the other students as they were already six months into their course, but Jack's father had assured the University of his Sons' Ability to catch up, his donation to the science wing had made them see sense. On any days free from lectures, a pound to a penny, you would find Jack sat in the library, pouring over books and documents trying to cram information into his brain.

Marcia was out, doing what Marcia did best, which was either shopping or visiting the beauty parlour, either way it involved spending John's money as fast as he could earn it. John resented being Marcia's cash cow, but divorce was frowned upon within his company. The men with stable home lives were progressing the fastest up the promotion ladder. He could put up with her spending habits as long as she kept her side of the bargain and played the dutiful wife when necessary. He picked the mail up from the table in the hall. Mary, the cleaner had placed them in a neat pile awaiting John's attention. John leafed through them, not giving them much consideration. Letters and bills were a chore he could well do without. A hand written envelope addressed to Mr J. Parrish caught his eye, he opened it. After the first line he realised that he was not the intended recipient. Until that moment he hadn't even considered the fact that it may have been for Jack, but John Parrish had no hesitation in continuing to read the contents. By the time he had reached the end of the letter, he was enraged. How dare she write to Jack claiming she was pregnant, of all the underhanded ways to try and get Jack to return to Preston! It would be over his dead body. There was no way on this earth Jack was going back to England to become a teenage father. Most likely it wasn't Jack's baby anyway, even if she was telling the truth regarding being pregnant. Jack had settled better than John and Marcia had expected. John Parrish had plans for his son and becoming a father at the age of eighteen was not one of them. John folded the letter, placing it back into the envelope and then hid it in his top inside pocket. Jack didn't ever need to know about this letter. He would make sure of it.

Annie stood vigilantly by the front door every day for a week waiting for the mail to drop through the letter box before one letter appeared with the distinctive airmail symbol emblazoned on it. Annie expelled a huge sigh of relief that Jack had answered her letter. She didn't know what the letter would hold, but at least he had cared enough to respond and quickly as she requested. No one had noticed her strange behaviour, but she never left the house until the mail had been delivered. Today, thankfully she was alone. mum and dad were at work - the house was empty, she didn't have to worry about her parents overseeing the contents of the letter. Carefully she pulled it from the envelope. A small rectangular piece of paper fell to the floor. It was a cheque made out to Annie for one thousand pounds. She was confused, why would there be a cheque? She read on.

Dear Annie,

It is with regret that I am forced to write to you on Jack's behalf. Jack no longer wishes to be in your confidence. He feels his life is based over here now and that he must let go of the past and that includes you. He is sorry for any upset he may have caused you, but he no longer feels the same about you.

If you are indeed pregnant he does not wish you to go through with it or to be acknowledged as the Father. Enclosed is a cheque to cover any costs and for your inconvenience. As you can see from Jack's lack of ability to deal with this subject, he is certainly not mature enough to be Father.

Please do not attempt to contact Jack again. You are his past. He has moved on and has a new girlfriend. If you do care for him, I hope you are mature enough to keep his best interests at heart and leave him to get on with his life. Let me make this perfectly clear, this is what Jack Wants. He will not make contact with you ever again. We do not expect to hear from you again.

Yours Sincerely

John Parrish.

Annie sank to her knees and sobbed uncontrollably. Jack has a new girlfriend! The words repeated in her head. Whatever she expected to find in the letter, nothing prepared her for what she found. She wrapped her arms around herself trying to stop her body from convulsing with anguish. How could he! How could he be so hard and so cruel? She could understand that his father would react in that way, but Jack she thought was made from different material. How wrong could she be and to have a new girlfriend already! She felt a pain in her chest and knew instantly that it was her heart breaking. Nothing mattered anymore, college, packing, what anyone thought, her mum, dad, friends. She was alone now. She was the only person who could decide what was best for her. She sat crying on the blue Axminster carpet in the hall until she could cry no more. Jack had let her down. He would *never* let her down again, of that she was certain.

Suddenly a wave of calmness and certainty washed over her freeing her from her indecision. She knew what she had to do. She picked herself up from the floor, took her jacket from the hook on the wall, together with her black leather handbag. She paused and looked at her reflection in the hall mirror to check how badly her face was stained from the tears and if anyone passing would notice. She looked red and blotchy, her eyes bulging like a fish pumped with too much air, but she didn't care. If anything it would help her case. She pulled the door shut behind her. It would only take her five minutes to walk to her destination. No time to change her mind or talk herself out of it.

The sun was shining; people were going about their lives as normal enjoying the last days of warmth before autumn took hold. The decisions she made today would affect the rest of her life. She knew it was a decision that she should sleep on and consider, but she knew herself too well. If she waited, she would lose her courage and be persuaded into a different path. Annie pushed the large door open entering the building which was to be her destination. The surgery was full of old men and Mothers with small children. Annie had managed to navigate the toddlers and push chairs and made her way to a middle aged woman sat at the reception desk, who asked if she could help.

'Yes you can help.' Said Annie. 'I need and emergency appointment to see a doctor - Now.'

Chapter 8

To Jack's surprise, he and Aussie life were well suited. He loved the open air life style, outdoor sports, barb-b-q's, sunshine and the relaxed attitude to life. There were only two major down sides to the move. Firstly, was sheer volume of work he had to catch up on at university and secondly the fact that he had a constant ache in his heart from missing Annie every day. He had made some friends within the university community, in the little spare time he found, and the locals had welcomed the new 'Pommy' with open arms, but it wasn't the same as having Annie next to him every day sharing all his adventures, as she had always done. He had to explain everything to his new friends, what music he liked, what TV, who he was and what he wanted to be. Annie already knew all of these things; he could just get on with living, now he seemed to spend his life explaining. It was more than simply missing her company. He missed her smile, her scent, her laugh – the list was endless. He was in love, nothing could erase her from his mind, not even distance, but John Parrish was about to try.

Jack's Father had immediately settled in to Australian life. He enjoyed being the new 'Top dog' in town. He moved around the city, meeting new people, working out in what capacity he could use them or discard them if they had no obvious purpose. John Parrish was out to impress his new work colleagues and Jack was part of the package. Each new set of 'useful' people John came into contact with, were invited to a reception at the house. Caterers were summoned at Marcia's insistence, then John and Marcia would host the perfect party. John also saw this as a perfect opportunity to find Jack a replacement for Annie. At John's request many guests brought along eligible daughters or nieces, Jack had caught his father on the phone on several occasions requesting that they bring along their teenage children, especially female, who were of a similar age to Jack, so that his son could make new friends. Jack had begged him to stop, but John Parrish simply defended himself by saying he was only asking them out of politeness. Jack constantly felt as if he was being set up by his father, but it wasn't going to work. Several of them were great company and he enjoyed the attention, as any young, red blooded male would, but when it came to the crunch and Jack could see the possibility of the girl wanting something more than friendship, he reversed out of the situation like a thief at a heist. His heart still belonged to Annie. No one came close to making him change his allegiance, much to John's annoyance.

It was at the end of such a night of entertainment that Jack excused himself from the party in order to write yet another letter to Annie. Tonight it had been the Peterson's, a middle aged couple, thankfully with no children in tow. Jack had been paraded around as a prize exhibit of the 'perfect son' and student. He had made positive noises about the land of opportunity he now called 'home' when asked. He served the drinks and re-fills on demand. The only reason he put himself through this on a regular basis was the financial reward delivered by his Father for attending. Jack had plans for the money; his goal was to get a ticket home to England to see Annie as soon as possible.

Jack had written numerous letters to Annie, but he hadn't yet received any replies – not one. He had phoned Annie's home a couple of times when his parents were out, but there had been no reply. Jack couldn't understand why he wasn't receiving any letters. He knew she would be busy with all the preparation for college, but surely she could find a little time to write even a brief note. Anything would be better than the silence he was suffering. Annie was not the type to be flaky or forget. He was starting to feel uneasy about the situation. Now, in the safe surroundings of his bedroom and knowing his father would be drinking until the early hours and unlikely to interrupt him, Jack started yet another letter to Annie.

My dearest Annie,

*I can't begin to tell you how much I'm missing you, but what's driving me crazy is the fact that I've not had **any** letters from you. I know you have to get on with your life and I have to get on with mine, but I did think you would have written at least a few times, but not even once Annie? Are you that cross at me? You know I had no choice in the matter of coming here. I'm longing to hear from you to find out what's going on in your life, how university is for you and what your new address is there. I'm assuming my letters are going via your mum at the moment as I don't have an address for you in Manchester. I've rung your mum's house a couple of times, but can't get a reply. Nothing is the same without you here and I need to know that you are okay.*

I don't want to fall out with you, especially at this great distance, but don't make me pay for my parent's choices - it's killing me. If you feel differently about me or have found someone else at least put me out of my misery and let me know. I'd rather have you just as a friend than not hear from you at all, but just to make it clear how I feel -

I love you Annie and always will.

Please write to me soon. My heart is always yours.

My Love always, Jack xxxxx

Jack was almost in tears by the time he had finished his letter. Writing his thoughts down seemed to magnify the loss he was feeling. What he wouldn't give to be able to speak to her now or hold her in his arms inhaling her fragrance. He sealed the envelope then wrote the address on the front and the return address on the back - just in case. He took it downstairs and placed it on the hall table. In the lounge he could see his father finishing the last of the brandy bottle, Jack had seen this scenario many times before - he knew his father was drunk, the amount of alcohol he had consumed during the evening, he couldn't fail to be. Jack hovered in the door way, not wanting to be forced in to conversation and keeping his father company whilst he drank.

'There's a letter for Annie on the Hall table. Please will you post it for me tomorrow?' Jack hated asking, but he wanted to be sure it reached the post as quickly as possible.

'Sure thing.' Replied his father, not even taking the trouble to look up at his son. Jack's father had offered almost from the beginning to post any mail for England through work. He said it got there faster because work paid to have documents couriered to Britain on a daily basis. So they had slipped into the routine of Jack writing the letters for Annie and leaving them for John to take the next day to post. The extra money Jack was saving went into his airfare fund, every dollar made a difference.

'I'm going to bed now,' said Jack turning his back on his father. 'Don't forget to take the letter - it's important!'

'Have I forgotten yet?' John replied curtly with a large dose of distain.

'No – you haven't. Good night.' At least it was one thing his father had done for him on a regular basis. There weren't any others.

John Parish sat for a while, enjoying the beautiful surroundings he had the privilege to live in, the culmination of the fruits of his labour. He had no regrets regarding leaving the UK, only regret that he couldn't have made the journey alone. John had played the part of family man to the letter as far as the outside world was concerned, but he had never compromised for anyone in his life, not even his wife. He had made it plain to her, put up or shut up – she chose the latter. The move to Australia was necessary to further his career and although he would have made the journey solo if necessary, having Marcia and Jack with him gave some gravitas to the 'Family man' image, he spent so long creating.

When John was sure his son was upstairs in bed, he went into the hall and picked up the letter and took it back in to the lounge. Marcia had taken herself off to bed as soon as the guests had left. She was as board of all the business parties as Jack was, but at least the people were company to talk to. John didn't converse with Marcia, if he could help it. He was married for practical reasons. It was important to have the home looking clean and neat and she understood how to entertain on the level necessary for his career. His friends had all been aghast when John Parrish announced that he was going to marry the C.E.O.'s daughter all those years ago, especially as at that point he had barely spoken to her, but true to his word two years later they were married and that was the point at which John's interest in Marcia ceased. John sat back in his favourite chair twisting the letter back and forth through his fingers. He took a last gulp of the brandy, draining the glass, then he ripped the letter open and read it. He shook his head in exasperation at the outpouring of emotion his son had written. In John's opinion, Jack needed a lesson in being a 'Man'. All this soppy romantic talk wasn't going to get him a good job or the sort of wife that would be expected of him. Jack needed to focus on his career, not some love sick tart, who was out to ruin his life. It was John's mission to make sure that they didn't speak or communicate. John folded the letter back in to the envelope, and then made his way into his office. He unlocked the filing cabinet and placed the letter in the bottom draw with all the other letters Jack had written – and the letters he had intercepted from Annie, before they got to Jack. What Jack didn't know wouldn't hurt him. He would soon tire of writing when he received no response. It was only a matter of time before John Parrish succeeded in his assignment and Jack forgot all about Annie.

It was three weeks since Annie had received the letter from John Parrish. Every day, she couldn't help herself, she had to check the post to see if Jack had changed his mind and written to tell her, every day she was disappointed. Each day she spent running through all the possibilities in her mind, driving herself almost mad with worry, hoping that she was doing the right thing. From somewhere, Annie had managed to muster enough courage to tell her parents the condition she was in, and to their credit, they promised to support the path she chose. She still found herself cross examining her motives for her decision. It was such a momentous event, how could she be sure? If she made the wrong decision, there would be no going back it was a decision she would have to defend for the rest of her life. Annie needed to get out of the house for some air to clear her mind. She hopped onto the first bus that stopped at the end of the street. Ten minutes later she found herself in the middle of the town centre.

It was a Saturday. The streets were busy with shoppers of all ages, families searching for school uniforms for the September term and young girls Annie's age, looking for the perfect party dress, without a care in the world, as they should be. She was just about to cut through Marks and Spencer's to miss some of the busy spots, when she bumped into Nick. At first she was too busy dodging people to see him coming towards her and she would have marched right passed, oblivious to him, if he hadn't walked in her path to stop her dead in her tracks.

'Annie. How are you? You look well – spending all your money on clothes and shoes as usual?' He joked hoping she was in the mood to accept his banter. He was hoping it would cover up the embarrassment he was feeling, after the way they had parted at the ball. He was hoping that now was a good time to sort things out, especially as Jack was long gone.

'I'm glad I've seen you.' He touched her arm instinctively to show his sincerity, 'I wanted to apologise for leaving you at the ball.' He said rather sheepishly. 'Too much drink is my only excuse and the fact that you looked so gorgeous I wanted you all to myself.' He hoped that she would accept his flattery and his apology. Annie felt her cheeks turning crimson. The memory of that glorious night came flooding back. She wanted to say, *'Don't worry – you did me the best favour ever by leaving.'* – but she managed to keep her tongue still. 'Did you get home okay?' Nick was asking.

'Yes, I was fine' Annie decided to stretch the truth a little; she didn't want to get into another Jack and Nick argument. 'Some friends took me home and as you can see I'm in one piece, so all is well.'

'Good, I'm glad, but it was still wrong of me to abandon you.' He looked down at the ground then tilted his head sideways, giving him large puppy dog eyes. 'Do you forgive me?'

Unexpectedly Annie felt very guilty. She could tell that Nick had been beating himself up over the past few weeks because of the way he had left her, when she wasn't bothered in the slightest and had the most exciting night of her life - after he had gone.

'There's nothing to forgive. I assure you I was fine. Let's just forget it and move on - as friends?' she thought she had better make it clear. She was in no emotional position to start any sort of relationship, other than friendship. She understood Nick well enough to know he would expect there to be an open playing field for her affections now that Jack was off the scene. It only took a second for Nick to hide his disappointment.

'Okay - friends it is. So what are you doing in town?' He plastered a forged smile on his face.

'Just a few things I need and some fresh air, nothing important.' She didn't want to confide her troubles in Nick. He was the last person to be sympathetic with anything that involved Jack.

'What about you? What are you doing in town and when do you leave for college?' She questioned, putting the emphasis back on to him as they walked.

'Actually I've got some news.' His enthusiasm shone through, dispelling the hidden disappointment he'd felt earlier. 'Have you got time to go for a drink? I do mean coffee. I don't think I mix well with alcohol, as you already know. I learned that lesson and I'm not going to repeat it in a hurry!' Annie decided that it was a better choice to spend some time with Nick, than going home to dwell on her situation alone and she had to admit, it was nice to see him.

'Okay, we can go for a coffee - but only if I can have a sticky bun too?' she looked at him returning the large doe eyes. He smiled – she'd won.

'You know how to drive a hard bargain. You'll want froth on your coffee next!'

They went to Brucciani's Italian coffee shop on the high street. It was always a favourite with students. The décor hadn't changed since it opened in the 1930's; its charm was its age, lots of dark wood and Formica tables. It was like an old grandmother's house, warm, cosy, a little chipped around the edges, very familiar, it was famous for its ice cream soda's and the coffee was great. The atmosphere inhabited the very fabric of the building, it wasn't something you could buy or replicate. Nick pointed her in the direction of an empty table and ordered two coffees and two sticky buns at the counter. He found her seated as instructed, at a small round table in the corner near the umbrella stand.

'So, what is this exciting news you have to share?' Asked Annie as he settled into his seat. Nick took a deep breath. 'I'm not going to university – well I am - but not full time. My plans have changed.'

'What – why? I thought it was all settled. You had your place and everything?'

'It was settled – still have a place if I want it, but I've been offered an apprenticeship at aerospace. My uncle heard there was one going, so he got me the forms and – well, they have accepted me. I work full time and go to university one day each week, and there are a few residential weeks I have to go on during the year. This way I get to study my chosen subject and earn at the same time. It's a no brainer really. Actually, I start next week, so my mum has sent me out to get some smart work clothes. It took me all my time to persuade her not to come with me! She still thinks I'm six and still need her to choose my clothes for me! If I left it to her I'd be going to work looking like my father!' He raised his eyebrows to the ceiling and shook his head wondering just what went on in his mother's head.

'So what have you bought so far?' Annie hadn't noticed any evidence of shopping.

'Nothing!' He exclaimed with exasperation. 'I don't know what to buy. I Keep finding things I like , but they're more for going out in than going to work - and if I get the wrong things my mum will just make me go shopping with her and that can't happen!' They laughed at the thought.

'I'll come with you if you like' offered Annie. 'Mind you, I can't guarantee I can do any better than your mother, but I'll give it a go? '

'Believe me; you can't do any worse than I did on my own and you are as sure as hell better than bringing my mum!'

After they had finished their coffee and cake they headed back into the throng of Saturday shoppers. They weaved and threaded their way through the crowds, trying to keep together and unscathed from mums with pushchairs and wilful children or elderly women who believed they owned the whole of the footpath and anyone who came within a three foot radius was in violation of the unwritten rules and was in need of a good dressing down. When they eventually managed to find their way back together Nick took Annie's hand as if it was the most natural thing to do in the world. He winked at her and gave her hand a gentle squeeze.

'I can't lose my best shopper to the walking stick brigade. I'm going to hang on to you!' He squeezed her hand again. She thought about pulling away, but she didn't want to seem churlish. It was doing no harm, he was only being protective, and his shopping trip needed her.

'If you don't keep up I'll have to put children's reins on you!' he scolded as he dragged her into the next shop on his list. She laughed and followed him obediently.

It took two hours of serious shopping before Nick was satisfied with his purchases. They bought two pairs of grey trousers, three white shirts, two ties and a smart Jacket. Nick had never bought so many clothes at one time.

'I'm glad I'm not a girl!' Declared Nick 'I couldn't do this every week!'

'Neither could I!' Agreed Annie 'You know not all girls spend all their spare time shopping. Some of us have a life and a personality! Besides - I don't have the money either!'

'Well you were in town when I met you and I do believe you were shopping?' She smacked him playfully on the arm.

'Yes, but for things like shampoo and other essentials. So, less of the cheek or I'll send you home with a 'red herring'. You're mum will insist on returning it and shopping with you, besides you owe me another coffee after all this hard work.'

'I suppose you'll want another sticky bun too!'

'You're starting to get to know me.' She confirmed.

After three months of writing to Annie, Jack gave up. No letters or phone calls in reply, nothing to give him any reason to hope. Finally, after six months anger got the better of him. Who did she think she was? - Just dropping him after being friends for all those years and especially after the night of the ball when everything changed for the both of them. If she didn't want him, he would find someone that did. That was the easy part for Jack, girls that had been hanging around him in college trying to gain his interest saw a flicker in his eye showing that maybe things had changed and he may be ripe for the picking. He wasn't going to waste his youth waiting for a girl who couldn't be bothered to write to him. Some of the women were hopeful of lasting, meaningful relationships with Jack, but he never gave his heart, he was never emotionally connected to them. He still thought of Annie every day and longed for her every night, but when his mind wandered he made a conscious effort to dis-guard all thoughts of her. Finally he decided that the only way to get over Annie was to 'get over' someone else and her name was Alexandra, Marsha, Belinda and Shona……….. There were many, but not one of them penetrated his heart like Annie had done.

Chapter 9

Three years later.

Jack sat on the train looking out of the window as the familiar countryside rolled past. Nothing seemed to have changed, but he had. His father had been outraged when he announced he was going back to England. No amount of ranting or raging deterred him. Jack had saved his own money during his time in Australia. He didn't need his Father to bankroll this 'jaunt' as his Father had called it.

Jack was a man now, and if his father expected him to act as such then he would have to accept that being a man involved Jack making his own decisions, besides his father promised he could go back to England after university had finished. Jack felt that if he didn't pull himself free from his father's grip now – he never would. Jack had managed to arrange a Job interview in Manchester; it was a global company that was looking for new blood. One of his lecturers' had suggested he apply and to his surprise he was offered an interview. The money he had saved paid for his ticket and he had persuaded his Aunt to provide him with lodgings and food until he got settled. His Aunt Sylvia was his mother's sister and never did like his father, so the persuasion had been minimal. Jack's Mother had pleaded with him to stay, in truth she was more worried about being left alone with his father. Jack was the only thing that made her life bearable. The marriage would have been over ages ago, but Marcia was not strong enough to fight against John and didn't want to live without the trappings of wealth he could provide. So, she had settled for a life of following her husband's wishes regardless of how much they differed from her own. Jack was unaware of the fact that Marcia had been against the move to Australia, but lifestyle had become everything to Marcia and without John everything would go. John Parrish was wise enough to make sure she had no cash of her own. She liked the lifestyle she had become accustomed to. She decided that it was better to be unhappy in luxury rather than happy in squalor – at least for the moment.

The p.a. announcement that they would be arriving at Preston station jolted him from his thoughts. He gathered his bags and waited for the train to come to a standstill. For some reason he expected it to look different, but it was exactly the same, even down to the coffee stand. He could see Aunt Sylvia was waiting for him on the platform as the train came to a standstill. She was smiling and waving with genuine pleasure – at least someone was glad to see him.

'My goodness Jack, you're a young man now and very good looking! You obviously get that from our side of the family and not your father's!' she laughed. 'Are you tired? I can either dump your bags in the car and take you out for lunch or we can go back to the house if all you need to do is sleep?' she was looking at him expectantly.

'Lunch would be great if that's okay with you? It seems ages since I ate something decent, you know what airline food is like!'

'Oh, you poor dear. Don't worry we'll get some food into you very soon. Anywhere in particular you would like to go? I suppose I'm the one who should know the best places to go as you're a bit out of touch, but I don't come into town for meals very often. Uncle Frank makes me go to the golf club instead. I can't tell you how boring it is! – But that's another story. So where should we go?'

'I don't mind?' said Jack who just wanted food of any description.

'Well, in that case I know a good Italian in town, we'll go there.'

Lunch was great. Aunt Sylvia talked easily asking question about his mum, where they lived, the differences between life in Australia and England and all about the job interview in Manchester. After a couple of hours exchanging news she slid a key across the table towards him.

'You're going to need this - It's for the house. I'm not getting out of my bed at all hours to let you in and out. At my age I need beauty sleep - all can get! The house rules are – Tidy up after yourself, keep safe, because it's me that will have to tell your mother and father if anything happens. Definitely no drugs of any description and lock the house up when you go out.'

'Is that all?' Jack asked in disbelief. He was used to the long list of rules his father expected him to live by.

'I can make more up if it would make you happier?' Jack shook his head; he was enjoying being treated as an adult for a change. '– if there's anything else we've forgotten.' She continued, 'well, we'll cross that bridge when we come to it.'

Jack was delighted. Not just at the short list of rules, but it was the first time that he truly felt that he had been treated as an equal by a member of his family. Aunt Sylvia was so completely different to his mother; it was hard to believe they grew up in the same house as children. Their conversations covered all subjects. She was a fountain of knowledge and a good listener. By the time they reached dessert, he knew that he could tell her anything. It reminded him that Annie was the only other person he had had this sort of connection with.

'There's someone I want to look up in Preston – and sooner rather than later?' He said, hoping she would understand what he was leading too. 'I don't want to push my luck, especially as I've just arrived, but is there any chance you would drop me off on the way back. It's not far from your house and I can walk round to yours later – if you don't mind me abandoning you hours after I've arrived?'

'Is it an old friend? Or an old school chum?' her question was inquisitive, not demanding.

'It's Annie, she……'

'I remember Annie. She was at every family party that happened. Lovely girl. I always thought she had a soft spot for you. Is she looking forward to seeing you?' Jack looked down inspecting the crumbs on the table cloth. Aunt Sylvia picked up on the vibrations.

'I'm sorry – Don't answer that. It's none of my business. I always have a habit of saying the things I'm thinking before I kick my brain in to gear.'

'No it's fine. I don't mind you asking. It's just that she stopped writing to me whilst I've been away and I don't know what happened to her. I just need to know that she's alright.' Sylvia held her hand up in the air signalling the bill from the waiter.

'Then you can go and see right now.'

Aunt Sylvia dropped him at the end of Annie's road. He paused and waved her off into the distance. He needed a few moments to compose himself before he knocked on the door. He couldn't remember the last time he felt so nervous. He wished he'd checked his appearance in the car's vanity mirror, for all he knew, his face could be covered with the tomato sauce from the pasta he had just enjoyed – another good impression. He took a deep breath and started walking towards the house. It was early evening, the light was starting to fade, some of the houses had switched on their lights. In the distance he could see a beacon of light shining from Annie's house. His stomach was churning; the Italian food wasn't helping the feeling of nausea trying to overtake him. He had to know why she didn't write. Maybe he wasn't going to like what he found but at least he would know. Anyway, Annie probably didn't live here anymore, but if her mum did still lived here, at least she would be able to fill in the gaps or tell him where she lived now.

Jack opened the gate into the front garden; it squeaked as all garden gates do, it's obligatory. His hands were shaking and his palms sweaty and to top it all he now definitely felt sick. He raised his hand to knock on the door before he had time to change his mind.

Inside the house Nick and Annie were bathing Violet. Annie's mum and dad had gone away for a few days and they were enjoying the luxury of having the house to themselves. It was hard at times, not having the space afforded to other young couples, but at last the light was at the end of the tunnel. They had found a house they liked and were waiting for the sale to go through, now that the wedding was over, they could concentrate on setting up home for their family.

'Was that the door?' Annie stopped making splashes in the bath for Violet to listen. They heard the loud precise knock again.

'I'll go,' Nick smiled at Annie, 'you carry on bathing Violet. I can see she's enjoying getting you wet.'

'Thanks a bunch!' said Annie passing Violet one of the small plastic ducks from the side of the bath.

Nick dried his hands on a towel at the same time as making his way down the stairs. He wasn't in the mood for a conversation on double glazing or how the Bible could save his life. He braced himself for a stream of questions and a quick exit line then he opened the door. When the solid wooden door revealed the person who had knocked, Nick decided he would have gladly swapped and put up with a hundred callers selling conservatories rather than deal with the person in front of him. Both parties stood in stunned silence for a few moments. It seemed like a life time to both of them. Neither one wanted to be the first to break the silence and speak. Eventually it was Annie who did. Jack recognised her voice in an instant.

'Who is it Nick?' She called from upstairs.

'It's nothing – No one - it's okay you carry on!' He called up the stairs. Nick stood staring at Jack, who by this time was looking extremely cross at being referred to as 'nothing' and 'no one'. They were both still shocked and at a loss of how to progress their conversation. Of all the people that may have opened Annie's door, Jack had never considered Nick as a contender; he had never been in the frame of possibilities. Jack was seething internally, but he knew that he had to keep his cool. The memory of the last time they had met came to the fore front of Jack's mind. He didn't want a repeat performance, although the end result was magical.

'I'd like to speak to Annie please.' Jack kept it polite, short and to the point, his eyes however couldn't hide his contempt, they were giving Nick a cold hard stare. Nick stepped out onto the doorstep pulling the door to behind him.

'She's busy Jack. She has a new life and she doesn't want to see you.' Nick was speaking in an aggressive whisper. Jack was having none of it.

'I'd rather she told me that herself!' Jack raised his voice hoping it would attract Annie's attention, wherever she was in the house.

'Jack, things are different now, you were her past. She's with me now.'

'That's as may be Nick, but I need to hear all this from Annie. I'm not leaving until I speak to her!' Jack stood his ground with no intention of being moved.

'We're married Jack!' Nick threw the words at Jack like a weapon. They hit him full force, piercing his soul. He physically staggered backwards, reeling at Nick's words.

'You can't be!' He shouted, beginning to lose his cool.

'We are and I'd prefer you not to shout as you'll upset the baby.' Jack shook his head trying to expel the words, refusing to let them enter his brain.

'You can't be serious. You're both too young!'

'Young or not, it's what's happened. - You left and…….' Nick stopped speaking as the door behind him opened.

There stood Annie in the doorway holding Violet. Jack's rage instantly evaporated. Annie looked beautiful, even more beautiful that the night of the ball. He couldn't believe his eyes, she was not only a wife, but also a mother. How could her life have changed so dramatically and for him to be so unaware? He was beginning to understand why she hadn't written. She knew this news would drive him crazy.

Annie stood transfixed to the spot, unable to move. The distant memory that she tried daily to forget was standing in front of her. She felt acutely embarrassed that Nick had opened the door. If she had opened it, she could have prepared him and let him down gently or simply kissed him and persuaded him to take her with him. In her fantasies that's what would have happened, but this was real.

'Jack I …..' Words failed her. His eyes were penetrating her soul. She knew nothing she said would soften the blow Jack had just received. She was distinctly aware of Nick in front of her with his arm across the doorway barring the way through, she didn't know if it was to keep Jack out or her in?

Annie wanted to keep her distance, she didn't trust herself. If she got too close there was no telling what would happen. Annie tried to get a grip of herself for Nick's sake. She owed it to Nick; especially after all they had been through over the past three years. Annie had tried to convince herself she was over Jack – she couldn't have been more wrong and she could tell by the look of horror on Nick's face that he knew it too. The tension was tangible. Both men were staring at her waiting for some sort of response. It was unbearable, whatever she said one man was going to get hurt.

'I only have one question Annie.' It was Jack speaking. 'Are you married to him?' Jack pointed at Nick; his words were full of venom. Annie hesitated for the slightest of moments. 'Yes. I am.' The words were spoken quietly and with an air of apology. Nick stayed silent; he knew by Annie's reaction that Jack Parrish still had the power to destroy his life. Jack threw his arms open wide in a gesture of defeat. 'Well then! There's nothing else to say – is there? – I hope you'll both be very happy.' His words were directed to Annie and smothered in insincerity. He gave Annie one last look then turned and ran out of the gate and down the street, never to be seen again.

Nick turned to Annie before she had time to react to Jack's leaving. 'Did you know he was coming?' His words were laden with accusation. She could see the fury in his eyes. She stared him down.

'You know I've had no contact with him since the letter his father wrote to me.' Nick Knew it was true, but he wasn't satisfied. He wanted her to have told him to go and never darken their doorstep again, that she was happily married and more important- in love with him, not Jack. Nick picked Violet out from Annie's arms.

'She'll catch cold out here. I'll take her in.' He walked past her leaving her stood alone on the doorstep dazed and confused, wondering if she would ever see Jack again.

Jack ran to the park where he had gone on that fateful day when he had been told about Australia by his parents. There was only a little light, but enough to see the paths. It all made sense now. Nick had made his move on Annie as soon as he had left for Australia. She was at a vulnerable point, he probably got her pregnant on purpose, to try and keep her. Well it worked. Now she was a married woman with a child. As much as he wanted to be with Annie, even with another man's child, he was no home wrecker. Annie had made her choice and Jack would have to learn to live with that and get on with his own life. It was too late for them; she would never be his Annie again.

Jack didn't go to the job interview; instead he took the first flight home. He knew his Father would revel in his unsuccessful return, but it was a small price to pay compared with staying in Preston. He's couldn't live in the country knowing she was with Nick – any other person maybe, but not him.

Chapter 10

14 years later.

Annie stood by the window and watched as the removal man took the last of the boxes and loaded them on to the van. The rooms in the house seemed larger and unfamiliar, which was silly, because they were still the same rooms she shared with Nick and Violet. The wallpaper was an old friend she recognised well, but it all seemed out of context without their familiar furniture and personal belongings and the long row of photographs plotting Violets growth from a baby to a young woman. Their whole life had been packed away, including Nick.

It had been a long and hard decision to leave the four walls that had been their family home for over twelve years. It was the only house that Violet remembered. In the early years it was full of birthday parties, Easter egg hunts and Christmas gatherings, then dramas about school and boys. The last set of memories were by far the saddest, the knock on the front door from the police to tell them Nick had been involved in a car crash, the endless flow of people gathering to bring their condolences, then finally taking Nick to his definitive resting place. Annie knew that if they stayed in this house she would never move on. Every room, wall, corner and space held at least one memory of Nick which would keep them in perpetual mourning.

With each box she packed she managed to slowly separate herself from the house, until she reached the point that she was at now - the point of no return. It was time to move forward. She didn't need familiar rooms around her to remember Nick. She carried him with her in her heart always, no matter where in the world she went. It had taken her time to understand this and separate Nick from the bricks and mortar around her. Many of her friends and family still didn't understand that if she stayed she would eventually suffocate and drown in her own memories', but the hardest part was convincing Violet. She had spent weeks shouting, crying, and pleading with her mother to change her mind when Annie had finally found the courage to broach the subject.

'But we can't move! Dad is here, all my friends are here and college is here. You can't take me away to a different part of the country where I don't know any one! I won't go!' Violet declared.

'You know it's closer to granny and we do know people. Try and think of it as an adventure.' Annie tried to sooth her, but the words were futile. Violet was like a stubborn mule, unable to move forward or compromise. Annie understood, Violet needed to feel close to Nick and she was still grieving, but Annie knew if she didn't do something now she never would. If she put it off for Violet's sake, eventually Violet would move out to University and away and that would leave Annie alone in the four walls she loved and hated in equal measure. Annie's nerve would have long gone and she would talk herself out of ever making a move. Annie was certain the time was right - it was now or never. Annie tried a different tack.

'Now is a great time to move. You are at the point where you have to change schools anyway to go to sixth form. I promise you will make new friends. Everyone who meets you can't help but love you!' Flattery sometimes worked with Violet, plus it was true, people did love her. Annie needed to use every tool possible on her side.

'You just want to forget Dad and move on! You're heartless and I hate you!!' Violet's words pierced Annie's fragile heart, leaving the conversation to end as many did, with Violet storming off upstairs or out of the front door. Annie's' response was always the same too. She would sit down on the floor on the spot where she stood and burst in to tears, tearing herself apart, assessing if what she was doing was the 'right thing'.

It had taken seven months for the house to sell and another year before that to make the decision. Annie had helped Violet to accept the decision bit by bit, a little at a time. She still wasn't happy, but she understood her Mother's reasons and decided to give up on her objections or at least put them to one side.

Annie walked around each of the rooms for the last time, checking to make sure nothing had been left behind, but also collecting a few final memories to store and safeguard. Some for herself and some she would hold dear for Violet, until such a time that she needed to be reminded of them. When the time came to pack, Violet went to stay with a school friend for a couple of days, telling Annie that she couldn't bear to be there whilst her mother ripped her memories apart. She wanted to remember the house just as it was, not full of boxes and then ultimately bare. Annie understood and made no objections. In some ways it was easier, not having to worry about Violet with every item she moved or packed or threw away. When everything was packed away Annie watched from the front bedroom window as the removal van ambled off down the road. All their belongings were off to a new life. It was time for Annie and Violet to follow.

When Annie and Nick had married they moved away with Nicks' job. Annie had been against it at the beginning. She was a young mum, who needed the support of her own mother, but it was a good move and meant promotion for Nick. In the end Annie gave in. She knew how much it meant to Nick and after everything he had done for her, it was the least she could do. Now it was time to come home. It took four hours, most of it stuck in traffic on the M6 before Annie and the removal van to reach their final destination. Annie decided that if she was going to change her life, she may as well change everything, including her job.

Annie had scoured the newspapers looking for a suitable job, but there was little she was qualified for and now that she was a widow she needed to support herself and Violet. Annie only knew how to do two things well, firstly, how to be a Mother and secondly how to work in a Florists' shop. Before Nick had died she had worked part time in her local Florist, partly to help supplement their income, but more importantly to stop her from going crazy, being at home all day. She loved the job and was a natural. She had taken part time courses at the local college, which had helped her to build her skills and her confidence, but now she needed a job in another town, where people didn't know her or her ability.

She had applied to every Florist in the Preston area once the house was definitely sold, but no one was hiring, except for part-time work. Annie needed full time, just to keep a roof over their heads. Nick had left them with some money, but not enough to spend life in part time work. When it was looking as if her plans were going to fall through, one opportunity presented itself. In Longridge, one of the villages surrounding Preston, a small family run Florists' shop was for sale. The advert read. 'Due to retirement freehold florist shop premises for sale including three bedroomed living accommodation and small garden'. To Annie it was an omen and a prayer. The money she had received from the sale of the house and Nick's life insurance policy would cover the cost of the purchase. The fact that it was already a going concern would mean that she already had a regular customer base, as long as she kept them happy. The remainder of the money would help her through the first year whilst she got on her feet. It sounded perfect; finally she was going to be in charge of her own destiny. The vendor had sent the books through to her solicitors, everything was in order. They had sent some photo's via e-mail. The overall size of the shop was good, but modernization was a must. If she had of been sane she would have been daunted by such a large project, in truth she wanted something she could lose herself in. The busier she was, the less time she had to think about Nick – this was the perfect project for that.

Annie drove her car up the main street in Longridge. In the distance she could see the removal van parked outside what must be her shop. It seemed strange, driving to an unseen destination to start a new life. With every mile her sense of trepidation had grown. Was she stark staring mad? Uprooting Violet, buying shop that she hadn't even seen? As always with Annie, rationality set in. The decisions had already been made – there was no going back. Annie pulled her car into the layby opposite the shop. She recognise the facia from the pictures she had been sent. Annie took one look and let out a gasp of exasperation. The premises looked unloved and uncared for. Paint was peeling, the windows needed cleaning. The sun blind was battered and torn in all it was a total mess. This wasn't new information, Annie knew all this before she signed on the dotted line, but seeing it in front of her, the reality was hitting home – what had she done. From behind the removal van a man appeared. He was looking in her direction and waving. She presumed it was Mr Stretford, the owner's son. It had been arranged that he would meet her to exchange the keys and show her around. He walked across to the car, greeting her with a large rugged welcoming smile.

'How do lass, you've found us then.' He held the car door open for her. 'It's all in order for ye.' Annie climbed out of the car.

'Mr Stretford isn't it?' Annie confirmed, still confused as to how he knew she was the new owner.

'Aye lass, it is. We moved the last of our mum's stuff out yesterday, so all that's in it is yours. She left some things she thought you might make use of. I'm not so sure mi sen!- But ye know what olden's 'r like fer not throwin' ewt 'owt.' He walked her across the road and up to the shop as they talked. He was a short man in his late forties or early fifties, Annie guessed, His hair was cropped short to lessen the impact of his diminishing hair line. His mother had owned and run the shop for the past forty years, but it was all too much for her now, age and Ill health had forced her to close, as there was no one willing or able to take the business over in the family, she had been forced to sell.

'We tewd all't 'customers we had you'd likely be closed fer a week or two, so the' know not t' bother ye til' ye settle in, but they'll be glad t'si thee when ye finally open th' doors!'

Annie stood in front of her shop. She smiled weakly at Mr Stretford, she was feeling extremely daunted by the task ahead. Whatever made her think she could run a business? Her own business? Which meant that if it failed she had no one to bail her out and no income to live on? For a split second she had the urge to run away, but that was not an option. The nearest she had ever come to being even slightly business-minded, was balancing the shopping budget at home. Running a shop wasn't in the same league. Why had she been blind to her shortcomings before she signed on the dotted line? It was nerves, that's all it was – nerves, she tried to convince herself everything would be okay in time. She felt Mr Stretford's hand on her back, gently moving her forward towards the front door of the shop and impending doom. To resist him was futile.

'Now I promised me mother I'd wait for ye and show ye where't switches are for t' lights and 'ow t'boiler works fer't hot water, an when I've done that a'm off fer m'tea – I'll be back t'morrow an I'll show thee all t'other bits and pieces ye may need or things I've miss'd - alright lass off ye go'. He had to ease Annie through the front door, like a child on the first day of school, reluctant and not sure what to expect. She dragged her heels, hoping that someone would step out from the side lines to tell her it had all been a big mistake, the money hadn't transferred and she could go back to her old life – of course that didn't happen. Mr Stretford or 'Stan' as he now insisted she call him gave Annie a whistle stop tour, from how to nudge the door with your shoulder if the key was sticking in the lock, to the preposterously outdated heating system and its temperamental tendencies. The whole tour took no more than fifteen minutes including time to stand aside for the removal men to get through with the furniture and boxes.

'– and if it's still cold, I gives it a good whack wi' mi shoe. Right lass you've got t' basics and I'll be back t'morro t'see if owt' else is pushin'.' Annie's mind was frozen. There was too much information to take in. She had barely understood the instructions on how to get through the front door and now she was being left to fend for herself.

'Ohh, t'keys!' Stan passed her a large bunch of dated rusting keys, 'thee'll not get far wee'out 'em. Tara lass! I'll si thi t'morrow.' Before she had time to ask any questions, Stan was gone.

It took the removal men a further hour and a half to unload their precious cargo. Annie stood in the middle of the chaos orchestrating where each box or piece of furniture should be placed. Apart from the obvious large pieces such as chairs, beds, fridges she opted for everything else to go in the spare bedroom. The whole premises needed to be decorated, so it was pointless putting everything out in its place only to move it again. Once everything was decorated she would be able to go through them at her leisure, but for today it was out of sight and out of mind.

By the time she finally waved off the removal men she was completely exhausted, more emotionally than physically. It had been harder than she expected, leaving behind all traces of Nick in the fabric of their home. There were no nails he had knocked in or shelves he had struggled to erect or paint streaks she had urged him to sand down and paint out. He had made no mark on her new home and never would. Her exhaustion made it all too much to bear. She crumpled in an emotional heap on the floor. Tears fell silently without sobbing; she didn't even have the energy for that. The task ahead felt insurmountable. She wished Violet was with her, even though she knew she would be moaning about the state of the building and the living accommodation. She felt as if she had ripped her life in two, her past and her future. She couldn't stay in the old house drowning in memories of Nick, but at the same time she wasn't sure that she had made a wise decision with the place she had bought. Annie missed having Nick to bounce her ideas off. He was always quick to tell her if her ideas were unrealistic or push her if she needed that extra boost to take something on. She wondered what he would have said about her current whim. Annie sat on the floor surveying the shabby interior around her. What she needed was a hug, but without anyone to provide this for her, she took matters into her own hands and wrapped her own arms around herself. After allowing herself a few minutes of self-pity, Annie picked herself up and began to decide which task was the most important and should be prioritised. Violet is what came to mind. Annie had promised to ring and let her know that she had arrived safe and sound. Annie took out her mobile and pressed the speed dial button for Violet. Violet's phone was switched off, so Annie changed tack and sent her a text. *'Arrived a little while ago. Tried to ring you. Lots to be done here. Missing you! Ring me when you get this. Love you loads Mum xx'*. Annie hadn't lied to Violet, there was a lot to do, she just managed to exclude the fact that it would take them a month of Sunday's to achieve it. Any other major decisions were impossible in Annie's present frame of mind. Annie realised that sleep was what she needed; all other decisions could wait until the morning. She pulled herself up from the floor and made her way in to one of the bedrooms. The bed was in place but without covers and linens. Annie didn't know if this was going to be her room or Violet's, she had promised to let Violet chose when she arrived, but for tonight it belonged to Annie. A few minutes searching through a stack of boxes didn't bring the reward of covers and duvets for the bed. Her patience was zero. She looked around to find an alternative. Finally she settled for a cushion from the settee and a car rug that had been wrapped around one of her large paintings. She led on the bed staring at the strange walls covered in faded blue wisteria flowers, trying to justify the decisions she had made regarding their future. She had gone from settled happiness to lonely disaster in little over a year and she had no control over any of it, but now she did have control. The rest of her life was in her own hands. The decisions were all hers – succeed or fail – it was down to her. She was just going to have to get on with it. Annie started to think of colours for the bedroom, she had just opened a paint brochure in her mind's eye when sleep took her to a place where it didn't matter what colour the walls were and the whole room was decorated before morning.

Chapter 11

The following morning Annie awoke with a more positive attitude. The sun slowly crept through the curtain-less window into the bedroom, it nudged her slowly into consciousness, bringing her back from her deep sleep in the land of oblivion. Her eyes focused on the blue wallpaper, she was disappointed that the makeover pixies had not been in overnight to decorate the room, as they had in her dreams. Annie realised she needed food and drink. She had been too tired to eat the night before, but now her body was encouraging her to re-fuel and get moving. In the kitchen the kettle and tea were out on the worktop. This had been an essential item which the removal men had insisted on carrying up front in the van, together with the milk and biscuits, in case it was needed in an emergency. She was now glad that they did. They had also left her a half-eaten packet of rich tea biscuits, not Annie's favourites and certainly not the most healthy and nutritious breakfast, but definitely welcome. She made a mental note to find the local shop at the first opportunity.

Ten minutes later she stood holding a steaming cup of tea and a fist full of biscuits. After a few sips she started to feel revived and ready to take a closer look at her new home and business. She took the stairs from the upstairs landing down into the shop workroom. She opened a side door that led in to a good useable space. Work benches around three sides of the walls and a large storage unit with draws and shelves holding all the essential items needed to run a florist's shop. Stan had shown her all of this yesterday, but nothing had sunk in, today she could see the potential. It was a positive thing, to have all the mechanics for floristry ready and waiting to be used. Sure, there were things that hadn't been in use since Adam was a lad and the décor was old fashioned to say the least. Annie doubted any of it had seen a paint brush since 1972, but all these things in time could be fixed and because it all needed was attention. She could justify spending the money on making it as it should be, rather than thinking she should mend and make do. Granted she didn't have bottomless pockets and some things would have to be compromised, but painting and decorating was not one of them. It was a project that needed putting back together and fixing a piece at a time, not dis-similar to her-self.

She made her way through into the main shop area. Old and tired plastic flower vases were stacked in the corner of the space, where she presumed the fresh flowers were usually displayed. The floor was covered in lino, in places bare, with holes showing through to the floor boards. The shelves were stocked with various antiquated and outdated vases, containers and flower arranging paraphernalia. It had been a busy , hardworking space in its day and was bound to be frayed around the edges, but in reality it wasn't any worse than she expected and it could all be fixed with a lot of hard work, another perfect reason to start from scratch again.

Annie hitched herself up on to the counter and continued sipping her tea. She started dreaming about which colours would look great with the available daylight and if she should keep the counter in the same place or move it, when she was interrupted by a knock on the front window. Through the grime and windowlene smeared across the glass, she could just see the outline of a man gesticulating to her that she should open the door.

'Hold on!' She shouted trying to let him know he had been noticed 'I need to find the keys!' It took her a few minutes to locate them in the flat. She had been so tired that she couldn't remember putting them anywhere. She finally found them on the floor next to the boxes she had been searching through for bedding. When she came back down the stairs the man was still standing there waiting for her. She hoped he didn't want flowers because he was going to be disappointed. The old lock took a little negotiating as Stan had promised, but eventually it relented. The door opened to reveal a young man in work clothes. His hair was short and functional and his hands bore the scars of manual work. He smiled broadly, she couldn't help but reciprocate.

'Morn'in are you Annie?' He was a charmer; there were no two ways about it. She was sure he could melt any young girl's heart. Luckily she didn't fall into that category.

'Yes – I'm Annie.' She smiled at him expectantly waiting for him to continue, to find out what he wanted.

'I'm here about the renovation of the building? You rang me last week and asked me to call today to give you some costing's on the work you have in mind? I'm Zach?' He could tell she had forgotten. He hoped this wasn't going to be another waste of his time.

'Oh God I'm sorry!' The penny finally dropped with Annie. 'I completely forgot I'd asked you to come today. Come in, come in. I'm just getting my first real look at the space. I under estimated the amount of energy I had left by the time I arrived, I'm afraid I haven't got down to deciding exactly what I want doing. There's so much to do, it feels impossible to achieve by the time I want to be open.' Annie was embarrassed that she had let it slip from her mind.

'Well it depends on when that is.' He commented at the same time as having a good look around. ' If it's next Monday you want to open, then you haven't got a chance in Hell, but let's find out what you need to be done, then I'll be able to give you a more specific timeline.' They walked around the building from the bottom to the top prioritising the jobs. He was just what Annie needed. Zach knew what he was talking about, even though he was a little on the young side. He explained to her that he had worked with his father since leaving school and up until his father's death two years previously. She didn't feel patronised or bullshitted. He was to the point, honest and he told her when he thought her ideas were mad. She liked him and was as sure as she could be that they would be able to work together.

'Assuming that your costing's come in on target – when can you start?' This was the most crucial part. If he couldn't start within a few days it would be impossible to hire him.

'I can start today.' He smiled broadly flashing his young perfect teeth.

'Honestly? I didn't expect you to say that!' Annie wasn't sure it this was a good or bad sign.

'The fact is,' he continued, 'that my next job has agreed to wait. They're not in any panic for the work to be done. In fact they are going on holiday and would have preferred me to start when they get back so that any snagging can be sorted out immediately rather than having to wait until they get back. So they are happy to let me do your job first.' He hesitated 'so long as you are happy with me?' He added hopefully. Annie took a moment to think. In the past she would have stalled by stating she would have to run it past her husband first, but that was no longer the situation. The decision and responsibility stopped with her.

'Okay –,' she agreed, 'let's give it a go and see how we get on. I do need a full breakdown of costing's for all the jobs, so that I can use what little money I have left wisely.' She didn't want Zach to think she was a bottomless money pit. He needed to know there were limits before he got carried away with ambitious plans.

'Of course – I'll start measuring up and sorting the basic repairs. Then there's the stripping out of the old stuff. That will give you a few days to get the feel for the place and decide how you want it to look. It'll probably take me a couple of days to get the costing's for you. I'm assuming you want me to start in the shop first and leave the flat till later?' He enquired. Annie hadn't given it much thought until that moment, but he was right she needed an income from the shop. The flat would have to wait.

'The sooner we get opened the better. I need to start earning some money to pay you!' They both laughed. Zach was as good as his word. He took a notepad and tape measure out of his pocket and as simply as that, the plans for the renovations began.

'Of course there is one sure way to make me work faster and get you open?' Zach added. Annie paused for a second.

'I get it! You're going to blackmail me with tea aren't you?' Zach nodded in agreement.

'Okay! Which way is the nearest shop? I need to stock up on supplies.' Enquired Annie. 'I haven't found my bearings yet. I had to have biscuits for breakfast!'

'It beats left over pizza which is what I had!' Zach admitted. They both pulled a face. 'It's out of the door and to the right just before the crossing and if it's a cooked breakfast you're after the bakery down the road does a great breakfast barm to go – just in case you were thinking of feeding me?' She felt as though she should be annoyed by his forward manner, but she wasn't, he was just young and full of fun.

'Actually I wasn't!' She responded with equal bluntness, 'You're safe to be left alone in charge of a tape measure whilst I nip out, I presume?'

'As long as your trip involves tea and more biscuits? I think I can spare you.' Zach extended his tape measure and held it up against a wall trying to look professional. It didn't fool either of them.

Annie nipped upstairs to get her purse before setting foot out of the door into new territory. She was enjoying the banter with Zach. He didn't know her or the fact that she was a widow. There was no treading carefully, afraid of upsetting her. It was a fun conversation with no undercurrent. She had forgotten what that felt like.

Annie found the shop exactly where Zach had said, it was well stocked and obviously well used and loved by the residents of Longridge and the surrounding area. She hoped to escape un-noticed by the locals as an outsider for the moment. It wasn't her aim to make a big splash on the first day. She wanted to integrate quietly and slowly, without a fuss, at least until the shop was ready to open, although any publicity is good publicity they say. It was the pile of cleaning materials and rubber gloves that blew her cover at the checkout.

'Looks like you're going to be a busy bee today with all this lot?' Commented the cheerful lady behind the counter. Obviously nothing ever managed to get past her – she was well trained, probably through years of practice and watching Miss Marple.

'Yes I am.' Stated Annie, not feeling the need to elaborate on the subject for the benefit of this stranger.

'Just passing through?' She wasn't going to let Annie get away so easily. This woman knew there was a story here and it was her duty to extract it.

'No – no I'm not.'

'I don't remember seeing you in here before and I have the memory of an elephant?' - *I bet you do'* thought Annie. It was no use; she was going to have to tell the woman. She would find out soon enough and the last thing she wanted was the woman telling everyone the new Florist was stuck up and wouldn't chat to anyone. She looked upon it as damage limitation and spilled the beans.

'I've just moved in to the Florists' shop up the road – hence the cleaning products.' There it was out. The world and his neighbour would know before tea.

'Ahhh.' A light switched on in the woman's head. 'Are you Annie?'

'Yes- yes I am.' Said Annie, picking up her purchases, not wanting to hold up the customers behind her.

'Yes, Stan told me you were coming yesterday. He was like a cat on a tin roof, up and down the street all day looking for you. He didn't want to keep you waiting. I love Stan and his Mother to pieces, but I dare say you've got your work cut out for you there. It's not had a penny spent on it for years, but you look like you've got a bit 'o sense about you. I think you'll do just fine. Well, good luck Love! I'm sure you'll be a great success and if you need any help in the shop for a few hours I know a dozen people who would bite your hand off fer a bit o' pin money.' The woman behind the till gave Annie such a warm and genuine smile that Annie could no longer give her the cool treatment. She had forgotten how friendly people up North can be. It was Annie's problem, she just had to change her mind set back to being Northern. Annie softened her tone towards her.

'I can't stop to chat now...'

'April! That's my name.'

'Eh April... but I'll bear that in mind. I will need someone to do part-time and driving in the future, but as you suggested, I've got a lot of hard work ahead of me before I get to that point.' Annie looked behind at the growing number of bodies, trying to make April realise she had people to serve, 'but I'm sure I'll see you again very soon...April.' Both women smiled understanding their common bond of dealing with the public's needs.

'I'm sure we will. Shout if you need anything. Now love do you need a bag?' April had moved her attention on to the next customer.

The encounter reminded Annie of what it had been like growing up in Lancashire. People were generally friendly. Smiles of acknowledgement between strangers and meaningless conversations brought people together momentarily on a daily basis, which in such a mad and busy world can't be such a bad thing -*'weather's bad today,' 'you look loaded up' and her favourite especially when she was carrying flowers, 'are they for me?'* These sayings were unimportant, but they gave people the chance to interact and maybe over time make new friends? In many places this art had now been lost. Annie remembered making remarks in the streets when she moved down south after she and Nick were married. The people looked at her as if she had just uttered a torrent of abuse at them or that she had just been released from the local mental home. After a few times of trying she eventually gave up. Now she was back up north she would have to brush up her skills. Annie walked back to the shop slowly, absorbing each shop as she passed it. There were many trades along the high street, which in turn resulted in many varied reasons for people to come here and spend their money. In some ways it seemed to have escaped the ravages of supermarket trading, but she wondered how long it would last, until there were superstores at each end of the village, squeezing the life out of it.

Within five minutes of returning to the shop she had made tea for herself and Zach. She had against her better judgement paid a visit to the bakery and bought two breakfast barms, recommended by Zach to keep him sweet. He had been surprised and delighted with his small tasty gift.

'Don't get used to this – it's a one off and next time it's your turn to pay!' She promised, as they drank their tea making mental lists of what they would keep. A list of what to keep was easier than making a list of what they were going to throw away. Zach announced that he had ordered the first of many skips that would be needed and it was on its way. They were so engrossed in their conversation that they didn't even notice the man and woman that walked in through the open door.

'Well hello there! It hasn't taken you long to get started had it?' It was Mr Stretford and his Mother making their way cautiously through the debris Zach had started to collect for the skip. Annie had expected a frail woman, but Mrs Stretford seemed quite sturdy and spritely even though she held on to Stan's arm for dear life, in fear of falling.

'It's just what it needs dear – a good clear out and start again, I'm Mrs Stretford – Stan's mum. You must be Annie?' Mrs Stretford put her hand out for Annie to shake.

'Mrs Stretford, it's lovely to meet you. Stan has been telling me all about you.' Annie charmed her immediately. 'We needed to get started straight away so that we can get opened – I hope you don't mind?' Annie was only asking for 'asking's sake, if she had said no she wasn't going to stop. Annie just wanted to be courteous. After all Mrs Stretford had been the owner here for a very long time, she was going to be a hard act to follow.

'Mind dear! I only wish I'd had the energy and drive to do what you are doing! – If you're not careful I'll roll my sleeves up and get stuck in with you...but this body of mine is making me slow down. If it wasn't I'd be here helping you! I wish you all the luck in the world lass. Just make sure you invite me when it's your 'Grand Opening'!'

'Ohh I don't know about a 'Grand Opening'? I thought I'd just open when we are ready? Just sort of creep into the village without anyone noticing.'

'Nonsense! You're doing something you should be proud of. Let the world know all about it and it's good publicity and although I've told all my old customers to come to you and support you when you open, you still need all the help you can get. Let me know when you set the date and I'll spread the word.'

'Mum's very good at that!' Added Stan who had been waiting to find a space to speak.

'I'll certainly think about it.' Smiled Annie surrendering to her enthusiasm.

'Mrs Stretford looks like she means business Annie? ' Zach was adding his pennies worth, 'I'd give in and agree to it or you won't get any rest 'til you do.' Stan nodded agreeing with him.

Annie felt pinned into a corner, but she could see the benefit of making more of a splash and if Mrs Stretford was willing to spread the word, well it would help get the shop up and running again.

'Okay I give in, but I'm counting on you to spread the word. I don't want to end up being the only one at the party!' Mrs Stretford smiled broadly, pleased that she had succeeded in getting her own way and on their first meeting. Sometimes people took a little more persuading before coming around to her way of thinking. Mrs Stretford had one final question for Annie.

'And one last thing before we go – are you going to change the name of the shop?' Annie hesitated not sure if the old lady was going to throw a hissy fit if she said 'yes'.

'I'm not sure yet – but probably?'

'Well I would. It's your shop now. Let people know it! A bit of change is good for people, even if they don't realise it. What are you thinking of for the name?'

'Well, I was thinking of naming it after my daughter, she's called Violet.'

'Eeeee, what a splendid thought and it's a flower to. It couldn't be more perfect!'

'Come on Mother!' Coaxed Stan, 'Can't keep the Vicar waiting; you promised to see to his roses.' Stan ushered her towards the door. As they were picking their way back through the same pile of rubbish, Annie noticed a young woman standing at the door, trying to catch Annie's Attention. It was like Piccadilly station this morning.

'Hello Pippa.' Mrs Stretford warmly enthused. 'I see you've thought about what I said?' The woman at the door was plainly embarrassed. 'Pippa used to work for me Annie. She's been to college and she's very reliable and a great worker. I told her she should pop in and introduce herself to you – there may come a time when you'll need a little help in the shop and I can't recommend her highly enough. I'll leave you to it dear – I've interfered enough. Come on Stan! The Vicar won't wait forever!' And with those words of wisdom she left the shop.

'Sorry.' Said Pippa, 'Is this a bad time? I know you've only just arrived. You haven't even had time to find your bearings. I can call back another day?' 'No, it's fine' Annie found it all amusing. The smoke signals had been working well in the area. She began to wonder who else was going to turn up on the doorstep. Pippa seizing the moment, launched into her verbal job application.

'….and I've been to college so you wouldn't have to start from scratch in teaching me things. I'm good with people and I know the area for delivering.' Pippa paused momentarily for breath, 'I do however have two small children and I am a single parent, but the children are of school age and my parents are always there to step in when I need them. I wouldn't want full time – just part time?' She stopped and smiled, 'I've said too much haven't I?' Annie couldn't help but like her. Her honesty and personality shone through like a beacon in the worn out debris of the shop.

'Well it was a lot to take in - Pippa, but it was delivered concisely, which is better than half an hour of waffle. I'm Annie.' She put her hand out to greet Pippa. 'I don't know how many hours I would need you at this point in time or when we'll manage to open. The hours will be variable; I'll need extra cover at busy periods. How flexible can you be?'

'I do have my mum and dad, as I said. They live close by, they help me tonnes, especially in the school holidays. I do work part time in one of the supermarkets, but my heart isn't in it. I didn't grow up wanting to be a shelf stacker. This would be my perfect Job Annie. I'm a hard worker and don't mind doing anything.' Annie heard Zach snigger behind her; she had forgotten he was there.

'Ignore him Annie! We used to go to School together. He used to think he was funny then too.' Pippa's words cut into his School boy humour, bringing him down to size. Annie like the fact that Pippa could stand up for herself, she was a great believer in gut instinct and it was telling her to say 'yes'.

'If you're willing to have a trial period to see how we both feel, I'm sure we could work something out?' Annie liked the Vibe Pippa was sending out. She was young, fresh, positive and like herself, for whatever reasons she had to carve a living for herself to look after her children at least she was being pro-active and not just sitting back waiting for an opportunity to come looking for her. It would have been easy for Pippa to let the state look after the children, but she was out there trying to make it work.

'Okay – we'll give it a try. Leave me your number and when we get nearer to opening I'll give you a call – I have to warn you at the beginning it'll probably be only a few hours a week until we get established. I don't know how busy we'll be?'

'That's wonderful!' Said Pippa scribbling her number on an envelope she found in her handbag. She passed it to Annie. 'Anything here is better than full time where I am now. I'll leave you to get on. It's looking good. It's going to be beautiful when it's finished.'

'Do you think so? We haven't even started yet?'

'Well, I know you have good taste. You're going to give me a chance! Besides, Zach is the best builder in the area, although it pains me to say it in front of him and I know he'll look after you, 'cause if he doesn't he'll have me to answer to!' Annie turned to look at Zach.

'It was Hell going to school with her.' He confessed. 'She knows I used to have a crush on her and she's not afraid to use the information to her advantage – even after all these years!' He was blushing ever so slightly, which led Annie to believe his crush was still alive and well.

'You locals don't let the grass grow under your feet, do you? I've never seen such a good network in operation!'

'Early bird and all that!' Zach shouted. Annie shook her head in wonderment.

'You'll soon get used to us.' Pippa remarked.

'That's what's worrying me!' She confessed.

As Pippa left the building, the first skip arrived, ready to be filled jam-packed with ancient tat. Zach went out to the skip driver to work out the best position to drop it, using the opportunity to have an extra chat with Pippa on his way, Annie meanwhile went back to her cup of tea, but it had gone cold. It was one of the few things she couldn't stand – cold tea! She pushed it aside. She wanted to help

Zach fill the skip, but she wasn't dressed for demolition, she went upstairs to find some work clothes. Annie ventured in to the jungle of boxes in the bedroom. To her amazement all the boxes with clothes in were at the top of the pile. At the bottom of the third box, she found some old overalls that Nick had bought her once for a joke. Nick didn't think she had a practical bone in her body. She wondered what he would say if he could see her now? She hoped he would be proud of her, but she knew for sure he would have been surprised. She pulled on the overalls; she was surprised that even just wearing them made her feel more capable. She went down stairs to find Zach, picking up her pink screwdriver on the way, ready to work.

Annie and Zach dragged, pulled and pushed things that needed to be removed from the shop to the skip. It was hard physical labour, harder than she expected, it had to be done bit by bit, with many tea breaks in between for them to catch their breath and take away the taste of dust from the back of their throats. Annie was moving the last few items that were ready to go, hoping to find space for them in the already bulging skip rather than having to wait for the next one, when her phone rang. It was Violet.

'Hi Mum, how are you? I got your message late yesterday, but I figured you'd be asleep, so I didn't ring back. Is my room ready yet?' Annie laughed out loud.

'It depends what you mean by ready?' She mused, 'If all you want is four walls and a roof, then we're fine. If you want more than that we may struggle!'

'Is it that bad Mum? I know you said it needed work, but is it liveable?'

'Sort of – it's not what you're used to; you may need to lower your expectations. If you imagine a cave with heated water and electric, then work from there, by the time you arrive you'll think it's a palace!'

'God Mum! Is it really that bad?'

'No! Think of it as an adventure. At the moment it's not decorated the way you would like, but in time we can sort that out. You'll need to bring your imagination. When you get up here you can choose the colours you want!'

'Do I get all new furniture and curtains, bedding, lamps……'

'Hold on a minute Violet, I'm not sure the money will stretch that far, we'll talk about it when you get here. Which train are you catching?'

'Well Mum…….Would you be really cross if I stayed down here for a couple more days? I've been invited to go camping with Amy and her mum and dad – it won't cost you anything, only a big box of chocolates to say thank you when I get back?'

'Are you sure they invited you and you didn't invite yourself?' Annie knew Violet wasn't shy at coming forward.

'No. I Promise...and I'll be good, but... if... you really want me to come now I will?' Annie knew when she was being manipulated, but Violets room wasn't anywhere near ready and the better she could make the place look before she arrived, the more chance Violet would settle and not kick up a fuss.

'Okay... but as soon as you get back ring me and we'll sort out train timetables for me to pick you up.'

'Okay, I promise - got to go Mum. I'll ring you soon. Love you!'

Violet hung up the phone and turned to her boyfriend. 'Bingo! She bought it! I told you she would. At least we've got a couple more days 'til your mum comes home. Let's make the most of it!' Violet pulled on the bed sheet that was hiding her boyfriend's modesty until it fell to the floor, next she flung her arms around the willing youth and started to kiss him fervently – all over.

Chapter 12

It was Saturday before Annie managed to lure Violet to Longridge. Each day disappeared in a flash, with the mountain of tasks thrown up by the renovation. Zach turned up every day on time as he promised. He listened to what Annie wanted and came up with ideas when she needed them. His knowledge and understanding of the building trade was a 'god send'. Annie felt completely safe in his hands. She didn't have the technical know how to make the best choice, he did.

Any spare moments Annie managed to find were spent trying to make some sense of the mountain of boxes and bags in the flat. Annie didn't want to unpack Violet's things until she had chosen her room, but she cleaned it up and made up the bed in the second bedroom, which was larger and the decoration was more up to date - slightly. Annie guessed it was the one Violet would choose, but she was by no means certain. Annie had demoted herself to the smaller room. It was a small price to pay, if it kept Violet from nagging about the décor until Annie could afford to redecorate her room. Annie searched until she found the box full of Nick's photos. Choosing special pictures and framing them was something they had done together after Nick's accident. Annie hoped that placing the pictures all around the flat would help Violet settle in. It was starting to look more homely, but even that was a far cry from what Violet had been used to. Annie knew it was not going to be an easy ride ahead, but no matter how difficult it had to be faced. Annie was the adult and Violet was just going to have to get used to their new surroundings.

Annie waited anxiously on the platform of Preston Station waiting for Violet's train to arrive. She bought a designer coffee from the shop and sat at a small table waiting nervously for Violet's arrival. The station didn't look very different to the last time Annie had been there, which seemed a life time ago. If only she had known she was pregnant when she was there to send Jack off to Australia. It seemed as if Annie knew that story inside out, but it belonged to someone else. It was a moment that was so detached from the rest of her life; she could have easily persuaded herself that it had happened to someone else. The pain of losing Jack, at the time seemed un-surmountable. She could still see the look of disapproval on his father's face and the smug satisfaction his mother showed, knowing she had won and Jack was leaving. Today she felt no connection to the events gone by. It was all history – water under the bridge. Jack had never attempted to make contact since the day he arrived at their house when Violet was a toddler and Annie had disposed of any feelings she had for Jack long ago, fate had brought Nick to her and the years between had been happy. He had never let her down. It wasn't perfect – no marriage is. At times his insecurities got the better of him, but they were momentary glitches, nothing insurmountable. In so many ways he was the complete opposite of Jack – that wasn't a bad thing.

The tannoy system announced the arrival of Violet's train pulling Annie back to the present. It was on time. Annie stood waiting impatiently for Violet to emerge from the train, eager for a hug. Annie had missed her greatly. They were not used to being separated, but especially since Nick's death, this was the first time they had been apart. Annie caught sight of Violets wild curly hair making its own entrance to the station. Within a minute they were stood hugging each other like there was no tomorrow. Annie grabbed one of Violet's bags as they made their way to the car which was parked on the car park.

'Good journey?' Asked Annie, linking arms with Violet as they walked.

'Okay – of course the old lady with a need to tell a stranger her life story came and sat next to me! And every time I tried to listen to my music she started chattering at me – telling me some story about how nice the trains used to be in the 'olden days'! Then! - She made me go and get her a cup of tea from the buffet cart. She said she couldn't carry it and walk back as her hands were unsteady!'

'You'll get your reward in heaven!'

'I want a chair next to St Peter after putting up with that! It didn't do my street cred any good.'

Violet pushed her holdall into the back of the car before climbing into the front seat. The journey to Longridge passed in a flash. Violet was full of questions, about what it was like, who she had met and was there any 'buff' blokes around, barely leaving time for Annie to answer each question, before the next was issued. Annie had expected a surely and resentful attitude from Violet, it was a pleasant surprise to see her smiling and relatively happy. Annie enjoyed the moment; they would be home soon enough – the wind was about to change.

'You have to be kidding Mum!!!' Squealed Violet when Annie pointed at the new shop as they pulled up outside. 'This can't be it! Tell me you're joking?' Annie just shook her head and smiled meekly. Violet folded her arms in a statement of disapproval at the same time tutting and shaking her head.

'It's better inside.' Annie encouraged, 'come and see?' Reluctantly Violet stepped out of the car and slowly walked towards her new home. She looked up at the windows on the first floor. It was not a pretty sight, with all the dirt collected on the glass from months of neglect standing empty, not to mention the peeling paint on every frame. It was the worst building on the street by far. Violet's face was thunderous.

'Don't forget it's nowhere near finished yet. We haven't even started on the outside! We've only been here four days and Zach has been a great help. He'll soon have it looking great'

'Who's ….Zach?' Asked Violet accusingly.

'Someone call my name?' He popped out from behind a large piece of chipboard near the front door. Violet smiled involuntarily. She didn't expect such a good looking man to be working in her mum's shop.

'You must be Violet?' Zach held out his hand for Violet to shake, 'I've heard a lot about you.'

'I wish I could say the same!' Violet shot a glance at her mother, chastising her for giving her no warning.

'Zach is our builder,' Continued Annie ignoring Violets moody looks, '– he's already made good progress. Come in and see' what he's managed to do already.' Annie ushered Violet through the door, followed by Zach.

'It's looking a lot better now we've stripped everything out in here….' Said Zach proudly.

'It's a dump! ' Violet was not impressed with the empty shell in front of her. How could her mother bring her to this broken down place and expect her to like it? Granted, Zach, as eye candy was a bonus, but it would take more than that to make this place feel like home. Violet made a silent vow to herself - If she didn't like it she was moving in to her boyfriend's house – not that his parents knew anything about it, he wasn't the love of her life, but it would be better living with him for a while than staying here if upstairs was no better. He had been good fun and the sex was okay, but she didn't see it going anywhere. He had been what she needed after her dad had died. He made her feel loved, whilst her mother was dealing with her own grief and Violet didn't feel she could lean on her too much. The boyfriend adored Violet and made her feel special. He was more upset about Violet leaving than Violet. Her plan was to let him down gently over time. In some ways - and not that she would ever admit it to her mother, she had been looking forwards to getting to Longridge – if only their home had been nicer.

Violet managed to keep her lips tightly shut as her mother showed her around the shop and the flat upstairs. She uttered any expletives internally on the journey around, as much as she loathed the look of everything, she understood how much this move meant to her mum, and besides, when college was over Violet intended to go out into the big wide world on her own. She had no intention of staying at home and working in the shop.

When that time came, her mum would be left on her own and Violet knew it would be better for her to have something of her own to concentrate on and if truth be told it would keep her off violets back. Violet acknowledged to herself that it was an unfair assessment of their relationship. It was understandable that after her dad dying so suddenly, her mum would be extra protective – at least for a while, but the time would come when Violet needed to escape, the busier her mum was the better.

To Violet's surprise the upstairs was more habitable than downstairs. The flat consisted of a lounge, three bedrooms, a small kitchen, bathroom and separate toilet and there was one surprise she wasn't expecting. In the lounge there was a door leading out on to a large balcony which covered the expanse of the garage roof at the back of the house. It was a great suntrap and an even greater space for a welcome party thought Violet, something to work on with her mother later, Violet was sure she would get her own way.

Overall the decoration of the building was well below any standard Violet had ever had to live with, but she could see that her mum had made an effort to make it feel like a home. The same furniture from the old house, the settee with a soggy bottom in one corner, which ate you whole and you had to fight for your life to get out of it. There were photo's up on the walls from childhood and special days out, then there were the special photos of her dad, they made her smile. One item that she noticed on the side table by the hungry settee was the blue table lamp with a chip on the base from where her dad had dropped it. Violet softened with a sudden rush of emotion, remembering how cross he had been with himself when it happened. She put her arm around her mum's shoulders and gave her a hug. Annie, slightly surprised responded and hugged her back.

'You okay?' Annie asked after a few moments.

'Yes - but I do have two important questions for you. Firstly - Did I get the best room? And secondly – can we have a party on that balcony!' They both laughed. 'Of course you got the best room – don't you always and we'll see about the party. You need to go out and make some new friends to invite first!'

'Oh I will. If you promise I can have a party?' grinned Violet.

'Let's just get you unpacked first! Let me show you through to the best room in the house!' Annie guided Violet into the bedroom with the blue wisteria wall paper.

Chapter 13

The two weeks after Violet's arrival were a blur for Annie. Violet spent much of each day under her covers in her room, trying to escape the possibility of being asked to work. She had no intention of spending her last few weeks of freedom before college started, working until she was so tired she couldn't be bothered to eat, like her mother. Zach turned up each day with a list of decisions to be made about the building. Items that needed to be sourced, where she wanted plug sockets and light fittings, if the old stud partition walls should stay in place or be pulled down, but by the end of that second week, the main repairs and structural changes were complete. Now it was time for the fun part, of choosing colours and styles, re-assembling the whole thing back together again and creating a new look and brand for the business. Annie to her own surprise had a very clear vision of how the shop should appear and feel to the public. The difficult part was making Zach understand and facilitate her vision on her shoe string budget.

Elsewhere in the building Violet was beginning to get cabin fever. It was the first week of September now and the new college term was due to start. Violet was looking forward to making some friends her own age. Everyone she had met in the village seemed to be on the wrong side of thirty – except Zach, but he wasn't far off. Violet had selected her clothes the night before. It was important to make the right impression on her first day. At least it was the first day for everyone, except those who knew each other from high school; everyone would be feeling the same. She had insisted that she would be fine going on the bus, when Annie offered to drive her in. Violet had always been an independent soul, so this came as no surprise to Annie.

'I'm off mum!' shouted Violet from the top of the stairs. Annie was in the shower, trying to wake herself up.

'Wait Vi! I won't be long!'

'I can't mum. I'll miss the bus!' Violet was itching to get going.

'Okay, well - I'll meet you at the gates when you finish! Good luck and you'll be fine. Just be yourself!' Annie shouted above the noise of the shower.

'I will – Bye!' Annie's mother hen instinct began to kick in. What if no one spoke to her? What if she hated her tutors? What if she lost her way? – Annie would have been much happier, if she'd been allowed to deliver Violet in person and give her a pep talk on the way, but as usual Violet struck out on her own. She had however conceded when Annie had offered to pick her up after college and take her out for a pizza as a treat to mark her first day, as usual Violet had an ulterior motive, as she had her eye on a little retail therapy after the pizza. Violet had tried to make Annie go shopping with her on several occasions, but Annie always claimed to be too busy to spare the time. This spree was long overdue and Violet intended to exploit it to the max.

Annie's day rushed by as its usual dizzy pace, she was feeling more useful now, her painting skills were being put to great use. Annie had settled on a pallet of vintage shades for the walls, muted creams and pastels, making sure to keep the space feeling light and airy. It was amazing how even the first coat of paint made such a large difference to the look and feel of the place. By three o'clock she was washed, her brushes cleaned and she had changed out of her work clothes, ready to go and meet Violet from college.

Annie pulled up in a parking space outside the college, close to the gates. 'The gates' – it had been a long time since Annie had thought of those college gates. Memories of moments in her past came flooding in. The countless times she had waited for Jack at those gates, then like magic he would appear, followed by the 'lip gloss posse'. She allowed herself a moment to remember him, with his cheeky grin and floppy hair, then reality hit home and she remembered the circumstances in which he left and abandoned them both. The gates also reminded her of Nick and the day he asked her to the leaver's ball. Annie found it odd to think that Violet would be walking the same corridors as she did – and her Father, but it had been Violets choice of college, not hers. There were a couple to choose from, but Violet was sure that she wanted to take her 'A' levels at the college her father and mother went to. Annie wondered if it was a way for Violet to still feel connected with Nick – She would never know. Of course Violet was one to the last to leave the college. She was surrounded by a group of peers, at the centre of everything as usual. Annie waved from the car, Violet noticed her immediately. After a brief exchange with the girls Violet made her way to the car.

'Well? How did it go?' Annie enquired as soon as the door was open.

'Good – it's quite cool for a college.' Answered Violet with a moderate level of enthusiasm.

'Of course it is. I went there!'

'I would say it's cool 'despite' you going there Mum!' Annie put on her fake hurt face – it had no effect. Violet was too busy re-counting the events of the day. She had stopped and looked at every old photograph she passed in the corridors, hoping to spot one of them in a sporting pose or amateur dramatic role, but she found nothing.

'Was Dad cool when he was at college?'

'He would have to be cool to be seen with me' Mocked Annie. Violet raised her eyebrows in exasperation. 'No, but was he?' Annie hesitated sensing a deeper need in Violet to know something she had never bothered to ask about Nick before. Annie was only too well aware that this was yet another major change for her daughter; at least progress was being made. There was a time after the funeral when Violet couldn't bear to speak about Nick and if it was possible would leave the room, but now in her own time she seemed to be re-opening the door she had once firmly closed. Annie was relieved and delighted to hear her questions.

'Your Dad was so cool; you couldn't help but notice him and when he smiled, everyone fell for his charms.' It was the truth, but in a version that Violet would understand.

'Did you fall for his charms?' Violet was staring Annie in the eye, searching for a truthful answer.

'Of course I did – We were married or had you forgotten!'

'No I mean, did you fall for him the first time you saw him? Did he sweep you off your feet?' The last thing Annie wanted was to diminish her marriage to Nick by adding in the details surrounding her getting together with Nick, but she also couldn't lie and say it was love at first sight. Annie paused, looking for the right words to sooth Violet without distorting the truth too much.

'Your Dad and I were in the same classes at college, let's just say it took me a little time to get to know him and understand all his good qualities. We were friends from the start, which is always a good way to begin, but any romance came a little later. Everyone liked him, just as they like you - Come on now enough questions! Let's go and eat.' Annie tried to change the subject; she was feeling on shaky ground.

'And then can we shop?' Added Violet with her killer smile.

'I wondered why you let me pick you up! Now I know. I'm just a cash cow to you!'

'Mum! – You're much more than that. You're my cleaner too.'

A normal pattern emerged over the following weeks. Violet spent her days at college, in between nipping into the town centre on breaks, and evenings out cementing relationships with her new friends or as you and I might put it - getting drunk in the bars. There were still moments when Violet wished that they hadn't moved to longridge. She was making new friends, which was a relief to her, but everything was such hard work, having to explain to everyone over and over again, where they came from, why they were there and where her Father was.

She even considered having a card printed and laminated to save her the trouble of explaining. Taking friends home was still impossible. The new shop was taking shape, but it would be a long time until they started on the decorating upstairs. The old décor was not uplifting to say the least. Violet didn't want her friends to come around and see what a 'Hell hole' her mother was forcing her to live in. The little credibility she had accumulated would vanish in an instant. When she wasn't at college or out socialising, she was on the computer, keeping track of friends on Facebook and Twitter. She had insisted that Annie got broadband to help her with her assignments as soon as physically possible, which Annie did, but its use was far more social than college orientated. Violet used it as her life line to her old life, she could touch base with old friends if she needed to and arrange to go and visit for a weekend when it was all getting too stressful. Violet used her Facebook account to tell the boyfriend it was 'over', she changed her status to single and let the network do the rest. It didn't take long for the message to reach him. Violet refused to answer his calls and texts, after a few days he stopped texting and changed his own status to ' in a new relationship', a little part of her was disappointed he didn't fight for her, but she didn't want to do the long distance relationship thing. She was young and had no desire to get tied down young as her mother had done. Violet found it almost impossible to believe that her mum was only a few years older than she was now, when she had her. Her mum was happy with her life; she met dad and fell in love. That was fine for her mum, but Violet wanted a different life. One perk she missed from losing her father was the extra pocket money he gave her without her mother's knowledge. Nick would pass her a few pounds to go shopping with, but it was always their little secret. It wasn't the money she missed, but the independence it afforded her. Annie gave her what she could, but money was scarce, as no income was being generated yet, which is why Violet took the bold step of applying for a job at a local hotel.

Violet had heard one of the girls at college, Nirah, talking about where she worked in the common room. According to Nirah, it was a good way to earn some money. The work wasn't difficult, okay, the wages weren't brilliant, but the tips from the guests made up for that. Nirah worked there in the evenings and at weekends, still finding time to fit in going to college and turning in her assignments on time. It sounded too good to be true.

The hotel was only a few minutes' drive from Violet's home and would be a perfect place to work. Violet couldn't rely on her mother for hand outs for ever. Nirah was sure they needed staff, as the turnover rate was high. Nirah's immediate supervisor, Miss St John was always complaining about being short staffed. Many of the workers only came once, and then didn't bother to turn up again. Waiting on tables wasn't every teenagers dream. Nirah also provided Violet with the telephone number of the staff manager. When she was sure she was on her own and wouldn't be interrupted, she would ring the number.

Nirah had indeed given Violet correct information. There were vacancies to start immediately. Violet was surprised and delighted, when the staff manager offered to interview her over the phone, there and then.

'You'll have to work the odd evening during the week and at least one day each weekend. There will be overtime offered at busy times and you will be expected to cover, if we are short staffed. We will provide you with a hot meal on each shift and a lift home in the minibus is available at the end of a night shift, as the hotel is not on a bus route. Your trial shift starts on Saturday. Be here by eleven forty five am to start at twelve noon. I need your contact details and your national insurance number – bring them with you when you come – Any questions?' Violet was having trouble keeping up with the conversation, let alone racing ahead to think of questions. 'No, I don't think so?' answered Violet without thinking.

'You need to wear black trousers or a black skirt and a white blouse – not 'T' shirt. No bare legs and the skirt not too short. No high heels or you won't make it to the break! No painted nails and report to Miss St John when you get here – make sure you go to the back door, which is the staff entrance. We don't want people clogging up the reception area. I think that's everything for the moment. Good luck and I'll see you on Saturday' with that her call was terminated. Violet thought they were either desperate or stupid to take her on so easily, but it didn't matter; now she would be able to save for driving lessons and eventually a car. Violet felt on top of the world – only one hurdle left – to tell mum.

Violet hadn't wanted to jinx her chances by telling her mum about the job in case she didn't get it, but now the job trial was confirmed, she couldn't wait to spill her news. The following evening, when her mum was having a rare hour off from sanding down paintwork seemed the perfect time to confess. Violet had cooked tea, which although a nice surprise made Annie on edge to begin with. There never was a free meal where Violet was concerned. Annie waited all throughout the meal for the bomb to drop and when the meal was finished and the plates stacked and still no demands made, Annie could stand it no longer.

'Violet - that was a lovely tea, but I know you too well. What do you want and how much will it cost me?' Annie threw her a knowing look hidden within her smile.

'Mother, Mother, oh ye of little faith, can't I make you a meal just because I want to?'

'Well you can – but you never have before, not without a few strings attached anyway?' Annie could tell there was something on Violet's mind. She didn't however have a clue what it could be. Annie prayed that it was nothing to do with wanting to quit college or move back down south.

'Well, now that you ask ……..' Violet fluttered her eye lashes, 'there is something I have to tell you.'

'I knew it! How much' laughed Annie 'and don't try those lashes on me, that trick never works – well sometimes on men!' Violet raised them again at her mother's comment.

'And that doesn't mean I want you trying that method out young lady!' Continued Annie.

'It's not going to cost you anything Mum – quite the opposite!' Stated Violet. 'I've just got something to tell you.'

Now Annie *was* worried. In her head she pleaded with God *'Please don't let her be pregnant or on drugs or thrown out of college or moving away'*.

'The thing is – well, I've got a Job!'

'A job!' Repeated Annie almost shouting with relief. 'That's great news – Hold on! You're not quitting college are you?'

'No, it's a part time Job - evenings and weekends at 'Priory Hall', waiting tables, cleaning rooms, whatever they ask me to do. Nirah from college recommended me for the Job and after the interview they said yes! I've got a trial day on Saturday'

'That's great news Vi! I'm sure they'll love you, but you'll have to make sure it doesn't interfere with your college work?'

'I will Mum – Promise. The first thing I'm saving for are driving lessons.' Violet wasn't well known for her co-ordination skills, Annie pondered on which poor soul was going to be blessed with the task of teaching her. Annie was sure of one thing though, it wasn't going to be her. Annie was pleased that Violet had found something for herself in the village, but slightly disappointed that Violet hadn't confided in her.

'Why didn't you tell me about it? I could have wished you good luck?'

'You were always so busy and I could never find the right moment, you were either working down in the shop or on constructing the web-site - also I thought you might be cross with me and I didn't know if I would get it?'

'Why would I be cross?' Annie asked in bewilderment.

'….because of college work and everything going on here. I thought you might expect me to be here to help you get opened and then when you're open work for free?'

'I'm not going to deny that there may be odd days when I may need to ask you to be here, but if going to work at this hotel makes you happy, I would never stand in your way. The florist's shop is my dream. I don't expect it to be yours too. You have your own path to follow. You are sensible and you work hard at college and as long as you don't start to neglect that for work as a waitress, all will be fine – but if you keep another secret from me Violet Pickering, I'll be forced to knot your hair in plaits and tie them together to make you look neat and tidy! – understood!' said Annie playfully grabbing at Violets wild hair.

'Understood loud and clear Mum.' The pair instinctively moved towards each other, arms stretched out wide for a hug. Annie loved these moments. She would be like a limpet constantly stuck to Violet given half the chance, but she was painfully aware that too much would be suffocating for Violet, she didn't want to transfer her need for support after the loss of Nick on to Violets shoulders, so she self-regulated her hugs aiming to get the quantity just right. After a minute or so they broke apart. Annie stole a kiss from her cheek.

'Am I neglecting you?' Annie asked with a serious tone, looking Violet straight in the eye, so that she could judge the honesty of her answer.

'No Mum - you're not – and don't beat yourself up just 'cause I didn't tell you first. Teenagers are supposed to have secrets you know. If we didn't we'd never grow up because you adults would stop us from doing everything! - Didn't you have secrets when you were a teenager?' Annie turned away just in time to hide her blushes from Violet.

'Me?' Annie professed 'Once a goody two shoes, always a goody two shoes.' The less Violet knew about her mothers' youth the better for everyone's sake. Diversion tactics were needed.

'Right! Fancy joining me? Do the dishes or sand the walls?' Annie looked at Violet expectantly.

'Sorry Mum – homework, I know you feel that it should come first and I need to keep ahead for when I start my job.'

'How is it you always remember things I say, then throw them back at me to bite me on the bum when I least expect it!'

'It's just a natural skill Mum.' They both air hugged and air kissed each other. It was one of their little ways. A sort of mutual understanding, that neither one was pulling the wool over the other ones eyes. Humour and sarcasm had always been prevalent in the house hold. The sadder times in past years had quelled its use. They both enjoyed the feel of another small step back towards normality.

Chapter 14

For some unknown reason in the cosmos things were going to plan for Annie. An opening date had been set for the following week and no major hitches had surfaced to scupper her plans – so far. Fascia's, stationary, labels, packaging and awnings had all been ordered, indeed packages and workmen were arriving on a daily basis. Pippa had popped in to the shop a couple of times when the children had been at school to pitch in and help with some of the mundane tasks, like sanding and preparing work surfaces for papering and painting, this was the one job Annie hated the most. Annie was very grateful for the help, especially as Pippa insisted that her time was a gift and didn't want payment. Pippa wasn't awash with money, and in truth she could really have used some to pay some bills, but she wanted to help Annie, the chance of this job was important to her. Pippa figured that if she helped to prepare the shop for opening, it would open sooner and as a direct result, she would feel the benefit in her pocket sooner rather than later.

It was six in the morning, but Annie was so hyped with the list of things to complete she couldn't stay in bed any longer. She pulled on her faithful work clothes, which were destined for the bin in the very near future and went down the stairs in to the shop, stopping to make a coffee on the way. As her foot hit the bottom step and she could see the shop before her, a smile of satisfaction crept on to Annie's face. Gone was the tired space with dated and chipped paintwork and it had been replaced by a clean, sparkling, warm and welcoming retail experience – well it would be when it was finished. She sat on the counter, which still needed its final coat of paint, with her pad and pencil in her hands trying to imagine the flow through of the shop, where she would place stock, that she yet to buy. This was something she had never done before. In all the shops she had worked in, she merely followed orders, putting things where she was told. Now, it was all her choice, it was a daunting prospect. She knew it was extremely important for her business to create the right shopping experience for her customers. She had no back ground knowledge or degree to base her choices on. It was a purely instinctive reaction, she hoped to god that she was on the right track.

She was still sat on the counter, surrounded by a pile of redundant paper scraps when Zach arrived at eight, letting himself in with the spare key. No matter which way she planned it, something was missing –she just didn't know what.

'You're eager.' He said dropping a bag of nails and a pair of brackets on to the top of his work box.

'I'm trying to make some sense out of the space. I'm going to have to start setting things up soon and putting everything in place - and there is still so much to do and …..' Tiredness had got the better of her and tears were spilling down her cheeks. 'The paint needs touching up by the door, all the windows need a miracle clean, there's stock to buy and price and........'

'Whoa, whoa .... Slow down a bit.' He tore off some kitchen roll that they used to clean the paint brushes and passed it to her.

'I'm sorry.' She said in between tears. 'It seems too much to do and what if I get it wrong?'

'We'll get it done. Even if I have to cancel my night at the pub, we'll do it and it won't be wrong. You need to have a little faith in yourself. I have faith in you, Pippa has faith in you. We need to transfer some to you!' Zach poked her in the forehead with his index finger. He knew it was going to take more than that to pull her out of the hole she had dug for herself.

'Right! Here's what we're going to do today.' Said Zach taking control, 'I'm going to start in the back corner of the shop, clean it, finish any jobs that need doing, then as I move forward you can take over the space and start to price and display. Whilst I'm starting there, why don't you go to one of those wholesalers and pick up the stock that's been put away for you? It's a perfect time to do it and once it's in the shop it might inspire you and help you to decide the layout?' He waited to see if she would take him up on his suggestion.

She stood up and threw her arms out to each side, showing him the full effect of her lovely work attire. 'Do you think I should go like this?' She asked as she twirled in front of him.

'It works for me!' Agreed Zach, pleased to see her smiling.

'Umm, remind me never to take fashion advice from you! I'm going upstairs to change.' She said jumping off the counter and made her way to the staircase. She stopped at the bottom and turned looking over her shoulder towards him 'On the other hand though, I like all your other ideas. You should take it up professionally. You might be able to make a living at it.'

'I'll think on what you've said Malady!' Zach tipped an imaginary hat on his forehead.

'See you do my good man!' Annie laughed all the way up the stairs. 'Women', thought Zach, they're not that hard to understand.

It was also Violets first day at Priory Hall. She had to be in by ten-forty-five. Her alarm was set for nine thirty, but Zach had been banging and moving things downstairs, which woke her way before she was due out of bed. She used the spare time to have an extra-long shower, followed by a breakfast of French toast, orange juice and coffee. She wasn't sure when she would eat again; she didn't want to be hungry all day. Violet didn't dress until after breakfast, she had a very bad habit of sharing her food with her clothes on a regular basis. When she was dressed and presentable she made her way downstairs to the shop.

'Where's Mum?' asked Violet.

'Gone to the wholesalers to fetch some stock.' Answered Zach at the same time as fixing the last of the skirting boards into place.

'Well in that case, it's going to be you that has to wish me luck for today.' She shouted to Zach as she left the shop.

'Luck!' He shouted after her, '- but you won't need it!'

The walk to Priory Hall would take her approximately twenty five minutes, if she walked quickly. She set off at ten, eager not to be late on her first day. Nirah had confirmed that she was also working today. Violet was glad to have a friendly face around, someone to ask questions of, if she needed. The footpaths were narrow running along the country lanes, but they were safer than walking on the road, as some of the cars came around the corners at breakneck speed, and if she'd been in the road, they would have certainly hit her, even from the footpath she could feel the rush of air.

A large sign in the distance announced the 'Priory Hotel and Spa' as she turned the final corner. As instructed she made her way around to the back doors. The door was locked, but there was a bell. Violet took a deep breath, and then rang it. There was no response. She rang it again, unsure if it was working - still no response. She waited for a couple of minutes then rang it one final time. She was just about to go in search of another entrance when the door opened rapidly. She was greeted by a man, obviously surprised to see her standing there. He was in his thirties wearing a dark suit, white shirt and purple tie, tucked under his arm was a pile of papers and documents.

'How long have you been there?' He said managing to throw in a smile at the same time. He looked familiar; perhaps she had seen him in the village shop? Or maybe he just had one of those faces that you think you have seen before.

'A few minutes. It's my first day. They told me to come to the back door and ask for Miss St. John. I did ring the bell – several times, but no one came?'

'Blasted bell! Follow me.' He said, crooking his finger at her beckoning her in. She followed him through the narrow corridors with spare tables and chairs stacked on either side. He was obviously in a hurry and had a fast pace to match. Violet found it hard to keep up with him. He spoke to her as they walked. This was a man used to being obeyed.

'Make sure Miss St John gives you the code for the back door, so you don't have to wait. It's a waste of your time and that of the person who has to open it. Watch the door!' He called as he took her through a swing door and in to a large function room, it was being set up for a wedding. Various members of staff were polishing silver cutlery or holding Chrystal glasses over hot water to make them sparkle. Others were rolling tables into position and covering them with white crisp linen cloths. No one was stood around idle, everyone had been allocated a task and everyone was doing it. The man leading the way pointed to a woman in her late twenties with blond hair tied up neatly in a chignon, stood in the far corner of the room.

'That's Miss St John in the pink blouse over there.' He directed. She was stood looking extremely efficient with a clip board in one hand and a pen in the other, orchestrating the staff, allocating tasks to anyone who came within ten feet of her.

'Miss St John.' called the man. 'I have a new recruit for you. I found her at the back door trying to break in!' Everyone in the room turned around to stare at the new blood. Her face went crimson. Violet wasn't amused.

'... and please get maintenance to check that the bell is working at the back door. We nearly had to dock her wages for being late, because she couldn't get in.' The man looked at Violet in a way in which she couldn't decide if he was being serious or not.

'Thank you Mr 'P'.' Called Miss St John, 'I'll get on to it straight away.' 'Mr P' was gone before Miss St John had time to finish her sentence. She turned her full attention to Violet.

'Now its Violet isn't it? Well don't worry we'll ease you in gently today.' Violet could see kindness in her eyes, but equally she knew that Miss St John would stand no messing. Violet was led to the staff rooms. Miss St John allocated a locker to her, then made sure her uniform was correct and in line with company rules.

'Now did you have everything explained to you over the phone? She was asking Violet.

'Eh, yes.'

'I'm afraid we are quite formal here and there are certain ways to address the managers. When you address me in front of a guest you should call me 'Miss St

John', but here behind the scenes you may call me Scarlett – Don't get the two mixed up! Now, put your purse and anything else in your locker, then we can get a coffee and I'll talk you through some of the do's and don'ts that will be expected of you. I know you won't remember everything all at once, but if you can't remember, ask one of your colleagues to help you. They all had to learn at some point. Now Violet – tell me about yourself?' Violet did as she was instructed. She told Miss St John about moving up from down south and going to college and about her Mum's shop that would be opening soon. She left out the part about her Father being killed in a car crash, she didn't want people to define her by an event she hated to talk about. She didn't want to become 'The new waitress, whose Dad was killed'. Miss St John passed her a biscuit to go with her coffee.

'Didn't you want to work for your Mum in the shop? Won't she need or expect your help?' Asked Miss St John.

'Do you know how much Mothers' pay their daughters these days?' They both smiled. 'Of course I will help her if she needs me, but she has to get on her feet first before she can afford to pay me, so I'm afraid you get first dib's on my talents!'

'Good. I like to see a little confidence. Right it's time we found out what you can do.' Violet knew that she was going to like Scarlett. They were just clearing their cups away when Mr P. came marching through the door on the hunt for Miss St John.

'I'm afraid I need you at Reception urgently Miss St John.' He said, catching her attention with a wave of his arm.

'I'll be with you immediately Mr P. - Violet, please go into the main function room and help to set the tables. I'll be in as soon as I can. Ask any one of the staff and they'll guide you as to what to do.' Violet watched them both scurry out of the room like shoppers trying to get through the doors first in the January sales, looking for a bargain.

Violet eventually found her way back to the function room after a few wrong turns into other parts of the hotel. All the corridors looked the same to her, she wondered if she would ever remember which way to go. Finally, one of the maids pointer her in the right direction. Violet could see two girls around Annie's age and one boy chatting whilst placing cutlery on the round tables at the far end of the function room. One of the girls, with the best cheek bones Violet had ever seen called her over.

'Did Miss St John send you in to help us?' She asked with a friendly smile.

'Yes, but I haven't a clue what I'm supposed to do!' Admitted Violet.

'Don't worry we don't know either!' They all laughed, 'I'm Kerry, she's Fiona and he's Spencer.' Kerry used the fork she was polishing to point at each person as she introduced them.

'Aren't you a friend of Nirah's?' It was Spencer asking her. 'She said one of her friends was staring today – grab a cloth and help polish these – What's your name?' He tossed a white tea towel across to her.

'I'm Violet.' She said picking up a spoon from the pile on the table and starting to polish it.

'She's a right laugh that Nirah. How d'you know her?' Asked Fiona. 'I think she starts at four today – I say start, but the lazy cow never does any work!' Fiona laughed, amused by her own comment.

'You're no better!' chipped in Spencer. 'I've never met anyone who takes so long to go and find an extra bread roll! – By the time you come back, they're on dessert!' Fiona scowled at Spencer.

'What's Miss St John like?' Asked Violet changing the subject.

'Oh don't ask Spencer what he thinks of her. He thinks she's the bee's knees. Don't you Spen!' Fiona piped up.

'Jealousy is a bad thing,' He said shaking his head, 'She wants me.' He pursed his lips and tilted his head towards Fiona, indicating that it was Fiona who wanted him.

'But she can't deal with the fact that I'm Gay darling! – and she's declared she's going to turn me!'

'And in truth, he can't cope with me rejecting him, which is why he says he's Gay! So he has this fantasy crush on Miss St John instead, but it's her clothes and makeup tips he's after. He fantasises about having a girly night in with her!' Spencer used a spoon to splash Fiona with some of the water left over from polishing the glasses.

'See the truth hurts doesn't it Spen!' Laughed Fiona.

'Miss St John is alright really.' Said Kerry bringing the conversation back to Violet's question. 'It's that Mr P. you need to watch – Nothing gets past him. He only arrived a few weeks ago, he was sent here by Head office. Apparently he's here for a year to sort this place out. Bosses said it was losing money and had the worst reputation in the whole hotel chain - and they own loads. If he doesn't fix us, there's talk they'll close us down or sell it. So where he's concerned watch your back, he's out to make his mark!'

'He seemed okay?' Violet was surprised to find herself defending a man she didn't know.

'Fluffy animals always do - until they bite you!' Warned Kerry.

'Quick – look hard at it! I can see him coming this way!' Said Kerry picking a fork up and dipping it in.

Annie wasn't having such a good day. It took her four hours to get to the wholesalers, choose some more stock, get through checkout, load up and get back to the shop. The traffic was terrible and some of the stock that had been saved for her couldn't be located. She'd had nothing to eat or drink and her head was pounding like a cleaver on a butchers block. Hours later than she expected she finally turned into the main street of Longridge – home at last. She could see ladders and activity outside the shop. Zach and the sign maker were fixing the last of the screws into the new shop sign. Annie stopped the car a little distance from the shop in a layby before she had been noticed. She wanted to look at it and admire her achievement , which also happened to be her biggest nightmare. Emotion overtook her, all the months of striving to survive without Nick and trying to be strong for Violet, not letting her guard down to grieve herself. Life without Nick was immeasurably different. She felt as if she had been left without a purpose, it had been difficult searching to find her own path, but what if her choice was wrong, what if she couldn't do it, run her own business. Maybe it was just a dream that should have been left to fester and dissolve? What if she was about to completely ruin their lives? Worst case scenario – they would be homeless. After holding on to all these doubts and fears for weeks, the sight of the new sign with 'Violet's' name emblazoned on it, shattered her defence and all her pent up emotions started to flood out. Her body heaved and rasped expelling tear after tear. Suddenly there was a knock at the window, bursting her bubble of anxiety. It was Mrs Stretford. Annie quickly tried to stop herself from crying and packed her emotions back in her heart, but it was easier said than done. She was embarrassed to be caught emotionally naked by a woman she barely knew. It would be the talk of the village before tea that the new florist was already cracking up. Annie reluctantly wound down the window, knowing that there was no way she could excuse herself without speaking.

'Is something wrong Annie?' Asked Mrs Stretford with genuine concern.

'No, no, I'm just having a moment – overtired, you know how it is.' Annie tried to brush it off.

'Don't give me that old nonsense! You get out of that car and come with me.' Annie was left with no option but to get out of the car and follow Mrs Stretford. Mrs Stretford took Annie to her home, a little cottage two doors away from where Annie had pulled her car in at the side of the road.

'I could see you from the window, getting all upset,' She said as she led them both through the front door, 'now sit yourself down and I'll make you a cup of tea. Stan's out so we won't be disturbed.' Annie did as she was told, still trying to stop the tears; it seemed that once she had opened the flood gates, there was no stopping them. Annie sat with Mrs Stretford for over an hour, pouring her heart out. Mrs Stretford just listened, encouraged her to talk and administered tea.

'You are very hard on yourself Annie.' She said at the end of the second pot of tea.' I do understand dear. I lost my husband a long time ago too and had to bring Stan and his sister and brother up on my own. Your shop was my salvation. It kept me going and gave me something to get up for in the morning, until I was strong enough to get up for my own sake. You lost your husband, but that doesn't mean you have to be lost too? It's true what they say dear -time is a great healer, trouble is you have to get through the time before you feel any benefit.'

'Do you think I can do it Mrs Stretford – make the shop work?' Annie was asking in all seriousness. This was a woman who had lived through the life Annie was about to start, she knew all the pitfalls.

'My dear I know you can do it! From that first day I saw you with your work clothes on, getting on with the job, not just standing around giving orders. To run a business you need to get stuck into it. If it needs doing – you have to do it, unless of course it's something you can't, then you have to get help, but help was there for me and it's here for you, you just have to be strong enough to ask for it. I know you'll succeed. Your biggest hurdle is your own self-belief, but you come again for tea and I'll sort you out!' She gave Annie a wicked grin and a wink. 'Now, pick yourself up, dry those tears and go and make sure that sign is straight. Frank Bickerstaff never could use a spirit level!' Annie did as she was told. It was only after all her emotions had been released, that Annie realised the weight of the invisible burdens she had been carrying around every single day. Now, she felt absolved from her worries – at least for the moment.

'Where have you been!' Scolded Zach when he noticed her approaching from higher up the high St. 'We could have done with you an hour ago to tell us if this sign was straight!'

'Traffic was bad and the staff at the wholesalers needed a bomb under them!' She was not about to admit where she had been, luckily Zach hadn't noticed her car parked a little way up the street for over an hour.

'Well do you like it?' He proudly pointed at the sign to make sure she had seen it.

'Looks fantastic!' She beamed, 'but we need to get it covered before Violet gets back! Remember it's a secret?'

'Your wish is my command!' Said Zach climbing up the ladder and covered the sign over with a dust sheet so that Violet wouldn't see it. Annie hadn't yet told her daughter that the shop was named after her. She wanted it to be a surprise on the opening day, her gift to Violet.

At Priory Hall the staff worked hard under the guidance of Miss St John. The wedding party was due to arrive at four, but they were running a little late. This allowed the staff a short break before the long haul of the night ahead. Chef wasn't too pleased though, they could hear him shouting, asking how he was expected to keep a meal for a hundred people warm and in top condition if they couldn't be bothered to turn up on time. Violet decided not to introduce herself to him today, if she could at all help it.

Half an hour before the guests were due, Miss St John called all the staff together for a pep talk. Miss St John was about to start speaking when Violet noticed Nirah and a boy she had never seen before creep in to the back of the room, trying not to be noticed. The boy was the most gorgeous thing Violet had ever seen. He was sex on legs. It was lust at first sight. Violet had the feeling that things might get a little more exciting at work and if she was very lucky, out of work as well. His eyes were dark and moody, his features were chiselled and even through his white shirt, she could tell he probably had a six pack. If he wasn't a model, he should have been. His aura oozed 'Sex God' and 'Bad boy', just the type that Violet liked. Nirah waved discreetly at Violet, acknowledging she had seen her. 'The model' standing next to Nirah looked across to see who Nirah was waving at. Violet was no 'Shrinking Violet' so she stared right back at him, keeping eye contact. He smiled, confidently, daring her to continue – she did. There was no way she was about to back down at this point. She could tell he was surprised that she had enough confidence to stare back at him. Suddenly they were interrupted by Miss St John, commanding their attention.

'Okay people!' She started. 'We have a hundred guests today for the sit down meal and an extra sixty joining us this evening. Those of you who have done service before please take your usual tables. Violet you can work with Kerry; she'll show you the ropes.' Violet blushed, she felt like she was back I school assembly. The 'Model' was still watching her, which made her begin to blush. She cursed her body for letting her down.

'Remember to always smile.' Continued Miss St John. Never ignore a guest if they beckon to you, even if you are not looking after their table. Take the message and pass it on to the correct person. Remember to fill wine glasses whenever you get a free moment and no standing gossiping during service. All conversations should be regarding the service of the meal and nothing else. Any questions? – No – good, let's move then people.' Violet had a million but decided she would ask Kerry or Nirah instead. As the staff moved off to start their respective jobs, Nirah and the mystery 'Model' boy came over.

'Hiya! Where did you get to last night?' Nirah asked critically.

'Couldn't be bothered to go in the end.' Violet was speaking to Nirah, but her eyes were focused on her side kick, Nirah noticed that she didn't have her friend's full attention.

'This is Harley – Harley - Violet. He's a bad boy Violet. One of those you're Mother tells you to stay away from. Don't mix with him!' Warned Nirah. Harley was obviously enjoying Nirah's description of his character. He smiled at Violet again, *'Christ'* his teeth were perfect too when you got up close thought Violet, almost drooling.

'Don't believe anything Nirah says about me. Wait till you find out first-hand.' His words were laced with innuendo.

' - And what makes you think I want to find out anything about you?' Questioned Violet, who was no push over even though she would happily have agreed to snog him right there and then in front of everyone.

'Oh – you will – when you get to know me!' His confidence was refreshing to Violet. He was good looking and knew it, but there was also a feeling of tongue in cheek with him. He didn't seem to take himself too seriously – she liked that.

'Are you as dangerous as your name suggests?' Violet teased him.

'What do you mean?' He asked.

'Well- 'Harley' - fast, high maintenance, expensive and wanted by many?'

'If you put it like that – then – yes.' He conceded. He was about to offer to give her a 'ride' when they were interrupted by Miss St. John who was on a mission to have everything done and everyone in their correct places by the time the guests arrived.

'Violet, please place the bread rolls on the side plates on the tables over there. Harley and Nirah, you both know where you should be.' Miss St John gave them both a stern look. Violet moved away to collect her bread rolls, but not before she had communicated to Harley without words, the fact that she found him extremely attractive.

A few minutes later Miss St. John clapped her hands in the air. 'Places everyone!' Violet looked at Kerry vacantly.

'You need to go and stand by the wall near your table, with your hands behind your back and smile.' Violet didn't understand why, but she did it.

'It's so that we look professional.' Whispered Kerry. Violet showed what she thought of the idea by crinkling her nose. Although it didn't show on the outside, Violet was extremely nervous. *'Please don't let me spill anything on someone's lap'* she pleaded silently. This was her first job and she wanted to keep it for more than one day. She couldn't go home and tell her Mother she'd been fired during the trial period, besides it was starting to get interesting. She was looking forward to a close working relationship with Harley.

The guests on Violet and Kerry's table were made up from the Bride and grooms old Aunts and Uncles that none of the younger generation wanted to be sat next to. The youngest member was a World War I veteran for sure.

'This is going to be fun,' whispered Kerry, 'they'll want extra everything or they'll want something that's not on the menu – they always do at that age and you'll have to re-fill the salt, 'cause they lace everything with it. I bet you there'll be none left! Right put your best smile on and keep calm.' Kerry moved closer to the table and cleared her throat, hoping that the guests would hear her and notice she was about to speak.

'Good afternoon Ladies and gentlemen. My name is Kerry and this is Violet.' She beckoned to Violet, encouraging her to move closer to the table, 'and we are your waitresses for the afternoon. If there is anything you need please ask.' Almost before Kerry had finished her sentence the first request was delivered.

'Yes, young lady. I'd like a pot of tea. That church was colder than Siberia. I don't do this fizzy stuff. Joyce! Do you want a pot of tea too?' By the time they had finished it was pots of tea all round – with extra hot water.'

'Certainly Madam, we'll have them for you in a minute.' Violet followed Kerry into the kitchens. 'Told you!' Said Kerry, 'and we haven't even got to the starters yet!' they both laughed.

'What you two laughing at?' Remarked Harley as he passed them.

'Never you mind.' Said Kerry Irritated by his interruption. When he was out of ear shot Kerry gave Violet the benefit of her wisdom. 'He's all mouth that one. Thinks he's God's gift. He's had more of the staff here than I've made cups of tea for old ladies.' Violet turned around to admire his physique, still not dissuaded by Kerry's description of his ways. She mentally added a tight bum to his list of attributes.

The looked that passed between Violet and Harley didn't go un-noticed by Kerry. 'I can see You!' She goaded whilst waiting for the tea to be poured, 'making cow eyes at Harley!'

'I don't have any idea what you mean.' Said Violet feigning innocence.

'I mean it when I say he's trouble – give him an inch and he'll take a mile. I guarantee he'll hurt you if you let him near you. Don't say I didn't warn you!' Violet just smiled, even though she could tell that Kerry was annoyed by her refusal to heed her words. They carried the trays of tea out to their table. On the way they passed a table of young couples, obviously the close friends of the Bride and Groom. Everyone on the table was drinking the wine as if it was going out of fashion. One of the men nearest to Violet caught her arm and almost pulled the tray of tea out of her hands as she passed.

'Oye, bring another couple of bottles of this stuff will you!' He shouted pointing to his almost empty glass of wine. Violet didn't have a clue where to get it or even if she should.

'Certainly Sir. I'll be back in a minute.' She said to appease the man. She took the tea to her table, and then went to find Miss St. John. She would know what to do. Violet explained what the 'lovely man' wanted.

'I didn't know if I should get it or who was on waiting on that table?' Said Violet.

'It's Harley's table.' Said Miss St John calling Harley over. 'It looks like it's going to be a heavy session for some of them.' Miss St John turned to Harley.

'Harley I want you to take my key for the cellar and pull out twelve more bottles of the house red. Make sure you write it in the ledger at the door, with the date. You know what to do. Violet, you go with him to help him carry them and be as quick as possible. I need you both back here!'

'Yes Miss St. John.' They both chorused. Once out of the main room Harley turned to Violet.

'It's this way.' He said leading her through the back corridors of the hotel. 'Do you think you'll be safe with me in the cellar?'

'I don't know? – do you think you'll be safe with me?' She replied. Harley was impressed by her candour. He turned to look at her and smirked. 'I hope not.' Suddenly, he halted. There was a small door off to one side. They had reached the cellar. Harley took the key given to him by Miss St John and unlocked the door. He flicked on the light then stood back for Violet to go in first. It wasn't as large as Violet expected. She had seen programs on television on wine cellars; they always seemed to go on and on underground. This was more like a large garage on the inside. Once they were both inside he locked the door behind them.

'Why are you doing that?' Asked Violet, a little un-nerved, but trying to sound perfectly calm. She was pretty sure it was for effect only.

'Some of the guests mistake the door for the toilets. It stops them coming in. The last thing we want is to be interrupted when we're doing such an important job.'

Harley went over to the section with the wines and selected the bottles that were needed back in the wedding reception. He handed a box over to Violet. 'Go and put them by the door.' He instructed.

'Please!' She reprimanded him.

'Okay – Please.' He added begrudgingly. Whilst she was busy moving the wine she saw him put two new full bottles of Jack Daniels into the bottom of a cardboard box, then fill the box with empty glass beer bottles. She crept up behind him. He didn't hear her coming with the sound of the clinking glass.

'What are you doing?' She asked accusingly. She knew it was something dodgy.

'Let's just call it a perk of the job.' He said moving the box to the back of the room where all the empties were stacked for collection by the dray men. She followed him. 'So how do you make that work?' She wanted to know more about the scam he was operating, as she had never seen anyone blatantly steal in front of her eyes before. She wondered if this stunt was just for her benefit or if it was a usual occurrence. He stopped what he was doing and starred at her, then he moved towards, making her move back towards the wall. He still continued to move closer, until he was a few inches from her face. 'You want to know a lot of things. How do I know I can trust you?' He said pulling a lock of her hair that was dangling by the side of her face and winding it around his finger. His gaze moved from her eyes down her chest to her cleavage. He leaned in even further to peep inside her blouse. The crisp whiteness' of her bra with the lace edging aroused him. He knew she wasn't as innocent as her underwear. He wanted to hitch up her skirt and do it to her now, he could tell, she would make him wait to have her. It would have been easy if she'd had a few drinks, but sober, well he knew he'd have to wait. Violet interrupted his train of thought.

'As you say, you don't know if you can trust me. – So isn't it best to keep me close. If I know what's going on, then I become an accessory?' She was calling his bluff. He let go of her hair and placed his hands on the wall, one on either side of her head. Then he bent forwards and kissed her. Not a gentle tender, tentative kiss, but one designed to show her who was in charge. It was intrusive and fervent. She responded, equally as passionately. She had never met anyone quite like Harley. He was intoxicating and exciting; she was enjoying the risk of getting caught. Harley wasn't content with merely a kiss. He decided he wanted more. He'd have to wait to screw her, but there was still fun to be had. He moved his hand from the wall and grabbed her breast. Her nipple instantly contracted, making it hard and easy for Harley to locate. He rubber his thumb backwards and forwards over it. She wanted to push him away, but it was such a pleasurable sensation, she delayed for a few moments. It was true, she wanted him too. She liked him, but she wasn't that easy. She realised that she was going to have to manoeuvre herself out of the situation before it went too far. She grabbed him by the balls, as roughly as he'd grabbed her. She took him by surprise. He froze, unsure of his next move. He was enjoying their game and her hands on his erection.

'So, are you going to tell me what you're doing with the bottles of JD or do I have to tell the management?'

'You play dirty.' He said trying to move forwards towards her to pin her back against the wall, but she was too quick for him, side stepping away from the wall and letting go of his 'Crown Jewels'.

'Then we're well matched - So…. Are you going to tell me?' She could tell he wanted her to know how clever he was and how he had worked out a system. It only took a moment for him to decide to tell her, but it was more about boasting than trust. Besides which, he knew she wanted more than just a kiss from him, if he played his cards right, he'd have that too one day very soon.

'I usually get the job of helping to move the empties to the outside bin area ready for the dray man to collect, I take the boxes outside with the drink already stashed at the bottom, get the booze and hide the bottles in the bushes and collect them later on my way out of work! I always make sure I park my car as close as possible to the bins. Perfect. – and I wouldn't want anyone to mess my little system up!' He was staring straight at her.

'I won't.' She said as if butter wouldn't melt, 'But what do you do with the booze? Drink it?'

'Sometimes and sometimes I sell it. Given a bit of notice I can nick to order. I once got the whole lot of champagne needed for my mates wedding and the stupid fuckers in charge here didn't know a thing. - If they're that daft to have such a crap system, it's their own fault. Anyway, come on, we'd best get back before they come looking for us, and...' He stopped just before they went out of the door, '..And I think I'm gonna have more of you one day soon Violet. Maybe in here?' Then he unlocked the door and picked up the wine. Violet didn't reply, but her mind was racing ahead imagining it – may be he would.

Jack leaned back on his swivel chair gazing out of the window at the Bridal party on the lawn. The afternoon meal had been served and the room was being cleared, ready for the evening reception. Many of the guests were out on the lawn, enjoying the last of the day's light and warmth. The autumn day was mild, with last of the sun casting large shadows under the old willow and oak trees. Everything was perfect for the couple. All the guests seemed happy and jovial, their every need taken care of. That was part of his job – to make sure that the hotel and the staff did everything they could to make the couple's special day go without a hitch. Jack had resisted the move at first, when they asked him to come to Priory Hall. There were plenty of other's who were equally capable of bringing it back up to standard, but a little part of him – the gambler, wanted to spend a year in the county he grew up in and possibly bump into Annie's Mother or someone from school that could tell him what happened to her, and if he was indeed a Father? At the very least he wanted to know that she was okay and hopefully happy with Nick, as much as it pained him to admit that – most of all he wanted her to know that he didn't get the letters. He couldn't bear the thought that she felt abandoned by him. He wanted her to know all the unforgivable things his Father did to keep them apart – he had to let her know in some way that he didn't know about the pregnancy. It was the one main fact that haunted him constantly, she didn't know, that he didn't let her down by choice. His Father let them both down.

The happy couple laughing outside on the lawn made him reflect on the short disastrous marriage he had embarked on many years ago after that shocking night when he found Annie and Nick together - married. Jack had met Cassie at head office, he had been so glad to find someone to love that he didn't stop to consider, if she really loved him. Cassie, his ex-wife and Annie were as different as night and day. At least he and Cassie didn't have children to complicate the divorce. That was a mixed blessing. Maybe he had missed out on being a Father twice. It was too late now for regrets. Having the ability to look back now, Jack understood that the marriage never stood a chance. He was still in love with Annie and Cassie; well she wasn't truly capable of loving anyone but herself. Finding the letters in his Father's filing cabinet had in a strange way helped him to justify the failure of his marriage.

He recalled the time immediately after his father's death when he came back to

Preston looking for Annie. He spent three weeks searching all their old haunts, looking for clues as to where she may be. He tried the house where he had found Annie and Nick living together as man and wife, all those years previously. He wondered for a moment if their wedding had been anything like the one he was witnessing on the lawn outside his window. The neighbour's at Annie's mum's house had told him that the family moved away some years ago, but she didn't know where to and there was no forwarding address. She wasn't on the electoral register in the Preston area, so, he knew she hadn't returned to the area. For all his searching, all he found was a big fat dead end. The blow of not finding her hit him sideways. It took him weeks to put things into perspective and move on with his life. He was less bitter now; time had softened the edges of the pain making it just bearable. He kept himself busy at work and because he had no ties, he was the person they sent to fix all the problems, wherever they occurred, anywhere in the world. Because he was single, he was cheap to house. He usually stayed in the staff quarters in the hotel or sometimes there was a small cottage in the grounds, as was the case in Priory Hall, but he could be sent off at a moment's notice to the next crisis. No worry about having to take children out of School or a partner that had their own career to consider before a move was made.

He still thought about Annie every day. He had intended to look for her again, now that he was back in the area, but Priory Hall was keeping him too busy at the moment, still, it would settle down when he had gained control of the situation. It was only a matter of time. Then he would try again to pick up a trail for Annie.

The new girl crossed the lawn in front of his office on her way to collect left over glasses from the wedding party who were now in the process of moving back inside after the room had been re-arranged for the evening reception. There was something about this girl that he liked, he didn't know why; she was just one of those people you take a liking to for no particular reason, you can put your finger on it. The girl didn't see him watching her. She was too busy picking her way over the lawns on her tiptoes, trying to stop her heels sinking into the grass.

Violet was alone in the hotel gardens. The best man had rounded up the last of the stray guests and lured them back inside with the promise of the Bride and Grooms first dance. Violets small kitten heels were annoying her. It was impossible to walk without looking stupid, let alone balance a tray with glasses as well. Every time she made a step she lost half of her shoe into the soft earth. She made a mental note not to wear heels of any description to work again. There were at least a dozen tables full of empty and dis-guarded glasses waiting for Violet to remove them and send them for cleaning. In the centre of the debris stood one un-touched glass of champagne, without thinking Violet picked it up and downed it in one. It would have been a shame to waste it, besides no one was watching. Her mind wandered to Harley. Was she doing exactly the same as he was? Stealing drink? She didn't think it was anywhere near as bad. She was only disposing of something that would be flushed down a sink. Violet understood a little more about what Kerry was trying to warn her about as far as Harley was concerned, but there was something magnetic drawing her in to his world – and the danger he emitted. Up until now she had always played it safe in life. She had never been a risk taker. Never bunked off school or smoked behind the bike sheds, maybe now was it time to try something different. She was tired of playing it safe, it was boring. No one here knew her here. She could be whomever she wanted to be – not the person everyone expected her to be. She was beginning to enjoy the benefits of moving to a new town. On the next table to be cleared stood another glass hardly touched, she did the same, down in one. The bubbles fizzed in her nose. She smiled, feeling the warmth of the alcohol trickle down her throat. She looked around, still no-one in the garden to see her – no harm done. She continued on inside and took the glasses to be washed in the kitchens. She decided there were some good points to working after all.

Mr P. watched the new girl from the window, tutting loudly. He made a mental note to search her out later and explain the error of her ways. Even if he liked her, he still needed to explain the etiquette of clearing dead drinks and what would happen if she ever did it again. He was shocked, but amused when she drank the first glass, but she second was a step too far. He pondered for a moment, if he should make it a sackable offence. Then he remembered it was her first day – a dressing down would be enough.

It was two a.m. before the last of the wedding guests were dispersed to their rooms. Harley was waiting for Violet by the back door of the hotel. 'Do you want a lift home?' He asked her, in such a way that she knew he was offering sex. She smelt of food, spilled wine and sweat and she couldn't imagine that he would smell much differently, besides which, she was shattered and she couldn't just decide not to go home. She knew her Mum would worry and in all probability waiting up for her to hear about her day.

'I've got a lift on the minibus – thanks.'

'Your loss.' He said walking away without another word. He was obviously used to getting what and whom he wanted.

'Maybe another day?' She called after him, not wanting to burn all her bridges. She definitely fancied him. He ignored her and continued walking. At least she didn't have to walk home. Mr P. was in charge of giving all the staff a lift home, but not before he had called Violet to one side for a quiet word regarding the pitfalls of drinking champagne on duty.

Annie had intended to wait up for Violet, but tiredness got the better of her. She remembered the beginning of the late film, but everything after the first ten minutes was lost. The plot was weak and she had fallen asleep on the sofa. The numbness in her arm woke her. It was after two and there was still no sign of Violet. Annie heard an engine pull up outside the shop, she dragged her tired bones up from the sofa and looked out of the window, just in time to see Violet getting out of a mini bus with 'Priory Hall' emblazoned on the side. Annie went in to the kitchen and click the kettle on whilst Violet let herself in and made her way upstairs.

'Well? How did it go?' Asked Annie trying to sound wide awake. Violet let out a grunt.

'It was fine until that shit Mr P. gave me a telling off for drinking a glass of left over champagne!' Annie stifled a laugh.

'He didn't sack you did he?' Questioned Annie trying her best to understand why Violet was upset by the reprimand.

'No! He told me that *'It's unprofessional to drink on duty'* and *'anyone could have seen me'* and *'not to do it again'*.' Violet mimicked him. 'Bloody manager! He should get a life - not spend his time looking out of windows trying to catch people out!' Annie decided to try and find a positive on the day's events.

'So? What about the rest of the day? - What were the other people like to work with?'

'Oh they were fine. A good laugh really. It's quite funny, being on the side-lines at a wedding seeing all the different characters getting more pissed as the day goes on. We got the table full of old biddies. They were really funny though; one of the old men left us, me and Kelly, a tip - ten quid between us. They were hard work, but I don't care if they leave us bloody big tips!'

'Language Violet!' Chastised Annie, 'we don't want Mr P. having a word with you for swearing do we?' Violet pulled a face to let her mother know she was less than impressed. 'So can I interest you in tea and toast before bed? Or did they feed you so well that you won't need to eat for a week?'

'The food was good actually. May be I'll take you there for your birthday – If you fancy paying of course!'

'I knew there'd be a catch! Anyway are you sure I can't get you anything?'

'Ah no thanks Mum. I just need sleep please – Night.'

'Sleep tight, mind the bed bugs don't ......'

'Yep, yep – Night.' Yawned Violet who in her mind was already in her bed.

Chapter 15

The day of Annie's 'Grand Opening' was finally less than twenty four hours away. Each day in the previous week had been crammed with endless jobs and decisions. Sleep was a very rare commodity and Annie was looking forward to knowing that once the shop was open, she would be able to have some time to herself, surely there was nothing left in the building to paint! Zach had been a God send. He worked above and beyond the call of duty, staying late on many nights to make sure the fine detail was finished in time for the opening. It wasn't just a work relationship; they had become friends, although this was not with the blessing of Zach's girlfriend, whom for some reason she was reading more into the renovation of the shop than was there. She had managed to convince herself that Annie was out to bed Zach, which was complete nonsense and fabrication. Annie was almost old enough to be his mother and besides which, Annie had already convinced herself that Pippa and Zach would make a perfect couple. Bringing the two closer together was on her list of things to do after the shop was up and running.

Annie Took a display of vases down from the shelves for the sixth time and started to look for another home for them. She found it hard to make the final decisions when she was tired. The more the decisions needed to be made, the harder it was for her to make them. Annie didn't want to get it wrong and the weight of that responsibility was paralysing her. It took Pippa and Zach, working together, to take her aside and explain some basic home truths. It was ten in the evening. Annie had eaten nothing all day, insisting that there was no time for food. In short they ambushed her, making her sit down with a sandwich and a cup of tea.

'Annie, we know you want everything to be right, but no one knows what it should look like but you, Zach and I, so if there are little details missing, we can correct them as we go along. If we find things are not working in the position we put them in, we can move them. I'm sure Zach will come back and lend a hand if we need to move something heavy?' Pippa looked at him, giving him the signal to jump into the conversation.

'Yes, I will – Pippa's right Annie. Sometimes you need to try things to see if they work. You can't always have all the answers first time around. At this point it's most important that it at least looks like it's finished for the opening tomorrow?' He looked at Pippa for reassurance that he was on the right track with his words of advice. Annie sighed deeply,

'I know you are both right. I've been putting too much emphasis on the wrong things haven't I?'

'We understand – you want everything to be perfect, but don't forget you haven't even got any fresh flowers in yet. When they arrive it will totally transform the space again and it will bring it too life and the spaces you feel are dull – well they won't be!' Pippa was talking sense, Annie could see that.

'Okay!' Said Annie, 'I get the message! I'll sit and eat this sandwich and then I promise to put things on shelves and leave them there!'

'I'm glad to hear it!' Announced Pippa, 'but I'm afraid I can't stay any longer. My children have already forgotten what I look like this week and I promised Mum and Dad I'd be back at a reasonable hour?'

'God Pippa! I'm sorry, of course you should go. Go on, away with you – You too Zach. You've both been great; I don't know what I'd have done without you both. I promise to send you both out for a meal to thank you both next week – and Pippa I'll babysit to give your parent's a rest!'

'You can't do that Annie? What will Zach's girlfriend will think, if you send us out together!' Added Pippa flustered by Annie's suggestion.

'Actually,' interrupted Zach, 'she's not my girlfriend anymore - we broke up a couple of days ago.'

'Ohh?' Pippa was lost for words.

'I hope it was nothing to do with working here and doing all the overtime to get things ready on time?' Asked Annie, suddenly aware that she may have unwittingly contributed to the downfall of his relationship.

'God no! It was something we both decided. Let's just say we didn't bring the best out in each other.'

'Well – in that case, there's no one to worry about now is there, you two can go out and have a laugh as friends? There's nothing wrong about that – is there?'

'But it would be better if you were there too?' Pippa was not giving in easily. She looked to Zach again for back up. He nodded in agreement, but Annie could tell he was rather smitten with the idea of them going alone.

'Now, it would be unfair to make your parents sit for the children – It's the least I can do to say thank you to the both of you. I'll hear no more of it! I'll book a restaurant!'

Pippa drove home in a state of shock; somehow she had been manipulated into going on a date with the very attractive Zach. She wanted to refuse to go, but wouldn't that be churlish? There really was no reason why the pair of them couldn't spend a few hours together as civilised adults, then go their separate ways. It was Pippa's imagination that was running wild. He didn't fancy her, so there was nothing to worry about – except for the fact that she fancied him.

Annie settled down to the remaining list of jobs after Zach and Pippa had gone home. She placed the last of the new products on the empty shelves and even if she wasn't completely happy with the finished look, she was going to leave it as promised. It was after twelve before she heaved her tired body up the stairs and to bed. She reflected on the weeks of hard work they had all gone through. It had been difficult, but they had done it. Now its success or failure was going to be down to her own ability. There was just one large piece of the jigsaw missing – the fresh flowers. Annie's alarm was set for four a.m. she debated whether to go to bed at all, but decided that a few hours would help her get through the next day.

Annie felt as if she had only closed her eyes momentarily, when the sharp trill of the alarm clock woke her abruptly. She switched it off swiftly, not wanting to wake Violet. She dressed and crept out of the bedroom, picking her car keys up on the way. The roads were empty on the drive to the wholesale market; vehicles were few and far between. The odd car and taxi's, a few Lorries setting out on the day's deliveries, including the milkmen, trying to keep awake as they looked as if they'd been out on the town the night before and hadn't seen a bed either.

Annie had already contacted the flower market, so they were expecting her. She drove off the main road and into the giant car park, worthy of any high street supermarket, but the vehicles were large articulated Lorries, vans and chilled wagons, not family cars and Range Rovers. The outside of the wholesalers was flood lit. It looked like a larger football pitch at night – except for the lack of grass of course. The lights helped customers to see their way in and out of the building, no matter what the time of day or night. As Annie grabbed her list from her bag, eager, yet a little apprehensive at the same time. She could see People passing by, pushing trolleys piled high of every type of floral delight and plant you could think of. Inside was even better. She felt like a child in a sweet shop. This wasn't her first visit to a flower market. She had gone on one occasion, a long time ago, when she worked part time in a florist shop. The owner had gone away on holiday and Annie was left holding the fort. It had been a different market, one down south, but the feel and buzz was just the same. She had been in to introduce herself and open a customer account at this market a couple of weeks ago, so she was familiar with the layout and set up. The last thing she needed was to be running around like a headless chicken searching for the right flowers, when there was still so much to do before her shop doors opened at 10am.

It was usual for each customer to have a regular salesman and Annie's was Simon. She had met him on her first visit. He had been the first person to speak to her when she walked through the large concertina door. This morning he was here again, ready and waiting to help her.

'Morning' Annie! You all ready for the big day?' He was wide awake and bushy tailed, which was more than could be said for Annie at this God forsaken hour. Was it normal to be so happy and chirpy at this time of day?

'Now I've put away all the things on t'list it's all ready for you. Have a look 'round and see if there's anything else I can do fer y. There's a grand display o' Ecuadorian roses over in't Cooler. Thee've got big 'eads and som' great colours!'

'Thanks Simon. I'll go and take a look.' Annie wandered around the large building, making sure to look at Simon's rose display. The choice of flowers and plants were wonderful, much better than the small market she had been to years ago. There was also an area selling containers, oasis, cello, ribbons and every kind of sundries you could think of. Annie had intended not to deviate from her list, but she succumbed to a tray of white exquisite orchids, some shades of the Ecuadorian roses, two bay trees to place at her front door - and several other incidentals that she 'might' need. She sent up a silent prayer, hoping that her extra purchases were not fool hardy. When she had finished buying, within no time at all Simon had all her goods booked out and loaded in the car, ready to make her way back to the shop.

The roads were a little busier now, but there was still nothing to delay her. When she arrived at the shop it was just after six a.m... *'Now let the work began.'* she said out loud to herself. All the flowers had to be cut, conditioned and placed in water. It was always quite a laborious job, but essential to get the full life out of the flowers. Once she had ferried all the flowers in from her car, she pulled out her new tools from the workbox on the bench, a knife for soft stems and a sturdy pair of secateurs for the woody stems, then she began to orchestrate the final display for the shop. She and Pippa had prepared all of the vases the night before, which was a job in itself. She just needed to get the flowers drinking and in place. Annie surveyed the field of flowers before her. If no one came to buy them, she would be putting these same flowers into the bin in a few days. She prayed to God that they would sell. The last vase of flowers was being put in position, when she heard Violet coming down the staircase.

'Good morning Mrs Business woman' Smiled Violet as she came over to Annie and gave her a big kiss on the cheek and a squeeze. 'You've just got time for a quick shower and breakfast will be ready. I'm not letting you lose in this shop again 'til you've eaten something.'

'Oh Violet I appreciate the……'

'Stop right there! I won't have any excuses.' Violet gave it her best serious look. 'The flowers are in water everything looks perfect, you can afford the time and besides, you never know when I'll make you breakfast again. It may be a very long time! And if you miss it?'

'Okay, okay I give in……..Thank you.' Annie was happy to shower. She hated to admit that her personal hygiene had taken somewhat of a back seat in recent days; she could barely remember the last shower she had taken. So much had been happening; she had just made do with a good wash each day. When she emerged from the shower, Annie felt refreshed and re-invigorated and ready to take on the world.

Breakfast was Annie's favourite, warm croissants and strawberry jam and de-caff coffee. She didn't trust herself with the real thing. She was already bouncing off the walls and didn't need any help. She had dressed in smart black trousers and a purple blouse to co-ordinate with the shops' theme. Large black half aprons with the shop name and logo were hiding down stairs to be added to the ensemble. Annie had still managed to keep Violet in the dark regarding the shops' name. The half an hour Annie had spent away from the shop was just what she needed to recharge her batteries and focus on those little jobs that still needed to be completed. Annie picked up her plate and cup to take to the sink and start tidying away.

'No! I'll do that. I'm good at it now. I can carry six plates at once!'

'And how many can you drop!' Added Annie, wincing at the thought of Violet carrying so many dishes on a regular basis.

'Cheeky! – go on now; I know you're dying to get back down stairs. I'll be down later.'

'Thanks Violet, you've been wonderful!' Said Annie catching a kiss from her as she passed to start the final assault on the shop.

Annie descended the staircase absorbing all the sights in front of her, the weeks of hard work that she, Pippa and Zach had put into the building had finally paid off. All the little extra details, only they knew and understood the effort that had been taken. The addition of the fresh flowers and plants had brought the whole place alive. All the things she had fretted about yesterday were insignificant now. The walls, with their soft tints and shades, blended beautifully and thoughtfully with the fresh flowers. It was a fabulous symphony of colours – Annie loved it. The floor had been sanded to within an inch of its life, to expose the natural beauty of the old timbers. Two chandeliers' hung high in the ceilings dazzling and sparkling, compelling the visitors to notice them, dominating the open space with great splendour and throwing jewels of light in multiple directions. The shop units were painted with a white shabby chic design. It had been a labour of love for Annie. She and Zach had sourced and painted most of what they needed, they looked as if they had been made to measure, fitting the spaces perfectly. Other than the chandeliers, the fresh flower display, in stylish glass vases were the next things to grab your attention. The candles and incense fragranced the shop wonderfully as they mingled with the heavenly scents from Mother Nature's perfume counter. Everything had come together in her little retail miracle. Annie took a moment to breath in the atmosphere. She had done it. They were ready to open. Now all that was left was to see how the people of Longridge took to her. She was interrupted by Zach coming through the front door.

'Morning Annie, how are you feeling'?' He was dressed in a pair of cream chino's and a blue shirt. He had obviously made an effort for the 'Grand' opening.

'Don't you look dapper, Mr Smarty-pants!' Annie was delighted and surprised.

'Couldn't let you down today of all days now could I? - I don't think my old jeans and 'T' shirt are the correct dress code for today and I wanted to show you that I do own another set of clothes!' He winked at her.

'Thanks Zach – I mean thanks for everything you've done over the past weeks. You've been a God send!

Everything you promised – you delivered! I mean it; I couldn't have done it without you.'

'Glad to help. I've enjoyed seeing the old shop change in to this great space. It's good to see everything finished.' He had a sudden thought, 'It is finished isn't it? No last minute hitches that need fixing before we let the public in?' There was panic in his eyes.

'No problems, - but we need to show Violet the name of the shop and uncover the facia. It'll be too difficult to do it later with people outside – hopefully, if they turn up that is!'

Annie shouted up the staircase asking Violet to come down and help them with a job. She bounded down the stairs with all the enthusiasm of a cocker spaniel, eager and ready to help. They coaxed her outside, telling her they needed help with the dust sheet covering the sign before the 'Grand opening'. Violet obliged without question. One swift tug from all three of them and the sign was uncovered.

'Oh my lord!' exclaimed Violet, 'You named it after me! I had no idea?' Violet was

stunned. Her mouth was open wide catching flies. Zach pulled out his phone and caught the moment on camera.

'Is it a good thing?' Asked Annie not sure which way Violet was reacting, 'I wanted to show you that even though the shop is important to me – you are more important to me and always will be.' Violet lunged at her mother, pulling her into a bear hug. The old familiar tears started to gather in the corner on Annie's eye. 'Right I'm not going to cry. I've not got time to re-apply my make-up!' She declared. 'I'm going to find the Champagne and open it before the press and villagers appear. I'm dreading having to speak in public – maybe the Champagne will take the edge off!'

'Thank God I made you eat breakfast!' Said Violet putting her arm around her mum's shoulders and guiding her inside towards the Champagne.

Pippa arrived just after nine. The school was only a short distance from the shop, so once the children were safely inside Pippa dashed across to the shop to do what she could to help. Pippa could see Zach through the shop window, giving the shop floor a final sweep. She could tell, even at this distance that he was looking hot – hotter than usual, even when usual meant scruffy jeans and 'T' shirt, he was still hot. Pippa unconsciously straightened her hair and her clothes. She was wearing black and purple, just like Annie. Zach Looked up and smiled as he saw her pass the window.

'Good of you to turn up eventually! I've been slaving all night!' He stopped brushing and rested his arms on the top of the brush.

'You forget we left together!' She added, not letting him get away any with emotional blackmail.

'We did! But I wouldn't tell everyone that. They may read something else into it!' He winked at her, which had the immediate effect of making her blush.

At the stroke of ten a.m. the Lady Mayor, who was dressed in a dark green twin set with the obligatory pearls, stood outside the front door. She was a friend of Mrs Stretford's and a similar age. Stan's mother had done a fantastic job of telling everyone in the area that they should come to the opening to make Annie and Violet feel welcome in the village. Because of this intervention a small crowd had also gathered outside. Annie wasn't sure if it was the lure of the shop or the free champagne advertised on the shop window that brought people out, but everyone seemed excited, Annie included, she felt a mix of high tension and elation that they had finally reached this point. Now they had to deliver what they had promised and turn themselves into a real florist's shop.

Zach called for hush from the crowd and introduced Annie as the new proprietor of 'Violet's Florist Shop'. Annie made a garbled speech, thanking everyone for their help and for accepting her into the community, then she passed a pair of floristry scissors to the Lady Mayor and asked her to cut the broad, lilac, satin ribbon that had been pinned to the front of the door frame kept everyone at bay and out of the shop until the speeches had been made.

'I would like to wish Annie and Violet every success in their new shop. Such a shop plays a vital part in the community and it's wonderful to be able to be here to witness it's re-birth. We need to support our small local businesses, for without them our town will lose its heart. I am sure we will all be in and out looking for those special gifts, so without any more delay I would like to declare 'Violets' open for business – 'God Bless' all who shop in her!' The Lady Mayor cut the ribbon with Annie's new scissors and the crowd erupted into a loud round of spontaneous applause. The local reporter snapped away, making sure to capture the moment for the 'Evening Post'. Annie and the gathered crowd followed the Lady Mayor in to the shop.

Further up on Longridge high street, Jack pulled the Priory Hall minibus to a holt outside the Village store. He wondered what the crowd had gathered for, then realised that it was where he had dropped the new girl after the wedding. It looked as if they were finally opening the shop. He made a mental note to call in one day, when it was quieter. His mother's birthday was coming up soon and he intended to send her some flowers, but there was no rush. Another day would do just as well. He got out of the minibus and went to the post office with the letter that had to be sent special delivery to head office.

Inside the shop Zach and Violet were holding trays of champagne or orange juice for those feeling less adventurous, at this early time of day. Annie stood on the side-lines for a moment, listening to and absorbing all the 'ooos' and 'ahh's' coming from the lips of the guests. She wanted to know their true feelings and thoughts about the shop. Maybe she could use some of the information to improve their experience. Mrs Stretford made her way over to Annie with the Lady Mayor in tow.

'Annie, this is Sylvia.' She pointed at the Lady Mayor, 'She wants to know if you'll do some flowers for the Mayoral Chambers next week. There's an important meeting on and they want to make a good impression? You can fix them up with something?'

'I certainly can Lady Mayor.' Said Annie smiling broadly at the thought of her first order. 'Would you like to follow me to the counter and I'll take some details from you?' It was as simple as that, the shop was off and running.

Zach and Pippa danced around each other, helping customers and people who had come in for a good old nosy. Zach explained in detail to the men, who had been dragged along unwillingly, the amount of work he had done, the new walls, plastering, electrics, plumbing, decoration and organising Annie, whilst Pippa explained the concept of the shop, their philosophy and all about the types of flowers and plants they would be stocking. There were many furtive glances between the two, but no direct conversation. To Annie it was as plain as the nose on her face. The pair were destined to get together, even if Annie had to make it happen. When there was a quiet moment Annie asked Zach to help her bring some more bottles of champagne down from the flat. Once they were alone she took her opportunity to find out what he was thinking.

'It's going well down there don't you think?' she said pulling some bottles of Champagne out of the fridge.

'You've got a smasher there Annie. Don't think you'll have any trouble at all - seems the whole village is behind you.'

'I hope so, but you and Pippa have been fantastic. Don't you think Pippa's great?' Zach was slightly thrown by Annie's question.

'Yes, she's worked hard for you. I'm sure you'll both work well together.'

'No Zach! – I mean do you think she's great?' Zach looked at Annie blankly. 'For God's sake man! Do you like her – you know – as in a going out sort of way?' Annie almost wanted to shake him into realisation.

'Well - I – eh.' This was the first time she had seen him lost for words.

'Zach, I can see it plain as day. You're sweet on her?' Suddenly the floor seemed very interesting to Zach as his eyes focused on it. 'She feels the same. I can tell. Maybe now you've finished the shop you'll have a little more spare time. You could take her out?'

'I can't ask her out. I've only just finished with my girlfriend. Pippa will think I'm some sort of womaniser flitting from one to the next!'

'No she won't. Just tell her straight. You fancy her and want to take her out?'

'But she's got kids – what if they don't like me?'

'Hold on cowboy! You're talking about a date not moving in together or marriage! One step at a time. Give the kids time to get to know you I'm sure they'll love you.'

'I'm still not sure.' Zach still couldn't meet Annie's gaze.

'Well, that's up to you, but remember a lot of men will come in here to order flowers, so it's only a matter of time 'til she gets snapped up!' Annie pushed some bottles into his arms and shoved him down the stairs, towards Pippa.

All day people filed in and out of the shop, coming to see what 'the new woman' had done to the place, asking questions, picking up bouquets of flowers and ordering flowers for events in the future. The day exceeded all her wildest expectations. Pippa and Zach stayed all day, working like troopers. Pippa's Mum and Dad had agreed to pick up the children from school and were bringing them to the shop so that everyone could have a good look around and see where Mummy was going to be working. The whole of Pippa's family were delighted with the shop. To Zach's embarrassment, Pippa introduced him to each member of her family, telling them what a fantastic job he had done. Zach, in his role of host, insisted on getting some juice for the children, then a little while later, he had the inspired idea to take them to the sweet shop to stop them getting bored.

'Pippa – you show your Mum and Dad around in peace. We'll just get a few sweets and I'll bring them back in twenty minutes or so.' He said ushering the children out of the door.

'Zach I can't leave you to look after my kids?' Protested Pippa, who was secretly delighted that he was taking an interest in them.

'Course you can. Go on, enjoy your glory!' There was nothing she could, but agree, anything else would have been churlish. Pippa showed her mum and dad around and plied them with Champagne, resisting temptation herself. After half an hour she started to feel slightly anxious. There was no sign of Zach or the children returning. It was taking too long to buy sweets, even with her indecisive children. Eventually her fear of what her children were putting Zach through took over.

'I'm just nipping out.' She mouthed to Annie who was in the middle of explaining the benefits of white orchids as house plants to a young woman. Pippa popped her head into the sweet shop, but there was no sign of the children or Zach. She walked further up the road keeping an eye out for them, but to no avail. She decided to turn back to see if they had returned to the shop, when in the distance and not far from the shop she could see Zach and the children running and laughing on the small playground attached to the main village car park. Internally she breathed a sigh of relief that everyone was safe, then mentally slapped herself for momentarily doubting Zach. She made her way over to them.

'Come on kids! Zach's too old to play for long. He'll need a good long sit down to recover and maybe a spell in hospital! – plus it's time we were going home.'

'No Mummy!' Chorused the kids.

'Sorry, but it's time.' Pippa felt mean, but she was dead on her feet and she still had to make tea, do homework and settle the children to bed before she could sit down.

'Maybe Mum will let us do this again?' Asked Zach tentatively. 'Maybe she'll come with us as well?' He looked at her hopefully.

'It's okay Zach, you've been great with the kids today, but you don't have to be burdened with them, as you now know, they can be a handful.'

'It's not a burden. It's a pleasure. I would like us all to go out some time. I've had fun. I can't remember the last time I went on a swing! – And I would like to take you out sometime soon if you can get a babysitter? – And remember Annie owes you?'

Pippa was about to decline, thinking that he was only being polite, when a sudden surge of confidence over took her. Why shouldn't she go out with him? Even if it was just as friends, she liked him and she knew they would get on. There wouldn't be any awkward silences as the menus were passed around. A little fun was what she needed.

'Okay,' She answered with hesitation, hoping she wasn't about to make a fool of herself by agreeing, 'I will – if you're sure?'

'Oh I'm sure.' Replied Zach, leaving her in no doubt that pity was nowhere on his list of reasons for asking her out.

'Come on Kids! I'll race you back to the shop!' He shouted as he started to run.

Chapter 16

It was five in the afternoon and Annie couldn't wait for the final half an hour of business to be over, so that she could to go upstairs and put her feet up. The opening day had gone perfectly, everyone loved the shop and sales were fantastic. She knew it was because she was a novelty for now. It wouldn't take long for that to wear off. Then she would be able to judge the true reaction, but at least she had made a splash and a small ripple in the large debt she owed on the premises. Fresh flower orders had been taken, so it seemed that the locals liked her style of work, which was a blessing. There were orders to be made up in preparation for the following day, but fatigue overtook her. She longed to crawl into bed and indulge herself in a good night's sleep. Tomorrow would be another early start to make the bouquets on order and top up the shop with items for customers to pick up, but she didn't mind, it was still all very exciting and new. She decided that a cup tea rather than making flower orders was a far better option. She had filled the kettle in the work room and was waiting for it to boil, when the phone rang. Annie hesitated, trying to remember how she should greet the customers. She picked it up, still feeling strange at announcing the name of the shop, she was sure it would become second nature in time.

'Good afternoon –'Violet's florist' - Annie speaking – How may I help you?' It sounded strange, but good to say the name of the shop down the phone. The caller introduced herself as Miss St John from Priory Hall. Annie recognised the name from her conversations with Violet.

'I'm ringing to see if you can help me?' she continued, 'I have a guest who would like a bouquet of flowers as soon as possible. He wants to spend around fifty pounds; I know it's very short notice. Do you think you can help? Annie knew that if she said no, she would be shooting herself in the foot. It was on her agenda to try and get herself known at Priory Hall, the fact that they had come to her was wonderful; besides, she wasn't in the financial position of being able to refuse fifty pounds.

'Of course I can do that for you. I can't however deliver it to you until I close. It will be around six before I get to you. Is that okay?

'That's absolutely fine; he wants to present them at dinner this evening. He said he'll leave the colour choice to you, but he did mention that the lady has a preference for roses, if you could include a few in there that would be perfect and if you bring an invoice with you, I'll pay you cash on delivery.'

'That's great' said Annie, delighted that the local hotel was already interested in using her shop, 'I'll see you as soon as I can.'

Once the phone was back on the hook, Annie allowed herself a small whoop of glee. Although the thought of making another bouquet wasn't so appealing, but the thought that it was going to Priory Hall more than made up for it. She took a little time for a quick cup of tea, then set to work choosing the flowers and creating the bouquet. She chose the beautifully fragrant red rose Naomi with hot pink gerbera's for drama and pink ginger flowers with lots of tropical foliage to set them off. When they were gift wrapped to within an inch of their life she closed up shop, placed them carefully into her car and set off to Priory Hall. As she was driving it struck her that she was going to have to employ someone to deliver part time for her. Not everyone would be willing to wait until the shop was closed to receive their flowers. It may be something Pippa could do? It would give her a few extra hours of work. They might be able to share the job between them, if not; she could always put an advert in the shop window or in the local paper.

This was the first time Annie had been to Priory Hall. Luckily, the road signs to the Hall were easy to follow. It was pleasant being out of the shop and driving through the countryside. She had been so busy with the shop; she'd had no time to go out exploring and sight-seeing. It was wonderful to have so much open space a matter of minutes away from the shop. Fresh air was something she was definitely lacking. She turned as requested by the sign post and followed the gravel drive towards Priory Hall. She followed the cut of the drive through the ample grounds, oak, ash and the many other trees which gave scale and grandeur to the landscape, the main house and buildings nestled securely within its boundaries. In the distance she could just make out the outline of a summer house by the lake, the perfect venue for a wedding she thought. Eventually the drive led her to the main house and even though it was dusk, she could see the splendour and magnificence of the old building basking in its setting. In contradiction the new wing of the hotel with the spa and sporting facilities with its cutting edge architecture screamed to be noticed. It should have looked odd, but to Annie's surprise the fusion of the two styles blended sublimely. She pulled her car to a holt in the car park near the front door of the hotel, retrieved the flowers from the boot and followed the signs for 'Reception'.

Once inside the décor was plush and opulent with a modern twist of furniture which was bold and dramatic to match the building. The colours in the furniture and drapes were rich and warming. The walls were neutral and muted as you might expect in a hotel, but the shots of colour injected some vibrancy into the main areas. The oversized chairs and sofas gave the large area some proportion. The reception desk was un-missable, with its chrome frontage, shinning and begging for attention. Annie headed towards the perfectly coiffured woman behind the desk and asked for Miss St John.

'I'll page her for you. I'm sure she'll be with you in a moment, if you'd like to wait?' Smiled the woman behind the counter. Annie placed the flowers on top of the desk and waited patiently. Within a couple of minutes Miss St John appeared from behind the scenes. She strode in with an air of efficiency, but she also had a warm, genuine smile. She was a little younger than Annie and like the woman behind the desk dressed impeccably with perfect hair and make-up to match.

'You must be Annie?' Deducted Miss St John, 'Ohh those flowers are beautiful. Thank you for making them at such short notice. I believe it's your first day open today, you must be tired by now. Did you put these together? They are exquisite!'

'Eh, yes I did make them – Thank you.' Annie felt slightly embarrassed to accept the praise. It had been a long time since anyone had complemented her on her abilities.

'And you're Violet's Mum aren't you?' Scarlett St John remembered the young girl who started work at the Hall a short time ago and the conversation they had had in the staff canteen.

'Yes that's right. She's enjoying work. I hope she doesn't cause too much trouble – I believe she got herself into a bit of bother with one of the bosses who caught her drinking some of the left over champagne?' Annie raised her eyebrows in an effort to show Miss St John that she disapproved of Violet's actions.

'She's only young and they all make mistakes at first. She seems like a hard worker. I'm sure it was an isolated incident that's best forgotten.' Annie could tell that Miss St John was very competent at making people feel relaxed. 'Right I'm sure you are dying to get home after such an eventful day. I'll get your money for you. It won't take me long, but I have to get management to confirm the release of the petty cash. I tried to catch him earlier, but he was in a meeting, I'll just get someone to Page him now.' Miss St John nodded to the woman behind the desk, who had been listening to the conversation whilst pretending to fill some spread sheets on the computer. She dialled a number on the phone and requested Mr P. to make his way to reception.

'I'm hoping I might be able to put some work your way.' said Miss St John, 'especially if this is the type of work you create. We don't have anyone at the moment who we recommend for our functions and to our Brides. Can you do bridal work?'

'Yes, yes I can. I do anything involving flowers. It's a beautiful place here for a wedding. There are lots of interesting things we could do with the surroundings. I can bring you some photos of things I've done in the past and some information if you like. Then you would have something to show the brides?'

'That would be great Annie, they always like to see photos of other weddings, by the way call me Scarlett.'

'Thanks - Scarlett. I can't deny I need all the help I can get starting up a new business. It takes time for people to find out about you and know what you are capable of. Any work you could put my way, well I'd be extremely grateful.' Annie confessed.

'So what brought you to Longridge?' Scarlett wanted to know some of the back ground of the person she was going to recommend. It was all well and good being able to make a nice bouquet of flowers, but wedding flowers were a completely different kettle of fish. Everything had to be right. There was no margin for error. For all Scarlett knew, she may have had a shop somewhere else and done moonlight flit, leaving wedding couples high and dry? A little light questioning wouldn't hurt anyone.

Annie sighed internally. She didn't tell people openly that she was a widow, because she didn't like the way they changed towards her. Happy faces became solemn and those patronising tones crept into their voices, and worst of all, the phrase - 'How are you dear?' followed by a pat on the back of her hand. Annie hated it with a passion, but if she wanted Scarlett on side she would have to open up - at least a little. Annie understood that Scarlett would have to be able to trust her and Annie would have to trust Scarlett with the outline of her life story.

'I grew up in the area – in Preston - moved down south with my husband and his work.' Annie paused for a second, taking a moment to compose the words in her head, 'He was involved in a car crash eighteen months ago and killed. So I eventually picked myself up and moved back up north to familiar surroundings. I had always worked for other florists and done my City and Guilds certificates. I thought now might be my time to do it for myself. As you know Violet is old enough to look after herself – most of the time! – And here we are - first day of the rest of our lives today.' Annie waited for the platitudes to begin after she had finished speaking, but there were none.

'There must be something in the air bringing everyone back to the Preston area. Our new manager used to live around here and he's come back from living overseas.' At the same moment the double doors next to the reception desk parted revealing the new manager.

'Ah speak of the devil! Annie, this is Jack Parrish our new manager, Jack this is……….'

'Annie!' Jack finished the sentence, utter shock reflected on his face.

'Don't tell me you know each other? God it's such a small world!' prattled Scarlett. Jack and Annie both ignored her. The world had suddenly vanished and all Annie could see and hear was Jack.

'Oh my God' whispered Annie, fighting for breath and not trusting what was before her own eyes, 'Is it really you?' The colour had drained from her cheeks, her knees started to buckle under her. The room started to spin; she couldn't hear anything now, even though she could see Jack's lips moving. The darkness began to close in around her - then she passed out.

Jack could see what was happening to her, he moved across the floor quickly and caught her in his arms, breaking her fall, before she hit the floor.

'Annie! - Annie!....Can you hear me?' He tapped the side of her face gently. She didn't respond. She was out cold.

'Scarlett please unlock my office door and someone bring water!' He called to the on looking member of staff.

He picked her up without effort and carried her to his office. He didn't know if it was because she was light or if it was the adrenalin kicking in.

'I'm pretty sure she's just fainted.' He reassured Scarlett. 'I think it's just the shock of seeing me?'

'So you know her?' Asked Scarlett sure there was a story here to be told.

'Yes, yes I do' He declared with a grin that wouldn't have looked out of place on a Cheshire cat. He assumed Scarlett would think he was a fruit cake – he didn't care. Fate had brought Annie to him. He couldn't have imagined the events of the past few minutes, if he'd tried for the rest of his life, how it happened didn't matter to him. The only thing that mattered was that he would have the chance to sort out the lies and destruction his father had generated.

He laid her out on the couch in his office, and then as one of the hotels trained first aiders checked Annie's pulse and made sure her airways were clear. It seemed a straight forward case of passing out. There was no need to call for help at this moment; he would wait a while first to see if she regained consciousness on her own.

'So?' Asked Scarlett, whilst they were waiting, 'What's the story between you two? –and don't say there isn't one, it's obvious.' Jack waited before answering, uncertain of what he should say, if anything - after all, he had no idea what Annie's situation was? - and if he blurted everything out, he may cause unintended damage.

'We went to school and college together – All a very long time ago. We haven't seen each other for many years.' It was enough to deflect Scarlett but not more than he had intended to divulge.

It was only a few minutes before Annie regained consciousness, but to Jack it seemed like all eternity. He watched her, recognising the same familiar features he had watched and observed in their years together. Obviously she was older now, the flush of youth diminished, but not her beauty. No longer was she the gawky teenager who hung on his every word, she was a woman with history and experience, he was even more intrigued to discover how her life had evolved. Even passed out on his sofa he longed to take her in his arms and protect her.

When she awoke she found herself led out on a settee with her feet higher than her head. She felt disorientated and confused as to how she had got there, not to mention stupid and embarrassed. It took her a few seconds to recall the events, had she been dreaming or did she really see Jack? She had the sense of someone close to the side of her, she turned her head to the side and like an apparition he was kneeling beside her holding a glass of water.

'Nice to have you back with us Annie. Would you want some of this?' He offered her the water.

'Jack? Is it really you?' She still couldn't believe her eyes. All the hard work and lack of sleep over the last few days could be causing hallucinations.

'It is Jack. I can vouch for that.' Added Scarlett pinching his arm. Jack squealed like a girl, 'See he's real enough!'

Annie sat up, still feeling slightly woozy; she took the offered glass and sipped the water.

'Thank you.' she said, keeping her gaze firmly on him, still not sure if he was going to disintegrate before her eyes. Jack couldn't contain his curiosity any longer.

'What were you doing?.....What brought?...God!... I just can't believe it's you!' Jack had lost all verbal skills and was struggling and failing to string a sentence together.

'Do you want me to call a doctor for you?' Scarlett was asking Annie. 'God no! No. I'm fine; I've just been burning the candle at both ends with getting the shop up and open.....'

'Shop? What shop?' Enquired Jack.

''Violet's florist' in town.' Scarlett intervened. 'Annie was delivering some flowers for one of our guests.'

'The one that's just opened? I nearly called in there today to order flowers for my mother! Oh my God!' Jack exclaimed. 'How long have you been in Longridge?'

'Only a few weeks. We've been working hard on getting the shop open for business and today was our first day. I'm sure the fainting was only due to tiredness and not eating. I'm fine now. I just feel very foolish for making such a show of myself on my first visit to you.' Her words were directed to Scarlett.

She looked at Jack before casting her eyes down to concentrate on the highly patterned beige and brown carpet beneath Jack's knees. There was a minute's awkward silence, each person waiting for the others to speak. Not knowing what to do next. It was Annie who reacted first.

'I feel fine now. I'll get going. I've taken up enough of your time. I'm sure in a busy place like this there's always something that needs doing.' She was waffling and knew it, her nerves had got the better of her. Jack lifted his hand and pointed his finger at Annie.

'There is no way on God's earth that I'm letting you walk out of that door in this state.' Annie and Scarlett exchanged glances of surprise at his masterful tone. 'Scarlett please will you get one of the staff to bring tea and sandwiches to my office. You need a drink and some food inside you. Did you never listen to your mother?' His teasing eased the tension in the air, casting her back to the way he was with her all those years ago. She would have argued with him and demanded to leave, but she wasn't sure her legs would hold her yet, they still felt like jelly. 'You do still drink tea don't you?' Annie just nodded like one of those dogs in the back of cars. Jack hadn't finished with his questioning, 'And you're not a vegetarian? Or Vegan? Or Wheat intolerant? Any other specific dietary needs?' Annie had shook her head after each question in turn until he was finished, 'Sorry, the job gets you that way after a while. Thanks Scarlett. If you could see to that for me.' She was dismissed. Annie couldn't help but notice the sparkle in his eye and the wide, familiar grin. She didn't know what to think or to feel, meeting Jack so suddenly after all these years had pushed her into emotional overload. A sudden thought struck her. He was the Mr P. Violet had been speaking about, the one who told her off for drinking. Jack took the empty water glass from her hand, jolting her back to the moment. Their fingers accidentally touched. She was startled by the old familiar fizz of electricity between them; she jumped back, deeper into the sofa in an involuntary move. He noticed, but said nothing. 'Annie, are you sure you are okay? I can call the hotel doctor to come and check you over?' He instinctively took her hand in his as he spoke. She pulled away sharply, as if he had placed her hand into a burning fire.

'Don't please!' She ordered, folding her arms across her body. He did as she asked, after all for all he knew, she was still married to Nick. At this point in time he was only concerned that she was physically well. After finding out how hard she had been working, he could understand her fainting, but he could also see that it wasn't just fatigue – she was also in shock. He hoped it was a good sign.

'I'm sorry Annie. I didn't mean anything by it.' He was sincere. 'I'm just so pleased to see you – I've spent years searching for you and now you're in front of me. It's just mad!' Annie didn't understand his words.

'What do you mean? Searching for me? Why were you searching for me?' You knew where I was all those years when you left!' she was about to launch into a verbal lashing over all the hurt he had caused, how broken hearted she had been, how Nick had looked after her and cared for her, eventually mending her broken heart – but now wasn't the time or place – to be frank she didn't know if that time would ever come. She bit her tongue, but let Jack know she was struggling to stay civil. Long lost, distant memories came flooding back. His letter cutting all ties with her, when she needed his help. Nothing could get past the fact that he abandoned her and left her to an unknown fate. He cared nothing for her then, she wasn't about to let him start now. Her thoughts and feelings, she believed submerged in her subconscious or eradicated permanently, now raced to the surface, filling her with anxiety and confusion – it was a place she didn't want to re-visit.

Jack could see the bitterness surfacing in her face. If he could only explain to her what had happened, that it wasn't his fault, but the door opened revealing one of the staff with tea and sandwiches. Annie realised this was her chance for escape She knew that if they were alone he would stop her from leaving. She could tell he wanted to talk, but he couldn't do this with a member of his staff in the room. She needed to get out, needed to think, to put things in order in her mind and sleep - she needed sleep.

'I'm sorry Jack, but I need to go now!' She stood up, trying to prove she was well.

'But.....' He tried to protest, but she cut him off before he had chance to start.

'NO! I need to go!' Without manhandling her in front of the staff, there was nothing he could do but let her leave.

'At least let me drive you home for safety. You can't drive so soon after blacking out. You may pass out again?' She knew he had a point, but there was no way she was putting herself in a car with Jack. It was too much to bear.

'No. I'm fine!' Nothing was going to move her from her intention of leaving.

'Annie, don't be so bloody stubborn! Not ten minutes ago you were out cold in reception!' He was angry; she could feel it in his voice. 'I understand if you won't let me drive you, I understand Nick wouldn't be very happy if I turn up out of the blue on your door step, but let one of the staff drive you home.' She almost burst into tears when Jack mentioned Nick's name, but somehow she managed to hold it together.

'Annie, there's no hidden agenda. I don't want you to walk out of here and potentially black out and crash. Let someone drive you home?' She hated to admit it, but he was right and if she did crash, well, it would be too much for Violet to bear. Finally she relented.

'I'll let one of your staff take me – but not you.' Jack wanted to object, but he knew it was futile, her mind was set. Her safety was the most important thing at this point in time.

Five minutes later, Jack walked her to the mini bus where Harry the handyman was waiting to drive her home. They were both silent now, each lost in their own thoughts of confusion. Jack opened the front passenger door of the mini bus. 'Make sure she gets home and inside safely Harry.'

'Right'o boss.' Said Harry starting the engine. Annie climbed into the front. It took her all the energy she could muster. Jack held on to the door, stopping it from closing. As she brushed passed him, he whispered to her.

'We need to talk Annie. I'll come and see you tomorrow.'

'No Jack – I don't want to talk.' She was whispering too, 'There's nothing to say. It was all a very long time ago. Let's just leave it there, in the past where it belongs. I have my life and you have yours. There's no point in raking over it all again. It won't do anyone any good.' Jack wasn't put off, he wasn't prepared to leave the past undisturbed.

'Annie. There are things you need to know, Things I have to tell you, I..'

'Stop Jack!' She whispered through the tears that had finally broken though. 'I can't do this Jack. You have to leave me alone. You have to understand it's a shock to see you. I'm unprepared and extremely tired. There's so much going on at the moment, I can't deal with this now. When I'm ready to talk - I'll come to you. You can't demand me to talk to you? I need time.' His heart was breaking to see her so upset. He longed to wrap his arms around her, tell her everything would be alright - but he still didn't know if she was with Nick. The last he knew she was another man's wife and no matter how much he hated the fact, he had to respect that and if she wasn't ready to talk, he had to respect that as well, no matter how difficult it was for him. To push her now would only serve to drive her away and that thought was agonising to Jack.

'Okay. I understand.' He said holding his hand up in a gesture of submission. 'I'll give you some time, but you will have to speak to me at some point. There are things you don't know and you need to know.' She nodded her head in acknowledgement. Jack slammed the door shut and watched Harry and the mini bus drive into the distance with the woman he loved. The ache in his heart had returned, but not dull and manageable as it had been for years, but searing pain like an abscess under a rotting tooth. Gnawing away, reminding him constantly of the deep pain he held within. He looked up to the sky and silently prayed that it wasn't too late for them. When the last glimmer of headlights had disappeared out of the grounds he turned to go into the hotel. A sudden connection flashed through his brain. The new girl – Violet. She was Annie's daughter; Scarlett had mentioned she was the daughter of the new Florist to him. He understood why she seemed so familiar to him now, but this realisation only brought more questions without answers. If she was Annie's child, then there was a small chance that she might also be his? – Then just as equally she could be Nick's?

As promised, Harry deposited Annie home safely. He had wanted to come inside and make sure everything was fine; but Annie assured him that there was no need. There was only one place she intended to go and that was to bed. Thankfully Violet was out with friends, Annie wasn't sure how she would have managed if she had had to put on a front and chat to Violet about the day's events. Annie didn't even know if she could have said 'Hello' without bursting into tears. She undressed and curled up under the duvet like a small child scared of the dark – but it wasn't the dark she was afraid of it was herself, more specifically her feelings. The tears began to trickle on to the pillow. It was all too much. She didn't know why or what she was crying for? Herself? Violet? Nick? – Or Jack? The sobbing was constant, her body convulsed automatically, nothing but time would allow her to stop. Eventually she ran out of tears and energy, drifting off into sleep, her cheeks still moist from tears.

Chapter 17

Annie lay in her bed starring at the ceiling. She was starting to like the woodchip paper hanging above her head which she found slightly worrying. The alarm buzzed its way into her brain. It was 6am. She leaned over and switched it off. She had been awake for the past hour. Her sleep before that had been fitful and sporadic to say the least. She had managed a few hours in between the dreams of Nick and Jack running a hotel together, of Nick and Jack playing tug of war over Violet, another one of Violet running off to live with Jack in a flat over a Florist's shop. So by the time six o'clock arrived she found herself feeling more drained than when she flopped into bed the night before. She wasn't finding being awake any easier; her insides were churning like the ice breaker in a slush puppy machine, with no sign of a moment's peace on the horizon.

Never in a million years did she think she would ever bump in Jack again, let alone find him living a few miles down the road. In her mind, she had him settled in Australia, working – probably for his father, maybe with a family and children of his own and never giving Annie a second thought. She couldn't adjust to the fact that fate or circumstance had brought their paths together again. Was it a good thing or something to run a mile from, she couldn't decide. One thing was certain, she would have to keep Jack and Violet apart – she didn't even want to contemplate what devastation could be wreaked if Violet found out that she knew Jack Parrish. Her life had been hijacked and she was no longer in control.

She replayed the events of the night before over and over in her mind, she couldn't help herself. She had recognised him in an instant, he looked the same, just a little grey hair around the temples giving away the years that had past. She hadn't noticed a wedding ring, but she hadn't been looking for one – What was she thinking. It didn't matter if he was married or not. There was no way she was going to get involved with him again. Not after what he did, her broken heart had been glued back together, but it had never been the same – it never would. She couldn't help recalling the look on Jack's face when he was insisting that they needed to speak to her. She could see the pain and determination in his face. She had not seen that look since the day he was told about Australia. She knew he wouldn't settle until he had told her what was on his mind, but for the life of her she couldn't work out what was so important that wouldn't wait. She knew it wouldn't be long before he came knocking at her door and presumed it was to give her the *'please don't blame me – I was young and had my whole life ahead of me. I was too young to be a father.'* speech. She didn't want to hear it; she didn't want to hear any of his lies and bull shit. He was her past and she wanted him to stay there. If she wasn't careful Jack would bring her whole world crashing down around her ears. Annie didn't know how much Jack knew – he was bound to suspect that Violet was his child. At some point she would have to find out what he was thinking, but not today.

Annie was about to drag herself out of bed and face the day when the door opened gently, revealing Violet, hair tussled and looking far from awake.

'Morning.' She yawned cheerily when she realised Annie was already awake; 'I forgot to tell you yesterday, I'm on breakfast duty today so I'm off. The mini bus is picking me up in a minute outside.' Violet crossed the bedroom and kissed Annie on the cheek.

'It was a great day yesterday Mum! You did a fab Job – I'll see you later!' Annie started to panic. What if Scarlett said something to her? She hadn't considered that Violet would be going to Priory Hall so soon. What if Jack was waiting for her, he had access to the rota's? What if he said something to her? She tried to suppress the fear. Was she being irrational? She didn't want to give herself away and alarm Violet.

'Okay love, but I hope you're going to brush that hair before you go. You'll be frightening the guests.' Annie smiled as best she could.

'I will, I'll do it on the bus. Have a good day. I'll see you later.'

'Take care and Vi - I love you.' The words slipped out, Annie felt the need to reaffirm her love for her daughter, just in case something went wrong – like Jack.

Violet wasn't surprised by her mother's declaration of love, but she did notice the lack of spark and enthusiasm in her mother. She looked tired, mind you, she should, the amount of hours she had been putting in getting the shop ready, but there was something else she couldn't put her finger on.

'You okay?' she asked with concern.

'I'm fine, just tired from all the working - and I think I've picked up a bit of a bug. I'll be okay with some coffee inside me. Go on, I'm fine.' But Annie wasn't fine. She was petrified. What if Jack had put two and two together, what if he already knew that he was Violet's Father. At this moment in time speaking to Jack was the last thing she wanted to do, but she had to get to him, before he got to violet. She jumped out of bed and pulled on the same clothes from yesterday that were lying on the floor at the bottom of the bed. She ran to the window where she could see Violet waiting for the minibus to stop in front of her. She tugged at the old window frame, trying desperately to open it, luckily it surrendered. Annie called out of the window to Violet.

'Violet! Tell the minibus to wait a second. I'm coming with you!' Annie pushed her feet into the first pair of shoes she could find, grabbed her bag and keys, then ran down the stairs and jumped in the bus alongside Violet. Violet was staring at her mother as if she had gone stark staring mad.

'Mum! What do you think you're doing?' Annie recognised the tone used by Violet signalling embarrassment.

'Don't worry! My car is at the hotel. I need to collect it – that's all.'

'Why is it there? Did you break down?' Violet was demanding answers.

'Morning Annie and how are you feeling today?' Asked Harry who was sat behind the driver's wheel again, as if he had been sat there all night.

'I'm fine thanks Harry.' Smiled Annie.

'What does he mean – how are you? - and why is the car there – you didn't crash it?' Asked Violet accusingly. Annie knew she wouldn't get away with anything less than the truth.

'The thing is – Well, it's nothing to worry about. I want to make that clear, but I had a little incident last night, whilst delivering an order to Priory Hall – I passed out. I'm sure it was only tiredness and over work, it was only for a few seconds, but I thought it best not to drive the car, so I left it there.'

'You did what! Why didn't you think to let me know?' Anger flashed in Violet's eyes closely followed by hurt.

'Because I'm fine and when you came in I was fast asleep. I didn't drive home just in case it happened again, but it didn't. I didn't want to worry you. There was no point in making you worry about nothing.'

'I don't like it when you keep things from me, I should know these things. You'd be cross it if was the other way around and I hadn't told you when I passed out! Wouldn't you?' Annie had to agree with her.

'I promise the next time I pass out I'll tell you. After I wake up of course.' Violet smiled despite herself. She starred out of the minibus window, giving Annie the silent treatment she was so good at.

It only took twenty minutes to reach the hotel, including the three stops to pick up the other members of staff. When the minibus pulled up outside the back entrance, everyone jumped out including Violet.

'You go on love and get inside. We don't want you to start late.' Said Annie encouraging Violet to leave her to her mission. 'I'm just getting my car then I'm off to open the shop. I'll see you when you finish.' She lied. It was better that Violet didn't know she was going on a 'Jack' hunt. Knowing where to find him was her first problem. She didn't want to go into the hotel and chance running into

Violet again. An explanation would be awkward to concoct. Then an idea came to her. Annie waited until she was sure Violet was out of ear shot.

'Harry! - Can you tell me where the staff quarters are for Jack? – I mean Mr Parrish. He has my keys for the car and I need to get back to work to open the shop?'

'I'll go and find him for you if you like?' Harry volunteered.

'No - no I'm sure you have lots to get on with. I've already taken up enough of your time, especially last night when you were good enough to run me home. Just point me in the right direction and I'll be fine – Thank you Harry.'

'Well if you're sure? - He lives in the little workers cottage behind that clump of trees.' Harry pointed into the distance, at the edge of the car park. 'If he's not in there, he'll be in the breakfast room checking everything is in order for the breakfast rush. I'm not sure if he's on the early shift or not today. Do you want me to check the rota?'

'No Harry, you've been a star. I can take it from here.' She gave him a cheeky wink, as she set off walking towards the trees in the distance. He blushed slightly. Handy men didn't get much female admiration in his experience. He watched all the programs on the television and films, where the women always fell for the handy man and the men had to fight off the women. He wished it had been like that, even occasionally, but it had never happened to him, not even in his younger days. Still, Annie managed to put a smile on his face for the rest of the day.

Annie walked with an easy air, until she was out of sight from the hotel, then she stopped and fell against a tree for support. What the hell was she doing? What was she going to say? This was the last place she wanted to be right now, but she knew, it had to be done. Annie took a deep breath and forced herself to put one foot in front of the other, heading in the direction Harry had pointed. Her mind was a blank, she would have to make it up as she went along.

There was only one building behind the trees, so there was no chance of choosing the wrong one. It wasn't fully light yet. She could see the porch light on and another light in one of the rooms to the right of the front door. It was only a small building, probably one bedroom, kitchen and bathroom, that sort of thing, but then this wasn't supposed to be a home, it was work and somewhere to rest in between shifts. She walked to the door with her fist clenched and held out in front of her; this was to make sure she knocked on the door before she could change her mind. Annie knocked timidly on the door with the brass knocker in the shape of a bell. Annie instantly regretted her actions, but it was too late. There was nowhere to run to, unless she went to hide behind a tree?

She waited impatiently, tapping her foot on the stone floor outside the door for a couple of minutes, until the door started to open slightly. She had to force herself not to run away – damn it, he was at home. When the door opened a little more, she could see Jack peering out into the autumn dawn. Her gaze started with his face, but her focus soon changed when she realised he was wearing only a towel and a smile. His hair was damp and his skin glistening with water molecules. He had eased into his body well. The gawkiness of youth had disappeared and now he was a 'man' –'Ohh god' she had to leave. She didn't care what he thought, she had to go now, but Jack had other ideas.

'Annie! I didn't expect to see you so soon. Come in.' She turned her back on him, afraid she was going to start blushing again.

'I can see it's not a good time for you. I'll wait here.'

'Don't be daft Annie. It's cold out here!'

'I can see you're busy. I'll come back later – another time.' Annie had one last try to escape, although she knew he was capable of following her back across the car park in his towel if she wasn't careful.

'No! Annie for Christ's sake get yourself in here. I'm not going to keep you hostage? She glanced back towards the door to see that it had opened further to reveal more of his exposed body. Annie didn't know where to look without felling embarrassed. Quickly she looked away again.

'I've just got out of the shower, as you can tell, but come in, just give me a couple of minutes to get some clothes on and I'm all yours.' The double entendre didn't go unmissed by either of them. She couldn't really afford to do 'later' and she didn't want to go in there with him semi- naked. She decided to offer a compromise.

'I'll wait out here - 'til you are dressed.' She stated.

'Don't be so silly, come in – I promise I won't seduce you if that's what you are worried about?' He was mocking her. Anger flashed across her face.

'I see some things don't change very much do they Jack? You're still very confident of your 'pulling power' aren't you?' Her words seethed sarcasm. He realised she was in no moods for jokes.

'Please yourself, but I'm catching my death out here. Come in if you change your mind.' He walked away leaving the door ajar and went to dress. Annie stood outside, feeling the cool autumn air swirl around her arms and legs, but she wasn't giving in. She would only enter the house when he was decently dressed. It was a matter of principle. She didn't want him to think that he only had to say the word and she would Jump. She wasn't that innocent school girl eager to please anymore. He no longer held the status of demi-god within her world.

In no time at all he was back at the front door, dressed in his suit, except for the jacket and his socks.

'Right I'm decent now – you can come in.' Decent was not a word Annie would have used to describe him. She followed him inside, wishing with her whole being that she was somewhere else.

The décor was dated, it needed a good scrub and a lick of paint, she wondered if a time would ever come again when she could look at a room and not focus on its decorating needs, obviously her mind was still set in restoration mode.

'This will be very short.' She said as he took her into the lounge, and hoping the right words would come to her. 'Violet, your new employee is on duty this morning and I'm sure you have already worked out – She is *my* daughter and it's really important to me that you don't tell Violet that you know me for the moment. I understand you probably think it's an unreasonable request and can't do any harm, but I have very good reasons. I hope you will respect my wishes – I'll see myself out.' Annie turned to leave the room.

'Hold on a minute! If you want me to do as you ask, then, trust me and let me know the reasons. I'm not an enemy here Annie!'

'Aren't you? I don't know what you are – except for a major inconvenience! Jack flinched as her words hit home. 'I don't want you upsetting Violet and going asking loads of questions about me and my life. She looks strong, but underneath she's actually quite fragile.' Annie considered how much she could trust him. She didn't know – he was a cad and a dirty low life who left her to fend for herself, but if she wanted him to stay away – well, then she would have to give him a good enough reason to respect her wishes.

'Okay – I'll tell you.' Annie paused for a moment to compose herself. 'There's no easy way to explain this. - Nick, her Dad, died in a car crash a couple of years ago; obviously it's not something she'll get over. She needs to be handled sensitively. So if not for her sake, please for mine - leave her be.' Jack didn't speak for a while. He turned away from her and looked out of the window on to one of the perfectly manicured lawns. He seemed genuinely stunned. Annie continued, 'I know you want to talk to me, but as I said last night I need some time. Seeing you again is a big, big shock and Violet is my first and only priority. Jack, if you ever thought anything of me – for the time being, you'll do as I ask. Do I have your word?' She expected and needed a promise from him.

'Annie there are so many things I need to say, maybe you'll see things differently if I ….' She cut him short.

'Did you hear anything I said? Nick died! Violet is devastated, she lost a father, I lost my husband! Stop thinking about yourself and think of her if you can! - I need you to promise me?'

'Yes. I promise.' The words slid out of his mouth without conviction. He was desperate to tell his side of the story, but if he pushed now, he knew he would push her away and maybe for good. 'I'll respect your wishes for the moment, but I *do* need to speak to you Annie.'

'I will talk to you.' She assured him. 'But give me time.' He nodded silently; it was all so nearly in his grasp at least, but at the same time still so far out of his reach that it may never be tamed. Annie turned and left without another word.

Jack watched out of the window as she melted into the distance. So - he was not Violet's Father. Annie had clearly stated that Nick was her *Dad*. God - what they must have gone through with the car crash. However much he 'disliked' Nick, he empathised with the pain that losing him must have caused Annie and Violet. When Annie was out of sight, he sat in the large armchair and again, contemplated the bizarre events of the last twelve hours. He concluded that, if he had waited this long, he could wait a few more days or weeks – after all, he had the rest of his life. There was no point in talking to her, if she was not in the state of mind to listen. In her eyes, he was still the one who left her and did nothing to help. Maybe, when he finally could voice the truth to her, she would see him differently, but he had to remind himself that she was a grieving widow and the shock of losing Nick may keep them apart forever. He felt selfish for thinking it would have been better if they had divorced, but if Nick was alive, they probably wouldn't have divorced and she wouldn't be here in Longridge. It seemed so cruel, as if fate were tantalizing him, showing him what could be, but giving him no opportunity to attain it.

It was violet's first taste of breakfast duties. Having to get up early had been a pain, it was bad enough having to get up early for college through the week, but getting up early at weekends was just plain sadistic. There was however one small pleasure to be gained, Harley was also on breakfast duty with her. She found him slumped against a wall in the locker room, trying to keep his eyes open and looking as if he hadn't yet sobered up from the night before.

'Morning.' He said as he noticed her come through the door.

'Morning.' She replied trying to sound laid back as she opened her locker.

'What time you on till?' He asked coming up behind her and making as much body contact as possible. She tried not to let it show, but she was enjoying it.

'Two – why?' She said deliberately standing still and pushing her body back against his.

'Wait for me when you finish. If you want we can go for a drive - or something? Unless you've got plans?' She smiled inwardly, thankful that he was still interested in her after she had snubbed him the last time they met. There was nowhere she had to be and nothing she had to do – well nothing that wouldn't wait.

'Okay. I suppose I can see you then.' She answered with indifference. She hadn't been able to get him out of her head since she met him, not that she was going to let him know that. It was the moth to the flame syndrome and she was willing to get burned.

Eventually, Jack moved his personal life to one side, put his socks on and went across to the hotel. As he passed the restaurant he could see Violet in the distance serving breakfast. Looking at her now, he now understood why she had had an effect on him. It was the simple moves, looks and nuances that reminded him of his precious Annie. He forced himself to carry on walking to his office even though the temptation to go and talk with her was immense, even if it was passing the time of day or checking that all the hot plates were being replenished as they should be, just some form of contact was all he needed. If he was lucky there would be time in the future. Even if she was not his child, she was Annie's and therefore important to him, especially as now she was Fatherless. He settled down to working at his desk and busied himself with checking staff working rotas, looking for ways to save money for the company. It wasn't the most exciting task, but it did need his full concentration, he was hoping that he would be able to block out all other thoughts of Annie and Violet. It didn't work. He kept making mistakes and when he wasn't doing that he was daydreaming, writing mental lists of all the things he wanted to say to Annie. With every passing hour his agitation increased, waiting had never been one of his stronger characteristics. These two women filled his every thought, each minute seemed to expand into an hour - he didn't know how long he could wait before he would feel compelled to confront them. He had to get a grip. His train of thought was shattered by a timid knock on his office door. He was glad of the distraction.

'Come in!' He shouted without looking up from his work. Violet walked in with a tray of coffee and a few home-made cookies from the kitchens. There was no smile. The last time they had spoken he was giving her a dressing down. He was definitely not on her Christmas list. She stomped up to the desk and placed the tray in front of him.

'Miss St John asked me to bring this for you, it's your coffee.'

'No spare champagne for me today?' he teased. She didn't take the bait, 'Don't worry, I'm happy to make do with coffee? 'He smiled, trying to be friendly after their exchange of words. She was having none of it. She didn't even give him a curt smile out of politeness. He could see the same stubborn streak that ran through Annie, also ran through the middle of Violet – granite. He wanted to tell her he knew her mother – and her father, but it would be too dangerous – and he had promised Annie. He had to prove to her that he was trustworthy, he managed to say nothing – but unfortunately Violet had other ideas after speaking to Miss St John regarding her mother's antics the night before..

'Mr Parrish?' She began, 'Miss St John was telling me that you were there with my Mother last night when she passed out. What happened? Do you think she's alright now?' Jack could see she was genuinely worried about Annie's health, so he chose his words very carefully and told her the highlights and edited version of the night's events, concentrating on the fainting. He was careful not to make mention of their past history together.

'Miss St John also said you know my mum. Is that true?' Jack hesitated. Annie was strict on her instructions regarding him seeking out Violet, she left no rules on what he should do if she came seeking him? If he lied, the truth would come out and she would have no respect for anything he ever told her again. On the other hand, he didn't want to tell her that he and her mother had been lovers, before she married her father. He opted for basic, minimal truth; it seemed to be getting him by so far.

'Yes - I did know your mother. It was a very long time ago. We went to the same schools and we grew up together.' - Surely there was nothing in there Annie could hang him for?

'So did you know my dad as well? Nick, Nick Pickering?' Violet couldn't and didn't hide her eagerness to know the answer to this question.

'Yes. I did know him – not very well, but our paths did cross from time to time.'

'What were they like?' Violet's questions were coming thick and fast. 'What were they like as kids; I bet you could tell me loads of stories about them. Anything juicy I can use to blackmail mum?' He had been plunged in to waters he would rather stay away from. He had to take control of the situation before the questions went too far and he said something he would later regret.

'I'm sorry Violet, but as much as I would love to chat about the past to you, we both have work to get on with. Perhaps some other time we can do this, when we both have more time?' Her face oozed disappointment. It was natural for her to want to follow any connection to her father, especially under the circumstances, but he couldn't risk saying the wrong thing – not now. There was too much at stake.

'Thank you Violet.' He said dismissively, burying his head and continuing with his work. When the door was firmly closed, she pulled faces at him and whispered a few expletives to the door frame. Harley witnessed her annoyance.

'What you doing? – You can get put away for talking to walls!'

'I'm not; I've just taken his lordship a drink. He hasn't even got five minutes to pass the time of day! He's such an arse!'

'Ignorant shit!' said Harley, 'Bosses – there all the same. I'll nick you a bottle for later, to make up for the 'fascist bastard' –what do you drink?'

'No! Don't do that! – one day you'll get caught and I don't want to be the reason.'

'I thought you were up for a laugh?' He goaded her.

'I am up for a laugh; I just don't want me or you to get fired!'

'Then as I said, I'll surprise you with my gift later.' He squeezed her bottom as he passed. She slapped his hand playfully. The last thing she wanted today was another dressing down from Mr 'P'.

Violet returned to her job of clearing the breakfast room and setting the restaurant tables ready for lunch. She hated moving all the slops that the residents had left. Whenever she had stayed in a hotel with her mum and dad, she had been taught only to take what she could eat. She was appalled at the amount of food people wasted without a second thought. Miss St John came in to the restaurant with the rota for the next week's shifts.

'Do the guests always waste this amount of food?' Violet asked pushing a plate of cold full English breakfast under her nose.

'I'm afraid they do. We've tried different ways to cut down wastage, but nothing seems to work. People seem to think that they've paid for it, so it's up to them what they do – Tell me did you remember to take coffee to Mr P.?'

'Yes.' Replied Violet with complete lack of enthusiasm.

'Do I detect that you're not a great fan of Mr 'P'. ?' Scarlett was unashamedly fishing for information.

'How do you put up with him? I know he's your boss, but I went in trying to be chatty and he told me he didn't have time to chat and to get on with my work!'

'He's actually okay Violet if you give him a chance? It's only because he had to tell you about the Champagne that you think you don't like him. Let me tell you, the manager before him would have sacked you without a second thought for drinking champagne! So think yourself lucky that he's not here!'

'Do they do that really – for stealing alcohol?'

'It depends on the circumstances, but yes. Stealing is a very serious issue and we treat it as such, but don't worry. You're past the worst now. I'm sure Mr P. won't bring up the subject of the champagne again. The thing is to make sure you don't give him reason to.'

'I wouldn't be so sure.' Muttered Violet as she took the plates through to the kitchens.

At the end of the shift, Violet left the hotel as usual by the back door exit. She could see Harley in the distance, leaning against a tree, smoking a roll up with one of the young chef's stood close by. He probably had a posh name and job description to go with it, but it all meant nothing to Violet. They were stood in a sheltered corner, under the trees at the far end of the car park, where they could have easily been missed. They didn't see Violet. Harley passed the chef a small plastic bag that he had been holding in the palm of his hand. The chef in return gave Harley what looked to Violet like some money folded up, but it was difficult to be certain at that distance. They looked around as they exchanged their goods. Out of the corner of his eye, Harley finally noticed Violet. He had a quick exchange of words with the chef and then made his way towards Violet.

'Ready?' He said walking past her towards his car. She followed him without any questioning. He was parked as Violet expected, right next to the refuse collection area. They had to pass all the recycle bins and where the empty glass bottles were put. As they walked past, to Violets amazement, Harley dipped down and picked up two bottles from one of the boxes and slid them under his jacket. It was so smooth and well-rehearsed, she almost missed it herself, she was sure no one in the hotel would have seen.

'Harley!' Chastised Violet, 'Its broad daylight you'll get caught! Miss St John was telling me that they automatically sack people here for sealing.'

'Have you been blabbing to her?' Harleys face changed, she could see that merely

the thought of her speaking about it enraged him wildly.

'No! I haven't. So you can change your face! I said I wouldn't say anything and I haven't! – But you seem to think you're invincible and can't get caught? What if one of the guests looks out of their window at the very same moment? It's going to happen one day by the law of averages.'

'It won't. There're as thick as pig shit in there!' He said putting the bottles of drink into the back of the car.

'Well? You getting in – or what? – And how long before you 'ave to be back?' He demanded to know.

'Doesn't matter what time. I don't have to be anywhere.' She answered with a glint, as she climbed into the front seat of the car.

'Good.' He said with a hint of innuendo. He started the engine, revving the car to the max, before speeding out of the car park at full throttle. Violet didn't admit it to anyone, but she had a fear of fast cars since the accident that killed her dad. She clung on to the door handle for dear life, hoping that Harley wouldn't notice the look of terror in her eyes. She considered asking Harley to slow down, but she suspected he would only drive faster and wilder if he thought she was chicken. He drove down the country lanes at break neck speed, taking them further away from civilization, until they reached a high point overlooking the Ribble valley and Pendle hill. Harley pulled the car off the road on to some waste gorse land, which was obviously used as a car park at weekends by the ramblers. He drove to the edge nearest the sheer drop, to give them the best view, and then turned off the engine. Harley reached across to the back of the car and picked up the two bottles he had liberated from the hotel. 'Which do you prefer?' He asked holding up a bottle of champagne and a bottle of Tia Maria. She took the champagne out of his hands and flipped the cork. She needed a drink to calm down after his frantic driving.

'It's not all for you!' He said grabbing the bottle back out of her hands after she had taken more than her fair share of the liquid. They passed the bottle back and forth until it was empty. Violet could feel a fit of the giggles coming on for no particular reason; maybe it was because she hadn't eaten anything all day, maybe it was just her frame of mind.

'God! If I drink that 'Tia Maria' now I'd never make it home!' She said turning the champagne bottle upside down, proving there was none left. 'Tell me what you were doing with that chef?' She asked him directly, hoping to catch him off guard.

'Never you bloody mind!' He answered with annoyance that he had been seen, and that she was asking about his business. 'You can be too nosy for your own good you know. What you don't know can't hurt you!'

'Go on, tell me?' she pushed 'I won't tell anyone. Was it weed?' He looked her up and down trying to weigh up if she could be trusted. She leant across and kissed him hard, as if to prove the point.

'It might have been.' He admitted when she released him.

'Do you want some?' He asked her as he passed her the Tia Maria.

'No, I'm fine with the booze. God its cold here, now the engine's turned off!' Harley moved his hand and slid it up and down her thigh.

'I could warm you up.' He offered.

'Or you could turn the engine on?'

'I can think of better ways to warm you?' He moved his hand closer to the zip on her black trousers.

'Not here you bloody won't!' She said slapping the back of his hand. 'We'd get frost bite!'

'We could go to mine?' He suggested undeterred by the knock back. He tried his luck again with her zip, this time she didn't push him away, 'Well? Are you up for it or are you all talk?' She looked at him as he drew her into his deep broody eyes. She felt a warm flush overtake her body, she wasn't sure if it was the alcohol or desire.

'Okay.' She said grabbing the empty bottle of champagne, 'but I hope you've got another bottle of this at home.'

'I've got a whole bar, all courtesy of Priory Hall, with everything you could think of. Shall I take you to see it?' She leant across to him and kissed him again. 'You show me yours and I'll show you mine.' She teased, letting her hand wander to the top of his thigh.

Annie had managed to get back to the shop in time for opening after her exchange with Jack and collecting her car. The pile of flower orders to be made up sat on the work desk waiting for her, luckily nothing needed to be made in a panic, which was as well, because Annie's speed was less than efficient. She grabbed a box and cello for a hand tied and then realised that the order was an arrangement made in oasis, she had to start again. Her mind was all over the place after the events of the previous day. She willed herself to focus, but her mind was happier replaying every word that Jack uttered the sound of his voice and the expression on his face as Annie told him of the tragedy in her life.

Annie's world had stopped, but to everyone else, it was still business as usual. New customers and strange faces came through the door, some to order flowers and some just to have a good old nosy and a chin wag. Annie did her best even though she was not in a chatty mood, people were asking inane questions like, why she had chosen that particular shade for the wall and what stock would she be expecting in for Christmas, these things were not at the top of her agenda. All the excitement over the shop that she should be feeling had been over taken by a greater feeling of trepidation and fear of the unknown. She felt as if her destiny was now out of her hands. If she hadn't put down roots and mortgaged herself up to the eyeballs, she would have seriously considered moving away, but this wasn't an option now. She had to stay and find out what havoc would be wreaked by Jack's appearance.

After a fully day of work without a break, Annie managed to turn the key in the front door of the shop at five thirty. No last minute orders or problems. Annie felt relieved that she had made it through the second day of trading without a visit from Jack. He must have thought about her words and decided to consider her wishes. Her visit to him seemed to have bought her some time. The problem was that she didn't know if she had weeks, days – or hours. It was a ticking time bomb with the detonator already set in motion.

Tea was a simple affair. There wasn't much in the fridge and Annie didn't have the energy or inclination necessary to go shopping. Violet had texted to say that she was going out with friends and wouldn't be back until late. So, with only herself to please, Annie made scrambled eggs on toast and a large mug of tea. She took it across to the sofa and settled in front of the TV – bliss. She didn't care what was on, anything would do, so long as she could lose herself in it.

Four hours later, Annie woke as she heard Violet coming up the staircase. Her plate was still lodged beside her on the sofa, with the remains of her tea. Annie had no recollection of falling asleep; she assumed exhaustion had got the better of her.

Violet appeared at the top of the stairs munching on a portion of fish and chips, 'Do you want some mum?' She offered, whilst thrusting the chip filled paper under Annie's nose, ' They're not bad. At least they can make good fish and chips up north!' The smell of them won Annie over and she pinched a couple of the hot tasty chips.

'You seem in a good mood Vi. Who've you been out with?'

'Oh just some of the girls from work, they're a right laugh. It was good fun.'

'And how was work?' Annie reached over and pinched another chip, dipping it into a red splodge of ketchup at the side.

'It was okay, but the amount of food they waste at breakfast is shameful. I'm going to start making the guests clear their plates before they leave the restaurant!' laughed Violet, 'and I had to take coffee to that bloody Mr 'P.' this morning.' Annie nearly choked on the chip she had just placed in her mouth. 'He told me he knew you and dad.'

'He did what? - What did he say?' Annie's internal panic button had been pushed. Her brain was on red alert, she was prepared should she need to come up with a barrage of red herrings, lies or excuses.

'Did he come looking for you?' Annie was trying not to sound panicked.

'No, why would he look for me? Miss St John sent me in with his coffee. He was a really grumpy sod! He just said he went to school with you and dad. Then told me to get back to work and that he was busy and basically I should be too. He was more interested in getting his money's worth out of my wages than being friendly and chatty. I almost liked him for a moment when I found out you all went to school. Go on Mum; tell me something really bad about him that I can tell everyone at work? It'd be worth it to see him squirm!'

'There's nothing to tell. I can't remember much. How's college going?' Annie tried a quick tactical manoeuvre to avoid disaster - it didn't work.

'There must be something that happened. Was he at all your schools or just college?'

'All the schools.' Admitted Annie reluctantly.

'Were you good friends then or mortal enemies?'

'Violet, you do have a very fanciful mind! At one time, yes we were friends.'

'Did you think he was buff?'

'What?' asked Annie confused.

'Buff – fit – good looking. Well did you?' Annie lifted her eyes to the ceiling indicating to Violet that she was far from amused, but Violet was having far too much fun to drop the subject now. 'Did you snog him?'

'I think I'm going to get a drink, those chips are very salty. Do you want one?'

'You did!' Violet knew her mother's decoy tactics well. 'You did I can tell!' Annie had had enough - She snapped.

'Violet I don't want to talk about Jack Parrish! – Understood – end of conversation!' Violet had never seen her mother snap over such a trivial conversation, she put it down to her tiredness.

'Okay, okay - keep your hair on! I don't know why you're getting so uptight about a Kiss! I bet he was quite hot when he was younger; I'd have probably kissed him if I knew him when he was younger, he's still quite hot now. Is he married?'

'For feck sake Violet!' Annie was shouting now 'Let it drop!' The last thing Annie needed was Violet developing a misplaced crush on her biological father. Was the world going mad?

Violet let the subject drop, but she was starting to feel there was something more her mum wasn't telling her. This wasn't her usual behaviour, Violet didn't know what, but something was un-nerving her.

Annie got herself a glass of water, then made an excuse to go down into the shop to check on a delivery time in the morning. In reality she wanted to escape all the questions from Violet. She sat in the dark on one of the chairs, in the area she used to take wedding and funeral orders. People were passing up and down the main road going about their usual day to day lives, a few cans or a bottle from the off licence, supper from the take away, walking the dog before bed, all of them unaware that she was watching them from a distance in the dark.

The stillness was relaxing and therapeutic. In her mind she ran through the conversation with Violet again. Trying to check if there was anything she had missed. It dawned on Annie that she didn't know if Jack was married or indeed if he had a family. There had been no sign at the cottage, but she had only been there a few minutes at the most. What if he had a wife next door in the bedroom – the thought had never even entered her head. It was all so messy. She wished that the company would send him away to another hotel – perhaps that was her answer? Could she persuade him to go or put a complaint in about him and get him transferred? In the meantime she vowed to stay as far away as possible. She wondered how long he would wait before he became impatient and came knocking - It wasn't long.

Chapter 18

Jack sat outside Violet's florist in his car trying to pluck up the courage to go in. It had been three days since Annie had searched him out at Priory Hall. He had waited each day, for her to materialise at the hotel or phone to summon him, but each day ended with a 'no show'.

It was true that he needed to order flowers for his Mother's birthday, it was the only way he kept in touch with her these days and although he could order them somewhere else, he wanted to give Annie his business to help with her bills, little as it would be. He considered phoning his order through, but in truth he wanted to see her and he hoped it might break the silence between them and give him an opportunity to speak to her. He waited until he was sure the shop was empty, and then he tentatively made his way across the road. The exterior of the shop and it's window display were creative and inviting. He would have used the shop even if it hadn't been Annie's. He pushed the door open; an old fashioned bell rang to announce his arrival. He strolled in as calmly as he could across the floor to the counter. Annie was nowhere to be seen.

'I'll be with you in a moment!' He heard her call from behind the scenes. He could tell by her tone, that she was unaware of the visitors identity.

He wandered around looking at the different items on the shelves, vases, plants, incense burners, all manner of things which he could imagine Annie having an appreciation for. He was only there for a few seconds before Annie emerged from the workroom with a half made bouquet of flowers still in her hands. She stopped dead in her tracks when she realised her visitor was Jack.

'I'm here on business. I need to order some flowers for my Mother's Birthday.' He held his hands up as if in a cowboy movie, showing he had no intention of reaching for his gun. He didn't want to raise her hackles even before their conversation had started. 'Finish what you're doing; I'm not in a hurry.' He turned away and started browsing at the shelves again.

'Jack - I said I would come to you when I was ready?' At least she was calm and not insisting he should leave at this very moment. Although he was aware it was a distinct possibility if he didn't tread carefully.

'I am aware of that.' He stated. 'But as I said, I'm here on business.'

'You could have phoned through?'

'I was already in town, posting her card.' Annie paused considering what she should do next.

'Give me a moment.' She requested, pulling a piece of string from her apron pocket and tying around the flower stems.

'Did you make all these bouquets?' He asked with genuine interest, pointing at the ones on display.

'Yes.' She answered curtly, not wanting to be dragged into idle chat.

'You're good at it from what's here. I never realised you were so creative.' He wasn't sure if a complement would work, but it was worth the try.

'Jack what do you want?' The limit on her patience level had just been reached. Jack coughed lightly to clear his throat.

'I need to order some flowers for my mother. It's her birthday in a few days. Can you organise flowers to be sent to Australia from here?'

'I can through one of the relay organisations. So your parents are still out there?' Annie found herself asking despite herself. She reconciled it by telling herself he was a customer and she would ask the same of anyone else.

'My mother is still there. My father died a couple of years ago, though why she stayed with him I'll never know.' He picked a vase up, and then placed it back on the shelf.

'I'm sorry.' Said Annie, who understood the heartache of loss.

'You wouldn't be if you knew what he'd done…..he..'Tthey were interrupted by the bell on the door, a young couple had arrived to talk about wedding flowers with Annie. She'd been expecting them.

 Annie excused herself from Jack and showed the couple to the seats at the rear of the shop and gave them some bridal design books to browse through. Then Annie eased Jack gently to one side so that the couple couldn't hear the conversation.

'I'm sorry Jack it's a bridal appointment. I have to see them.'

'It's okay, I'll wait. It's my afternoon off.'

'Jack – Do you know how long these consultations can take? It could be an hour or two. Write down the address for your mother and a phone number, your card message and how much you want to spend and I'll see to it for you.'

'I really don't mind waiting.' His eyes were pleading with her, 'I can go for a

coffee and come back?' But he could see she was not going to give in.

'Jack you know there's no point. I'll contact the hotel if there are any problems.' He conceded to her argument. Reluctantly he wrote down all the details, whilst Annie asked the couple if they would like a drink. Whilst he was writing, he looked across at Annie. She seemed so confident and assured, miles away from the young girl, he had left on the train station years ago. He was in awe of her; she had 'blossomed' in every sense of the word, if anything he was more attracted to her now, if it was possible. She looked up and caught him starring at her. He lowered his gaze and concentrated on the matter in hand. When he had finished, he caught her attention pointing to the paper and gesticulating that he would ring her. She nodded to show she understood, the couple completely unaware that her focus was anywhere else but with them. He closed the door as he left, saddened that another opportunity had slipped past without a chance to tell Annie the extent of his father's lies.

At the end of the consultation, which was a good hour later, the couple, Ben and Sophie, booked Annie to design their wedding flowers. They seemed inspired by her ideas for their theme and had confidence in her ability. Annie had to work hard to hide her inexperience in taking such orders. In the past she had been the trainee, sitting on the side-lines, making notes, but this was her domain now. She took the approach of speaking to the couple as if they were already acquaintances, giving her honest opinion generously, but being careful not to push the couple into a direction alien to their dreams or desires. The wedding wasn't until next spring, but it pleased Annie to know that advance orders were coming in and who knows, perhaps Ben and Sophie's friends were in a similar position of planning a wedding.

Only when Ben and Sophie finally left to go to their meeting with the event co-ordinator at the venue, did Annie pick up the piece of paper Jack had been writing on. His hand writing was still the same, scrawled and messy, more like a teenager in a hurry than a responsible business man. She remembered the many time she had sat with him whilst doing homework, when she would chastise him and tell him to be neater – he never was. Annie realised she was thinking of him fondly, something she hadn't let herself do since the letter came from his father. She reminded herself *why* he had no place in her life. This was business – that's all. She went to the computer to send the order right away, with all the other things going on, if she left it, she'd probably not remember until after the delivery date and he would never have believed that it hadn't been done purposefully. She dutifully copied all the information on to the computer and sent the order off to headquarters to be forwarded to Australia. It was a new system that she hadn't used before; she was still trying to get to grips with it, even after spending hours sat using the practice system. She crossed her fingers and hoped it had all gone well. She was just about to file the paper away, when she found a postscript at the bottom from Jack. It read -

'Annie, I know you need time, but other people interfered in our relationship. Things happened that we were both unaware of. As desperate as I am to speak to you – I will wait until you are ready, My Love Always Jack x.

It was the 'My love Always Jack' that threw her. Her heart was beating fast, but why? She hated him for what he did. How could he write that, when he had abandoned her! She screwed the paper up and threw it in the flower waste bin. Her feelings were in turmoil, she didn't know what to think about anything anymore. She cursed the fact that she had moved back up north. If she'd stayed where she was none of this would have happened. She needed a good long chat to someone impartial, but there was no one. She would just have to work it out for herself. Half an hour later Annie passed the flower bin and picked out the screwed up paper and slipped it into her pocket.

Chapter 19

One of the pleasures involved in Scarlett's job was making everything perfect for a couple's wedding day. It wasn't always the easiest Job, but ever since she had been a little girl she had played 'Weddings' whenever possible, so it seemed only fitting that she had ended up in a job where she made other peoples wedding dreams come true until the day came for her to organise her own wedding, but she suspected that even then she would remain in the same business. Her job gave her the chance to relive the excitement and romance on a weekly basis.

Today she was preparing the reception room for Lisa and Jasper. Their wedding wasn't until the following day, but it was a large wedding and there was lots to be done. The couple had hired most of the hotel's bedrooms for their guests. There was a pre-wedding dinner for both sides of the family tonight before the formalities of the wedding tomorrow. It was mid-afternoon and Scarlett was organising the seating plan for the evening dinner, when one of the girls from reception came in to the function room looking for her.

'Miss St John, tomorrow's bride had been on the phone from her room in floods of tears. There seems to be some kind of problem. I couldn't make any sense out of her. She was asking for you. I promised her I would come and find you and ask you to go up to her?' She's in the blue room.' Scarlett left what she was doing and made her way up the stairs and to the blue bedroom. She was used to dealing with all manner of problems. Over the years she had dealt with almost everything, she just hoped it wasn't a case of cold feet on either side. Scarlett knocked on the bedroom door gingerly; she didn't want to startle her if she was already highly strung, also she had a degree of apprehension, as to what she might find. The mother of the bride opened the door, also in floods of tears. Whatever it was it 'Must be bad' thought Scarlett. She entered the room where the bride was sat on the edge of the bed with her head in her hands. Scarlett reminded herself of the golden rule, which was to keep calm, no matter what might be said in the next few minutes. A hysterical bride was not a pretty sight, especially when you're in the line of fire.

'Hello Lisa. Is there a problem?' Scarlett asked tentatively.

'It's all going to be ruined! We'll have to call it off. Mummy, I can't bear it, why does it always happen to me?' The Bride's Mother moved forward to console her daughter. Scarlett looked at the Mother for some indication as to what the problem was. She knew better than to second guess it. She'd done that before with disastrous outcomes. Eventually the bride was calm enough to let Scarlett in on the 'big' problem.

'I've just.' sob 'had a call.' *sob* 'from the florist's.' big sob and pause, ' she's fallen and broken her arm - and leg!' wail, ' She can't do the flowers!' The final sentence tumbled from her lips followed by *sobs* and *howls*.

'I see - That is a problem.' Said Scarlett, who needed a little time to think about the best way to proceed. She asked a few more questions, searching for any possible solution to the problem.

'I can't get married without flowers and a bridal bouquet. What will people think??' *Sob*

'So, has the florist managed to make any of your designs before her accident?

'Nooooooo!' *Sob.*

'Can she make any of any of the designs for you?'

'Nooooooo!' *Sob, sniff.*

Has she got all the flowers to make everything?'

'Yes!' Lisa almost smiled.

'Right, give me half an hour and let me make a few calls.' Reassured Scarlett. 'We'll sort something out. I don't want to raise your hopes up too much, but I do have an idea.'

'It's just a big mess. We'll have to cancel!' Sniffed the bride who had missed Scarlett's glimmer of hope. Scarlett crouched down on the floor to the same level as the bride; she often thought it must be similar to calming small children, having to calm a bride.

'Lisa, the most important thing to remember is why you are getting married tomorrow? And I presume it's because you love Jasper. You have to keep that as the most important thing of the day all the other things are lovely, but they don't compare in importance. You will have flowers. I will sort something. Scarlett was looking Lisa directly in the eye, trying to use it as a form of calming technique. She'd seen it work on TV programmes with animals, she considered blowing up her nose, like they do with horses, but then thought better of it. Lisa appeared slightly calmer even without that technique.

'I'll be back soon with news.' Said Scarlett letting herself out of the room. When the door was firmly shut, she let out a large sigh. She had given the very same speech at least once a week since she started this job over minor and major problems that had occurred. Words were great, but she had to fix the problem. She went down to the office, picked up the phone and dialled a number that had recently been added to the hotel's phone system.

'Hello Violet's Florist. Annie speaking, can I help you?'

'Annie - It's Scarlett. I need your help!' Scarlett filled her in on what had happened to Lisa's florist and asked her if she could do anything to help them.

'The problem is,' said Annie 'I haven't got the flowers to make all these things? And she might not like my style of work?'

'Annie, your work is great. I don't mean this the wrong way, but she's so desperate I'm sure she'd be happy with anything you do and as for the flowers, I've thought about that. I can send Harry and the minibus to pick up all the flowers from the other florist and bring them to the hotel for you? You could work in one of the conference rooms?' Annie thought how she would feel as a bride if the same thing had happened to her. She wanted to say 'No'. She was tired, emotionally drained and wanted to stay as far away as possible from Jack, she was also aware that Scarlett would lose confidence in her ability if she turned them down.

'Okay.' Said Annie with false enthusiasm, 'but I can't come over till I close up at five thirty?'

'Annie you're a star! Whenever you get here is fine, but it may mean you have to work through the night, or at least very late? There are a lot of places to be decorated with flowers?'

'Are you trying to talk me into or out of it?' Chipped in Annie.

'And I will be eternally grateful?' Added Scarlett. Annie didn't want to do it, but she couldn't stand by and see someone have their wedding day ruined when she had the power to save it — she sounded like super woman — pity she didn't feel like it.

'I'll do it. I may be able to get some help, but either way I'll be there, but the bride will have to realise that if I run out of time, she may have to settle for fewer designs, but I will make sure the main bridal party have their flowers.' Annie had caved. 'But you'd better keep me supplied with copious amounts of coffee to keep me awake!' Scarlett squealed with delight.

'I promise and sandwiches and cake! And even a glass of champagne when you finish!'

As soon as Annie rang off from Scarlett, she re-dialled Pippa to see if she could help.

'Oh Annie, I'm really sorry, but Mum and Dad are out tonight. It's their wedding anniversary. I can't get a sitter?'

'Never mind.' Said Annie trying to hide the disappointment in her voice. 'It was a long shot any way.' Annie was going to have to do this one solo.

'I can come and run the shop for you tomorrow, if you have to work all night tonight - if that's any help?' Suggested Pippa offering a ray of hope.

'Yes – yes please.' Annie nearly bit her hand off. She could stay up all night working, it was the day after she was dreading, but now at least she could look forward to some sleep.

'I'll find a way to get the shop key to you. Thanks Pippa.'

Scarlett checked Harry was able to go and get the flowers for the wedding, then she rang the florist with the broken arm to explain her solution and get her address, only when everything was in place, Scarlett went back up to the brides room.

'I've got good news!' She beamed as she went in. 'I've got hold of a florist for you, she's going to come to the hotel and do your flowers.'

'You have? How did you do that?' Asked the bride's mother with great interest.

'I can't tell you that, its top secret, you might take my job if I tell you, but I can tell you that a member of staff from the hotel will drive to your florist's and bring the flowers here.'

'I can't thank you enough Scarlett,' Added the bride, '– but are you totally sure it's sorted?'

'Yes totally. The only thing is, the florist will need to be paid for her time?'

'That's fine.' Chipped in the bride's mother, 'Tell her it doesn't matter what it costs as long as it looks fabulous!'

'I'll tell her.' Promised Scarlett, hoping Annie would have the sense to add something for her inconvenience.

At the close of day, Annie gathered all the things she thought she might need together in a large pile next to the front door, ready to load into the car. If she had a van she could have made the designs at the shop and transported them up to Priory Hall, but with such short notice, she would have to take everything up there and make things in situ. She had gathered oasis, dishes, ribbons wires, cutters, her work box and if it would fit the kitchen sink. She had no idea what she was expected to design, what colour the flowers were, it was all one big mess

– but if she pulled it off she would surely get more wedding on recommendation from Scarlett and the bride's family and friends. The downside was the possibility of bumping into Jack, but there was no point worrying about that now. Annie texted Violet to let her know she was working at Priory Hall and not to worry if she didn't come home, which was a laugh really as Violet had gone straight from college to a party and told Annie not to worry if she didn't see her until Sunday.

By the time Annie arrived at Priory Hall, it was already past seven. Scarlett was waiting for her behind reception, pacing a track into the carpet. I thought you had changed your mind and weren't coming! I'm very glad to see you!'

'It took me longer than I expected to gather my things and load them into the car, but at last I'm here as promised.'

'I can't tell you how grateful I am.' Her greeting was genuinely warm. 'I owe you big time! Now - I've got some of the lad's on duty waiting to carry your things in from the car and I've set one of the conference rooms aside for you. There's plenty of space to work. The flowers are already in there waiting for you. What else do you need?'

Annie was taken aback by Scarlett's efficiency.

'I know why you got the job here – Miss Efficiency! 'Laughed Annie. 'The only thing I need is a guide as to what the bride is expecting? Do we know what she ordered in the first place?'

'We have the original order; the florist sent it with the flowers. She also said to say a huge thank you to you and if you ever break your arm or leg, you know who to call!'

'Don't worry I will!' Vowed Annie. As the staff carried in the sundries out of Annie's car, curiosity got the better of her. 'Is Mr Parrish on duty today?' Annie needed to be prepared in case she bumped into him.

'No. He's been away at a conference all week. Men! Never there when you need them, not that he would have had a clue how to sort this one out! I'll show you through to the conference room now.' Said Scarlett marching off efficiently with Annie in tow. Scarlett showed Annie which door was hers, then carried on to supervise the pre-wedding banquet in the main room.

When Annie opened the door to her work room, she was met by a sea of the most heavenly flowers. Pastel pinks, creams, peaches and soft greens. There were at least five shades of roses, hydrangeas, gerberas, viburnum, phlox, lilies and various foliage's.

In no time at all, the items from the back of Annie's car where inside the hotel and she was ready to start. A young girl, about the same age as Violet came in with a tray laden with sandwiches, cakes, pastries and coffee.

'Miss St. John has sent these for you. She said if you need anything else, just ask.'

'Thank you.' said Annie, not realising until that moment how hungry she was.

The best plan Annie decided, was to sit and eat, to recharge her batteries, at the same time looking through the flower order to work out if she had brought enough containers with her and to see if she understood the type of designs required. Annie said a silent prayer, hoping that it would all make sense to her. The list was longer than she anticipated, a brides bouquet, five bridesmaids, various buttonholes, wrist corsages, normal corsages, pedestal arrangements, table arrangements, top table arrangement, flowers for the cake, thank you flowers, flowers for the ladies toilets, the list went on and on. She didn't know if she would manage to do everything, but she decided she would die trying.

Annie planned the full scale operation in her head. Firstly, she would start with some of the larger arrangements as the flowers would be drinking and would take no harm. One of the problems of making bridal flowers in a hotel was the heat. It was the end of October and chilly outside; but the hotel heating had been cranked up to keep the guests warm and toasty. Luckily she was on the ground floor and there were double doors to the gardens which she could open to cool down the room and the flowers. She would leave the main bridal flowers until later, as some of them would be without water until the time of the wedding – shit - she didn't know what time the wedding was. It could make a difference of hours in the amount of time she had to work. She made a mental note to check with Scarlett later. Annie took a deep breath and cleared her brain. *'Right Annie you need to concentrate and work fast!'* she said to herself as she bounded across to the flowers with scissors at the ready.

Jack found the drive back to Priory Hall slow and laboured due to the road works and traffic jams, not to mention the commuters heading home for the weekend. Jack could have stayed another night at the hotel after the conference, but he knew he would drink too much and then regret it when he had to get up early to drive back, besides, there was no one there he knew especially well and would want to spend time with. It would be another evening sat alone in a hotel bedroom. He preferred to drive home and be closer to Annie – at least distance wise.

The conference had been very informative, but the socialising was as hectic as the conference. Colleagues had arrived from all points on the globe, many he had worked with over the years of travelling from city to city and continent to continent. The daily schedule was full, leaving evenings as the only free time to catch up. This meant that Jack and many of his colleagues continued their 'catch up' through until the early hours with their conversation and drinking, by the last day Jack was exhausted and had no intention of repeating the mistake s of the previous three nights. His colleagues were surprised when he announced he was leaving. Jack had a reputation for always being at the centre of the party and usually the last one to leave, mainly because he was the one person with nothing and no one to go home for. Somehow, Annie's arrival in the village made Jack feel differently about home and even though the chances of reconciliation were slim, he would still prefer to be near to her. His friends tried to cajole him to stay, there was no changing his mind. Jack set off for home at the first available opportunity.

It was with relief that Jack parked his car at the back of the car park, in his usual spot, near to the cottage he called home. He needed a shower and some food, followed by sleep. The lights in the hotel started to have a familiar feel to him. He was settled here; even more so now knowing Annie was just down the road. He retrieved his bag from the back seat of the car and walked the short distance to the cottage. As he opened the door to the cottage, he was met by a warm blast of air, luckily the heating had switched itself on and the rooms were warm and cosy. He dumped his bag on the bed and then stripped off his clothes. His first task was a shower. The water was hot and refreshing to his skin, washing away the weariness of the journey. He dressed in casual jeans and a 'T' shirt, finally feeling relaxed after a week of suits and ties. Next on his agenda was food. He pulled open the fridge door to find something for supper – nothing – it was bare. Not even a few eggs for an omelette. There was no other choice; he would have to go across to kitchens and butter up the chef to make him something, but he least he wouldn't have to cook now. There were two entrances to the kitchen area from where Jack lived. He decided to take the door which was furthest away, but was the most direct to the kitchens. This meant that he would be less likely to bump into staff needing a managerial ear for problems, when he was still officially off duty. They had managed for a week without him; another night would make no difference.

The ground was firm and dry, so Jack took the short cut across the lawns. It also allowed him to view what was happening in the hotel without detection, as the dark night would conceal him. He turned the last corner of the building before the kitchens. In the distance he could see that the patio doors from one of the conference rooms were wide open. He was sure there were no conferences booked in for evening sessions before he had left. This door being left open and unattended was a security issue. Someone was for the high jump. He passed the entrance to the kitchens and continued to the open doors in the distance. As he neared, he thought he could see someone in there moving around. A few more steps and he was sure that someone was in there. He considered calling security, before venturing any closer, but a delay might mean their escape, whatever they were up to he was sure they were up to no good, besides which, he wasn't scared – not really. He crept forwards, making sure to keep out of sight. He wanted to check how many of them were in there before rushing in. He didn't want to end up in hospital brutally beaten. Slowly he leant forwards, peeping around the corner to see – he couldn't believe his eyes, it was Annie. She was the last person he expected to see; surely she hadn't reduced herself to breaking and entering?

'What are you doing?' He shouted a little too loudly. She turned quickly to see who was there, almost knocking over a large bucket of roses. 'Christ almighty!' she declared. 'What are you trying to do to me?' She hadn't expected anyone to come in through the garden.

'I'm sorry – I saw the door open and it's a security issue. I was checking it out.'

'Scarlett said you were away on a conference?' Declared Annie defensively.

'I am, well I was – I just got back. What are you doing here?' Jack was confused to see her surrounded by buckets of flowers.

Annie looked around her and then at Jack. 'Take a wild guess?' She didn't have time for stupid questions. She had a deadline to be met.

'Yes - I can see you are making arrangements, but why here?' Annie realised she wouldn't get rid of him unless she explained what had happened, so she did.

'……. So you see why I'm here and it's going to be a late night and probably all night!'

'I'll help you.' Jack offered with true intent.'

'What do you know about making bridal flowers?' She almost laughed in his face.

'Nothing – but I'm willing to do whatever you say. I can go and soak that green stuff you use.. –'

'Oasis.' She educated him.

'Yes – and I can carry the arrangements into place for you. It must be handy to have a bit of muscle around?' Annie ran her eyes around the room as if looking for someone to fit the description.

'Okay I don't spend all day in the gym, but I am a man and do come equipped with some muscles, even if they are under developed.' Her precious time was being wasted.

'I can manage thank you.' She wanted him gone, he was interrupting her concentration.

'You're refusing my help?' Jack couldn't quite believe his ears. He had come to save the day and he was being dismissed, but he wasn't going without a fight, 'I can ...'

'Jack! – be told - go away you're slowing me down. I don't have time to argue.' Jack's arms went up in submission.

'If you're sure? You're missing an extra pair of hands?'

'I'll get over it.' Said Annie sternly.

'I'm going to get something to eat from the kitchens, would you like me to bring you anything back?'

'Jack – go!' Annie stood with one hand on her hip and the other pointing in the direction of the door. He gave in and left- for the time being.

It took Annie a few minutes to get back on track after Jack's appearance. She tried to work as fast as she could, but she was a little rusty, which slowed her down and when she had done weddings before it was with other staff to help, it had always been a combined effort. Working on her own, everything seemed to be taking forever. It was usual to prep for a wedding the day before to make the most efficient use of time on the day, but that luxury had not been afforded to her. Normally bases would have been prepared, bows made for corsages and buttonholes, boxes covered for packing the flowers. All little jobs, but lots of extra time, time she didn't have.

She was just putting the finishing touches to the last of the pedestal arrangements when she heard the door open behind her. Fully expecting that it was Jack coming back to torment her, she was about to turn around and give him a mouthful, but luckily the entrant spoke before she did.

'Wow, these are wonderful. You must be Annie - I'm Lisa the bride. I can't thank you enough for stepping in like this. I thought I'd have to cancel everything. You truly are my guardian angel!' Annie could feel the colour rising in her cheeks.

'I'm glad I could help.' Answered Annie. Lisa started to prattle on about all the disasters and calamities that had befallen the 'Happy' Couple on their route to the 'Big Day'. Annie didn't feel as if she could carry on working, as Lisa was demanding her attention. Next, Lisa talked Annie through the whole concept for the look of the day. 'I think it's good for you to know this Annie, to help you design?' Annie couldn't get a word in edge ways; all she could do was make the appropriate grunts to affirm she understood. Annie was mentally wishing Lisa would leave her to get on with the job of 'designing'! When the smallest of gaps in the conversation arose, Annie started to make little comments about having a 'lot to do', 'not wanting to be late with anything', 'tight schedule', but nothing sank in. Lisa still continued to talk and babble on incessantly about her concept. It was at least another twenty minutes later, after Annie had learned how the couple met and where they were going on honeymoon, but not the same hotel as the 'Blyth-Smyth's'. Annie was reaching the point of telling Lisa exactly where to stick her flowers, when the door opened again and there stood Jack, the only thing he was missing was his underpants on the outside of his trousers. She knew this was an opportunity to move Lisa on and she had to take it. She cut Lisa off mid-sentence.

'Ahh, don't stand loitering in the doorway. Do come in Mr Parrish. Lisa have you met Mr Parrish. He's the manager of the hotel.' Lisa moved forwards to shake his hand. Lisa's back was facing Annie, giving Annie the chance to mouth *'get her out please'*. For one moment she hoped that Jack was still on her wave length and got the message - he was and he did.

'Lovely to meet you Lisa. My you're going to be a very radiant bride tomorrow.' Jack settled into schmooze mode. 'I trust everything is to your liking with the Hotel? Now, I think we had better leave Annie to get on with your flowers; it's going to be a tight time schedule as it is for her. Shall we? He held his arm out pointing at the door. Lisa had little option but to follow. 'And - Annie asked that you show me the exact placement of those wonderful pedestal arrangements she has made for you and let's go and see if they've started the preparation of the ceremony rooms yet shall we?' And with one swift smooth move, Lisa was history. Annie was amazed at how easily Jack dispersed with Lisa, especially as Annie had tried for the last thirty minutes and failed. Annie made a mental note to brush up on her schmoozing.

Annie was way behind; the time she had spent with Lisa was time she could ill afford. She was also beginning to run out of work space, all the arrangements she had made, were cluttered around her feet, hampering her working speed. She needed to get them in to the correct places and make some space. She hadn't even started on the main bridal flowers yet. She stopped and poured a coffee for herself. The caffeine would at least keep her awake and a couple of small pastries would give her energy. Comfort food was certainly needed. Five minutes later she was back working as fast as she was able. She would leave it for half an hour, to make sure Lisa and Jack were long gone, then she would move some of the arrangements to their places.

It wasn't long before Jack returned – alone this time. He had managed to shake Lisa and send her off to bed, as all brides need their beauty sleep. It was nearing midnight and Annie was far from finished.

'How are you doing?' He asked, already knowing the answer.

'Still a long way to go. It's getting a bit short for space in here. I think I'm going to need to ask Scarlett to borrow one of the boys to help me move all these.'

'Scarlett has gone home. She finished her shift. She was going to stay, but I said I'd be here to help. She's back on at eight and is working through till the end of the Wedding reception, so she needs some sleep – Now are you ready to accept my offer of help yet? I can get one of the lads to help you, but do you really trust them not to drop your designs?' Don't you think I'd be better?'

'Why? Because I can trust you?' Her words were scathing.

'You can trust me.' She could see the hurt in his eyes that she felt differently. 'I just need to prove that to you – but that's a conversation for another day. I promise I won't try and bring up the past or tell you all the things you 'do' need to know. At this moment we need to get these flowers finished! Right! Let's set up the ceremony room and do this in order, so if we are last minute at least we can be finishing the room for the wedding breakfast whilst they are actually getting married?' Annie was too tired to argue. She needed help and to be frank she didn't care where it came from. Jack showed Annie to the ceremony room and she showed him where each design had to go. Whilst he was doing this, she could get on with the next task at hand. To her surprise, Jack was easy to direct. He didn't argue about her choice of placement and his eye for detail was as fine as hers. Moving all the large designs gave Annie space and also made her feel less on edge, in a strange way it de-cluttered her brain allowing her to focus on the bridal flowers. Twenty minutes later he returned.

'Right,' said Jack 'all the arrangements are in their correct places? Do you want to check them?'

'No I can't spare the time; I'll do it when everything is done.'

'Okay what's the next job?' He asked eagerly. He was enjoying just being with her, spending time, nothing more or less.

'Do you have a torch?' She asked him.

'Are you pulling my leg?' He was on his guard, 'Is this like sending the new boy for a long stand?'

'No I'm serious. Do you have one?'

'No, but I'm sure maintenance will have one. Why?'

'I need you to go out and pick about sixty ivy leaves around the size of a fifty pence piece.'

'You are kidding right?' He was laughing.

'No. I need them to make all the buttonholes!'

'But its pitch black out there? I won't be able to see anything?'

'I know – that's why you need the torch brain box!'

'Is this some sort of test to see if I'll do anything for you, because.....'

'Do you think I have time to waste on mind games? Do it - Don't do it I don't care!' Annie was tired and losing patience. She sat at one of the tables and started to chop the heads off white roses to make buttonholes.

'Okay, okay I'll do it, but if I get spotted by the staff or guests, you'd better tell them what I'm doing. I don't want to get a reputation for being a 'perv' out in the gardens!' He disappeared out of the room and in search of a torch. A little while later she looked out of the double doors, she could see the flicker of a beam of light in the undergrowth of the garden. She couldn't help but laugh. He was definitely out to impress. She made sure she got the laughing out of her system before he returned. It seemed to take forever for him to find the right size of leaves in the dark. The torch was of little use, still, he promised he would get the leaves and so he would. Twenty minutes later a cold and miserable Jack made his way back through the patio doors.

'It's creepy out there!' He said making his entrance through the open patio doors. 'Will these do?' He emptied a bowl of leaves on to one of the tables. 'It's hard to see what you're picking in the dark. I don't know how many spiders I caught as well.' She moved closer to inspect the leaves.

'They'll do fine. Thank you. Now all you need to do is stitch them.'

'Shit Annie! I'm not sewing. I never could do it. You're worse than Mrs Redman in art when she made me sew a whole tea towel by hand! It took me three weeks! '

'It's not with a needle and thread, it's with wire, it's much more macho. I'll show you what to do. Come and sit down with me over here and bring the leaves.'

'Now you take a leaf, turn it over and then take one of these thin wires and place it through the spine of the leaf about two thirds up, pull both sided down and twist the wire.' They had to sit closely together for Jack to be able to see in detail what she was asking him to do. He wasn't listening, he was close enough to smell her scent and although they weren't touching, he could feel how physically close she was. To emphasise a point she briefly touched his arm. A surge of testosterone took him by surprise, he tried to re-focus and keep Annie out of his brain.

'Do it again – slowly.' He said finally giving the task his full attention this time around..

'They need to be wired to make them flexible in the buttonholes, to sit in the correct position. Go on have a go.' The first ones he messed up, ripping the leave. It was fine work and needed a delicate touch. 'Try again.' She encouraged. After about five, he had the hang of it. 'It's a good job you've got it now or I'd have to send you out for more leaves!' She teased. He gave her a look that would have frozen the sun. They both sat working in silence for a while, Annie because she was tired and Jack because he was concentrating on his sewing. Annie's mind began to wander. As mad as she had been at Jack for the last eighteen years, she had to admit that he was good company and still managed to make her smile, even against her will. At that point in time she couldn't imagine sitting there with anyone else helping her, it was strange, she couldn't forgive him, but there was still something binding her to him. She could feel her guard starting to slip slightly. It was probably tiredness. She would make sure it was back to full height tomorrow, there was no way she was going to let him back into her brain or her heart again.

At three a.m. Jack went for fresh coffee and bacon sandwiches – his idea. They worked and munched at the same time. Jack's pace was slow stitching the leaves, but it was still saving her time in the long run, leaving her free to make the bridesmaid's and bride's bouquet. When she had finished the bride's bouquet she turned to Jack, still holding it in her hands.

'What do you think? Does it look okay?' She asked him. He paused and looked at her. Her hair was messy and tangled from all the times she had run her fingers through it with the stress of the situation, her eyes were blood shot from lack of sleep and her cheeks were flushed from the tiredness.

'I think you look beautiful.' He said with tender honesty. Annie's cheeks flamed even more.

'Not me! The bouquet you fool!' She said feeling embarrassed and vulnerable. 'It's lovely. I didn't know you were so clever. You never seemed to show much creativity at school?'

'That's because you nicked all the good paints and crayons and left me with the crap!' She smiled sarcastically.

'Well at least I didn't wee in the Wendy house on my first day!' He reminded her. Annie pretended to look wounded.

'How could you bring that up after all these years? I probably weed when I found out I had to sit next to you all year!' They were both laughing now. Somehow the distance of years between them had dissolved for a moment, but it was Annie who pulled the guard back up.

'So the bouquet, it looks okay to you. I usually hold it and look into a mirror to check. You could hold it for me, but don't drop it!' She passed the bouquet to Jack. 'Don't you care anything for my reputation with my staff do you?'

'Don't worry, you haven't got one – but you might have tomorrow, 'dearie'. Now stand straight so I can see.' Jack stood up as requested placed one hand on his hip and struck the campest pose he could think of.

'Perfect!' She said 'Now it's just the buttonholes to finish until the final details on the morning.'

'Technically it is morning.' He corrected.

'Technically these wires will hurt if I sick one in your eye! You know what I mean, nearer the time of the wedding.' They continued working together. Annie made the buttonholes, Jack made sure that they all had a pin and then packed them in tissue to keep them fresh. By five a.m. they were both dead on their feet.

'That's it!' Cried Annie 'That was the last one. We can't do any more until a little later and god knows I need an hours sleep. I'm sure you do to.' It was her way of acknowledging the work he had put in on her behalf. 'I'm going to go home, and then I'll be back in a couple of hours. I need to get a key to Pippa; she's going to open up for me.' Annie covered the last of the buttonholes with wet tissue paper.

'That's stupid! Going home, just to come back again? I can get Harry to drop a key off, he'll be going to pick up the breakfast staff in an hour, he can easily drop it off with Pippa - and you'll lose time you could be sleeping whilst you're travelling. Come across to my place. You can crash on the bed. I'll sleep on the sofa.' He continued without giving her chance to chip in, ' Firstly, you are so tired it's dangerous, secondly you could over sleep because you are so tired and I can order a wakeup call and thirdly the chef makes a really good breakfast.'

'How can you invite me to sleep at your home when, well, - I don't even know if you're married! What if I come across and then your wife walks in? What's she going to think?' Jack could see her tired mind trying to make sense. He had been so desperate to find out about her life, he had omitted any information regarding himself in their conversations.

'I'm not married – well not any more. I was once for a short time, but we went our separate ways a long time ago, so no one is going to march in asking what your intentions are towards me.' She could tell that his patience was also starting to wane.

She looked at him longing to say *'yes'*, because it did make sense and she was scarred of over sleeping as there was still work to be done - but she felt that she should say no. It was all so easy to stay there, but it would lead him on and make him think she was ready to open old wounds, which she wasn't. She stood still not knowing what to do for the best.

'Annie, on my life I won't try anything on, believe me I'm so tired I couldn't if I wanted to and I won't try to make you talk, we both just need to sleep?' She nodded in silent approval. He rang reception and arranged for Harry to take the key then they both walked across to his cottage in tired silence.

'The bedroom's in there.' He pointed to a door on the left. 'I'll just grab a blanket then I'll leave you to it. It seemed strange, both standing either side of a large bed, as tired as she was she couldn't help but remember the passion they shared all those years ago on the night of the ball. She was appalled to discover that a tiny part of her still wanted him, even after what he had done – tiredness – she put it down to tiredness. She would feel differently in the morning.

Jack was as good as his word; he started to leave the room as soon as he had the blankets tucked under his arm. 'There are some clean pyjamas or 'T' shirts in the drawer if you want them.' He offered 'Well goodnight.' Jack started to close the door behind him as he left. He congratulated himself on resisting the urge to kiss her. Annie called after him, he opened the door again.

'Jack – you will wake me won't you?'

'Annie, you don't need to worry. I'm going to ring for a wakeup call now. You can trust me.' She couldn't find any words to respond, so she left him to go in silence.

It was strange lying on Jack's bed. This time the room wasn't full of sporting trophies and pop posters. There was very little to show what kind of person he had become. The walls were bare, no pictures or prints, everything placed neatly away in the draws and cupboards. She decided not to undress, somehow it seemed improper. She merely flicked off her shoes and jumper, leaving her leggings and 'T' shirt on. She vowed she was only going to lie on the bed and rest her eyes, but she was out for the count before Jack had managed to shake out his blanket.

'Annie.' She heard a faint familiar whisper in her brain. She opened one eye. Jack was standing at the side of the bed holding a cup of tea and a slice of toast. 'It's seven thirty. Here have this.' He placed the tea and toast on the side table. 'I'll leave you to wake up.'

'Thanks.' She said managing to open the other eye, whilst inwardly praising herself for deciding to remain fully dressed. She sat up on the bed. She couldn't decide if she felt better or worse for the sleep. Her bones were tired and aching, but no wonder, she had just worked nearly all night and she still had work ahead of her. She took a bite out of the toast and carried the tea into the lounge. Jack was sat on the sofa looking equally as rough.

'God! I hope I look better than you do!' She commented. Jack turned and scanned her from head to toe. 'No. No – you don't.' He said in a way only he could without her taking offence. She flopped into the chair by the fire place. She knew she should feel awkward in his home, but she didn't. They sat in silence, munching toast, drinking the tea, trying to force life back into their bodies. It was Annie who broke the silence when she had eaten her toast.

'Do you have to work today?'

'A little later. I'll go in for a couple of hours. I can make it up tomorrow. I'll just show my face to let them know the boss is back!' Annie thought it was nice to see he didn't take himself too seriously; it was a trait that could have easily changed.

'I want to say you were great last night. You were such a good help. I wouldn't have finished it all if you hadn't been there.' She said graciously. He looked deeply into her eyes.

'You would have done it Annie. You underestimate yourself and your ability and I would like to announce now, that I never want to be a florist! – Are you ready to get this baby finished then we can get off to work!' Jack was far too perky for Annie's liking. Annie groaned loudly.

Across at the hotel the day staff were arriving in dribs and drabs. Annie and Jack went to the ceremony room and checked all the flowers were still in perfect condition. She sent Jack around to each arrangement with a water spray to keep them fresh and moist, whilst she finished the last details on the bridal flowers. The wedding was due to start at eleven o'clock. At eight thirty she had received confirmation from Scarlett that the bride was up and getting ready, so she and Scarlett took all the bridal flowers up to the brides room. This was a moment of trepidation for Annie; she always had a rush of insecurity, fretting that the bride would hate them. Scarlett had already cooed over all the flowers, telling Annie what an incredible job she had done and that she would definitely be her florist of choice to recommend to potential brides, still the judgement on the bouquet had not been made by the one person who counted – the bride.

Lisa was in the middle of having her hair put up into a chignon. She squealed with

delight as she caught the first glimpse of her flowers.

'Annie they are divine! You exceeded my wildest dreams with the bouquet. I think I'm going to cry!' The makeup lady looked alarmed. 'I'll try and hold it in.' she promised. I'll tell all my friends how wonderful you've been stepping in at the last minute! At least four of them are getting married in the next year.'

'I'm glad you like them.' Said Annie modestly. 'Everything is set up for the Ceremony and the reception. I hope you have a wonderful day.'

'Thank you Annie, I'm sure I will. Mr Parrish told me not to worry last night, he said that you were fabulously talented and that everything would be wonderful – and he was right! Everything is perfect.' Annie's colour deepened even more at the mere mention of Jack's name, unsure of how to respond to the platter of flattery Annie simply smiled.

As the door was closed behind them Annie let out a large sigh of relief. She felt like the walking dead, but she was glad she had helped Lisa.

'So, is that everything sorted and in its place now?' Scarlett was asking.

'Yes! All done – and it time to get to work!' Annie pulled a disgruntled face.

'There's just one thing we need you to do, if you can just call into the breakfast room on your way out?' Scarlett tried to hide her smile from Annie.

'What have I missed?' Annie was racking her brain trying to think what could need to be done. 'They don't expect flowers in there do they?'

'It's nothing to be alarmed about. I just need your opinion.' As Scarlett led her into the breakfast room, she noticed Jack sat at a table for two in the corner. Scarlett led her straight to him. She turned and indicated for Annie to take a seat at the table with Jack.

'We wanted to say 'thank you' for making out bride happy and to make sure you get a proper breakfast before you go to work.' Said Scarlett picking up the linen napkin and placing it on Annie's lap.

'She's right,' said Jack, 'we both want to 'thank you'.'

'It's the least we can do for all your hard work.' Added Scarlett.

'But I don't need to be fed. I've had breakfast.' Annie realised the words would lead to questions from Scarlett, whom she assumed didn't know she had slept in Jack's bed.

'One of the staff got me a slice of toast.' Annie added to clarify.

'Well one slice of toast isn't a breakfast, we can do much better than that.' said Jack 'The important thing is you made someone feel special because of all the hard work you did and we want to make you feel the same..' Jack nodded to the waiter in the distance, who brought over a tray with bucks fizz on it. He passed one to Annie, Scarlett and Jack.

'A toast to team work!' Announced Scarlett.

'To team work.' Jack and Annie reciprocated.

'Aren't you joining us for breakfast?' Annie asked Scarlett, uneasy about being left with Jack in a situation where she would be forced to talk without the distraction of work.

'I'd love to join you, but I have a bride and a wedding to organise. My day is just beginning. I'm sure Jack will look after you. Won't you Jack?'

'Without a doubt.' He smiled his killer smile. Annie didn't want to come across as churlish and ungrateful, which she would have if she had refused, so she accepted for the sake of an easy life.

'I can't stay long.' Annie pre- emptied as their breakfast was served.

'I know. You have to get to the shop.' Jack finished her sentence for her. She was ashamed to admit it, but she had enjoyed their time together. Maybe it had broken a few barriers down; maybe she now had the patience to listen to his version of events, not that it would change anything, but now for some reason she wanted to hear what he had to say – she was ready.

'What are you thinking about?' He asked after they had been eating in silence for several minutes.

'Just that life is strange and if someone had told me a month ago I would be eating breakfast with you, I would have had them certified.'

'Sometimes we have the power to shape things?' He stated mystically.

'What do you mean?' She asked.

'Well, meet with me and let me explain what happened – what I think happened, because I'm not really sure. I know we're both tired and you have to go and we can't talk properly here, but let me tell you just one thing.' Jack's voice was starting to tremble, it was very slight, but she could tell he was trying to keep his emotions in check. 'Annie, on my life. I *never* received your letter telling me you were pregnant.' Annie's world stopped.

'So you are telling me that you never knew I was pregnant? Not even when you came looking for me just after I'd married Nick?'

'No I knew nothing. - I found the letter hidden in my father's office after he died – that was the first I knew about anything. Please let me meet you to explain everything?' His words did change everything. They had both been the puppets of John Parrish and oblivious to the truth. The emotion of being able to finally say those words to Annie brought tears. Jack tried to stem the flow as best he could, Annie wasn't doing much better either, luckily because they were in the corner no one could see. She had the urge to put her hands out to him and share the pain he was so plainly feeling, but she stopped herself. She didn't want to give him false hope. They both sat silently staring at each other. It took a few moments for the full realisation of his words to hit her. If he didn't know about the pregnancy - he hadn't abandoned her?

'So?' He eventually asked again, 'Will you meet me?' Annie just nodded not trusting herself to speak without sobbing loudly. Jack was relieved, he sighed loudly. Now he could find out the truth after all these years of waiting and he would be able to make Annie understand that he hadn't ignored her plea.

Chapter 20

It was Sunday lunchtime the following week, before Jack and Annie managed to find a window of opportunity, in which they were both free and Violet was occupied. Violet was working at Priory Hall on the lunch shift, Jack made sure she had arrived before he left for Annie's home. Whilst he was driving, he kept going over and over the words he wanted to say to her, he couldn't remember a time when he had been more nervous. He felt as if the rest of his life depended upon this meeting.

Annie, was no better, she had been pacing up and down the lounge since Violet left, looking out of the front window every few seconds to see if he had arrived. She was having second thoughts about letting him come to their home. It was as if, as soon as she let him in, he would somehow blend himself into their lives. She felt as if she was losing control over her family and she could hear a constant voice in her head telling her she was tainting Nick's memory– but there was a big question that needed answers and to find the answers she would have to let him in.

As if on cue the doorbell rang. She ran to the stairs, and then stopped herself. She needed to be calm. So she walked to the door, her legs going only a tenth of the speed of her heart.

'Come in.' She offered with a watery smile as he came across the threshold for the second time. ' We'll go upstairs. Did Violet arrive alright?'

'Yes I made sure I saw her before I left, just in case she had phoned in sick or something.' Annie nodded, confirming the sense in his actions. Jack followed her up the stairs into unfamiliar territory. The décor was not what Jack expected, not that he could figure out what he did expect.

'Sorry about the state of up here.' Annie felt as though she should apologise for the dilapidated décor. 'We finished the shop because it was most important to get open for business, but up here hasn't been touched yet, I'm afraid the whole building was in this sort of state when I took it over, but you know what they say, Rome wasn't built in a day.'

'I think you've worked wonders with downstairs, especially if it looked like this to begin with. I'm sure you'll get there. I didn't know whether to bring a gift or not, but I decided if it all got too much we could just get drunk! – so..' he passed her a bottle of wine that had been secreted in his jacket. She hated to admit it but the thought of just getting wasted sounded extremely appealing. Maybe a little Dutch courage would help to loosen their tongues for them to say all the things they had wanted to say for years.

'Do you want some now?' She offered.

'Not just yet – but I reserve the right to change my mind.' He said looking around at all the photos of Nick and Violet watching their every move. 'I could go for a tea though?'

'Have a seat.' She offered. He sat down in a chair opposite where Annie was making the tea.

'How is it going in the shop?' He had been reduced to making small talk, but he didn't want to start their conversation until he had Annie's full attention. It was important she didn't miss any of the words.

'It's okay. Early days yet, but the wedding at your place seems to be helping, I've had three wedding enquiry's since then.'

'Good.' He said sounding unsurprised. 'People know when they find something good.' Annie turned around momentarily to look at him.

'Em, I gave your name to a couple of people when they came to view 'The Hall', Seems they took my advice when the topic of floral decoration came up.'

'You probably scared them into it.' She said passing him his tea.

'Well, there is that point of view. ' They both smiled weakly, aware of what was coming next.

Annie sat in a chair as far away as possible, but facing Jack. She felt like she was about to go for a job interview and her life depended on it. She placed her tea cup on the table so that he wouldn't notice her hands were trembling, then pulled one of the cushions from behind her back and placed it on her knee for protection. It was no use putting off the inevitable; she decided to take the bull by the horns.

'What did you mean Jack, when you said you never got my letter about – being pregnant.' Jack sat forwards in his seat giving the conversation his full attention.

'Just what I said. When my father died, I went through his papers for my mother. At the back of a filing cabinet I found a pile of letters, in your hand writing and mine, all tied together. I swear Annie - I had never seen any of the letters before in my life. He must have hidden them from me when they arrived. I wrote letter after letter to you and I couldn't understand why you never wrote back. When I had finished my university course I came back to England to find out what happened to you and that was when I found out you married Nick!' there was distain in Jacks voice. Annie was left no choice but to defend the dead.

'Don't you dare blame him in any way? He was a good man, no matter what you thought about the 'boy' you knew. He looked after me. He was all I had and I loved him.' She paused; Jack was trying to swallow the bitter words which were trying to form in his mouth.

Annie stood up. 'I want to show you something.' She disappeared into the bedroom for a moment. When she came back she was carrying a letter. The paper was folded and torn. He could tell it had been read many times. She passed it to him. 'Read this.' She sat down opposite and waited. It was the letter she had received from his father all those years ago. He started to read it. After the first few lines he started repeating 'No!' – 'No!', he was shaking his head in disbelief. Tears rolled unashamedly down his ashen face. Even though Annie was trying to remain detached from him, she could feel his pain. Part of her instinctively wanted to go and put her arms around him to comfort him, as she did all those years ago when he was taken away from her, but she remained distant.

'He can't have been that cruel - Can he? I know he was a controlling bastard and as fathers go, he could have done a hell of a lot better, but to deliberately write something hurtful like this? Surely the man had some sense of right and wrong?' He looked at her for assurance. These were questions Annie had asked herself many times.

'In his own way he probably thought he was protecting you.' Now she was older and had a child of her own, she could just about understand that point, but not the way he went about it. She asked one of her many questions.

'Did you know he had written this letter to me? Saying you wanted nothing to do with me or any baby I might be carrying? - and that I should leave you to your life?' She was staring at him intensely - testing him. She would know it, if he was lying when he answered.

'I swear on my life that I had no idea about anything. If I had known you were carrying my baby, there is no way I would have left you to be on your own, which my father probably knew, considering the amount of letters I wrote to you, he must have known how I would feel. I would have come home to you, regardless of his opinion. When I left for Australia I was in love with you. For me, nothing changed.' He hesitated, 'I still felt the same. You just stopped writing or as we now know my father took and hid your letters before I saw them.' He stopped. 'Did you get *any* of my letters?' Annie shook her head. 'I gave them all to him to post. He said he would do it through work and it would save me the postage! He never sent any of them did he? 'Annie shook her head again. Jack was beyond anger.

'I never received one letter from you when you went. The only letter is the one you are holding from your father.'

Jack threw the letter on the side table. He walked over to the wine, opened it and scoured the cupboards until he found the glasses, then poured two drinks, all without speaking. He passed one to Annie. She took it without hesitation. She willed the alcohol to numb some of the memories that were being exhumed. The anguish at the time was so deep routed that a mere simple scrape brought the pain to the surface, opening the old scar tissue. Jack downed his wine, placed the glass on the side then moved over to where Annie was sitting. There was still unfinished business between them, she was afraid to stir old feelings, but they were both in pain. This was the first time either of them had heard the truth. For a moment Annie wondered how different her life would have been if Jack had received the letter – she stopped herself, not wanting to wish away her years with Nick. He crouched down on the floor in front of her. He took her glass from her before taking her hands in his. She gave in reluctantly, but still clung on to the cushion.

'Annie,' He said lovingly. 'I need you to be totally honest with me. I have tortured myself since I found the letter. - What happened to the baby?' This was the question Annie was dreading having to answer. Tears rolled down her face accompanied by large sobs, 'Did you have the baby Annie?' He was crying too.

'Yes.' She said in a whisper, but it was loud enough for him to hear her.

'Annie – Is Violet my daughter?' Annie pulled her hands out from Jacks grip and placed them over her face crying into her hands she said 'Yes - Yes she is.' Jack pulled Annie in to his arms. They held on to each other, both weeping for a missed life they could have had together as a family, the one John Parrish stole from them. Independently, they were both thinking what might have been, had Jack received the letter – but that was not what happened. Their lives were different and that had to be faced. It wasn't Jack the boy in her arms; it was a grown man, a man who was a stranger to her and especially to Violet. Annie pulled away; she was starting to feel guilty for telling Jack her secret, a secret Violet didn't know. She felt as if she were a traitor. Nick had brought Violet up as his own daughter and indeed she was his. Never once had Nick thrown back at her, the fact that he was bringing up another man's child. She made Jack look at her; she would have to be careful in what she said to Jack, she didn't want to force a reaction.

'Jack, I know we're both hurting now, but the most important person in all of this is Violet. We are both adults, but she is still a child at heart.' She was praying he would agree with her. 'All Violet knows is that Nick is her Father.' Annie could see Jack visibly wincing. 'She knows nothing else. We can't tell her Jack. It will break her. She's already had to go through the trauma of losing him. I'm not sure that's she's strong enough to take this?' Jack pulled away from Annie, displaying his anger at her words.

'I find out that I have a daughter and you tell me I should keep my mouth shut and pretend I'm not her father!' Jack's fury was overflowing.

"Fucking' me does not make you a father!!!!!' Annie stood up to him, equally enraged. 'Nick was there for me when I needed him.' Jack opened his mouth to speak, she silenced him in a second 'I know now that you didn't know about the pregnancy, but I can't change history. We have to deal with what we've been given. We have to deal with what happened, not what we wanted to happen!!! The reason I told you the truth about Violet is because you were lied to by your father and you deserve to know the truth – but – Violet must come first! Do you understand?' She was stood holding his shirt in her first, to stop him from moving away and not hearing her words. Jack had never seen Annie so single-minded, but then, he had never seen her defending her daughter before – their daughter, he tried to make the words sink in. In his head, Violet being his daughter had been his fantasy, the unreal wish he carried around since the day he met Annie again, but the fact that his dream was a truth came as a shock, an amazingly wonderful shock. He breathed deeply trying to calm himself down.

'So what are you saying?' He asked, 'That I should just disappear and pretend she doesn't exist when I've only just found her?'

'No.' she was calmer now, 'I just don't want you to rush into telling her now, to make you feel better. It has to be about her. In the last two years she has lost a father, moved home, moved school and lost her circle of friends. Do you really want to be responsible for pushing her over the edge?'

'Of course I don't!' He was annoyed that she thought he could be so selfish. 'Don't you know me at all?' He asked. Annie stared at him for a few moments pondering her answer.

'No Jack – I don't know you. I know the boy, not the man, just as you knew the girl, not the woman I've become. We've both lived a lifetime on our way, we're not the same people. We can't be.' Jack moved to pour himself another glass of wine.

'When I left for Australia Annie, as I said before, I was in love with you. For me, nothing has changed. I have loved you my whole life, my marriage was a disaster, because I couldn't get you out of my mind. I may be a man now, but the boy who loved you and who you loved is still in there.' Annie turned away, they were words she would have killed for once, but today they made her feel sick with fear.

'Jack, this is not about us. There is no 'us' anymore. This is about Violet and I won't settle until you promise me that you won't tell Violet?'

Jack had missed nearly seventeen years of her life, he didn't want to miss any more, but Annie was right they had to put Violet first. If he disregarded Annie's feelings, it was a sure bet that he would lose her for good. Eventually he spoke. 'Okay I promise.' Annie grabbed her chest in relief. 'But – I do want to see her and get to know her. You can tell her I am an old friend which is true and maybe we can all spend some time together?'

'You're blackmailing me!'

'No Annie – I'm just not prepared to lose her and you when I have waited all these years to find you!'

'You seem to have forgotten that I might not want this! It's not your divine right to be with me just because our paths crossed again and it's what you want!'

'Had you still been married to Nick, well, it would be different, I concede that, but that's not the situation, is it?'

'You arrogant bastard! He's dead Jack, I didn't divorce him. In my head I'm still his wife!' Jack had said too much, letting his feelings get the better of him.

'Okay I'm sorry. I presumed too much, but the truth is that I'm scared to lose you again and I'm probably going about it all the wrong way, but please don't punish me for my father's actions, by keeping Violet away from me. I will honour your request. I won't tell her, but equally, I won't wait for ever!'

Annie was just about to respond, when there was loud knocking on the front door of the shop and someone was calling through the letter box. Annie's first thought turned to Violet – maybe something had happened to her. She ran down the stairs, followed by Jack. It was Stan, frantically banging on the door. Annie unlocked it as quickly as she could.

'Annie, Annie, its Mum, I can't wake her –you need to help her.' Annie, Jack and Stan ran across the road to Mrs Stretford's house. Jack being the most athletic arrived first, with Annie closely behind. Mrs Stretford was sat in her favourite chair in the front room; she looked as if she had fainted. With his first aid training Jack was the obvious candidate to take charge. Jack tried to wake her, but could get no response. Although he had never met Mrs Stretford, he noticed a droop in her jawline. It wasn't a good sign.

'Stan have you called an ambulance?' He shook his head.' I knew she was breathing, I just can't get her to wake up!' Stan said.

'Go and ring one now.' Instructed Jack, 'tell them you think she may have had a stroke. Annie go and find a blanket to keep her warm.' Annie found one in the bedroom folded up at the top of the wardrobe. When she came back Jack was talking to Mrs Stretford, calmly telling her not to worry, that we would take care of her and the doctors were on their way. Annie knelt down at the other side of the chair. Jack looked across at her. 'Just be calm and positive.' He encouraged. Annie took Mrs Stretford's hand and spoke words of encouragement. A couple of minutes later Stan burst back into the room. 'They'll be here in a little while. The paramedic is on the line in the other room, she wants to talk to you, he directed the words at Jack, 'I said you were looking after her.' Jack got up to go to the phone,' Just do what Annie's doing.' He patted Stan on the shoulder as he left. Mrs Stretford's phone was fixed in position, leaving him stranded in a different room to the patient, so Jack gave the operative his mobile number. A minute later his phone was ringing, allowing him to move back to the others and report first hand on Mrs Stretford's condition.

It was ten minutes before the nearest ambulance made its way to them, Jack sent Stan to watch out for them and show them in. When they finally arrived, Annie, Jack and Stan moved back to let them do their job. After a couple of minutes a decision was made to take her to hospital.

'Who is next of kin?' Asked the paramedic.

'I am.' Said Stan, 'She's my Mother.'

'She might need some personal items; they'll most likely keep her in.'

'Shit – I don't know where she keep's everything! I've never been through her draws in my life!'

'I'll sort it Stan, if that's okay with you?' Offered Annie,' I'll put some things in a bag and follow you up to the hospital in my car?'

'Ehh, that's grand Annie. Thank you.' In no time at all, Mrs Stretford was safely on her way to hospital with Stan keeping a watchful eye on her in the back of the ambulance. Annie went to find a bag she could use for the overnight items, Jack followed her.

'Do you think she'll be okay?' Annie wasn't sure she wanted him to answer her question truthfully, 'I think her eyes were rolling and her mouth had dropped at one side? It wasn't usually like that.' Annie had observed the changes.

'All I do know,' Said Jack 'Is that she's on her way to the best place to make her well.'

'How did you manage to keep so calm?' She asked him.

'I've done my first aid certificate many times and unfortunately over the years at work, I've been around when people are taken ill. It happens more often than you think. If you go in panicking, you're no use to anyone. After a while it becomes second nature.'

Annie gathered a nightdress, cardigan, slippers, a book that was on the bed side table, a hair brush and a wash bag she found hanging on a hook on the bathroom door.

'Can you think of anything else she might need?' Annie asked.

'I'm sure Stan can bring anything we've forgotten later. I don't think she'll need much today, she's going to be out for the count for a good while. Come on. Let's get these up to the hospital.'

'I'll take them.' Said Annie who hadn't expected Jack to volunteer to go with her. 'I'm sure you have things to do.'

'Whatever I have to do will wait. I'm not leaving you on your own to go to the hospital. Stan needs all the support he can get at this moment.' She didn't argue. She hated hospitals. The last time had been when Nick had died. She had sat by his bed for three days and nights while he lay in intensive care fighting for his life. If she never saw a hospital again it would be too soon.

The journey took them twenty minutes. The conversation was non-existent. Jack was lost in the battle between his heart and his head over Violet. He was replaying the first moment he met her and wondered why he didn't recognise his own child. Annie was sitting worrying that Jack may not keep his side of the bargain. She just had to hope and pray that he would.

There was no sign of Stan when they arrived at the Accident and Emergency unit. They sat in the reception waiting for news. It was two hours and three vile cups of coffee before Stan came out from the trauma ward to find them waiting. When he saw Annie, he started crying. Annie went to him and hugged him.

'I've lost her Annie –She's gone.' Annie wrapped her arms around him and just hugged him. Annie could feel Jack's presence stood behind her unobtrusively, patiently waiting for Stan to compose himself.

'It was a stroke. She gave up in the end. Still, doctor said she wouldn't be able to talk or walk if she'd lived. Perhaps it were a blessin. I know she'd ne want to live like that.'

'Do you want me to call anyone for you?' Asked Jack. Stan shook his head.

'I have a sister who lives a few miles away, but I can't tell her by phone, I'll have to go and see her.' Stan was trying to pull himself together and think rationally.

'I'll take you.' Offered Jack.

'No lad, I can't put you out any more. Besides I've rung me mate Billy. He'll be here in a minute. He's more than happy to take me. You and Annie get yourself off. You've done more than enough. See' He said pointing through the window, 'Billy's here now.'

'If you're sure?' said Jack.

'Do you want me to come over later?' Annie was worried about leaving him on his own.

'No lass. I might stay at mi sisters. Likely she'll not let mi out 'o her sight, but I'll be in touch.' She kissed him on the cheek; Jack gave him a man hug.

The emotions of loss flooded back to Annie as she stepped out into the autumn air. She tried to fight it, but it had been an emotional day, the slightest thing would have set her off, the mood she was in, so to lose Mrs Stretford was way more than she needed to tip her over the edge. 'Did you know her well?' Jack asked assuming that Annie's silent tears were for her.

'No, not very well, but I would have liked to get to know her better. The shop belonged to her before I came so we're sort of linked. She ran that place when she had lost her husband and I did the same. Can we walk for a bit? I need some air and space.' Jack twigged that she probably wasn't only thinking of Stan's mum.

'Are some of those tears for Nick?' He asked cautiously. She nodded.

'What happened to Nick?' Jack had never asked before, maybe now was the right time.

'It was a car crash. He was coming home from work it was raining; another car side swiped him into a lorry. He didn't stand a chance.' Annie broke down. Jack wrapped her in his arms. It was becoming a habit. She realised that the rawness of Nick's death was still only just under the surface. She had spent so long being brave for Violet that she had never given herself chance to grieve properly, it was the only way she could reason her feelings at this moment. She was sad to lose Mrs Stretford, but they were not close. Some of her tears were for herself and the uncertainty of her future, now that Jack was around and desperate for Violet to be told the truth. A few minutes later Annie had composed herself again and they continued walking.

'Were you happy – married to Nick?' Annie felt it was a brutally frank question to be asked whilst she was in this vulnerable state, but she decided that honesty was needed.

'Yes. We were happy – Does that disappoint you?' She could be just as cutting.

'No, of course not. I'm glad you were happy, but remember – events were taken out of my control. I wanted us to be together. I'm bound to feel sadness for what was taken from us.' Jack somehow felt he still had to compete with Nick.

'I understand that, but Nick didn't steal it from you – your father did.'

'Yes. - But if you hadn't been married when I came looking for you after college, we might have repaired things and worked it out?'

'That's one thing we'll never know the answer to Jack. Nick and I had only been married a matter of weeks when you turned up on our doorstep. I couldn't wait forever, especially after the letter sent by your father was so final. I couldn't spend my life waiting for you to show up?'

'No. I understand that. When I came to your house, the baby you were holding that night, it was Violet wasn't it.'

'Yes, it was.'

'I was too busy being cross at Nick to even consider how old she was or that I might be the father.'

'Sometimes we only see what we want to see.' Annie said wisely, 'I was very confused when you left that night. I thought you had come wanting to acknowledge the baby, but now I understand you didn't even know I had been pregnant, so you assumed the baby was Nick's.

'I just saw red! I couldn't believe you ran off with him – of all people.'

'It wasn't a case of running off with anyone. I was pregnant, couldn't go to college. I had no Job. As far as I knew you were never going to come looking for me, it said so in the letter. Nick and I started off as friends. A lot can happen in three years Jack. It took time for me to get over you and start to have feelings for Nick, but I did. My only alternative was living life as a single mum longing for a man who wanted nothing to do with me.'

'Did you long for me?' He held on to the words hopefully.

'We can't go back in time Jack. All we have is the moment we're in and the memory of what we felt in moments gone by. Now I know – you didn't know anything about the baby, but this was how I perceived it at the time. Eventually Violet was born. Nick was with me at the birth, he looked out for her from the moment she was born. We didn't get married until later, in fact, as I said, a few weeks before you turned up on the door step. Afterwards Nick told me that he was so uptight, because he didn't know if I would throw my arms around you and leave him.' Annie stopped walking and looked at Jack 'and the very sad thing is, that at that moment in time, if you had asked me, I would have gone with you – God forgive me!' Jack was stunned. He had never thought for a moment that she might have still wanted him all those years ago. He cursed himself for not asking her to go with him. He was so self-obsessed, all he could see and feel was his own anger at finding her with Nick.

'Then we worked together at bringing up violet, she was the most important thing to both of us, and over the years I grew to love him very deeply, as I've said before I owe him a lot.'

'But you can't just love out of gratitude!' Jack still couldn't deal with the ghost of a dead man.

'Don't twist my words Jack! I loved him and if it wasn't for the accident, I would still be with him!' She had lost her patience, 'I think we'd better go back now!'

'Just one thing Annie!' He pulled on her arm to stop her walking away from him. 'You may not want to hear it, but Violet was conceived out of Passion, our passion for each other. It was the most passionate and important night I've ever known. No one has ever come close to matching the way I felt for you that night and you can't tell me that you didn't felt the same way too at the time. That can't be a bad thing. I loved you then and no matter how many years or events have passed between us or other people. I still love you – I always will, even if this is the last conversation I ever have with you. I won't ever stop loving you.'

'Jack! You can't say that to me!' She pulled away and began walking to the car.

'Why not it's true?' He followed her, keeping pace.

'We can't go back to what we had, what we were! We're strangers now, there's too much time between us and even if I did feel the same there's Violet to consider.'

'Do you feel the same?' Annie ignored him and continued walking towards the car. Her silence spoke volumes to him. For if she felt nothing, it should have been the easiest thing in the world to tell him so, but she couldn't.

'You do, don't you. You do have feelings for me?'

'Not now Jack – Not now!' Without meaning to, she had presented him with a glimmer of hope. Just maybe, in time, there was a possibility that things could work out.

Chapter 21

Violet was on her knees by the time she arrived back at the shop. The Hotel had been full to capacity after the weddings over the weekend. The dining room was at bursting point for lunch, with birthday celebrations and anniversaries and to complete her day, two members of staff had called in sick, which meant more work for the staff that were in. To add to the torment of her day, she had a hangover from hell, brought on by too many Bacardi breezes and tequila shots the night before at Harley's.

Violet shouted as she went up the stairs, to let her Mum know she was home. There was no reply. Annie hadn't said she was going out, but violet thought she was old enough to do what she pleased on a Sunday afternoon off from the shop. She'd probably taken herself to one of the wholesale cash and carry places looking for new stock, she was sad that way. Violet kicked off her black work shoes, what a blessed relief, they had been pinching her little toe all day, she instantly felt better. All she needed now was a drink, some chocolate and a film on TV, if she could stay awake. She went to the kitchen to make the coffee and found a bottle of wine half drunk. This wasn't usual behaviour for her Mum. She became more suspicious when she saw the two glasses on the coffee table; someone had been round that was a definite. She hoped it was Zach coming to look at the flat for renovating or Pippa calling in for a chat. Anyway, whoever it was, they had good taste in wine. It was the stuff they sold at Priory hall. Violet decided that wine was preferable to coffee after a hard day, the hair of the dog and all that, so she abandoned the idea of the coffee and helped herself to the last of the wine. She picked up the remote and started flicking through the channels looking for something she fancied watching. There was a film just starting, she'd seen it advertised, she decided to give it a go. She flopped down on the settee and turned to place her glass on the side table. There was an old folded letter in her way, she moved it to the side to make space for the glass, and that would have been the end of it, but her curiosity got the better of her and she read it. At first it made no sense. Who was pregnant? She looked for the date on the envelope. It was dated seven months before she was born, she re-read it and that was when the pieces started to fit together, but she couldn't be the baby being talked about in the letter. Her father was Nick, not Jack, not Jack her boss! The reality of it hit her. She was the baby being discussed in the letter.

It was at that moment Annie arrived back from the hospital; Jack had dropped her off outside. He had wanted to come in, but she had insisted he went home. Annie was tired and an emotional wreck from talking to Jack and the sad news of Mrs Stretford's death. She mounted the stairs unaware of what she was about to find. Violet was stood next to the settee frantic with rage. Her cheeks were red and her eyes inflamed from crying.

'What on earth is the matter?' Annie asked moving forwards to comfort her. Violet wrenched herself away from Annie's hug.

'How could you! How could you lie to me for all these years!! ?' Then Annie noticed the letter from John Parrish screwed up in her hands. The letter she never wanted Violet to see. It had been left on the side in the rush to help Stan and his Mother. In that one moment Annie's world had come tumbling down around her ears.

'Violet........I can explain........Just...'

'Just what! Let you fill me with more lies! – Is it true? I am your bastard child?' she was screaming at Annie.

'Violet don't speak like that! You don't........'

'I don't what – understand that my mother is a slut who couldn't keep her knickers on! Having affairs behind my dad's back!' There was no possibility of reasoning with Violet in this mood. Annie wanted to shout back, *'Don't be daft, everything is just as it was.'* But she couldn't.

'Is Jack Parrish my father?' Screamed Violet. Annie didn't answer. She couldn't bear to confirm the news that she never wanted Violet to know, that Nick was not her biological Father.

'Tell me!' Violet was two inches away from Annie's face, she was totally out of control.

'Tell me the truth. That's the least you owe me after a life of lying to me!' Annie tried to think. This wasn't supposed to happen. Why was the world conspiring against her? It wasn't as if she had deliberately set out to deceive Violet, it was circumstance. Why and how had she been turned into the baddie in this situation? Annie needed to regain control.

'Violet, love, you need to calm down.' But Violet was not going to give up her fight for the truth.

'Is that who was here – drinking wine, having a good laugh about the fact that I didn't know he was my Father? Poor little Violet's not in on the joke that her boss is her father and the man she loved and called father is no one to her!' Annie's patience finally snapped.

'Don't you dare say that Nick is no one! He looked after you and gave you everything. Don't you dare put him down!'

'Oh my God! You never told Dad I wasn't his child did you? You lied to him and to me? Did you trap him into marriage?'

'No Violet………………… No. It wasn't like that…..' Annie stumbled trying to find the right words.

'Mum! Tell me the truth or I'll go to 'The Priory' and ask him!' Annie could tell she meant it. She sat down on the chair, she needed something to support her legs that were about to give way.

'Alright, alright!' Annie took a deep breath, '– Yes. Jack Parrish is your biological parent, but it's Nick that brought you up, he is and always will be your father.'

'Screw you Mother! Screw you!!!' Violet grabbed the shoes that had been nipping her toes all day, she didn't care how much pain they would cause her, she ran down the stairs and out of the front door. Annie tried to stop her but it was no use she was gone.

Annie sat crying wondering what to do next. She had no idea where Violet would go – or what she would do.. She would give her time to calm down, and then ring her mobile. Then a thought struck her, what if she had gone to have it out with Jack. He needed to be warned. She rang Priory Hall. The switchboard couldn't find him anywhere. She couldn't leave it to chance; she grabbed her keys and set off to find Violet and Jack. Annie looked down every Side Street and alley that she passed looking for signs of Violet, but she was nowhere to be seen. She drove straight to Jack's accommodation and knocked on the door as if her life depended upon it. She could see a light on in the lounge. She peered through the window, but she couldn't see him. She banged again, this time harder, so hard she hurt the side of her hand. She rubbed it to try and take away some of the pain.

'Annie?' She heard a voice calling her from behind. It was Jack coming across the car park from the hotel. 'What are you doing here?'

'Have you seen Violet?' She asked with urgency.

'Annie you have to trust me! I promised that I …..'

'Stop Jack! – Just answer – have you seen her since you left me?'

'No – why? I'm sure she finished her shift a good while ago.'

'No, no, it's just.' She paused, unsure how to phrase it.

'She knows you are her biological father.'

'What? How? I've not said anything?' He was confused, but quietly comforted.

'I know you didn't - She found the letter. We left the house in a hurry to help Stan and I forgot to put it away! It's my own stupid silly fault and now she's run off and all upset and I don't know where she is or how to find her!' Annie was shaking, partly from fear of not knowing what Violet would do and partly because when she ran out of the house she forgot a coat.

'How did she take it?' He was concerned.

'How the fuck do you think she took it!! Her whole world has just been turned upside down. She's upset, mad, bewildered, confused and a thousand other nameable emotions -and she definitely doesn't want to speak to me!'

'What did she say?' He wanted to know all the details.

'Well, there were a few choice words, but basically I am a liar and a whore.'

'Come inside a moment, you're freezing out here.' She didn't argue. Once inside he went to find something to warm her up.

'Here.' He said passing her one of his jumpers. 'This will be too big for you but it's warm.'

'Thanks.' She said pulling it on, looking forward to its warmth.

'What do you want us to do next?' He asked expectantly.

'I don't know Jack! It's all such a great big shitty mess and I don't know what to do? I've been looking for her on my way here, but there's no sign of her – She may have got a bus to a friend's house. I rang her mobile, but of course she won't answer, it just goes to voice mail. Jack what have we done!'

'What's your best guess for where she'll go?'

'I don't know? Maybe a friend? Either from college or here?' She looked at him hoping he would have a magic answer.

'Do you have any phone numbers for any of her friends?' He was being logical and calm. Thank Christ someone was, it was what she needed.

'No I don't. She's only started college a few weeks ago, so I haven't even met any of them yet! I've no way to trace her.'

'Do you want me to check at the hotel if anyone has seen her?' Asked Jack.

She nodded in response.

'It's worth a try, because you're in the firing line as well. I think she'll come looking for you at some point. She's got it into her head that we were having an affair behind her dad's back. I tried to explain , but she was too upset to hear my words. 'Jack told her to stay where she was and get warm whilst he went across to the hotel to make some enquiries.

'Think of any other places she could be while I'm gone. There's a pad and pen in the desk write it down.' he shouted as he closed the door.

Jack swept through the hotel like professional detective, asking each member of staff if they had seen Violet in the last hour. Eventually he came across Nirah.

'I saw her with Harley.' She confessed. He was just going off duty.' Nirah hesitated. 'She looked quite upset, she wouldn't say why? I don't know where they went?'

'How long ago was this?' Jack demanded. Whatever Mr Parrish wanted Violet for it was important. Nirah thought it best not to stand in his way. 'Not long ago, about fifteen minutes.' Jack didn't thank her for the information he just ran off in the direction of the staff car park. Once outside he scoured the area for Harley's car. It was nowhere to be seen.

Annie was pacing up and down the lounge when he returned. 'Any news?' She asked as soon as she heard the door open.

'She went off with Harley not long ago. We don't know where she went.'

'Who the hell's Harley?' Asked Annie, stunned by the addition of this male to the scene.

'He's an employee. He works with Violet. I think they're quite friendly.'

'What do you mean quite friendly? And what's he like?' Annie was trying to get the measure of the man, trying to guess what they would do.

'I don't know him very well at all. He comes across as very sure of himself, lots of the female staff think he's very attractive. He's not the stay at home studious type, that's for sure and that's about all I know.' Annie didn't feel re-assured.

'What do you think I should do now? I can't think straight.' Asked Annie.

'Let's give her a little time to cool off. She has to come home some time. Why don't you leave another message on her phone, or text her. When she's had time to think she may answer one, even if you ring her just asking her to let you know she is safe and fine. At least we know who she's with and if she doesn't turn up in a few hours, I'll find out his address and we'll go and see if she's there?'

'Don't you think I should go there now?' Annie couldn't sit waiting doing nothing.

'Do you? Do you think she'll be in the mood to listen to you right now? Or do you think a little time may help?' Annie was torn. She knew Jack's words made sense. She knew dammed well Violet wouldn't listen at the moment, yet, she needed to see her and know she was safe. Annie hoped Violet may have even gone back home.

'Okay.' She eventually agreed 'I'll leave it a while to see if she calms down, but I don't think she will, I don't think I would if I was in her shoes. God I don't know what I would do.'

'You're still her Mum and she still loves you, she will come around in the end.' Jack's voice of reason was trying to keep her calm.

'Jack she hates me for lying to her. Nick and I thought we were doing the right thing at the time. Nick didn't want Violet to know he wasn't her biological Father; there seemed no reason to tell her. Nick had read the letter your father sent. Neither of us ever expected to see or hear from you again. That's why he was so upset when you came to my mum's house that time. We were both so shocked to see you. He thought his world was about to come crashing down around his ears. He thought you had come to snatch Violet.' Jack turned away hiding his face from Annie. If he had known then, what he knew now, he probably would have taken her and tried to take Annie too. The pain of that day was still strong for Jack, now magnified by the fact that he was never told the truth. Lies and circumstance had robbed him of his daughter; he understood the pain Violet must be going through. It's never good to find you've been living a lie your whole life, but now she knew the truth and maybe in time she would let him explain to her, the actions his father had taken to wreck their lives. Violet was still unaware of the full situation and the truth. The letter was a pack of lies. He had to find a way to get the truth to her as soon as possible. She needed to know that he never said he didn't want her or her Mother. Annie noticed a change in Jack.

'Are you alright? You seem upset?' It was the first time she had shown any real concern for him since their reunion.

'I'm just wondering what Violet will be thinking after reading that letter of lies. She's going to hate me even more. In her eyes I'm the one that left you and abandoned her to an unknown fate. Nick will be her hero even more now as he stepped in and saved the day!'

'I know it's hard for you too, but he already was her hero. That's the way little girls are with their dad's. I know now it wasn't your fault the way things turned out, but it's not her fault either. You can't make Nick into the villain, just because you didn't see eye to eye. You were both young and – well to be frank idiots!' Jack looked at her reproachfully. 'She's hopefully going to find room in her heart for both of you – it can be done – I did it.' The words were out before she had realised their implication. He was about to pick her up on it, but she was too quick for him.

'I need to go home and see if she's turned up there.' Annie headed for the door.

'I'll come with you.' He started to follow.

'No Jack I need to speak to her on my own. If she sees us together it's going to add fuel to the fire. I promise I'll ring you if I know anything.' Jack started to protest. Annie turned and touched his arm. It was the first time she had done so by choice.

'I understand you're worried too, but if she turns up and you are there, she's just going to run off again. I need to be on my own, that way she may stay and talk to me.' Annie could see the pain of helplessness in his face, she knew what it looked like, she was feeling it herself. She touched the side of his cheek with her hand. He felt that old buzz of electricity they used to share. Quickly he kissed her hand before she had time to move it. She flinched with shock, but didn't pull away. Annie was too concerned with finding Violet to hear the argument taking place between her heart and her head.

Chapter 22

Harley had his foot down to the floor on the accelerator pedal in the car. He didn't know what had happened to Violet, only that she was upset and desperate to get wasted in whichever way she could. He regarded it as both his civic duty and an opportunity to be her comforter, he was sure she would be grateful. She had already helped herself to the bottle of whiskey sat on the floor under a jacket in the back of the car. He drove to their usual spot overlooking the valley. Harley turned off his head lights and the engine, just leaving the ignition on enough to power the music. The Wanted rang out from the speakers. It was dark outside; lights pin pricked the view in sporadic bursts like hundreds of minute tares in a giant piece of dark fabric covering the sky. Violet watched the lights fading in and out with the movement of the trees. The bottle sat on her lap was already three quarters gone. She hated whiskey, it was leaving a burning sensation in her throat, but she needed something to destroy the new information that was already imprinted in her brain and playing constantly on a three minute loop.

'God I needed that.' She said as she released the bottle and passed it to Harley. He drank it like it was lemonade. 'How the hell do you do that – it burns!' She asked him.

'Don't you know? Practice makes perfect! Did you never listen at school?' He took another swig.

'I don't remember being taught drinking skills – maybe I was off that day! Have you anything else to drink?' Harley reached under his seat and pulled out a bottle of peach schnapps. Violet's face lit up.

'That's better! Something I can drink without burning my tonsils. Why didn't you tell me you had that before?'

'I was enjoying watching you struggle with the whiskey!'

'Bastard! You know I don't like it!'

'Yes, but look at it this way. You made me smile, watching you struggle with it and you're in a shitty mood, so serves you right!'

'Don't go there Harley! I don't want to talk about it!' She decided to distract him, 'You're right it has been a shit day and I need to forget everything and I was hoping you would help me to do that?' She reached across the handbrake and placed her hand in his groin. Harley almost choked on the whiskey he was swigging, not because he wasn't willing to participate in helping her forget whatever it was she was running from, but he was taken by surprise by her brazenness. It wasn't a tactic she had used before, but he liked it.

'Let's move into the back?' Violet suggested, 'There's more space for what I've got in mind!' she climbed over the seat and into the back with ease. Harley didn't argue. He was in the mood for whatever she had to offer. He followed her.

'God its cold in here without the heater on!' She complained.

'Here.' Harley passed her a blanket from the boot. Telling her it was one he kept one there for 'emergencies'.

'Oh ye! And do you have emergencies often?'

'Now and again. It's good to be prepared. I used to be a boy scout.' He lied.

'Now that I can't believe, but if you show me your woggle I might!' she kissed him again, but her teeth started to chatter with cold.I think we'll have to share body heat to survive.' He said as his fingers slipped between the gaps in her blouse, unfastening the buttons as he proceeded.

'You're right. I've heard it's what you do when you find yourself stranded in freezing conditions.' She added whilst helping him with his own buttons. Violet suddenly pulled back.

'I need more drink!' she demanded. He passed the bottle of schnapps back to her that he'd been holding whilst she climbed across the seat. She started to gulp it like she was in a drinking race. It was a mission to obliterate the details of the letter. She would drink anything and do anything until she forgot that she was Jack Parrish's love child.

Harley had no idea what had got into her. He was looking forward to sex which was a certainty, but he did prefer his conquests to be conscious. 'Hey, slow down Vi. There's no rush you know!' He pulled the bottle back so that he could have some more. It was his; it had been his neck on the line when he took it. Violet was dis-content, waiting to get her hands back on the bottle. She would have to try other methods.

'Have you got anything on you, you know – to smoke, and I don't mean cigarettes? The sooner I can't remember my name, the better.'

'I thought you didn't do that?' He was surprised by her request.

'Well, today I think I'll try anything!'

'Okay – If you're sure?' He pulled out a splif and lit it.

'Here – try it. This is quite a strong one though.' He passed it to her. She took a large drag on it and in hailed the smoke. Her lungs unused to being contaminated rebelled and spat it out; her chest was heaving leaving her choking on fresh air.

'You weren't kidding were you?' Laughed Harley. 'You really haven't done this before. Don't breath in so deep 'til you get used to it.' Violet did as she was instructed and waited for a change to take place within her. She didn't feel any different.'

'It's not working.' She took another drag.

'Give it time. It's not miraculous you know. You don't have one puff and it turns your world upside down.'

'I think I'll stick to the drink!' She said passing him the joint and taking another swig of the schnapps.

'What's with you today?' Harley's curiosity had got the better off him.

'Nothing – everything – I don't know! I don't want to talk about it. Kiss me again.' She pulled him forwards and wrapped her legs around his waist. 'Kiss me 'till I forget everything and when you've done that you can show me your woggle!'

There was no sign of Violet when Annie got back to the house. She checked the cupboards in her room, just to make sure she hadn't been back and cleared out her things whilst the flat was empty. Annie checked her phone again to make sure she didn't have a missed call – she didn't. She felt helpless. She didn't know what to do for the best. Should she wait a little longer or should she phone the police? Annie split her time between pacing and sitting. Every car that passed on the road, pulled her towards the window like a magnet, but each time the car passed without stopping, shattering her hopes that Violet would come home. At ten she decided to text Violet again, it read –*text to let me know you are fine or I'm ringing the police! I love you. Mum xxx.* Annie waited impatiently for a reply. Eventually it came. It was very short and to the point. It read –'Go *to hell!!'* At least she was alive and well somewhere. Annie could breathe at last. There was nothing for it but to wait it out. Violet would come home when she was ready and not a moment before. She was probably staying with this 'Harley' person. At least she wasn't on her own. She hoped he was sensible and looking after her.

Jack had been doing his fair share of pacing too. He understood why Annie wanted to speak to Violet alone, but keeping out of the way was against his nature. He longed to be there to see what was happening, as it was, he could only wait to be informed from Annie, should anything happen. He looked out of the window. As expected there was no sign of her. The cars were beginning to frost over lightly. Jack liked winter, there was no dramatic change in the Australian weather, yes it was cooler, but the changes were more subtle. He missed knowing the season, from just stepping out of the door. It was late when Annie rang to tell him that Violet had been in touch. He could hear the relief in her voice. He offered again to go and sit and wait with her, but Annie told him she didn't hold out much hope that Violet would come home tonight. The conversation ended with them both promising to keep in touch if the situation changed in any way. Jack waited for the phone to ring again, but it didn't. He couldn't sleep, so he settled for the late films on the TV, hoping they would at least give him some distraction from the worry.

Jack awoke to loud banging. He was disorientated; he had fallen asleep on the sofa, whilst watching the film. It took a moment for him to realise where the banging was coming from – it was his front door. The banging became louder and he could hear shouting. On opening the door he found Violet leaning against the wall, looking more than worse for wear still holding a bottle of booze – this time it was vodka.

'Well - Hello - 'Daddy'! Surprise! It's your long lost daughter here'. I'm sorry my mother didn't have me aborted! I'm sure from the wonderfully caring letter, you got your father to write, it's what you would have preferred!! So here I am. The mistake that was never supposed to happen! Her vicious words cut him to the core. He wanted to shout the truth at her, but she was too drunk, in the morning she wouldn't remember. It was better to wait and speak to her when she had sobered up.

'Violet, come inside where it's warmer.' He opened the door wide for her to come in. She was too drunk to move. Jack grabbed her arm to help her inside.

'Get your fucking hands off me Mr Peeeeeeee……' She screamed. He let go of her arm.

'Violet come inside! Let me ring your mum. She's very worried about you!'

'The only thing she's worried about is that her sordid little secret has come out. What's it like having a bastard daughter? Are you pleased with what you got or am I a disappointment to you?' Violet goaded.

'Violet you're too drunk to have a serious conversation with at the moment. When you're sober we can…'

'We can what! Play happy families? You me and Mum, all together and let's forget Nick – My father. Nick! Nick! Nick! He is my father and always will be. You never will. So why don't you fuck off back to Australia 'cause I don't want you, Mum doesn't want you and we never will!' She tried to stand alone without the support of the wall to leave, but she stumbled. Jack put his hand out and stopped her from falling.

'I've told you before, take your bloody hands off me now!' Her words were scathing and final. He stood back, not knowing which course of action was best. If he had been her father in the real sense of the word and on an everyday basis, he would have picked her up and tucked her under his arm and marched her inside, but at this moment he didn't have the right or the courage to do that.

'Okay.' He called after her. 'If you are leaving then let me drive you home to your Mum. She needs to talk to you Violet. She's very upset, she loves you.'

'Ahh, poor mummy. Does she need to confess all her lies? Well it's too late! I don't care anymore! – and I've got a lift thanks 'Dad'!' each of her words stung him like nettles on the leg of a small child. In the days when he had longed to know if he had a child, he never dreamed that in their first meeting the word 'dad', would be used as a weapon. Violet made her way towards a car in the distance, he recognised it as Harley's, the engine was running ready for a quick getaway. Her feet were unsteady and her movements erratic. Jack decided to follow her we was worried for her safety, he also wanted to have another go at talking some sense in to her. His feet were bare. He quickly grabbed his trainers then ran to catch her up. She was already in the car and about to close the door.

'Violet!' He shouted as he approached the car. Violet showed him the finger as she shut and locked the door. Jack ran round to the driver's side.

'Harley! Open the window.' Jack banged on the window. Harley wound it down a fraction.

'Where are you taking Violet? You should take her home!' He wanted to be sure she was safe.

'Mr P. – I'll take her where ever she wants to go!' Jack knew enough of the world to know that Harley was high on either drugs or alcohol or both.

'Harley turn off the engine now!' Jack was shouting trying to get his point across.

'Mr P. I'm not in work if you haven't noticed, so I think it's probably best if you go screw yourself!' Harley laughed as if he had said the funniest thing in the world then drove away, kicking up a shower of gravel as he left. Jack raced back into the house to grab his car keys and his phone. He couldn't leave Violet with Harley, the state they were in they would end up with the car wrapped around a tree. He would never forgive himself if anything happened to her - and neither would

Annie.

Jack took the road into town. He had made sure to watch which direction Harley went in when he pulled out of the gates, the noise of the engine alone would give them away, it was enough to waken the dead. The roads were dark and winding with ditches on either side. Side roads were few and far between, so it was relatively easy to guess their route. Large elderly trees guarded the fields, over hanging and gently teasing the cars as they passed. Street lights were non-existent. To drive safely on these roads, you had to have your wits about you. He drove as fast as he could through the darkness. He had to catch them before any ill befell them. Jack was on one of the narrow stretches. He could see some tail lights in the distance. They disappeared around a bend. He was sure it was Harley and Violet. He put his foot a little harder to the floor, increasing speed in order to catch them up. His phone began to ring. It was on the seat next to him. He looked down to see who it was – it was Annie. He reached for the phone taking his eyes off the road momentarily.

Jack didn't see the car coming in the opposite direction towards him. It was going too fast for the conditions of the road and sped out of control as it hit a patch of black ice coming round the corner. The oncoming driver slammed on his brakes. Jack looked up to see the headlights coming towards him. It was too little, too late. The two cars collided head on, sending Jack and his car into a spin. The tyre hit the side of the kerb, his car rolled and landed in the ditch. Then there was silence except for the ringing of Jack's phone.

When the phone rang at two a.m. Annie's heart leapt, at last Violet was ringing at last, but she was wrong. It was the police, ringing her on Jack's mobile, one of the fire brigade had found it, when they were cutting him free from the wreckage. The local policeman, who had been first on the scene, re-dialled the last number showing on the phone – it was Annie's. The policeman's words had been brief but precise. Jack had been in a serious car crash and taken to Preston Hospital – in the policeman's words –'He's a very poorly man, but he was still breathing when the ambulance took him away.' Annie wanted to scream at the thought of history repeating itself. How could God be so cruel to Violet? She was torn, She wanted to go to Jack, after all, there was no one with him and what if the worst thing did happen? What if he died all alone in the hospital? She couldn't live with that on her conscious, but what if Violet came home to find an empty house. She sat like a stunned animal for a few minutes, not knowing which way to turn, tearing herself apart, before she eventually reasoned that as far as she knew, Violet was safe and well and the likely hood of her returning in the middle of the night was slim. She forged a plan. She would text Violet when she knew more. There was nothing she could do for Violet at this point in time – but she may be able to help Jack.

Annie pulled the car on to the car park in front of the hospital A&E. department. The mere sight of the sign for A&E brought back unwanted memories of Nick's accident. She couldn't believe this was her second visit here within 24 hours. Just a few hours previously it had been Jack consoling her and Stan, now she was unsure of what she would find once she walked through the doors. She tried to remind herself that this was different to Mrs Stretford. Jack was young and healthy; both things would be bound to work in his favour. She sat in her car for a moment, collecting her thoughts and courage. Last week she would have been glad to see the back of Jack. There was no place for him in their lives, but now Violet and Jack knew her secret, it seemed cruel to think he may die before Violet had time to know him. Losing one Dad is bad enough, but two, would be unbearable. As she walked across the car park she considered how accidents and disasters had a way of putting things into perspective, which normal events can't. Annie didn't even know if they would let her see Jack. She wasn't family. He had no family over here that she knew of, surely they would let someone see him, they wouldn't leave him all alone? The thought that he might die alone and without her having the chance to tell him that she still loved him was almost too much to bear. She shook her head to dispel the thought. She followed the signs to the accident and emergency reception desk and gave the woman Jack's name.

'Are you a relative?' Came the expected question. Before she gave herself time to think she answered.

'Yes – I'm his partner.' She didn't care that it was a lie. There was no way she was going to leave him there all by himself, thinking that she didn't care – she did. More than she was prepared to admit to even herself.

'Just wait here please.' The woman directed Annie to sit on one of the waiting room chairs. Annie chose the same chair she had used when she came with Jack on the previous afternoon. The fact that they made her wait made her even more distraught, it wasn't a good sign. Maybe she was too late? Maybe he had been dead on arrival? Maybe she was going to have to bury another man that she had loved? - Did love? God she didn't know what she was feeling, she just knew he couldn't die. Her train of thought was interrupted by the voice of the receptionist.

'They've taken him through to the intensive care unit. If you go up the corridor to the left and follow the signs.' Annie was already out of her seat and on her way before the sentence was finished. 'Thank God' he was still alive. That was one prayer answered, but she still had a long list pending. The corridors seemed endless; each one looking identical to the last and nothing to help distinguish between them, finally the signs brought her to her destination. When she asked for Jack at the reception, she was again told to wait.

'He's only just arrived with us.' Reassured the nurse. 'The doctor is with him and we are trying to make him as comfortable as possible. It's best to let them get on with the important stuff at the moment. I'll let you know when there's any news and when you are able to go in.' Again she was directed to a chair.

'But I need to see him!' Annie's voice indicated her desperation. She grabbed the nurse's hand. 'I really need to see him, to tell him...' The nurse patted the top of Annie's hand.

''I Know, but it's not about what you need at the moment, it's what he needs and he needs the doctors to assess him and make sure he is getting the right care. I promise, as soon as they have finished and he's settled I'll call you in.' Annie knew the nurse was right. She nodded and released her grip on the nurse's hand, showing submission to the nurse that she had resigned herself to waiting. She sat impatiently on the chair staring at the notice board, yet reading nothing. Her thoughts swung like a pendulum between Violet and Jack, she was worried for both of them, but for different reasons. She was afraid of losing Violets love and afraid that Jack would lose his life. At least Violet was safe and well. She tried her best to concentrate on the positive. Annie contemplated whether or not she should text Violet to inform her of Jack's accident. It wasn't something she would normally text, but the chances of Violet answering her phone were slim to none existent. If Annie withheld the information, she was taking away Violet's choice of coming to see Jack. God forbid, it may be her last chance. Annie decided to try ringing first, but as expected there was no response. So against her better judgement, Annie texted the upsetting news to Violet.

After an hour of waiting, Annie went to find coffee from one of the vending machines. She didn't really want it; it was just something to do to pass the time. The base of her spine was beginning to ache from sitting for too long on the hard plastic chair, stretching her legs seemed an obvious way to relieve it. When she returned, one of the nurses was looking for her.

'The doctor says you can go in to see him for a few minutes.' The nurse led the way, talking as they were walking through the corridors. 'He is sedated and he needs a little help breathing at the moment, so he's on a ventilator. He has a broken leg, three broken ribs, he's unconscious and there is some internal bleeding on his brain, but at the moment we don't know how severe it is or how much damage has been caused. He is very poorly and the next forty eight hours are critical – but we have him settled now and this is the best place for him. We will do everything in our power to help him recover.'

The nurse paused outside his room. 'I have to warn you that there are lots of tubes and machines in intensive care, only I don't want you to get too overwhelmed, it can be daunting with them bleeping every few minutes.'

'I have actually spent more time than I would like to admit in intensive care units. My late husband was in a car crash. I'm sad to say I know what to expect.' The nurse placed her hand on Annie's shoulder.

'Let's hope and pray that this time we have a different outcome for you.' The nurse opened the door to reveal Jack and his machines. There were two beds in the room and a nurse's station. Jack was in one bed and the second bed was empty. The nurse encouraged Annie to move forward, pushing her slightly like a child being coaxed into class on the first day of school.

'It'll be alright.' Said the nurse, 'Just talk to him as normally as you can. We're not sure exactly how much he can hear, but it all helps. I'll leave you to it.' Annie edged nearer the bed. It was hard to recognise Jack at first under all the tubes and wires. His face was battered and bruised, lower down on his body, his arms and chest bore the marks of the impact. His body was limp and listless. He was completely oblivious to his surroundings and the worry he was causing everyone.

Annie placed her exhausted body into a chair that had already been positioned by the side of Jack's bed. She wanted to reach out and touch him, but at the same time she was unsure that she should. She hadn't read the book on etiquette of how to behave when the father of your child, but not someone you are in a relationship with, is in hospital very ill and she was afraid of disturbing the tubes and wires keeping him alive. Eventually courage came to her; she reached across the bed and took his hand, being careful not to move the machine checking his pulse, which was clipped on to his finger. He showed no signs of responding when she touched him. Gently she stroked the back of his hand, hoping to invoke some reaction, either large or small; at this point in time she would take any sign of life. Annie decided to try using her voice, to see if it would cause any reaction.

'Jack. –Jack its Annie – I don't know if you can hear me? You've had an accident and you are in hospital, but you are going to be okay. You just need to fight and get better.' She felt silly, her words felt strained and un-natural as if she were speaking to a stranger – and yet only part of him was a stranger to her, the modern man that she hadn't seen for many years, but at his core, even though he was lying unconscious, she could still feel his essence. The time they had spent together over the past couple of weeks had led her to consider the possibility that he was still the same man she had fallen in love with all those years ago. She sensed it was the right time to tell him how she felt, especially as he was unconscious. She needed to be truthful; at the very least she owed him that, before it was too late to tell him anything. It was like telling a secret to a deaf man – it was safe.

She turned to check that they were alone. She didn't want anyone to hear other than Jack what she was about to admit – and part of her hoped that when he work up, he wouldn't remember her words, but non the less she had to say them. The nurse had left her post for a moment, as if on cue, he was all hers. She shuffled the chair a little closer to the bed.

'I don't know where to begin Jack. I would never have believed that our paths would cross like this. I didn't bargain for all the hospital visiting needed, being in your company, they're going to give me my own chair if I'm not careful, being here two days on the trot.' She turned to check they were still alone, 'Jack, I'm so sorry that you missed out on Violet's life growing up - and I'm sorry I blamed you for abandoning us when it was all down to that stupid, miss-guided man who called himself your father. When I received the letter saying you didn't want anything to do with me ever again my world fell apart.' Tears dripped from Annie's cheeks. 'I couldn't believe that you didn't love me anymore, but after time and not hearing from you, I started to believe it and I'm ashamed to say I started to hate you for letting us down. I saw the hurt in your eyes the day you found Nick and I had married. I knew at that moment that you still loved me, which is why it was so hard for me to watch you walk away. Nick and I did grow to love each other, but it was a different kind of love from the love we had. He was a good man and a good father to Violet. You have a lot to thank him for. Violet was his world, he kept her safe and she was loved beyond measure. When he died my world crumbled again, and I had resigned myself to living a small quiet life with Violet and to be content with her being the centre of my world – then without warning, you came crashing into my life turning every truth as I understood it upside down and inside out. They were words I didn't want to hear. I had spent so many years hating your actions; it was hard for me to admit that I might have been wrong. You know what they say about love and hate Jack – Two sides of the same coin- it's true. When the phone rang to say you'd been in an accident it made everything clear for me.' She paused and took a breath knowing that once said, these words could not be undone. Even if Jack didn't hear them she couldn't deny the truth to herself any longer. '– I love you Jack. I always have, somewhere buried deep away. So you had better start fighting to get better 'cause I'm not going to lose you again Jack Parrish!' There she'd said it, the truth was out there. She felt strangely liberated, they were words she had been afraid to say and now she found that a great weight had lifted from her. She didn't know if Jack had heard, if he did, he made no visible sign.

The nurse breezed through the double doors. 'The doctor will be back to see Jack shortly. Why don't you go and get a drink and stretch your legs, I'll call you back in when the he's finished?'

Annie wandered out to the waiting room feeling like a spare part. She didn't want to leave Jack, yet she still hadn't managed to speak to Violet. Annie wondered what state of mind she was in and where she had spent the night. More than anything, she wanted to give Violet a hug and tell her everything would be alright, as much for her own sake as Violets. Annie made her way out to the front entrance to get a little fresh air. It suddenly dawned on Annie that no-one had told Scarlett or anyone at Priory Hall – or Jack's mother. Annie didn't know what to do. Should she ring Australia and worry his mother? She had her address and telephone number from the flowers' Jack had sent her. Annie thought how she would feel in that situation and she would want to know – but, Annie was unsure of their relationship now, after John Parrish had betrayed his son, would she be doing the wrong thing? It wasn't something she and Jack had got around to discussing. Annie decided to ring Scarlett, to tell her about Jack's accident, from that point on Annie would let the company decide if Marcia Parrish should be informed. It was 6.30 A.M., if Scarlett wasn't on duty now, they would be able to find her, after all, it was an emergency, Annie rang Priory Hall.

Scarlett was shocked at the news; she hadn't had cause to miss Jack yet, as he wasn't due on duty until later. 'I'm sure the company will want us to contact Mrs Parrish. I'll get on to it straight away and when that's sorted; I'll come down to the hospital. I'll be as quick as I can!' Scarlett assured.

'I don't mean to put you off Scarlett, but there're not letting anyone in to see him, so you would only be sitting in the corridor with me. Why don't I ring you when I know something?' Annie was definite in her tone.

'–but Annie I don't want to leave you there on your own? After all, I don't mean to be insensitive, but he's not your responsibility.' Annie fell silent on the end of the phone.

'Annie? Are you still there?' Asked Scarlett, afraid that she had upset Annie.

'Yes. I'm here – I know I'm not responsible for him, but in case you hadn't worked it out yet, Jack is Violet's father and because of that I think I should be here.' Scarlett's jaw dropped as if the hinge had gone, it was a good job Annie was on the end of the phone and not face to face, as swiftly as she could she covered her tracks.

'Really? I didn't know. I'm sorry. I didn't mean...'

'Look Scarlett, its fine. Jack didn't know for sure until yesterday and Violet only found out then too, but I would appreciate it if you kept it to yourself at the moment, life is tough enough for Violet I don't want people making it worse for her?'

'My lips are sealed Annie, but I still want to support you?'

'Look the doctors are in with Jack now. There's no point both of us sitting here. I'll ring you when I know anything and maybe you can come up later – Oh, and if you see Violet – please will you ask her to ring me, as you can imagine, I'm not her favourite person at the moment.'

'She'll come round. I'm sure. I'll tell her if I see her.' Scarlett hung up.

The clock hands ticked by at a snail's pace as Annie waited for news, trying to keep her mind occupied; Annie turned her attention to the next problem on her list and rang Pippa. She explained the situation and asked her if there was any possibility of her looking after the shop for the day and possibly longer, depending on how things went. It was only when Pippa answered in a very sleepy voice that Annie realised it was still very early in the morning. Annie apologised for the early call, but Pippa didn't mind in the least when she had heard Annie's news.

'What about taking the children to school and picking them up?' Asked Annie, 'will that be a problem?' Pippa hesitated ever so slightly.

'Well, Zach is here. I'm sure he'll take them and pick them up, if I ask him.' Annie could tell by her tone that Pippa was smiling.

'Oh, that's good.' Said Annie delighted that they had finally got together. Pippa was as usual a great strength, reassuring Annie and telling her to do what she needed and not to give the shop another thought. Annie also told Pippa the sad news about Mrs Stretford and their dash to hospital the previous day.

'I'm worried that he may be on his own. I was going to pop in today and see how he was, but I don't think I'm going to get away from here.' Confessed Annie. Pippa promised she would pop round to see how Stan was doing and to do anything she could to help and that she was sure Zach knew Stan, between them, they would see he had all the help he needed.

'You're a God send.' said Annie 'I don't know what I would have done without you!'

'It's just what friends do.' Said Pippa modestly.

It was seven fifteen in the morning before the doctors came out of Jack's room. Annie stood up, as if she were appearing in court as they made their way towards her.

'Mrs Parrish?' The older doctor asked.

'Eh, no, it's Pickering – we're not married.' Her deceit seemed to be back firing on her.

'Well, Miss Pickering. Mr Parrish is stable for the moment. As you know we have found some bleeding in the brain which is a concern. We are keeping him sedated for the next few hours so that his body can try to repair itself. He has a good few injuries to overcome, mostly bumps and bruises and a couple of fractured ribs, a few broken bones, but it's his brain we are most concerned about. We won't know the full extent of the damage until we try to bring him round. I'm sorry I can't be more reassuring.' Alarm bells started to ring in Annie's head. These words were familiar; she had been told similar phrases when she was at Nick's bedside. 'What do you mean 'damage'?'

'I mean that we have to consider the possibility of Mr Parrish suffering brain damage as a result of the crash. He hasn't been conscious since it happened, so until we wake him, we can't be sure.' The doctor seemed to be handling this news in his stride – Annie was not. The thought of brain damage hadn't even entered her head. She knew Jack well enough to know how frustrating he would find life if he had lost his independence, but this was all conjecture – no point dwelling on things that hadn't yet been confirmed.

'We'll know more when we wake him. Until then, let's just hope for the best and pray.' The doctor may have thought he was delivering words of solace, but he would have got the same effect had he slapped her across the face. Annie tried to hide the extent of her devastation.

'Can I go back in to sit with him?' She asked hopefully, not wanting to prolong her conversation with the doctor when she wanted to be with Jack.

'Yes. That's fine. Just don't expect too much at this point in time. Remember he is sedated.' Annie knew all about not expecting too much when she had lived through the horror of watching Nick linger and eventually die.

Annie could tell that Jack hadn't moved an inch when she returned to his bed side, no wrestles fidgeting or involuntary movements. The tubes and machines still dominated the area around his bed, overshadowing him like some mechanical monster in an old black and white movie. Her seat was waiting for her; she sat down and resumed her position. The time dragged with no one to talk to and nothing to stimulate her to keep her awake except for the coffee. Her mind wandered amidst the bleeps and vibrations of the machines in the room. Nothing in her life had ever been straight forward and simple. It seemed that Annie's path through life was littered with mountains to climb and swollen rivers to cross. She wondered if things would ever go her way. More than anything she wanted Jack to pull through and survive this latest test in one piece, but what then? What did she want from him, if anything and what would he expect from her?

Chapter 23

Violet was woken by the feeling of something fury crawling around the inside of her mouth, it felt as rancid as a three week old kebab. A vow of never drinking again popped into her head. She dismissed it before it had time to take root. She had no idea where she was or even what day it was. She squinted trying to focus her eyes, to see if she could recognise her surroundings. The light shone in through the aged red and grey stripped curtains of yester year, giving her just enough light to make out the silhouette of Harley, sprawled out on the bed, naked, next to her. He was dead to the world and showed no sign of life. She pushed him to the side of the bed to free a sheet to wrap around herself. She stood up too quickly for her body to cope with, then swiftly sat back down on the edge of the bed to stop the room spinning and her head imploding from the pain of her brain bouncing against the inside of her skull. She urgently needed water. It took her ten minutes to slowly get up from the dishevelled bed and make her way in to the kitchen. Violet couldn't remember which door led to the kitchen, so she opened each one she passed. The first two were the lounge and one of the bedrooms belonging to another student, luckily they were out. It was at the third door she struck lucky and found the kitchen. Violet poured herself a large glass of water from the tap, and then drank it in one large satisfying gulp. She re-filled the glass and took it into the main shared lounge, looking for somewhere to sit and rest her head. She curled up in the corner of the dirty, well-worn sofa staring into space, trying to remember everything that had happened the day before. Some of it was Chrystal clear, like finding the letter, but some of it was a definite blur. She had a vague recollection of shouting at Jack Parrish, but she wasn't sure if it really happened or if it was a dream? Hopefully Harley would know when he finally woke up. On the side table, in between the empty beer bottles and shot glasses sat Violet's phone. She didn't remember leaving it there, but that was no great surprise. A list of eight missed texts and voicemails from her mum came on to the screen. A fragment of Violet's conscious was remorseful for the way she had treated her mum, but not enough for her to make her phone her. Violet scrolled though the texts reading each in detail, as the events of the previous night had unfolded, jolting her memory.

The fifth text was completely different to all the others. It contained the news that Jack had been in a car crash and that her mum was on her way to the hospital. Violet didn't think it had been anything to do with her, she remembered screaming at Jack, but she wasn't in a car or was she, there was a vague recollection of Jack banging his fists against a car window. Surely she would have remembered if she'd been involved in any way?

Violet didn't know if she felt relieved or saddened by the news. He was still a stranger to her. She felt as she might when watching the news and some tragedy befalls someone you've never even met or heard of before. You feel sorry for them, but in reality it has little or no impact on your life on a daily basis. However, she couldn't help being pulled back in time to when her father had died. She remembered being kept away from the hospital because her mother felt it would be too traumatic for her to go through. She had never been given the opportunity to say goodbye, it was something that she had always regretted, and whilst she understood her mum's motives, there was a small part of her that felt guilty for not being there when her dad needed her. For a second Violet compared the two situations, but it wasn't the same. Nick was her dad – Jack was just some man who slept with her mum. She felt no need to rush to the hospital - well not for his sake. Violet closed her eyes and willed her body to repair itself. Her extreme hangover did nothing to help her confusion; her emotions were all over the place. She didn't want to see Jack, but she didn't know how seriously he had been hurt – he may die? What if history repeated itself? She wanted to ditch her mother after all the lies she had told. It was her mess , she could clean it up, but no matter how cross she was with her, she still loved her and knew how hard it would be for her to sit by a hospital bed waiting for news again. It wasn't a case of sleep on it and everything will be fine in the morning – it wouldn't be!

Violet scrolled on to the next message from her mum, explaining how sorry she was about everything and how severe Jack's injuries were and the next and the next, all begging her to get in contact and let Annie know she was alright. Violet could feel the sorrow and despair in Annie's words. It took about half an hour for Violet to put her pride and feelings to one side and ring her mother, she had lots of questions that needed to be answered and only her mother knew the answers. Violet knew she wouldn't be able to answer her phone in the hospital so she sent her a text which simply read – *ring me*. Ten minutes later Violet's phone rang.

'It's me.' Annie said simply, not knowing what sort of reception to expect.

'Where are you?' Violet asked coldly.

'I'm at the hospital. I got your text so I came outside to ring you. I was so glad to hear from you - Violet – How are you? We need to talk don't we?' Said Annie hoping she had had enough time to calm down enough to talk reasonably.

'Suppose.' Answered Violet in a non-committed tone, 'What happened to Jack? Are they keeping him in?' Annie almost laughed at her daughter's innocence over the gravity of his situation.

'Yes they are keeping him in. He's in intensive care Violet. It was a bad crash and he's not in a very good way. Do you want to see him?' The question was too direct, Violet felt backed into a corner. 'What do I want to see that bastard for? What has he ever done for me? He wanted rid of me even before I was born! Well now I want rid of him!"

'Violet that's not true. You don't mean that. Look the best thing is for us to get together and talk – face to face.' Annie decided she needed to lay it on the line. After all violet had insisted she hated being lied to, so if she wanted to be a grown up, she had to deal with grown up decisions.

'You can either come here or I'll come to you – but before you make your choice, Jack has no-one here with him – only me. He has no other family in this country and he is unconscious and may have brain damage. It's too early to tell, so if you want to see Jack at all, now might be the best time, because frankly Violet, I don't know what will happen to him!' Annie's voice was broken and emotional; the lack of sleep was beginning to show. '–and in truth Violet. I need you. I love you and I want you with me. I hate us not talking and yes there are plenty of things I need to explain to you. What do you say?' It was the first time Violet had ever known her mother to ask her to be there for her. Even through her father's death, her mum was always the strong one, the one everyone else leaned on. Violet wasn't happy about the situation, but she couldn't refuse her.

'Do I have to see him?!' She hissed.

'No – you don't. Visitors are at a minimum. There's a relatives room we can sit in to talk.'

'Okay, but I'm doing this for you - not him. I hope you understand that. It's you I care about – not him. I'll get there when I can.'

Violet sat for a moment contemplating if she was doing the right thing, but how was she supposed to know what the right thing was? She didn't know, she went to wake Harley to ask him for a lift.

'Christ Violet, I'm not getting up now. It's only eleven o'clock – get a taxi if it's that fucking important!'

'..But it's important Harley! Jack's had an accident and my mum needs me. She decided to tell him the truth and the reason behind her wildness the night before, it was a secret she had guarded preciously until now. 'Jack Parrish is, well – he is my father and I've only just found out. I have to get there for my mother's sake.' Her confession brought no response from Harley who was more interested in getting back to sleep.

'Surely you could run me down there. It won't take you long? You can come back to bed after.' She jumped on the bed and tried to kiss him, hoping he would change his mind. He pushed her away.

'I'm not your bloody chauffeur Violet! Sort it yourself! He wasn't your fucking father yesterday, all the things you called him!'

'It's mum I'm going for, not him. Oh go on! I'll make it worth your while later?' Violet grabbed at him under the bed clothes. He slapped her hand away.

'You're not that good Violet! Nothing happened last night that makes me want to go back to you for more! Now piss off and leave me to sleep.' Violet was hurt by his comments. He hadn't made any complaints in the night.

'Shit-head!' She shouted at him at the same time as throwing the left over water in her glass over him.'

'You bitch! You're a fucking nut case!' He shouted at her. If she had been near enough she was sure he would have struck her. Violet grabbed her clothes and took them into the bathroom to get dressed. Harley shouted after her.

'Take everything with you, cause you ain't coming back here. You're no pissing fun! You're a crap fuck and a lush! – And you owe me for the booze!'

In the end Violet decided to walk to the hospital. It was only about a mile from Harley's place. The weather was cold and fresh. She didn't know the bus times or the routes they took and she didn't have much cash on her, besides the longer it took her to get there the better. She needed time to sober up. The overnight frost had been dissolved by the winter sun which was shining through. Violet hoped the fresh air would clear her hangover and her mood. She wondered what she had ever seen in Harley, he may have the looks, but the personality was non-existent. The girls at work were right when they warned her about him. She made a note to self that next time she would listen to what her friends had to say.

Violet found her way to the hospital more speedily than she hoped. As she went into the front entrance she texted her mum to tell her she'd arrived. Violet spotted the café. She dug deep in to her pockets looking for enough money to buy two coffees. It was close, she only had ten pence spare. Violet sat at a table nursing her coffee and waiting for Annie to come down from the ward. Ten minutes later Annie appeared. Violet passed her the tepid coffee.

'It might be cold now, thought you might need it.' Annie smiled at Violet in that motherly way, her face showing the pride she was feeling at having a thoughtful daughter.

'What?' Asked Violet, sensing there was an underlying conversation going on without a spoken word?

'Nothing?' Said Annie. 'Come on, there's a relatives room. We can go and talk there without people listening in.' Violet followed Annie through the corridors passing all manner of ailments and illnesses. Violet hated hospitals every bit as much as her mother. They had only ever brought her grief and sadness.

The visitor's room was close to intensive care. Annie told the nurse on duty, where they were should Jack's situation change. The nurse asked who violet was, clearly wanting to keep visitors at a minimum. Annie introduced her only as 'my daughter', she didn't let slip that it was her 'daughter's' father in the intensive care bed nearby.

Annie closed the door to the relative's room. They were alone; at last Annie was going to be able to explain the truth to Violet – as long as Violet would listen. Annie followed Violet and sat on the sofa next to her. She took Violet's hand in hers.

'Firstly, I want to say that I love you very much and always have and anything I-we, that is your dad and I have done in the past is to protect you. I know you don't see that at the moment, but I hope in time you will.' Violet was sitting tight lipped listening but being firmly uncommitted to any conversation her mother may suggest.

'Will you let me tell you everything that happened before you judge me and your dad?' Violet's vow of silence erupted.

'But that's the whole point. He wasn't my father! You lied to me for all those years! He lied to me too! How can I trust anything you say now?'

'I understand, I'm asking a lot of you, to listen and accept what I tell you, but there are reasons. Let me explain and if you still feel the same, well, I'm going to have to deal with that.' Violet nodded her silent agreement to listen to the explanation.

It took Annie over an hour to explain and answer all of Violet's burning questions. Some of them were very difficult to answer, requiring Annie to honestly question her own motives and why Nick had been so keen to keep everything a secret. Then she explained how Jack had been totally unaware of Annie's pregnancy until he found the hidden letters in his father's office. Violet needed clarification.

'Are you telling me that Jack didn't know I existed?'

'He had no idea about any of it. There were no mobile phones or internet in our day, God I sound old now don't I! All we had was letters and a land line, but calling Australia cost an arm and a leg. We were both students and broke, so our only means of communication was by letter – Jack only found out for sure yesterday that you were his daughter. This has been a shock for him as well.'

'But that letter said....'

'The letter that you read was a lie! They were not Jack's thoughts and feelings. He has spent years looking for us, hoping to find us and then fate intervened and we showed up on his doorstep. I only found out yesterday myself that the letter was a complete lie. I'm still trying to get my head around it too. Maybe it's time for the truth to come out, but don't blame him Violet. I've spent years hating him and blaming him for leaving us, but now I know the truth and the only person responsible is Jack's father and if you still feel you have to blame someone – blame him.'

'Did you love Jack?' Violet wanted a direct answer. It was no time for half-truths.

'Yes. I did love him. That's one thing I'm not ashamed of, the fact that you were born out of our love and as we're talking truthfully, that's why I went through with the pregnancy on my own. I couldn't abort the child of the man I loved.'

'But why did you marry dad when you loved someone else? It makes our whole lives a lie! How did he bear it, knowing you wanted to be with someone else?'

'It wasn't a lie! I didn't want to be with someone else. I loved Nick. I still love Nick. I didn't marry him out of pity or so you would have a name and be respectable. I married him because I loved him. It wasn't an immediate thing, over time we grew close and I could see what a good man he was. He loved us both and wanted to build a family together. It was a marriage based on love Violet – not convenience! - And the letter you saw, well any respect and feelings that I had for Jack went the moment that letter arrived. My feelings for Jack were long gone by the time I married Nick. Violet I don't want to play the 'I'm older and know better' card on you, but in life you will find that things are usually a lot more complicated than they look at face value. There are all kinds of 'love'. Nick loved you as his own daughter; to him you were his and no one else's. We did the best we could to bring you up in a loving home and if you can't see that, well then, we must have done a crap job!'

Violet sat silently gathering her thoughts. There was so much new information to process. The pair sat in silence. Annie stared out of the window wondering if she should go back to Jack or stay with violet. She hated being torn in two directions. Why couldn't life be simple?

Violet gave great thought to her mother's words. She had been loved, she knew that, but it was the lies she hated. Her centre point of gravity had been shaken and now she didn't know where it was, who she was. Violet couldn't help but think of moment's in her life when Nick had called her his 'special girl' and she did feel special and loved, now she had to work out if she believed him.

Annie couldn't bear the silence any longer and announced that she was going to sit with Jack. 'Would you like to come with me?' She asked Violet in a voice that was expecting rejection.

'Mum – I don't think I can. All this is reminding me too much of da...' she stopped unsure if she was still entitled to use the word.

'Violet you can say 'dad'. Nick was your father in every sense of the word except biologically. He paced the floor with you when you were teething, he taught you to swim and to ride your bike. He scolded you for not doing your homework and loved you as much as any man could love his daughter and he did all this knowing he was not your biological father. It didn't make a difference to Nick and I hope you can see past the biology lesson and love him for who he was regardless of whose blood runs through your veins. It didn't make a difference to him and it shouldn't make a difference to you. He chose to love us, without any strings – unconditionally – and nothing can ever change that or take that away from us.' Violet broke down in to tears, swiftly followed by Annie. Annie moved across towards Violet and enveloping her in her arms. They hugged without speaking until all their tears were spent. It was Annie who spoke first.

'Right, I'm going to see how Jack is doing. It's up to you if you come with me or stay here?'

Violet thought about the way she had spoken to Jack the night before- what little she could remember of it. She knew it wasn't pleasant. Now she was even more confused. It was her mum who had lied. Jack was almost an innocent bystander in all the events, if what she had been told was true. How could she blame him if he had been treated as she had and kept from the truth?

'Mum, I can't just forget Nick and start thinking of Jack as my father. Whether he knew or not – he wasn't there. He doesn't know me and I don't know him!'

'That's true' Said Annie agreeing with her daughter 'but I know Jack and he's not trying to take Nick's place – he couldn't and he knows it. What you both need is time to get to know each other – the thing is?' Annie paused wondering if Violet could deal with the truth '– I'm not sure what he will be capable of, if anything after this accident. I'm not trying to be melodramatic, but this might be the only time you have with him and I'm not trying to push you, but you asked me to be honest and not to lie – so I am telling you as it is?' Annie offered her hand to Violet.

'Mum – I just can't.' Violet turned away.

'Okay – I understand,' Said Annie with empathy, 'and I hope you understand that I do have to go and see how he is?' Violet nodded.

'I'll wait here for you - if you like?' Suggested Violet. It was the best she could do to compromise at the moment. Annie understood the massive concession her daughter was making.

'I would like that very much.' Annie kissed her on the forehead as she passed on her way out of the relative's room and back to Jack's bedside. ' I won't be long.'

There was no improvement or deteriation in Jacks condition. The nurses and doctors came every hour to monitor his progress. Annie took his hand in hers and told him what had happened with Violet in the visitor's room. As expected he made no response, but at least she knew she had told him. Annie split her time between Jack and Violet, half an hour at a time. On the third time Annie went back into the visitor's room Scarlett was waiting with Violet.

'How is he?' Scarlett asked immediately.

'No change I'm afraid.' Relayed Annie.

'I've tried to contact Mrs Parrish, but all I keep getting is the answerphone. In the end I left a message. I know it's a horrible way to find anything out, but I couldn't think what else to do and it's better that she finds out that way than not at all. I left the details of the hospital for her, including the phone number if she should want to ring them here.' Annie could tell that Scarlett was unsure that she had done the right thing.

'You couldn't do anything differently than you have – unless you jump on a plane yourself and I can't see the company paying for that!' Scarlett nodded in agreement. 'I'm sure Jack would be very grateful for your help.' Annie corrected herself, 'will be very grateful.'

'And how are you coping Annie – under the circumstances?' Enquired Scarlett. Violet looked sheepishly at her mum.

'I've told Scarlett, you know, what I've found out about Jack.' Confessed Violet.

'Oh.' Annie was surprised that Violet had confided in Scarlett, but it was a good sign that she was accepting that changes. It was Violet's news to tell and if she wanted to discuss it with someone that was her prerogative. It was obvious that Scarlett had had the good sense to deny any knowledge of Jack being Violets father. Annie sighed inwardly.

'I'm fine.' Replied Annie giving Scarlett her stock answer. 'It's Jack I'm worried about –and Violet.' She added. 'It's just so hard standing by. Not being able to do anything.'

'The fact that you're here and caring is plenty. If you weren't he'd be on his own, with no family over here – well –he has family now hasn't he. He has you Violet.' Annie wasn't sure how Violet was going to react to Scarlett's comment. Annie could see Violet's eyes crammed with tears that she was desperately trying to hold back, Scarlett noticed too. The three girls moved in for a power hug. It was Scarlett who spoke first 'Who want's coffee?' She asked breaking the circle. It was agreed that Violet and Scarlett would go for coffee whilst Annie went back to Jack. She took his hand in hers, just like she had been doing over the past few hours. She lent in closer to him, so that he could hopefully hear her more easily. She spoke softly but firmly.

'Jack. It's Annie; I need you to pull through this. It's time to start fighting. I don't know what will happen between us, but I do care for you. Now Violet knows you are her father, you need to pull through so that she can find out what a good man you are. You know I said I wasn't sure if I loved you – well I do, but if you tell anyone I'll deny it.' She stood up and gently leaning over the machines, kissed him on the cheek. Jack was lost in his own silent dream world. He didn't flinch or move to give any indication he had heard anything.

Throughout the rest of the day and night Annie refused to leave the hospital. Eventually she managed to persuade Violet to go home and get some sleep, under the pretext of not wanting the shop being empty overnight. Violet didn't buy her excuse, but the hospital atmosphere was starting to get to her, so she surrendered and went home.

'I'll come back tomorrow.' She promised.

'Good. I'm glad and will you bring me a change of clothes. These are starting to hum.'

'Maybe you can appeal to Jack's sense of smell and wake him up by smelling appalling!'

'Thanks Violet, you've done wonders for my self-esteem.'

'Only kidding. You don't smell – yet, but it's only a matter of time!'

Annie managed to get a little sleep, taken in short bursts when she could, sometimes in the chair next to Jack's bed, sometimes curled up on the sofa in the relative's room. She constantly prayed silently for Jack to survive and to make a full recovery, hoping that her words would not fall on deaf ears and that all those hours in church as a child would count for something. Her sleep was fitful, her dreams surreal. In one dream, she was sat by Nick's bed in a hospital, but holding hands with Jack. All three were chatting away like good friends. It was just a symptom of stress, but she found it un-nerving. Every time she awoke up, it took her a few seconds to sort out the dreams from reality, sometimes there was little difference.

On day two the doctors asked specifically to meet with Annie in the relative's room. 'We're going to take Jack off the sedation and see if we can get him to regain consciousness.' Announced a young doctor who didn't look much older than Violet. 'It will be a few hours before we expect to see any difference in Mr Parrish – if at all. I have to warn you Annie that this is a dangerous and crucial time for Jack. We'll be keeping a close eye on him and we'll keep you informed.' Annie was distraught with fear for him. She could do nothing but wait.

In the afternoon Violet came to the hospital to check on Jack's progress. Her mother wasn't in the visitor's room, so Violet settled into the lounge to wait for Annie's return. Violet still couldn't bring herself to go in to the ward to see Jack, but at least she was there, in the background, supporting her mum. There was one niggling thought making Violet feel uneasy and that was the amount of care and attention her mother was pouring into Jack. Although her mother had stated otherwise, she wondered if she was still in love with Jack and if there had ever been any space in her mother's heart for Nick.

It was three in the afternoon and the doctor was in with Jack when Annie returned to the relative's room. Violet sat reading one of the ancient magazines from the coffee table.

'Hi sweetheart. When did you get here?' Annie crossed the room to give Violet a Kiss. The smile on her mother's face told Violet how pleased she was that she had come back.

'Not long ago. I've been at work this morning and before you say it I asked to go in. It's driving me crazy all this sitting around. I needed to do something – Scarlett brought me here. She's gone to do some errands for work, but she said she'd call back later.' Violet didn't tell her mum that Harley had been on the same shift and completely blanked her. She had seen him taking one of the new girls by the hand into the wine cellar. He caught sight of Violet from the corner of his eye. He stared her down making it clear even without words, what he intended to get up to in there. Violet knew she had been replaced. She thought she would have been upset, it turned out to be a lust thing with Harley, but he had shown himself to be a 'prick', she didn't need or want him any longer.

'Mum, Scarlett and I were talking and – we both think you need to go home! It's ridiculous, you spending all this time here, putting your own health at risk. Not to mention ignoring the business.' Violet didn't shout, but Annie could tell her words were spoken with a serious edge. Annie wondered if resentment was creeping in.

'I know you think I should go home Violet, and I understand your concerns - but

I'm sorry, I just can't leave him until I know he's going to be alright. When I know that for sure, then I'll leave.' Annie's words were direct and immoveable.

'You're afraid he's going to die aren't t you? So you don't want to leave in case it happens again like it did with dad! That's the truth isn't it?' Annie was stunned by Violet's equal frankness. Annie hesitated, wondering if the truth would do more harm.

'- Yes Violet. Yes. I am scared. No one expected your dad to die that day and I'll never forgive myself for not being with him at the end. Every one persuaded me to leave the hospital and I did and I have to live with that decision every day and I won't make the same mistake again. So if it means I have to stay here for a few days to be sure Jack will pull though – I will.' Annie was looking petulant with her hands on her hips.

'Is it because you're in love with him - ?' Violet had a string of accusations waiting to be voiced.

'What??' Annie thought she had miss heard her daughter.

'You heard me! Do you still love Jack? I think I deserve an answer.'

'Don't be absurd Violet!' Annie was not going to fuel any fire and admit the truth, 'I haven't seen him for years – I don't know him anymore, but whatever else you think he is your biological father and we are linked for life and beyond. That won't ever change. You can't bring yourself to be there for him and I understand that you can't – then I must.' Annie hoped her outburst was enough to throw her off the scent. Annie didn't know what she felt for him, well that was a lie. She did sort of love him, but she didn't know if it was the old Jack that she had known that she loved or the present day one who was still a mystery to her. She felt like her past was mixed up in her future. There was no way to figure it out at the moment, so denial was her best option. Violet stood up and made her way to the door.

'Where are you going' Annie asked concerned that she had said too much and had managed to alienate Violet even more.

'I'm going to see Jack.' she answered calmly 'Will you come with me?' Annie was shocked by the change in Violet's attitude, but she didn't question it.

'Of course I'll come with you, but are you sure you want to go in there. He's not a very pretty sight and there are lots of machines?'

'I'm sure. Oh come on mum. If I don't do it now I never will.'

Annie and Violet walked hand in hand down the corridor until they reached Jack's room. Even with warning, Violet was unprepared for what she found. She had not been allowed to go and see Nick when he was in hospital. Everyone thought she was too young at that time. Her only knowledge of the events was based on what she pieced together from conversations she had overheard. At the time she thought her mum and family were wrong to keep her away, but now looking at Jack, she was glad her memories of her dad were not of him lying dependant in a hospital bed. At least in her last memory of Nick, he was laughing.

Annie guided Violet to a chair at the side of the bed. She explained the machines, what each one did, the noises they made and that it was normal and not to panic.

'What do we do now?' Violet asked cautiously, looking to her mother for guidance.

'We just sit and hope that he wakes up and that there's no permanent damage. You can talk to him if you like or hold his hand. Sometimes, it helps to stimulate the brain into action.' Violet shook her head at the thought of holding his hand. She had visions of him waking up and asking her who the hell she was. There was no way she was going to risk it. Annie pulled up an extra chair. At first they sat in silence. Annie could tell that Violet felt out of her comfort zone, which was only natural, but at least she was there making an effort to be with him. Eventually, the boredom of silence and curiosity got the better of Violet and she started asking questions about Jack.

'Tell me about you and him? What was he like when you were at school together?' Annie was both startled and delighted by her interest.

'Well, he was the most fancied boy in my year.'

'Really?' Violet wasn't inclined to believe her mother's version of events. True, his face didn't resemble the back end of a bus and considering his age, he was wearing well, but to imagine him as the Robbie Williams of his day was a big stretch.

'Truly. There used to be this group of girls........' Annie started out on the journey of explaining their history. She included anecdotes she thought Violet would find amusing, but her main purpose was to try and give Violet an insight into the man lying in the bed in front of her, who had the same blood running through his veins.

The time passed more quickly with Violet to talk to. Annie repeatedly told Violet to leave, if it was too much for her or if she had other things she needed to do, but to her credit Violet stayed. At five the doctors came on their rounds, it was then they were told the important news. The sedation had been cut down over the course of the afternoon and if he was going to wake up at all, it should be soon. The doctor and nurses recommended talking to him, playing favourite music and holding his hands to stimulate his senses. Annie didn't have a clue what his favourite music was now, she would have known if you'd asked her twenty years ago. The only things she could remember were the songs they had listened to on cold winter nights, when there was nothing on the TV, which was often as this was the pre sky and cable era, when people were limited to a handful of channels. Violet had the brainwave which was to contact the hotel and ask Scarlett to go into his accommodation to see if there were and Cd's or an iPod, something they could use to give an insight into his musical tastes.

'That's a great idea Violet!' Said Annie, impressed by her logic. 'I'll go and ring Scarlett. I'll be back in a minute. Will you be alright here for a few minutes on your own?' Violet nodded reluctantly.

'I'm not on my own. He's with me.' Violet tilted her head towards Jack. Violet was curious about Jack, her 'biological father', she didn't feel able to say the word 'father' without the prefix. It felt dis-respectful to Nick somehow. He looked quite lost and helpless, lying surrounded by the machines. She was finding it hard to keep the charade up of hating him. She didn't, she felt nothing for him, but she didn't want him to die – of that she was sure.

Violet turned around to check her mother hadn't returned, she leant forwards and placed her hand on top of Jacks. It felt strange, she expected there to some sort of connection the moment they touched - but there was nothing. Violet told herself not to expect too much, after all he was unconscious, it wasn't as if he could respond. She squeezed his hand hoping for some kind of sign – again there was no response. She decided to try another tack, talking to him, but he didn't know her well enough to know her voice, so she held out little hope. She spoke with hesitancy, feeling like an idiot, nothing about this scenario felt natural, but the sooner he woke up, the sooner her mother would go home.

'Err – Jack It's Violet – I'm sorry for the things I said to you when I came to see you last Sunday night – before the crash – well in truth I don't know what I said to you because, as you know I was very drunk, but I know the things weren't pleasant, so I just want to say sorry.' She wasn't sure if his hand twitched in response. It was so slight that it could just have been her imagination or a muscle spasm. 'Well - I want to you get well, so I can tell you properly that I'm sorry and maybe we could try to get to know each other a little, as mates, cause I have to tell you straight that Nick is my dad and he always will be.' She pulled her hand away. Her embarrassment level had maxed out. She didn't want anyone to know what she'd said and besides, her mother didn't yet know that she had been to see Jack on the night of the crash. The longer it took for that one to come out the better.

Unbeknown to Violet, Annie had come back to the ward to ask the nurse if there was a CD player available for the music. Through the doorway she witnessed Violets actions, but not the words that went with them. Annie left discreetly, not wanting to spoil the moment for Violet. Annie lingered in the relative's room, giving Violet ample time to say whatever she needed to say to Jack.

'That's organised.' Annie stated when she finally emerged from the relative's room. 'Scarlett is going to look for some music, then send Harry up with it as soon as possible.'

'Did I miss anything?' Asked Annie.

'No, nothing.' Answered Violet, smoothing any creases out of the sheets where her arm had been leaning as they held hands.

The music was at the hospital within the hour. Annie noticed Harry skulking outside the door, not wanting to intrude; he was waiting to be noticed.

'How's Mr Parrish doing?' He asked with concern.

'We're still no nearer. They hope he'll wake up soon. That's what we need the music for, to try and encourage him to wake up.'

'Aye, well, here it is. I'll leave you to it. If he wakes up tell him I was asking after him.' Harry passed Annie a small silver iPod and a portable docking station that Scarlett had found in Jack's the bedroom, which was perfect for playing in the hospital. Violet found a spare socket, up by the top of Jack's bed; she plugged it in and switched it on. Annie felt it was best to leave it to Violet to organise, as there were some technical things were still a little alien to Annie, she still couldn't accept that such a small box could hold upwards of a thousand songs. She still had her Walkman, which she pulled out of her bottom draw, when the mood struck her. Violet scrolled through the songs in the memory, taking great amusement from the song choices that were downloaded.

'One thing is a bonus.' Said Violet after scrutinizing his play lists 'at least my taste in music is better for having Nick as my dad!' Annie smiled despite herself.

'Do we want something soothing or upbeat?' asked Violet.

'Well the whole point is to wake him up, so I'd go for upbeat.' Decided Annie. Violet selected a playlist labelled 'work out'. The first song to play was 'The Jam – a town called malice'. Violet stuck two fingers into her mouth pretending to be sick. Annie threw her a cautionary glance.

'You young people just don't know a good song when you hear one!' Scowled Annie. 'I've danced to this at many a good party!'

No song managed to play to the end without a comment from Violet on its place in modern pop history or if it should be deleted from his iPod for ever. In a strange way the music normalised the situation. It was easier to cope with all the technology that surrounded them. The music covered up the intermittent bleeps and electrical buzzing. They started to talk more easily and without realising, involving Jack in their conversations, with comments like 'You can't be serious Jack. This band was shit.' And 'How old are you? This is a grannies song!' Violet was unafraid to comment on Jack's taste and nearly choked laughing when the theme from rocky came on. She had visions of him running up and down the drive at priory Hall in his shorts, with the music playing in the background. In the middle of one of these impromptu appraisals, Violet took Jack's hand in hers, pretending to slap it for his choice. This was a natural growth in their relationship – if you could call it that, with one person in a coma. Annie didn't comment, on what she observed, she just let the moment pass as a normal occurrence, her heart quietly skipping a beat.

Eventually a track by the band 'Cherry ghost' came on. 'At last! One I know.' she exclaimed. I'm not saying you've got good taste Jack, but at least this one was written this century!' they both laughed and started singing along, hoping something would stir in Jack's brain to bring him back to them.

They didn't hear the person come into the room mid-way through the song and stand behind them, watching their exhibition. It was only when the song reached its natural ending that the person cleared their throat to announce their arrival. Annie and Violet turned to see who had invaded their therapy session. Annie wished the ground would swallow her up as she realised she was face to face with Jack's mother.

'Do you really think that this is the appropriate pace for such insensitive frivolity? - Turn that dreadful music off now!' Marcia's words were harsh and scolding. It had only taken Annie a few moments to recognise the woman. She looked just the same as the last time Annie had seen her, only a slightly fuller figure and hair that was obviously died within an inch of its life to hide the grey. Without speaking, Annie indicated to Violet to turn off the music. Annie automatically stood up.

'Mrs Parrish – We weren't aware that you were coming? It's lovely to see you.' Annie was flustered. She just said the first thing that came into her head and promptly wished she had kept her mouth firmly closed. It sounded more like a welcome to a party.

'This is hardly a social visit! – And it's not the place to have a party!' Sneered Mrs Parrish moving closer to Jack, her nose so high in the air it was nearly touching the ceiling. Annie moved sideways, so that Mrs Parrish could sit by the bed next to Jack. 'I'd like some time alone with him.' This was not an invitation but an instruction for them to leave.

'Wouldn't you like me to fill you in on what they are doing for him and...'

'Have you taken a medical course since I met you last?'

'Well, no.' Mumbled Annie.

'Then I'll speak to someone who knows what they are speaking about – after you have left!' Annie could see that Violet was about to kick off. Out of the sight of Mrs Parrish, Annie waved the palm of her hand downwards in a gesture for Violet to keep calm and let it pass.

'Of course you want to be with him. We'll go and sit in the relative's room for a little while and leave you two alone.' Conceded Annie.

'I don't know why you are going in there! You never were his 'relative' Annie! He has me now. You can go and get on with what you would normally be doing. Jack doesn't need you. You've done enough damage to my family already!' Annie was hoping that it was probably the shock of the situation and tiredness from travelling that was making Mrs Parrish so hurtful - it couldn't be that Mrs Parrish had spent so long with Mr Parrish that their personalities had merged could it? Annie chose not to acknowledge Marcia's last comment.

'We'll be in the relative's room.' Annie spoke calmly and sweetly, not rising to the bait, she wasn't going to give Marcia the satisfaction. Violet was somewhat less convinced that they should leave and had to be dragged away. Annie guided Violet with a firm grip on her arm, afraid that she would break away and give Marcia a piece of her mind. Annie closed the relative's room door behind them, so that no one would hear Violet let rip.

'Who does that fucking woman think she is?' Seethed violet who would have had steam coming out of her ears if it was at all possible.

'That Violet – is your grandmother!' Said Annie knowing the only way to silence Violet was to shock her. It worked.

'You can't be serious? That stuck up, obnoxious, rude, overbearing, crass woman is actually related to me?'

'I'm afraid so. Luckily Jack is nothing like her. So you should be alright, you may not turn into her.' Violet was about to blast her mother when she realised she was laughing.

'It's not funny Mum. Who does she think she is to order you away? It's you that's been there for him.'

'Unfortunately I don't think Marcia sees it that way, but maybe it gives you a little insight into the way Jack was treated by his family when he was younger. It's not such a large leap now that you've met Marcia, to believe that they could have kept the letters from Jack and if you think she's bad, well compared to her late husband, she's a mere pussy cat!'

'Do you think she knows - who I am?' The thought that this woman could know who she was and still treat her mother this way was upsetting to Violet.

'No – I don't think she knows. I know Jack hadn't told her, because he didn't know for sure until the day of the accident, like you – but don't worry. When she does find out she won't treat you any differently!' Violet opened her mouth aghast, unable to comprehend the woman's point of view. They were interrupted by a member of the senior nursing staff coming through the door. Annie could tell from her inability to look them in the eye that she was the bearer of bad news. She asked them both to sit down.

'Oh my God –It's Jack, something's happened! I knew I shouldn't have left the room….' Annie was on the verge of hysteria.

'No Annie. There's no change with Jack. That's not what I need to speak to you about - the thing is,' She spoke hesitantly. 'Mrs Parrish has requested that only family visit and since she is the only legal family, she should be the only visitor.'

'What!' Annie and Violet shouted in unison and rising to their feet.

'She can't do that! Mum's been here since the accident. He'd want her to be here!' Violet was going to stand her ground for her mother's sake.

'I'm sorry, but I'm afraid she can 'do that' because she is next of kin.' Annie could tell that the nurse did not agree with the request she was delivering. 'Mrs Parrish says she will keep you informed of any developments, but I'm afraid I can't let you back on to the ward – and I'm going to have to ask you to leave the hospital.' The nurse looked Annie and Violet in the eye. I'm very sorry about this.' Her eyes were saying much more than her lips were allowed. She was clearly mortified.

'But I am next of kin!' Piped up Violet. 'Jack is my - he's my father.' Violet looked at Annie to back up her claim.

'Is this true?' The nurses words were directed at Annie. Annie nodded in compliance with Violets admission. 'That does change the situation. I'll see what I can do.' The nurse left the room, giving them a watery smile as she left, indicating that she didn't hold out much hope.

'Do you think Jack's mother is serious about not letting us see him?' Violet asked.

'I wouldn't put anything past her. It's a long time since I've known her, but she was always very controlling. Jack was the apple of her eye and she would have done anything to keep him close to her. I used to think he was the only reason she stayed with John Parrish, but she is a mother with a son in grave danger, so she's doing what she thinks she needs to do – right or wrong.' Annie was trying to find a logical reason for her actions.

Annie and Violet paced the room as they waited for news from the nurse. It wasn't long before she returned. 'I'm sorry – Mrs Parrish is adamant that she is the only next of kin. She says that to her knowledge Jack has no children and unless you can bring written evidence to prove the fact – she will remain the only next of kin.'

'That bitch!' This time it was Annie who was out of control.

'I am very sorry.' Stated the nurse again. Annie understood the nurse was only the messenger; there was no point in making things more difficult than they were.

'I understand your hands are tied.' Annie addressed the nurse, 'I'm not next of kin, she's right - but Violet is Jack's daughter, Marcia just doesn't want to admit it. We're not going to cause a scene, because that's what she would want and we'll leave in a minute, but please, if I ring, please will you let me know how he is? I don't trust Marcia to keep us informed.' The nurse contemplated Annie's request.

'I can't make any promises, but I'll see what I can do. The mornings are the best time to phone- except Thursday.' The nurse winked at Violet.

'Thank you. I really appreciate your kindness and we won't tell a soul.' Promised Annie. The nurse nodded and smiled before leaving the relatives room.

'Are we really going to leave?' Violet asked not understanding why her mother had given in so easily.

'We have no choice sweetheart. Marcia has the upper hand being his next of kin. If we give her a day or two to think about it we can always come back and try to change her mind. She'll soon see that it's not so wonderful sitting hour in and hour out, alone with no one to speak to, but at this moment the most important person is Jack and what he needs, and what he doesn't need is us arguing over his sick bed - So Come on lets go home.'

'I can't believe you are taking this so calmly and easily.' Violet was shaking her head in disbelief.

'Violet I'm not, but fighting her at his moment in time will just lead us both to say things we may later regret and the most important thing is that he's not alone when 'god willing' he wakes up. Marcia will be there and for now that will have to do.' Annie led the way out of the hospital with a heavy heart. She would give Marcia twenty four hours to think about her rash decision and then she would be back. Annie just prayed that Jack was strong enough to pull through and that she would get to see him again. She couldn't bear another funeral.

Pippa was surprised to see Annie and Violet when they came thought the shop door. At first she feared the worst. 'Has something happened?' She asked tentatively, hoping she wasn't saying the wrong thing. Annie explained the whole messy situation with Marcia. Violet just chipped in with various swears words and expletives when the opportunity arose.

'She sounds like a very cold woman.' Commented Pippa

'She makes the waters around where the titanic sank positively tropical!' Scathed Violet.

'So what's going to happen now with Jack?' Asked Pippa with concern.

'In truth I don't know, but I'm hoping a little space will help Marcia to change her mind. I'll try again tomorrow.'

'Well, what you need at this moment must be sleep. I don't mean to comment, but the dark circles under your eyes are terrible. You both look all in, go and get a few good hours sleep. It'll do you both the world of good. I can cope down here for the rest of the day. Go on with you both!'

'Are you sure Pippa? I've left you to it all week. You've been so good already and there's so much to do getting ready for Christmas – all the stock to put out and....'

'Annie - it's a crisis. People pull together and do what needs to be done. I can sort the Christmas stock. Christmas will come and go regardless. It's you and Violet I'm worried about at the moment and if you don't get some sleep you won't be fit for Christmas! Go on with you, less talking and more sleeping!' Annie and Violet both hugged Pippa before climbing the stairs to the flat and heading straight to bed. Contrary to Annie's expectations, she slept through the night without waking once. She hadn't realised just how exhausted she was, until her head nestled into her clean white cotton pillow – bliss. A thin shard of light edged its way in through a crack in the curtain, eventually bringing Annie to consciousness. Her first thought was of Jack. There had been no news in the night, which was a good sign, then again, Annie didn't expect that Marcia would let the Hospital contact her, even if there was. It was seven a.m., She slipped on her dressing gown and went out on to the landing. Violet's door was not fully closed. Annie could see her, still fast asleep in a world without worry. Annie tiptoed past, making sure not to wake her, picked up her phone, then settled herself on the stairs, out of earshot and dialled the hospital. She had to try and find out what was happening and if Jack had regained consciousness. Luck was on Annie's side, as the nurse who had been so kind to them in the relatives room answered the phone. She immediately put Annie's mind at ease.

'Jack is doing well Annie. He regained consciousness in the middle of the night – only for a short time, but he knew his name and other details. As far as we can tell at this moment there seems to be no permanent damage. He's sleeping now and that will do him the world of good. He needs plenty of rest to put him on the right road.'

'Thank you!' Said Annie giddy with relief. Tears of relief rolled down her face. She felt elated as the weight of her worries lifted from her shoulders. She would never doubt the power of prayer again. Annie brushed the tears aside like an unwanted interruption. 'Was Mrs Parrish with him when he woke up? Did he recognise her? Is she still there?'

'I shouldn't really tell you this, but Mrs Parrish doesn't know yet. I believe she left sometime in the evening yesterday, saying she would be back later today.' Admitted the nurse with irritation.

'You mean to tell me when Jack woke up he was alone? Thinking no one cared about him?' Annie couldn't believe the insensitivity of the woman. Her elation morphed into anger.

'He did have the staff with him Annie. He was very groggy. I don't think he realised who was there. As I said it was only for a very short time.' The nurse tried to reassure Annie.

'Of course –thank you.' Said Annie gratefully. Annie didn't understand Marcia's behaviour; surely as a mother she could put herself out and miss a little sleep to be with her only son when he needed her. She couldn't understand why she and Violet had been sent away when Marcia had no intention of staying with him the whole time? In Annie's mind that was pure cruelty.

'Mum?' Violet was stood behind her, woken by the sound of voices. 'Is everything alright?' Annie rose to her feet and hugged Violet.

'Jack's regained consciousness – only for a short time, but they think he'll be fine!' Annie was smiling broadly. It was at that moment Violet realised that her mother still had some sort of feelings for Jack. She had seen the look before, when her mum used to look at Nick. Maybe it was possible for her mum to love two people in her lifetime equally? She wasn't sure, but it was unquestionably more than friendship her mother was feeling.

'Are we going to see him?' Asked Violet.

'I'm sorry Violet, nothing has changed, they still won't let us in to see him at the moment, but at least he's mending. He needs lots of rest, then soon he'll be out of hospital and then there'll be nothing she can do to stop us seeing him!' They both smiled at the thought.

Chapter 24

It was back to work as usual in the shop for Annie. Pippa had been fantastic at holding the fort. The shop looked great with everything in its place as it should be. The wholesalers had been delivering Annie's order every day under the circumstances, making it easier for Pippa. Zach who had been a great help too, taking the children to school on the days Pippa's parents couldn't manage to be there and when he was passing the shop, he called in to make sure Pippa was managing with everything. Even though life had been just as hectic for Pippa, her life seemed to be going in a whole new and happy direction. Some days had been busier than others, but that was only to be expected, especially in a new business, so at least Pippa's work load had been manageable, things were slowly picking up day by day as people heard about the shop and needed flowers, but now Pippa deserved a rest and it was time for Annie to pick up the reins and settle back in to normal routine. Annie planned to go visiting in the evenings, and after she'd had a few days' rest, she was sure Pippa would come in for a couple of hours to allow Annie to make afternoon visiting, after all, now Jack was regaining consciousness he would be able to keep his mother in check.

Annie had to admit that Jack was in safe hands –even if they were his mother's. There was nothing Annie could do for him at the moment, so the best thing was to keep herself busy. It was only when she sat and thought about the situation that it became unbearable. She had to keep telling herself that his mother was right; she wasn't next of kin and his mother was perfectly capable of looking after him – so why did she feel so guilty? Annie tried to shake off the bad feeling she had and pick some lilies, roses and genister to make a hand tied bouquet for an order. Somehow it felt good to be back in normal routine without the sterile atmosphere suffocating her. Annie was about to add the water in the bouquet when Stan came in.

'Morning Stan. How are you feeling? I'm sorry I haven't seen you since you lost your mum. I think you heard why?' Pippa had informed him of Jack's accident and Stan had come in to find out if the 'kind man' was making a good recovery. Annie told him the little she knew, playing down her involvement with him, but Stan wasn't fooled one little bit.

'Isn't he your young man?' He asked with the adeptness of his Mother's prying talents.

'No, no – he's an old friend. We went to school together a long time ago.' She hoped it was enough to throw him off the scent. He caught the message, that she didn't want to discuss it and graciously changed the subject.

'I was wondering? - Will you be able to make it to Mum's funeral tomorrow? I know that you didn't know each other well, but she held you in high regard and that's saying something for my Mother!"

'Of course I'll be there Stan. I held her in high regard too. - I know Pippa took your flower order and I'll make them later today and see that they are at the house in the morning in plenty of time.'

Stan nodded in silent acceptance of tomorrow's events, all of which he was dreading. Annie could see a tear collecting in the corner of his eye. 'How are you doing Stan?' Annie asked with genuine care and giving him permission to talk about what he was feeling if he wished.

'I miss her greatly - the old bag!' His moment of sentimentality was over, displays of public emotion were not in his nature. 'Make the flowers nice for her won't you. Flowers were important to her. She used to say that there was nothing sadder than a funeral without flowers. She said she knew it was daft, but it was as if people didn't care – if there were no flowers. It didn't matter to her if they were large or small tributes or flowers picked out of the garden. It was the sentiment behind and the understanding that the flowers bring passing beauty, just like the short time we have lived and loved ones in our lives.'

'Stan, that was almost poetic. What a lovely thought. She was a wise woman that mother of yours.'

'Aye -and cantankerous too!' they both laughed.

The funeral was beautiful, if you can say that about a funeral. Most of the village turned out. Mrs Stretford had lived in the village all of her life and was well known and well loved. Stan's heart was lifted, by the number of people that sent or brought flowers for his mother. The hearse was laden with all kinds of flowers. Some were professionally made tributes, many made by Annie, these sat side by side with an array of small bunches picked from the last flowers and foliage's of the year from people's gardens. The result was a hearse filled with flowers and fond sentiments. The sun made an appearance, melting the last of the previous night's frost and faintly warming the mourners as they waited. Stan and his family led the way into the church behind the coffin. Stan's eulogy was fitting and appropriate for his mother, filled with love and straight talking and ever so slightly amusing, even though it was unintentional. Pippa sought out Annie in the crowd outside the church after the service.

'You okay?' She asked Annie. Annie nodded. It was the first funeral she had attended since Nick's, it was all too familiar.

'You did a beautiful job of the flowers.' Commented Pippa. 'I heard lots of people talking about them.'

'We do what we can with god's ingredients. Anyway - How are you? Glad to be back with your children and away from the shop?'

'Em, I was - and then all I hear is where's my P.E. kit, what's for tea or I don't want to do my homework! - I enjoy being at work and it's easier!'

'I remember that time well, but now I get 'can I have some money' and 'will you take me to work'.' Said Annie empathising.

'Have you heard anything more about how Jack is?' Enquired Pippa. Annie shook her head.

'They still won't tell me anything else, as I am not 'next of kin'. They just say he's stable. I don't know where his mother is staying, so I can't get in touch with her, although I would expect she'd be at Priory Hall. I have a delivery to Priory Hall later. I think I'll look for Scarlett to see if she knows anything more - Just as long as I don't bump into Marcia!'

'Scarlett may know something; I suppose they'll have to keep Jack's place of work informed?'

'I wouldn't make any assumptions as far as that woman is concerned! The only rule book she follows is her own. I'm thinking about sneaking in this evening and trying to see Jack. Only problem is I don't know her routine, when she takes a break or if she goes to stay somewhere?'

'Well you've nothing to lose?' Encouraged Pippa, 'It's not as if you owe Marcia anything and the worst that can happen is you get turned away? Why don't you go and deliver some flowers to him? You may get through the door on that pretext?'

'Good idea Pippa! Not just a pretty face – except – they don't let flowers into the intensive care unit?'

'You and I know that, but you can pretend you don't know? Take a plant or something you're happy to leave in the relatives' room?' It was a good idea; Annie only hoped she had the courage to carry it through. The two women watched as the mourners started to clamber into the large black limousine.

Are you going to Mrs Stretford's wake?' enquired Pippa.

'I can't. I have orders and deliveries to finish. I've closed the shop for the funeral, out of respect and I'm sure people will understand, but I can't go AWOL all day.

Will you give my regards to Stan and explain?' The shop wasn't the only reason Annie didn't want to go, it was her acute aversion to funerals. She needed some space.

'Of course I'll tell Stan, but he'll miss you?' Pippa patted Annie's arm, aware that there was more behind Annie's disappearing act than she was letting on.

'I'm sure he won't miss me, there are so many people here. I thought you said Zach was coming?' Annie scoured the crowd looking for him.

'He couldn't get away from work, but he'll be along later - he promised.'

'So? How is it going with Zach?' Annie was dying to know.

'Okay.' Blushed Pippa.

'Just okay? I thought you'd be on cloud nine!'

'I don't want to get too involved yet. It's early stages and there are the kids to think of? What if he decides it's too much hard work taking on someone else's children and wants out?'

'- But he's not going to. I can tell you that for nothing! He knew they existed before he asked you out, so it's no big surprise and you can tell, he's a natural at it! You'll be having another one before you know it.'

'Annie! That's outrageous, then he would run a mile. I'm taking it slowly and we'll see what happens.' Pippa stated firmly.

'That's good, but don't push him away because you think he doesn't want to be there, when it's as plain as the nose on your face that he's dotty about you!'

The crowd parted and the funeral car procession moved off to the crematorium. Annie was sure she had made the right decision in not going with them. Instead she went back to the shop and immersed herself in her work.

Later Annie took the delivery of flowers to Priory Hall, she asked the receptionist to Paige Scarlett once she had handed over the flowers and given the receptionist the name of the recipient. It would have been impossible for Annie to leave without at least trying to find out more information regarding Jack's progress. Within minutes Scarlett was at her side, she knew very little about Jack's condition. However, she did know that Marcia had moved herself into Jack's place to make it suitable for his release from hospital and that the way she was talking; she had no plans to go back to Australia for the foreseeable future. Annie's mood, which was already low, dipped and hit rock bottom. If Marcia was intent on staying, life would remain very difficult and being allowed to see Jack would be virtually impossible, at least until her was well enough to make his own decisions, but who knows what damage she would do before that day arrived, dripping poisoned words in his ears every day. Scarlett continued with her story.

'Marcia did say that he's progressing well and that they are pleased with him. She seems to think he'll be released in a week or so. I've tried to visit myself, but she won't let anyone in. She just insists that he doesn't want to see anyone and wants total rest and that we can visit when he's home convalescing.' Scarlett checked there was no one around to hear their conversation. She continued 'I know she's his mother, but she's a complete control freak and a dragon! I wouldn't like her to be looking after me if I was ill. Friends cheer you up and give you other things to think about besides your own problems and illnesses. She doesn't see that she's slowing his recovery down by keeping everyone away!'

'She does things her own way, that's for sure!' Annie tried not to let her true feelings for Marcia show through. 'Will you let me know if you hear anything? Asked Annie with an air of desperation in her voice.

'You'll be the first to hear anything I know – but I'm going away tomorrow on a fortnight's annual leave. Why don't you just go marching up to the hospital and demand to see him? Or when he comes home go hammering on the door. If Jack doesn't want to see you he can send you away – but at least then you know it's Jack not Marcia making the choices?' ' Annie thought for a while, 'Pippa's been telling me the very same thing.'

'In truth I'm scared – scared of his mother, scared of how I feel, scared that he might think I care and want him in my life if I go...'

'Don't you want him in your life?' Interrupted Scarlett. Annie looked at the floor wondering how she should answer.

'I don't know?' She said truthfully. 'It's all a mess. So much has happened in the last couple of weeks, I don't know if I'm coming or going and I don't' even know if he wants me? – Then there's Violet and what she wants? It's all too much.' Annie hid her face in her hands, trying to keep er emotions under control.

'You're bound to be confused, but from what I understand other people kept you two apart for a very long time. Don't you think it's worth giving it a go, even if it goes wrong, at least you'll know, instead of spending your life wondering what if all the time? – and the only way to find out what Violet and Jack think is to ask them?' Annie pondered Scarlett's words. There was some sense in there, but where did she start, she couldn't get anywhere near Jack and how would Violet feel if Annie told her that she might still have some feelings for Jack – that was an

explosion waiting to happen.

'Look Annie, it's none of my business, but as an outsider looking in, it's clear you both still have feelings for each other. Do yourself and Jack a favour and find a way past his mother.'

'Scarlett – I can always count on you to give me the easy jobs in life!'

'You know what they say Annie. If it's worth having it's worth fighting for!' Annie suspected he was worth fighting for; she just had to work out if she had enough fight left in her to make things work out.

'Annie – he still loves you. Any idiot can see that!' Annie blushed on hearing the words, but that small ember of hope inside grew a little larger and burned that much brighter.

Annie stood behind the swing double doors that led to the intensive care unit. She realised that she was holding the orchid plant so tightly that her fingers ached. She didn't know what she was going to do if Marcia was still there? It was past visiting times, Annie hoped that she had gone back to Priory Hall for the night, but the only way to find out for sure was to go through the doors and find out for herself. She and Scarlett had hatched a plan that if she got caught she would say she was making a delivery on behalf of the Priory Hall management group, thus giving her a legitimate reason to be there delivering. Annie was glad that espionage was not a part of her everyday life, she was hopeless as it, she looked guilty even when she hadn't done anything! Annie took a deep breath, stood tall with her chest out for confidence and pushed the doors wide open. The corridor was empty, fifty meters to go undetected and she would be in sight of Jack's bed. In the distance she could hear the clatter of a hospital trolley heading towards her. She quickened her pace to get on the ward and out of sight as soon as possible. Through the glass windows and doors to the intensive care unit, she could see Jack's bed. There was no Marcia looming over him, but worse than that there was no Jack! His bed was empty. Annie gasped involuntarily. All the machines had gone and the bed was stripped. Surely nothing had happened? They would have let her know? Wouldn't they? Annie marched in to the unit to get a closer look. She didn't see the nurse sat at the desk at first. It was only when she stood up to challenge Annie's appearance that Annie stopped in her tracks. It was no one Annie had seen before.

'Mr Parrish. Where is he? Is he alright?' Annie wanted to shake the nurse for a quick answer.

'Mr Parrish has been moved to another hospital.' She answered without concern for her ex-patient or Annie's obvious distress.

'What do you mean transferred? Has he had a relapse? Is it the bleeding on the brain? Have they sent him to a specialist? Annie realised she would have to stop speaking if she wanted an answer from the nurse.

'Mrs Parrish wasn't happy with his care, so he has been transferred to a private hospital.' Annie shook her head in disbelief.

'What a stupid bitch!' The words fell from her lips before she could stop them, besides which she was a stupid bitch and Annie didn't care who knew it. The nurse was unruffled by Annie's choice language and secretly agreed with Annie.

'Isn't it dangerous for Mr Parrish to be moved so early in his recovery?'

'I'm afraid I can't discuss Mr Parrish's case with you as you're not next of kin and I've not been authorized to tell you.' – *'Shit'* thought Annie, he's disappeared and there's nothing I can do about it. Annie knew to argue would be futile. She thrust the plant into the nurses' hands and then removed the card.

'It's for the relative's room.' Annie left the hospital without another word.

Chapter 25

Jack looked out of the window. From his chair by the fireplace, he could see the lawns at Priory Hall. He had been starring at the same view for over a week now. He watched the frost settle every evening, and then melt slowly through the following day. The gradual disappearance of the frost was indicative of the pace of life he now had to suffer. He had watched the grounds men at Priory Hall place Christmas lights in all the large dominant oak trees lining the main drive, reminding him that Christmas was only a few weeks away. It had seemed a life time ago that he had been privy to the decisions regarding the hotel and ordering the fairy lights. If Jack strained his neck he could just see one of the back doors to the hotel. It was one of the few amusements he had to pass the time away, checking on the comings and goings of the staff, wondering how they were managing without him. His sense of responsibility was still keen. He was a perfectionist that would never change. He made several notes on small incidents and procedures that weren't followed to his specifications, things he would have to repair on his return. He wished he had the kind of personality to sit back and take things as they came, but that had never been the case for Jack and all this spare time was only making his keen eye even sharper.

It had been four weeks since his crash and time was dragging. Watching day time TV was a novel experience at first, it was something he had never done, except for the odd day when he was ill, which wasn't often. He could count the days on one hand – until now, but it didn't take long for his patience to wane and the appeal of the programs vanished. He had had his fill of Jeremy Kyle and loose women, although homes under the hammer appealed to his business nature for a short time, but even that had run its course. It was too cold for Jack to sit outside, he couldn't walk far yet and no one seemed to want to come and visit him. He longed for Annie or Violet to come knocking on the door to see how he was and spend some time, just a different face and other conversation than his mother's constant nagging. He didn't even have Scarlett to count on to come across and relieve the tedium of the day. She was away on annual leave and wouldn't be back for another week.

He still didn't know what had happened to Violet on the night of the crash and how she reacted when she finally came home – *shit,* he didn't even know if she did go home? Jack had asked his mother repeatedly if his mobile had survived the crash and if it hadn't could she please go and buy one for him. Marcia claimed to have no knowledge of his phone and insisted that whilst he was convalescing he didn't need it, when he was well enough; maybe in a couple of weeks, she would drive him to town to choose one, but what he needed now was rest and no interruptions.

It was difficult, watching people living their lives, in and out of the back door to

Priory Hall, not that their lives were exciting, it was more the fact that he was only capable of sitting and observing, he longed to participate, but at the moment he had to be contented with the fact that he survived the crash, however lonely he felt.

The doctors and Nurses had been keen to tell him just how close he came to death. Jack had no recollection of being in hospital, up to the point where he woke to find his mother sat by the bed. To say it was a surprise was an understatement. He had a brief recollection of some weird mixed up dreams involving Annie and Violet speaking to him, whilst he was sat on the top of a mountain. He put it down to the crash or the medication and his vivid imagination. The doctors had assured him that he would make a full recovery; he just needed time to let his body heal and mend - and rest. It was the 'rest' part he found most challenging. He was itching to get out and about and back to his normal life. Every time he suggested that he would like to go and get some air, his mother came up with a string of excuses as to why he shouldn't. – 'It was too cold' or 'it was too windy' or 'his lunch would be ready in a moment'. A couple of the staff had managed to get past his mother and had popped over to say 'Hello' since his release from hospital, but that was all. The chef had brought him one of his favourite meals on a tray, but chef had been working and needed to get back to the kitchens, with a big hint from Marcia. She was extremely over protective of him and relentless in her mission to keep everyone possible away. No one and nothing got past her.

His brush with death had affected him far more than he would ever admit to anyone, leaving him with no reserves of energy to fight with his mother, although the opportunity to do so presented itself almost hourly. So far he had resisted temptation and given in to her demands of a quiet life, but the time was nearing when his pressure gauge would blow and he would break free from his maternal jail. Jack didn't want to upset his mother, as she was the one who had flown over and stayed with him all the time in hospital, being with him, reading to him in the hospital when he was too weak to hold a book, speaking to him, playing his favourite music that she had sent for from his cottage. Jack had asked his mMother if he'd had any other visitors in hospital. She said 'No, not that she was aware of.' He specifically asked her about Annie and Violet. Marcia fained surprise at this news and claimed that she didn't even know Annie was living in the area and hadn't been to see him once. A small gut instinct told him that this was not the behaviour of the Annie he knew and loved, but the feelings of pain, abandonment and sadness he felt, drowned out the small voice inside his head and he began to believe his mother. He hoped that it was Violet's reaction to the news he was her father that was making Annie stay away. He tried to understand that she would have to put Violet first for the moment – it wasn't easy. She could have sent a note or card, just to put his mind at ease, if she couldn't come herself.

On one of the cold winter nights, when the TV had been switched off in frustration and Marcia had joined him in the lounge to take warmth from the roaring fire she had set earlier in the day, Jack broached the subject of Violet's parentage. Each day since leaving hospital he became stronger and more capable of making decisions, eventually he felt strong enough to lock horns with his mother.

'There's something I need to tell you with regard to Annie and Violet, her daughter.' He knew his mother was already aware that Annie was living in the area, as he had asked if there had been any word from Annie on several occasions. Marcia turned to face Jack. 'The thing is, there's no easy was to say this – Violet is also my daughter. She's the child referred to in the letter Annie sent to me and that father hid. So bluntly, you're a grandmother.' Marcia didn't flinch or show any sign of surprise - or joy.

'And you want to believe Annie?' Marcia's words were cold and insensitive.

'What do you mean, 'want to believe?'– Violet is my daughter. I am sure. There is no doubt.'

'Jack my dear; you've spent your life chasing a dream, something that isn't real and never will be. What you 'think' you feel for Annie, well it's a fantasy! You're lost in your adolescence. It's about time you grew up and realised Annie isn't your future – she's your past.'

'So you're advocating that I walk out on my responsibilities as a father?'

'Have you had a paternity test?' Marcia was quietly enjoying twisting the knife.

'Well, no...'

'Then you only have Annie's word that the child is yours. Who knows how many adolescent boys she lured into her bed after you left the country? And what about that 'Nick' boy she went to the dance with. It's very likely that he's the father of Annie's bastard.'

'Mother! – You've gone too far!' Jack struggled to his feet. He didn't want to listen to any more of the filth his mother was spouting. 'I am Violet's father and that's an end to it!'

Marcia grinned when Jack could no longer see her face; at least she had managed to plant the seed of doubt.

Jack slumped in to a depression. The one thing Jack had too much of was time. He replayed his life over and over again, with different endings, wondering if Nick and Annie had been together sooner than Annie suggested. He still couldn't understand why Annie and Violet hadn't been anywhere near him. Not even to see if he was alright after the crash? Surely someone had told her? He hadn't expected Annie to be so cold to him, even if she didn't want to be involved with him. They had been getting on well as friends, surely, even as a friend she would have enquired about his well-being? Not to mention the fact that he was Violet's father – or was he? Unconsciously he moved into self-preservation mode. He had spent his whole life chasing something, someone, that it seemed didn't care for him in the same way. Maybe it was time to move on and stop living in the past – but how could he – he needed to know once and for all the truth about Violet – if indeed she was his daughter.

Jack heard faint footsteps on the gravel making their way to the back door of the hotel. He leaned over as far as he could; looking out of the bedroom window to see if he could make out the owner of the feet, but the view was more obscured than in the lounge, but he was sure it wasn't Violet. He closed the curtains, disappointed yet again.

The following day a large pile of books, chosen by his mother, sat on a table trying to tempt him; it was obviously a peace offering from Marcia after her behaviour. His concentration levels were nil, besides which his taste in books was completely different to that of his mother's, not that she listened when he pointed this out when a previous pile of books appeared. There was still the light dusting of frost on the ground, making him aware that it was too cold to sit outside and get some air. He felt as if he were a child again, with no say and no control over his life, especially as his mother was ever present – he didn't like it one little bit.

As for Marcia, she felt very differently. Jack's accident had given her the purpose she had lost since John passed away. The house was too large for one person, but the thought of having to sell up and move filled her with fear, friends didn't bother to come over after John had died. So, each day melted into the next, with a little help from a large dose of gin and tonic. Now, at last she felt useful again, she would have never admitted it, but she was enjoying every aspect of looking after Jack – that was apart from his bad moods. Marcia had decided it was in his best interest not to tell him about Annie and Violet being at the hospital. She had already lost her son once, when he went in search of her. She didn't want it to happen again. Marcia would never admit it, but she was more like her late husband than she cared to be. Jack's peace was interrupted by Marcia walking in.

'Do you need anything darling?' She moved across to him and plumped the cushions he was resting on, disturbing his comfort.

'No thank you.' He was polite, but to the point. He wasn't in the mood for chit chat with his mother. 'Actually, I think I'll have a soak in the bath, the one I had yesterday seemed to help my muscles to relax and I managed a little longer at the physiotherapy exercises they sent me home with and they didn't ache as much afterwards.' Jack stood up carefully.

'I'll go and run it for you.' His Mother was out of the door before he could say bubble bath.

'I'm fine Mother! I'm capable of running my own bath thank you!' He shouted after her, but it was no use she already had the taps running. It was all he could do to get his mother to leave the room for him to undress, but there was no way he was going to let her stay. He locked the door behind her, knowing that if he left it undone he wouldn't get a moments peace. It was a little tricky, getting undressed, but at least he didn't have to dress in a suit and tie as he usually did, casual clothes were definitely the order of the day. He caught sight of all the bruises in the mirror. Over half of his body was black and blue and marked in some way. *'Not the most attractive I've looked.'* He thought to himself. Gingerly he lowered himself into the warm comforting water. He reached for a bottle of manly bubble bath that travelled around with him from home to home for at least two years. Now his Mother was out of sight he poured a liberal dosing into the water, then splashed with his fingers in the water to make bubbles. The last piece of the jigsaw was his IPod. He placed the ear plugs in firmly, then lay back in the water, making sure to keep the wire out of the bath. Peace at last. It was only a matter of moments later that he faintly heard a knock on the front door. It would have been futile trying to get out of the bath and to the door in time. His mother would undoubtedly be there first. He turned the tap on fully, letting more hot water in to his bath. He had no intention of leaving this bath for a long time, no matter who was at the door.

Annie was shaking as she knocked on the front door of Jack's cottage. She didn't know why, it was a perfectly reasonable thing to go and visit a friend that had come out of hospital. She had brought a gift of another orchid plant for him out of the shop. She was hoping he would get this one. She thought about bringing cut flowers, but she didn't even know if he liked them and she didn't want Marcia to think they were for her. It didn't take long for the door to open, but to Annie it seemed an eternity. Marcia's face dropped when she realised it was Annie. Annie wasn't too chuffed either. Still, at least the door was open.

'Hello Marcia. I've come to see how Jack is. I've brought him a gift.' Annie held the plant up for Marcia to see. Marcia glued her best fake smile on her face and put her hands out to take the plant from Annie.

'Oh that's lovely Annie. I'll see he gets it. Thank you for calling.' Marcia was an expert on dismissing people.

'I was hoping to give the plant to him myself?' Annie stood her ground, holding on tightly to the orchid.

'I'm afraid it's not convenient at the moment, but I'll see he gets it.'

'Surely that's for Jack to decide?' Marcia paused for a moment; she didn't like being put on the spot. For a minute or two the two women stood in silence, each standing their ground. Marcia was surprised that Annie had the backbone to oppose her. This was not the young Annie she used to know, she would have caved at the first obstacle. Marcia received the message loud and clear that Annie was no going to disappear easily, so she turned and shouted into the hallway. 'Jack are you decent for visitors?' Bloody typical thought Jack, just when you give up hope of ever having visitors again they turn up, but the relaxing sensation of the warm water against his aching muscles outweighed the promise of idle chat.

'No – ask them to call another time I'm in the bath!' Came the response through the bathroom door. Jack cranked up the volume on his IPod, he wanted peace from Marcia.

The look on Marcia's face was so smug Annie wanted to punch it right there and then. Annie wasn't going to give up.

'Jack. It's Annie, I've brought you a present from me and Violet!' but there was no response. Jack didn't hear her calling; he was oblivious to the events taking place less than twenty meters away. If it was possible to name Marcia's facial expression, it would be called 'conceited bitch'.

'As I said Annie – it's not convenient.' Marcia pulled the orchid plant from Annie's hands and closed the door before Annie had time to respond.

Annie was as mad as a wasp. Marcia had won again. She considered knocking on the door and barging past her to the bathroom to ask how Jack was himself, how he was recovering, but she had suffered enough humiliation for one day. It was Jack that hadn't answered when she called. It was Jack that didn't want to see her.

Jack waited for the water to go completely cold before he managed to drag himself out of the bath. He found it so therapeutic and best of all he was out of his Mother's reach. He lingered there until he was wrinkled beyond the state of 'prune'.

'How do you feel now?' Marcia asked him when the bathroom door eventually opened.

'The heat makes such a difference. I feel great. I'll be back to work tomorrow!' He joked, but he would if he thought he could get away with it. 'Who was at the door?' He asked rubbing the last of the water from his hair with a towel.

'I don't know who he was dear. It was one of the workers from the hotel. He didn't leave his name?' Marcia didn't even flinch. Telling lies was second nature to her. 'He said he would call again. Now go and sit in that front room before you catch cold. I'll bring you some tea.'

'Well? How did it go?' Pippa was eager to find out how Jack was when Annie returned to the shop. 'You haven't been long? I didn't expect to see you this side of closing?' Pippa tied off the bouquet she was holding, ready to give Annie her full attention.

'I didn't get to see him after all that!' Annie couldn't hide her disappointment and anger.

'NO! I can't believe that!'

'He was in the bath and didn't want any visitors!'

'Did he know it was you?' Pippa clicked the switch on the kettle to make Annie a cup of tea for her nerves.

'I don't think so. Marcia didn't say who it was. I can't go again though. She is such a horrible woman! I'm not going to give her the satisfaction of turning me away again!' Annie screwed her face up with distain.

'Do you think she will she tell Jack it was you at the door?'

'I doubt it very much. She took the orchid and shut the door in my face! She'll probably chuck the plant in the bin so he never sees it!' Annie collected two mugs from the cupboard and slung a tea bag in each ready for the boiling water.

'What a prize bitch!' Hissed Pippa.

'Don't I know it!' Annie snapped the head off one of the carnations not used in Pippa's bouquet and shredded it petal by petal in temper, anything to release some of the pent up frustration that Marcia was causing her.

Annie's mood sank further down as the day went on. Everything felt hopeless. She wondered if it would be less complicated if she had no feelings for him, but she did. She was too old to be running around after men, even one man and making a fool of herself. She resigned herself to living the quiet and leaving Jack to convalesce. He knew where she was if he wanted her. She wouldn't be repeating the afternoon's humiliation.

Following a good night's sleep her outlook had been revitalised her outlook. She was feeling positive and decided to only focus on what Violet needed and getting her business off the ground. She couldn't and didn't want to control Jack, whether or not he wanted to be in contact with Violet was up to him – and Violet. Annie was out on delivery duty with a birthday bouquet to one of the teachers at a local primary school when her mobile began to ring. Annie pulled over in a layby before she answered it; she didn't want any more hospital visiting. It was Scarlett.

'Hi Annie. The bad penny has returned! I'm back from my holidays and wanted to catch up on how you and Jack were? Did you go and see him yet? I thought you might call me on my mobile and tell me all the juicy gossip!' Scarlett couldn't contain her eagerness at dipping into other people's lives, like it was a weekly soap opera with Annie and Jack in the starring roles. Work had never been so interesting.

'I did go Scarlett, but he was in the bath and 'Mother Superior' wouldn't let me in!' Annie's annoyance was apparent in her tone.

'So, go back again!' Scarlett said eagerly. 'And keep going back 'til you get through the door!'

'I'm not ever going again! So don't ask me. I'm not going to allow that woman to humiliate me again and I can't spend all my time thinking about him. I have a business to run and a daughter to look after. I think that's plenty without going looking for more trouble, don't you? It's not going to happen Scarlett, so just let it go! I'll speak to you soon.'

Annie felt remorse as she clicked the phone off. It wasn't Scarlett's fault things were so mixed up. Annie immediately texted her back, *'Sorry. I am a miserable bitch today. Forgive me?'* An answer came back almost immediately. *'Forgiven x – but don't let Marcia win!'*

The total rest imposed on Jack by his mother was working. He was feeling a great deal like his normal self, which unfortunately created a severe bought of boredom. He was sat flicking through a book from the pile his mother had provided, 'The life of Mary Queen of Scots.' He had always hated history, even the desperation of boredom didn't make him want to learn now. He was flicking through the photographs, ignoring the text. Marcia came in to do her hourly matron's round carrying a tray of tea.

'Do you mind if I pop to the shops for a few items. There are several things missing from yesterday's delivery from the supermarket. I rang to complain, but they don't seem to care. They want to charge me another £5 to deliver the things they missed! So I'm going to go myself and buy them elsewhere. I won't be long. Now you just sit here and rest. I see you've started reading the books I brought you. I knew you'd like them. I've brought you some tea and your favourite biscuits, so you have no need to move anywhere. Is there anything you would like me to bring back for you?'

'Yes a mobile phone. I don't care which one, even one of those cheap pay as you go ones will do for the moment, but don't come back without one!' Marcia laughed as if he was joking, but he was deadly serious.

'Jack you don't need a phone yet, when you are well enough you can go and choose your own. It will only make you want to work and it's a waste of money to buy a phone that's not the right one. Be patient and wait a while.'

'Mother, I'm serious. If you don't bring one back with you I will order a taxi and go and get one myself!' Jack's tolerance level had finally been exceeded. Marcia was not happy.

'If you insist,' She conceded, 'but I think it will be a mistake!'

'You know there's no hurry for you to get back. Why don't you go and look around the old town for a few hours, it'll be a change for you? It's been years since you were in Preston. I'm going to be fine here and I think I'll go for a sleep after this tea, so there's no point in rushing back?'

'You know I don't like to leave you on your own.' Marcia had already given in once; she didn't want it to become a habit.

'I'm not on my own. There are thirty staff less than a hundred yards away. If I need help I can get it. Go on and enjoy a little time for yourself, you've been running around after me for ages now. I'll be fine.'

'Well - I won't be too long. Promise me you'll rest?'

'I promise.' Said Jack's with his fingers crossed out of sight.

Jack waited until he was sure she had gone, giving her a few minutes head start to Preston. He had no intention of sitting still and resting. There was only one place he was going and that was out. He slowly eased himself up from the chair, making his way to his trainers and coat which were in the hall. It took him a while to get them on; his body was stiff and un-flexing. Finally he was ready for his walk and fresh air.

The cold winter air engulfed him as he slowly ambled around the grounds. He had taken a large golfing brolly from the hall to lean on for balance – just in case. God it felt good to be outside. He inhaled deeply, then regretted it as he had momentarily forgotten about the broken ribs still mending. He decided to be sensible and keep to the perimeter of the buildings rather than heading off in to the woodland grounds. It was a good opportunity to take a mental note of any repairs or improvements than needed to be implemented when he returned to work. One or two of the old sash windows needed a coat of paint and there was a cracked pane of glass in one of the summerhouses. Jack remembered how easily he had slotted into life at Priory Hall. It was a great hotel with an enormous amount of potential; the management structure had been to blame for its earlier failings. He was sure that in time and with his strong management, he could bring Priory Hall back on track and make it one of the leading hotels within the chain, he was already making good progress in that direction. There were many reasons to stay here, including its proximity to Annie and Violet, even if they were giving him a wide berth for the moment, but it wouldn't be long before his task here would be complete and the company would move him on to pastures new.

Scarlett was setting up the large dining room for a Silver wedding Anniversary celebration party in the evening, when she noticed Jack walking gingerly through the gardens. She tapped on the window. He looked across to see who was trying to attract his attention. Scarlett opened the fire door revealing herself.

'Hello stranger!' She shouted across to him. 'How are you feeling?' Jack slowly made his way across to her.

'Ah I'm getting there. I just need to get my body working again. The hardest part is getting past the prison guard!'

'I assume you mean your mother?' Scarlett held the door open for him to come inside and rest a while.

'She means well, but I can't blink without her permission. If I have to put up with her much longer I'm going to be charged with murder!'

'So how have you managed to escape now? Or is she in the grounds searching for you whilst we speak?' Scarlett pretended to look for Marcia behind him.

'She would be if she knew I was out – she's gone in to town for a little 'shopping' and a mobile phone for me. I can't speak to anyone. I've no idea what's going on in the world. I may as well be on a dessert island - so as soon as she was out of sight I escaped for some air, anyway enough about me. How are things here? Are you missing my firm command?'

'Desperately!' Said Scarlett hoping to convince him. Jack didn't believe her.

'The worst part is having no one to talk to all day. It's so different from being at work, I'm used to being surrounded by people all the time.'

'Well it would help you if your mother let your visitors in!' Scarlett couldn't let the opportunity pass to fill Jack in on his mother's antics.

'What do you mean?' He asked, unsure of the point she was making.

'Well, did you know that Annie came to see you a few days ago?'

'No? – She did? - To see me?' He clearly had no idea thought Scarlett. He couldn't hide the delight her words brought.

'Your mother told her you were in the bath and you weren't accepting visitors.' Jack recalled the short conversation he had with his mother that day regarding visitors, but she never mentioned it was Annie. 'Annie was quite upset, especially after everything she did for you whilst you were in the hospital.' Added Scarlett.

'What do you mean what she did for me!' Scarlett could see Jack's defences rising, his eyes flashed with anger. 'She didn't do anything. I may as well not have existed; I'm surprised to hear she called at all. It took her long enough! The accident was weeks ago. She couldn't be bothered to see if I was okay then. So why is she bothering now? She probably never did care in the first place. Even Violet hasn't been anywhere near...' Scarlett was exasperated by Jack's line of thought, she cut him short.

'Jack Parrish – For a manager you're sometimes very thick! I think you need to stop wallowing in self-pity and see the bigger picture!'

'What?' Jack couldn't believe his ears. He was the injured party in every sense of the word. 'I'm not wallowing in self-pity! It's true they both don't care!' Scarlett was becoming cross at Jack's skewed view of events. True, he was unconscious and couldn't be expected to know what events went on, but now it was time for Scarlett to set the record straight.

'You had better sit down Jack, this may take a while, there was things you need to know! – Right, Annie and Violet sat by your bed for days on end whilst you were unconscious! Annie never left the hospital from the time the police rang her, to when your mother turned up and barred her from the hospital!'

'My Mother did what?' Jack was so incensed he tried to stand up too quickly and had to sit down again.

'You heard me right the first time Jack...and Annie told them at the hospital that Violet was your daughter and your mother still wouldn't let her in!' Scarlett relayed the full details of the trauma he and his mother had caused.

'But my Mother told me that she had been the only person at the hospital? She said no one had been near?'

'Well, that's true, once she arrived in the country because she forbade everyone else from coming to see you! – But it was Annie that sat with you for the first crucial nights and days. Marcia wouldn't even let Annie know how you were progressing, let alone visit. Annie has been beside herself with worry, not knowing if you had brain damage or if you would pull through with all your senses intact – well you did lose one sense Jack – your common sense!' Scarlett hoped she hadn't pushed her luck too far. He was still her boss and at liberty to fire her. She softened her approach. 'Annie cares deeply for you. She may not know it yet or be ready to admit it fully, but no woman lives at the hospital for days on end for a man she doesn't care for!'

'I can't believe my Mother lied to me? Why does she want to keep Annie and Violet from me? It doesn't make sense?'

'That one I can't answer for you Jack. You'll have to ask her.' Jack was suddenly very tired. He needed to go home and rest – and think.

Marcia kept her time away from Jack to a minimum. She did need to buy a few extra warm clothes that she hadn't bothered to pack in her rush to be by Jack's side, but they would wait a while longer. She parked Jack's car in the car park at the back of the hotel as near to Jack's cottage as was possible. She had several bags of food shopping and household essentials. Men never did seem to buy all the cleaning, materials needed for each job. Marcia decided to correct that oversight on Jack's behalf. As she neared the house she could see Jack stood on the doorstep waiting for her. Why did son's never follow their mother's advice?. She was about to shout at him for being up and about in the cold, then she noticed the look on his face. There was something wrong; His face looked contorted and harsh, she decided that it must be something very serious. She waited until she was closer before speaking; she never understood why people made such a show of themselves, shouting across a distance. She continued towards him struggling with the bags and their contents. He made no effort to help her.

'Is something wrong Jack? You look upset?' She asked placing the bags on the floor and reached her hand out to touch his arm. He flinched and moved away from her.

'I have a few questions for you to answer mother.' He stated abruptly.

'Well, we'll go inside and I'll make some tea and you can ask me whatever you like. You know you shouldn't be stood in the cold like this if you want to get better.' Marcia bent down to pick up the bags.

'No - we'll have this conversation here and now.' Said Jack standing his ground in the doorway, making sure she couldn't pass.

'Don't be silly Jack. It's cold out here and....' Jack interrupted her; she wasn't going to wriggle out of this one.

'When I was in hospital, did Annie stay at my bedside until you arrived?' Marcia was taken by surprise. She fiddled with the carrier bags to buy some time before answering. It had obviously been a mistake to go out and leave Jack on his own, she wondered if Annie had come calling again?

'Well she may have called in there once or twice. I'm not sure? I was more concerned with seeing how you were. You were in a dreadful state.'

'I want a direct answer mother. Was Annie at the hospital the day you arrived?' Marcia was tempted to lie, but obviously that medalling woman had been to see Jack and poisoned his mind. She could see from his anger that she would have to be careful how she played this one.

'Well our paths did cross momentarily. She was leaving as I arrived I think?'

'Did you send her and Violet my daughter away from the hospital?'

'I keep telling you Jack, how can you be sure that child is your daughter? Annie could tell you anything, you so desperately want it to be true, so you'll believe it! She could have slept with any number of boys after you went to Australia and oh how convenient to tell you it's yours!'

'How dare you refer to Violet as an 'It'. Mother, you know Annie and you know she wasn't that kind of person. You are being disrespectful to her!'

'What about the dis-respect to me - and to you! - Jack they were playing loud music in the hospital, you needed rest. It was more like a party. How were you ever going to get well with those strangers there? You needed your family, you needed me! Now, let me come in, I'm getting very cold out here!'

'I'm afraid I can't do that mother. You're not staying here anymore – All your things have been taken across to the hotel and a room has been booked for you there until you can sort your return flight to Australia.' Jack was calm, but with a firm 'no nonsense' tone.

'Jack, now stop being so silly. I'm going nowhere. You need looking after. You're far from well and you don't want to listen to all that poison Annie's been telling you. Surely you're not putting her before me! I am your mother! Your own flesh and blood! You haven't even seen this woman for the past eighteen years or so. Don't be a fool Jack!' You're father and I didn't raise you to be a fool!' Jack was far too old to accept this dressing down from his mother; he was not a child, no matter how much his mother treated him like one.

'Don't mention his name to me ever again after what he did! Whether or not you accept it, Violet is my flesh and blood and not that I need to tell you, but I haven't seen Annie, she's said nothing about you, though god knows why, she owes you and my father nothing!' Marcia was starting to feel embarrassed; she wondered if any of the staff were watching her humiliation through the windows behind her, she didn't give them the satisfaction of turning around to check if they were there.

'Mother, this will be the last time you ever lie to me, as I want nothing to do with you ever again. All my life you have known how I feel about Annie and yet you blatantly do things you know will hurt me. This time you went too far. Your room is paid for until you leave. For all of our sakes please make it soon.' Without another word Jack closed the door, leaving his mother stood on the doorstep with the shopping bags. Marcia realised that she may have lost her son to Annie – maybe for good? – But she wasn't going to skulk away with her tail between her legs and she had been brought up too well to cause a scene, especially at Jack's place of work, had he lived off the premises it may have been different. She left the shopping on the doorstep; after all, it was for Jack. She would have little need for oven cleaner and pork chops in the hotel. She threw her chin in the air, walked back to her car and sat in the driver's seat to contemplate her next move.

She needed time to come to terms with what had happened, to say nothing of the embarrassment of having to stay in the hotel and not with Jack. She would be the talk of the kitchens. Not that she cared what they thought, but appearances should be kept up as much as possible and in that respect, Jack had let her down. Marcia wiped a single tear from her cheek. It was for her own loss, her plan had back fired and she had been evicted from Jack's life. Marcia had no remorse for her behaviour, only regret that she had not won.

Chapter 26

Violet stared aimlessly out of the minibus window, as it wound its way around the country lanes to Priory Hall for the breakfast shift. There was very little to see as the darkness still enveloped her world. Only an occasional street light or the light from the farm buildings in the distant fields lit the landscape around her. She was on the early the shift yet again. Violet wondered why they kept putting her on a shift that didn't lend itself to bringing out her good points .It was an understatement to say that she was not at her best early in the mornings, she found it difficult to smile at the residents when inside she felt like crap and wanted to be at home, curled up in her bed. The importance of how soft their eggs should be didn't even register on her radar; let alone how lightly the toast should be browned. The only benefit of being at work was being away from home. Violet felt as if she had to tread on eggshells. She was afraid to say the wrong thing or not to say the right thing, it was a nightmare. Her mother was throwing herself in to work, pretending that she didn't care about Jack, instead of just admitting how she felt. If Violet so much as mentioned his name a black cloud seemed to hang over her mother's head waiting to rain on her, so Violet kept her mouth shut. The subject of Violet's parentage was still mainly off-limits as a conversation. Most of the time Annie walked around with a false smile permanently on her face, then when no one was looking the disguise slipped and Violet could see the raw pain she was feeling. Once or twice she tried to speak to her mother about it, braving the cold wind she knew would blow over the household, but Annie denied constantly that she had any feelings for Jack. The more she denied it, the more certain Violet was that she was lying. It was slowly dawning on Violet, how intense her mother's feelings for Jack must have been when they were younger. Even the fact that Violet was here today was proof of her love for Jack. Abortions were available in her mother's day too, even if frowned upon. Her mother had given up her place in university and given her youth to her daughter. Violet was starting to understand a little of what her mum had gone through for her. Violet had never thought about it before, but her mum was a strong woman, she must have been to stick to her guns when she had been alone and pregnant. Violet began to feel something new for her mother – admiration.

The minibus ground to a halt outside the back doors of Priory Hall. Violet looked across to Jack's cottage, looking for any sign of life on offer. There were no lights on and no one to be seen. It was possible he would be in the hotel later. She kept hoping that she would turn a corner and there he would be, dishing out orders with vigour and enthusiasm, telling her to get back to work and keep away from the champagne. She just wanted some kind of contact with him, anything to break the silence between them all, but he seemed to be keeping well away from everyone and the hotel or more likely Marcia was keeping him away.

The news of Marcia's change of residence from Jack's cottage to the hotel had spread through the staff rapidly; it seemed as if everyone knew what was happening in Jack's life, but for some unknown reason this important piece of gossip had evaded Violet. Perhaps it was because Violet's parentage had been the focal point of discussion on the local grapevine that Violet had been left out of the loop. Some were unsure if her loyalties lay with management or staff now that she had been proclaimed as Mr Parrish's love child. So, the fact that Marcia was now resident at the hotel went unmentioned. Another surprise for hotel staff was the fact that the usually even tempered Mr Parrish had resorted to banishing his mother from his home. Whatever his reasons, the staff were itching to get to the bottom of the mystery.

Once inside, Violet went through the same old routine. Coat and bag in to the locker, then out to greet the guests with a smile for breakfast and if you were lucky a cup of coffee behind the scenes first. The hotel was almost fully booked. Christmas party nights had begun and many guests took advantage of the lower room rates offered to party goers and stayed over, meaning that Violet had no time to slink off to a corner and waste some time. It was all hands on deck; everyone seemed to be running back and forth at double speed to keep up with demand for tea and toast. Violet wished she had a recording of the words - 'Would you like tea or coffee?' and 'Would you like some more toast? – White or brown?' It would save her voice from being on a perpetual loop. Violet was in the middle of clearing the debris from one of the family tables, where three children had sampled every available breakfast option on a different plate, then, left most of everything, when Marcia walked in. It was a face Violet would never forget. The duty restaurant manager showed Marcia to a table in Violet's patch of the restaurant.

'I thought you might like to serve your grandmother?' Said the duty manager as she passed Violet on her way back to greet more guests, but if challenged, she would swear blind that she had no intention of causing embarrassment to either Marcia or Violet, but other staff members knew the truth.

Marcia was the last person Violet wanted to see, let alone to serve and be polite to. She marched past Marcia's table with her head down, trying to keep out of sight. Marcia showed no recognition of Violet. Violet almost threw her collection of discarded plates on the floor, when she was out of sight in the kitchens. She needed to call in a favour, she simply couldn't serve that overbearing 'bitch'. Kerry was first on the scene, trying to make her way out to the restaurant with two coddled eggs on toast and a fresh pot of coffee for table six. Violet headed straight for her.

'Kerry. Please will you do me a favour and see to table seven for me?' Violet's

hands had adopted the position of prayer subconsciously. Kerry was not having a good day either and an extra table was going to be more work that she didn't need.

'You have to be kidding Violet! I'm on with dim witted Janine who keeps screwing up all the orders. I'm too busy correcting her mistakes to take your tables as well. Whoever it is they'll be going in half an hour. Just get on with it – It can't be that bad!'

'Kerry please!' begged Violet. 'I can't serve her! – Truly I can't!'

'Violet get a grip. Its only breakfast you're serving. Do me a favour and stop being so over dramatic!' Violet stood in front of Kerry blocking her exit.

'I mean it Kerry – I can't serve her! Her breakfast will end up in her lap or over her head if you make me do it! That's Jack Parrish's Mother – My grandmother and she hates me! Please I'll do anything. I'll swap and work your tables with Janine? Then you don't have to do both and I promise the next time you need someone to swap the rota with you, I'll do it? Even if it's Christmas day? Please Kerry - please?' Kerry considered the offer for a few moments. She quite fancied not having to come in on Christmas day.

'Okay – if it means that much to you, but you don't know what you're taking on with Janine!'

'You don't know what you're taking on with Marcia!' Violet muttered under her breath, just low enough not to be heard as she moved aside for Kerry to pass, she didn't want to put Kerry off.

As expected Janine was a nightmare to work with. The plain and simple truth was that she didn't listen to the customer requests. Brown toast would become white and coffee tea by the time her brain had reached the kitchens, but no matter how many riled customers Violet had to pacify with a smile and an extra round of bacon on their plates, it was far better than the alternative. Violet wasn't sure if Marcia had recognised her, she was after all out of context. Unless Jack had told her, Marcia wouldn't know she worked here and she showed no signs of recognition when Violet passed her table, which was far too frequently for her liking. There was one occasion when Violet thought she had seen her glancing her way, when she thought Violet was busy, but she couldn't be sure. Suddenly Violet's wandering mind was brought back to reality by an almighty crash. Janine had dropped a large tray of used plates and dishes on her way back to the kitchen and in close proximity to Marcia. The restaurant manager indicated for Violet to go and help with the clear up operation immediately. Violet tried to indicate she had other work to see to, but she was not excused. Violet cursed Janine under her breath and through gritted, smiling teeth as she made her way over to the disaster area that was Janine.

'I'm sorry Violet' Said Janine in hushed tones. 'It slipped from my hands when that man from table fourteen pinched my bum as I passed - Dirty old man. He must be at least forty.' Violet turned to look at table fourteen. The man, who was sat with his wife didn't bat an eyelid. The wife looked very refined, the sort of woman who had a housekeeper that was found through an advert in 'The Lady or 'Horse and Hound' magazine. The woman had no wrinkles or lines on her face which proved what Violet suspected, that she had never laughed or smiled in her life. He was reading the paper in-between mouthfuls of cereals and showed no remorse or responsibility for his actions.

'Never mind,' said Violet, 'at least he has a lifetime of punishment - living with his wife.' They both giggled. The Restaurant manager gave them a stern look. They both bowed their heads, clearing the mess away as quickly as physically possible. There was still no indication that Marcia had recognised Violet. - Thank the lord.

An hour later breakfast was nearly over. Most guests had left the dining room, including table fourteen. Violet had managed to slip a piece of half eaten toast and jam in his jacket pocket as they left, with the compliments of Janine. One guest not for moving was Marcia. She had ordered Kerry to bring her another pot of fresh coffee, a round of wholemeal toast and the papers. It was getting harder and harder to ignore Marcia as there were fewer distractions and customers to hide behind. Violet was just setting the last of her tables ready for luncheon when the restaurant manager interrupted her.

'Violet, Mrs Parrish has requested a word with you. You can go now, leave that table.' Violet glanced over at Marcia. She had her head bent down, immersed in the paper.

'I'd rather stick pins in my eyes. Can't you tell her I'm working and she can't disturb me?' The tones were hushed, but firm. Violet had no intention of passing the time of day with Marcia Parrish, after what she'd done.

The manager looked at Violet as if she hadn't spoken and simply barked 'Go now!' Violet had no choice. She walked over and stood in front of Marcia, oozing attitude. Marcia didn't even bother to look up from the paper. After a few seconds Violet cleared her throat to make sure Marcia knew she was there, after all, for all Violet knew she could be deaf and blind – she was old after all. Marcia didn't look up, she simply gave Violet instructions.

'Sit down Violet.' The words were cold and unwelcoming.

'I can't – I'm working.' Retorted Violet. Marcia was going to have to do better than that to get Violet to obey. They were an evenly matched pair.

'You can sit down - silly girl. I've cleared it with the manager, now sit down I want to talk to you.' Violet stood her ground without moving, unsure of her rights. She wanted to tell Marcia to 'F… off' but she was sure that would get her the sack and there was a small part of her that was intrigued as to what she could have to say.

'Well don't dither girl. Sit!'

'Have you no manners Marcia?' Violet was enjoying being defiant and overfamiliar by calling her by her Christian name.

'Very well. Please sit down.' Marcia was not amused. Violet relented and sat, by the end of the conversation Violet hoped to have annoyed Marcia so much she would never want to speak with her again. Marcia folded her paper and then took a sip of coffee from her cup.

'You don't look anything like Jack?' Marcia commented, looking at Violet as if scrutinizing a forged piece of art, thus beginning their game of verbal ping pong.

'Jack doesn't look like you?' Replied Violet curtly, who was surprised at how quickly her brain was working considering the early time of day.

'How can we be sure that you are Jack's daughter?' Marcia was pulling no punches.

'Believe me I wish I wasn't. I had a perfectly good father that I thought the world of and now I find that he wasn't my father at all – Life's shit!' Marcia flinched with the use of bad language, especially in a public place. It crossed her mind to reprimand Violet, but she decided to let it pass.

'So where this man now, the one you thought was your father? Is your mother a divorcee? – Or did he never marry her?'

'No she is not a divorcee – My mother is a widow!' At this point Violet expected Marcia to show some expression of regret for the way she was asked the question –but not Marcia. In her eyes, she and Annie were already condemned as liars. Marcia let Violet's comment pass without acknowledgement. The two women who had nothing in common except for DNA starred at each other across the small wooden breakfast table. It was Violet's turn to go on the offensive.

'Why did you chuck us out of the hospital?' The question had been burning on Violet's lips since she was made to sit with this arrogant, unfeeling woman.

'You both seemed to be having such a good time playing your music at the hospital bed side, but, it was wholly inappropriate!' Marcia screwed her face in to a knot, like she'd tasted something bad and sour.

'It was Jack's music! Not mine or my mother's! The nurses suggested it may help to stimulate his mind, if he recognised the songs that were on his own iPod – you don't think I actually like Michael bubble do you?' The corners of Marcia's mouth curled into a very slight smile, despite her trying to conceal it Violet noticed it. It was the first time she had behaved humanly and not robotic. Violet got the chance to see a faint glimmer of the person she used to be before she became the sour faced old trout everyone knew.

'I'm leaving today Violet. Jack had made it perfectly clear that he…. he is well enough to look after himself. If you indeed are his daughter, I expect you to look after him and behave as a daughter should. I need to know I can contact you to make sure his health and wellbeing are progressing well.' It took a second for Violet to sift through the words to gain their true meaning.

'You mean you want me to spy on him and be your messenger!' Violets nostrils flared in anger.

'No. I merely want to know that he is well. That he hasn't relapsed and…'

'If you want to know how he is – ring him or come and see him! I won't be spying for you!' Violet stood up without waiting to be excused. 'Have a safe journey Marcia. I'd like to say it's been a pleasure meeting my grandmother, but I can't. My parents always taught me not to lie. Unfortunately, it's not a quality that was drilled into you or Jack's dad!' Violet had opened the flood gates; there was no stopping her now. 'You and your husband have meddled in my mum's and Jack's life, causing untold distress and un-necessary heartache. Don't you think it's time to let them find their own way? Either together or apart? I don't know what will happen or if they'll be happy - but honestly Marcia it's nothing to do with you or me, it's between them!' Violet pushed the heavy dinning chair back under the table and walked away without a backwards glance. Once out of sight in the safety of the kitchens, Violet started to shake with temper. If she never saw that woman again it would be too soon, but giving her a piece of her mind did feel exceptionally good.

Jack had heard via Scarlett of his mother's departure. He felt a slight twinge of remorse for the way he had disposed of her, but she had meddled enough. He wasn't a child that could be manipulated. Those days were long gone; he wasn't going to make the same mistakes again. He didn't trust her any more – and probably never would again. He decided that he'd keep in distant contact with her, after all she was all the family he had, but she would never be close enough to affect his choices and those he loved. She had well and truly shop her bolt.

Two weeks had passed since her departure; no contact had been made on either side. The silence spoke volumes. His mother would have found it impossible to accept Violet and Annie. It was just the way she was made. She would be forever sowing seeds of doubt regarding Violet's parentage, undermining the huge task he hoped he had ahead of him, the chance of getting to know her – providing she was willing. He had decided to concentrate on getting fit and well first. The frequent flash back's to the accident were hard to handle, catching him unguarded and leaving him feeling vulnerable. The last thing he wanted was to breakdown in Violet's presence and scare her away, he wasn't a mad man, but he had been left with some emotional scars, that he was sure would fade in time. Physically he had made vast improvements over the past weeks, pushing himself, when it would have been easy to give in.

Another reason for keeping busy and exercising his body back to health, was that it gave him less time to dwell on his thoughts regarding Annie or to be more precisely less time for him to wonder on Annie's thoughts about him. He didn't know what move to make next when it came to Annie. He didn't want to hobble in to the shop as an invalid and have her thinking he was expecting her to look after him – that's why he had kept his distance after Marcia had left. He didn't have the slightest clue what she was thinking or feeling, whether she wanted to be with him or never wanted to set eyes on him again - it was all conjecture, when he was fit and well, he would contact her and not before. He was too proud to admit that fear was also a major component in keeping him away from Annie. As long as he didn't know what she thought, he had hope. He knew he wouldn't survive emotionally if he was to lose Annie again and that was why he had to be physically strong, to overcome what may lie ahead.

One of the advantages of living in a hotel and being the manager was the supply of cooked meals three times a day and the use of the gym. After his mother's forced departure, he had allowed the staff to pamper and cosset him. This was done willingly, the need for him to ask for help never arose. It was as if his recovery was a staff mission, building him back to strength and with it the chances of the hotel's survival. The use of the gym was especially relevant in regaining his strength. Jack usually waited until the gym was closed to the public before venturing across. There had been an instance when he found himself the centre of attention from some of the mature female staff. It seemed that every time he arrived for his workout that several would appear, with seemingly nothing better to do than ogle. So, it had become his routine to exercise late into the evening. On one such occasion, on his way through the hotel via the kitchens, he stopped to complement the chef on making a delicious supper of oven baked salmon with ginger and honey, new potatoes and seasonal vegetables, when Violet came flying through the swing doors into the kitchen, nearly running into him.

He looked very different to the last time she had seen him in the hospital, she noticed his hair had started to grey a little at the sides and it was still very short from where they had shaved it to dress his head wounds. He was slightly thinner, but still looking a lot healthier than when he was in hospital, in fact he looked almost as strong as when he had chided her for drinking the champagne in the garden. Violet was unsure if she should speak or simply continue with her task. Jack too was unsure of his next step. Everyone around them seemed to be oblivious to their awkwardness. The chef was shouting orders at the sous chef and pots and pans were being juggled on and off hot plates to keep up with the orders from the restaurant. With no idea of what the right thing to do was, Violet resorted to a smile. Jack took this as a positive sign and he was swift to act. Before she could think or react, he took her arm and pulled her to one side, away from the bustle and madness of service. Violet let him guide her; she was surprised how good it was to see him. He waited until the busy corridor was empty and they were alone.

'I'm glad I've bumped into you Violet.' His sincerity shone through his eyes. 'Is there any chance you would meet me, when it's your break so we can chat?' Violet couldn't refuse – she didn't want to refuse. There were things she wanted to say to Jack, if she missed this opportunity, who knew when or if she would get the chance again.

'I finish for the evening in half an hour – if that's okay we could meet then?' Jack's heart leapt in his chest, thankful that she would see him.

'Do you want to come over to the cottage? – We can speak without interruptions or people listening?' Jack scanned the rooms with his eyes referring to the staff who had finally noticed the events taking place and were gaining interest. Violet nodded in agreement.

'I'll see you later,' he said finally letting go of her arm, 'just come across when you're ready.' Jack had lost all interest in going to the gym. Instead he went to the restaurant to find some cakes to go with the coffee he was planning to make for Violet. He wanted her to feel welcomed; after all it was the first real conversation he was going to have with his daughter.

The frost cracked under foot as Violet made her way across to Jack's cottage. The thin material of her uniform was no protection against the cold. Her body wanted her to run, but her mind was nervous of what lay ahead and it made her walk. Her teeth were chattering by the time she knocked on the door, she stamped her feet to try and keep her circulation moving. Violet's limited knowledge and understanding of Jack, was as his employee, he played the part of her boss, not a father. She wondered if the two sides of the man would be different. She found it hard to imagine him in the role of 'father', changing nappies and playing foolish, childish games. Luckily for Jack she was past that phase, just the last of the teenage years to get through. She could see thought the front lounge window that the fire was lit and a tray with cups was sitting on the coffee table. It only took moments before Jack opened the door. He had been ready and poised, waiting for her to arrive. In truth he had been pacing and watching out of the window for her arrival, but he didn't want to scare her and open it too quickly. On opening the door, Jack had the impulse to hug her, but he managed to stop himself, just in time. Her last words to him on the night of the crash had been extremely dismissive of him in a parental role. He didn't want to assume anything and scare her away, after all he didn't have the slightest idea what she felt or thought – yet.

'Come in, go through to the sitting room and sit by the fire. You look frozen! Haven't you got a coat?' Violet flashed him a glance letting him know he as barking up the wrong tree if he thought he could get her to wear a coat. Not even Annie managed that. Jack closed the front door and followed her into the sitting room. The rooms were less spacious and stately than she had imagined. It was in essence, a cosy little cottage. It had none of the grandeur she associated with management. Jack showed her to a seat by the fire, then took a seat opposite. For a few moments, the silence drowned them, each waiting for the other to start the conversation. In the end it was Jack who took the initiative. Violet noticed that he looked nervous and not as confident as he usually did in public, she found it quite endearing.

'Thanks for agreeing to see me Violet……..I'er…. I wanted to do this, to talk with you, since I came out of hospital, but I didn't know what to say to you or even if you would speak to me? – Especially after the last time we met.' Violet lowered her eyes and focused on the fire, embarrassed at her behaviour on the evening in question. 'I suppose there's no point in dancing around the subject, so I'm just going to dive in and say what needs to be said. That is unless you want to speak first?' He felt he should give her the option. She shook her head; she had no idea where to begin. Jack continued, 'There is one thing that I want to make absolutely clear to you – I didn't abandon you and your mother. My family were- well – they hid the truth from me and I only found out the whole truth on the same day that you did.' Jack paused and waited to see what Violet had to say. Violet found the courage to look him in the eye. She nervously cleared her throat before beginning -

'Mum has explained everything to me. I know now that's what happened – when I came to see you on the night of the……..crash, I didn't understand everything.' Violet took a deep breath, 'I'm sorry for the things I said to you. They were hurtful and cruel. I didn't mean them, as you know I was very drunk. I don't know exactly what I said, but I know myself well enough to know it wouldn't have been

'nice'.' Jack smiled at her choice of words.

'No, your words weren't 'nice' – but I understand why you said them. I hate to think what I may have done, if I was in your position. I know how furious I was when I found out that my father had stolen your mother's letters to me. The best thing we can do is forget that you ever came to see me on the night of my crash.' Violet nodded in agreement. It was an event she would be glad to forget. Jack continued, 'I mean, I was reckless, I was so worried about your safety in the car with Harley. I shouldn't have chased you, I wasn't concentrating and I brought it upon myself.' Violet was visibly shaken by his words.

'You were chasing after me when you crashed?' Her eyes were wide with amazement. Jack realised his mistake, adding the burden of his accident to their conversation. It was a piece of information he should have kept to himself – maybe he wasn't going to take to parenting like a duck to water?

'It wasn't your fault Violet. I took my eyes off the road. It was totally …'

'But you wouldn't have been there if it wasn't for me?' Violet felt dreadful. It never occurred to her that she may have been the cause of him being on the road in the first place. Jack could feel her distress. He decided to take a chance; he leant forward and took one of her hands in his. She didn't tug away, she accepted the gesture politely.

'If we're going to get past this you need to stop thinking that my crash was anything to do with you. You're safe, I'm safe now and that's all that matters.' Violet looked down at the carpet, she couldn't look him in the eye. Jack decided to change the subject; keeping on this tack would get them nowhere fast. He let her hand go free and started to pour the coffee.

'I don't want to presume anything, but I would love to get to know you properly. I don't mean as your father – I know Nick was your father and a good one! I don't want to take his place, but if you feel like want to get to know me too, well that would make me very happy. We can take it slowly. I promise not to ground you before you leave here tonight?' He smiled hoping she would take the joke for what it was, an attempt to lighten the mood. Violet couldn't answer, she was so riddled with guilt for the crash, she stared into the fire.

'What does your Mum have to say about all this?' This question was big enough to jolt Violet from her silence and get her dander up.

'Why haven't you been in touch with her? She spent days sitting by your bedside, willing you to live and recover. She didn't leave that hospital for one moment, until that toss pot of a mother of yours turned up and chucked us out! Mum didn't deserve treating that way!' Violet's burning anger began to shine through. Jack took it all in his stride. He hadn't expected it to be an easy ride and Violet's description of his mother was extremely accurate. He was glad to see she had a backbone.

'If you were there Violet, you'll know that I had nothing to do with sending you or your mother away! My mother made some wrong decisions and she has been punished for those, as you know she is no longer here...'

'....But why haven't you been round to see mum? You're almost fully recovered now! For God sake you could have phoned her, just a few words to put her mind at rest and let her know you are fine! So tell me Jack - why didn't you?' Violet was on her feet now, staring down at Jack with distain. She was not going to leave until she had an answer. Jack rose to his feet and paced the floor searching for the right words.

'Things in the adult world as not always as easy as you first think Violet, things get complicated and ...'

'Don't try and fob me off with some bullshit about when I'm older I'll understand about the 'adult world'! You learn quite a lot when your dad is killed in a car crash!' Mistake number three Jack calculated.

'I'm sorry. That was patronising.' Jack admitted.

'If you want to get to know me Jack, then I'm going to have to trust you and the same goes for you. You have to trust me too and tell me the truth! I don't want or need a plastic father figure in my life, I want to get to know the real you, cause if we pretend now, it'll never work in the long term?' Jack was astonished by Violet's words of wisdom and her insight into human nature at such an early age. She was certainly her mother's daughter thought Jack. Inside Jack a beam of pride was ignited, thank the lord, the girl had common sense too.

'Okay.' He said 'The truth is .... Well there are lots of reasons.' He was floundering at the prospect of putting his thought into words. One slip of the tongue and their relationship could be over before it began.

'I'm listening?' Said Violet sitting back down and giving him her full attention.

'I suppose I'm afraid.... I spent so many years wanting to be with your mother and through our life so many things, people were in our way – stopping us.'

'You mean my dad?'

'Yes - No – partly, but things went wrong way before that, when I was sent to Australia. When I didn't stand up for what I wanted and I let my parents bully me into something I will regret for the rest of my life. I'm glad Nick was there for your mother and you, but by lying to me and keeping me in the dark, I never had the chance to stand up and see If I could have made it work, if I could have been a good father to you and husband to Annie. My parents stole that from me and now - I'm afraid that I may not be up to the job. Everything I do will be compared to Nick's way of doing things – I don't think I can compete.'

'What a load of shit!' Violet stood up again to look at him on the same eye level. 'You sound like a five year old winging and moaning about what people did to you! Your future is in your hands. If you want it – Fucking make it work!' Jack laughed openly at her directness. It had been a long time since someone had told him he was talking shit.

'Violet, I don't even know if she has any feelings for me?'

'You never will, so long as you stay away from her! I don't know everything mum's thinking, because she's as stupid and stubborn as you are, but I can see she cares for you and if it doesn't work out at least you'll know and you'll be no worse off than you are now!' He was about to give Violet a list of reasons why he shouldn't follow her suggestions, but she stopped him.

'Do you love her?' Her words were plain and simple.

'Violet, you can't ask me to tell you how I feel about your mum when I haven't even told her?' Jack was blushing.

'Do you want me on your side or not?'

'Violet...I..'

'Just answer the bloody question Jack. It's not difficult? – Yes or no?' It was Jack's turn to take a deep breath.

'Of course I do! Do you think I'd put up with your interrogation if I didn't? – Yes I love her. Always have, always will.' They both smiled.

'Then do something about it Jack, before someone else snaps her up! Joe at the garage always asks me about mum whenever I walk past?' Jack was pleased to see her relax a little and feel she could joke with him.

'I think I'm a better catch than Joe! I have all my own teeth!'

'It doesn't matter who's the better catch. It's who gets there first!' Violet wanted to punch him into action.

'And how would you feel if we did get together?' He asked with trepidation. 'It would be really weird. I've never seen her with anyone else but my dad.' Violet was conscious of using the word to describe Nick, 'but I'd get over it. I love my mum and I want her to be happy. If however, you think there's the smallest chance that you'll hurt her – then stay away. I don't want to see her hurt again.' Jack nodded, contemplating her words. 'In fact I have a favour to ask you. I know I said you should get in contact with mum, but please will you wait a few more days and let me have this Christmas with my mum before you bound in. If all goes well with you two, then it will be my last Christmas with her, with just the two of us?'

'I wouldn't turn you away at Christmas you know, if we did manage to work things out. I'd want to spend time with you as much as your mum would. I've got a lot of Christmases to make up for!'

'I know – but do you understand what I mean? Since Dad – I mean Nick died; it's been me and mum. I just want to have that one last time. It's only a few days?' Jack couldn't refuse her. It was the only thing she had ever asked of him. He had waited this long to find Annie, another few days wouldn't hurt. He would be stronger then, not an invalid needing to be looked after. He could explain everything to Annie in the New Year.

'Okay, I agree to wait, but in the New Year I'll come knocking.' Violet jumped to her feet.

'Right I'd better go or I'll miss the minibus home.' To Jack's surprise Violet hugged him, Just a short brief hug, but it was wonderful to hold her in his arms. He felt choked with emotions, a reminder of all the birthdays and Christmases he had missed was almost too much to bear, but it was more important to look forwards now – not back.

'Will you come and see me next time you're working? Maybe we could go for a walk in your lunch break or something?' He didn't know if he was asking too much of her.

'I'd prefer or something. I'm not the outdoor type. Let's get that clear now. I don't want you surprising me with a bonding session that involves walking, climbing, diving or skiing. Now a shopping session would be a different matter or a historic building at a push!'

'I won't do anything before I run it past you first.' Jack was elated at the thought of future meetings with his daughter, now he was getting to know her, he felt entitled to use the word, but only to himself. It was far too early to let her hear him.

'Oh and the next time I see you, I've got something to tell you about Harley.' Shouted Violet as she made her way towards the minibus.

Chapter 27

Annie switched on the lights in the shop. It was five a.m. and still pitch black outside, it wouldn't be light for hours. It was four days until Christmas and the rush had started. A stack of orders for holly door wreaths and garlands was waiting for her attention. She tried to get to the orders during the day when the shop was open, but somehow fate was conspiring to keep her busy in other directions. She had no alternative than to make an early start, hoping to make some headway into the mound of work ahead of them. Annie watched the beams from the florescent lights bounce on to the glittered items that filled most of the shelves, against the back drop of the darkness outside, it was almost magical. Annie hated Christmas in the shop. As other people were winding down for Christmas, enjoying the festivities and planning presents and surprise and outings and work parties, she was working harder and faster than ever. She had been through it before when she worked for someone else, but she got to go home and leave them working, a privilege given to her because she had a young child, but those days were long gone, now it was Annie letting Pippa leave at a reasonable time, so that she could prepare Christmas for the children. Annie was glad that it was going to be a very quiet Christmas this year, just herself and Violet. At one time she wondered if Jack would be a part of their celebrations, but she had still heard nothing from him. She knew from Scarlett that he was back on light duties at work, as far as she could see there was nothing and no one standing in his way of contacting her – yet he still kept his distance. Annie questioned Violet each time she returned from working at Priory Hall, but according to Violet she had never seen or contacted Jack. Annie worried about the effect of Jack's apathy towards Violet. She seemed settled and didn't mention him, but she must be feeling the effect of knowing he had not tried to become involved in her life. Regardless of what he felt for Annie, she felt he was letting Violet down and after Christmas she was determined to have it out with him.

To Annie the arrival of Christmas day meant just veg'ing out in front of the TV and relaxing, although in likely hood she would spend most of the day asleep or trying to keep awake for Violet's sake. Violet's presents were wrapped and ready, that was one benefit of being a florist, mountains of wrapping materials at her disposal. A small turkey was ordered with the butcher and Violet had promised to go to the supermarket in the last few days to get the fresh produce they needed, at this time of year there was no chance of Annie leaving the premises even for an hour. If Violet didn't go it would be turkey without the trimmings.

Annie gazed at the pile of holly and wished it was New Year already. Luckily, the holly wasn't too prickly this year. Stan had told her about Jeff, a local farmer with an abundance of holly trees in his fields. He was only too glad to let Annie harvest some for use in the shop for a reasonable fee and a holly wreath for his own front door. Collecting it was the easy bit. Now it had to be wired and sculpted into place - not a job for the faint hearted. Annie started by finding a large bough of lush holly, heavy with berries and cutting it in to small pieces, then she took two or three pieces and wired them together. She screwed her face up every time one of the sharp edges penetrated her flesh, which was every few seconds. The first day of using holly was always the worst, she knew by tonight her hands would be sore and swollen, but in time her hands would become used to and eventually oblivious to each prickle, at least with no visitors this Christmas, she wouldn't have to sit on her unsightly hands during Christmas lunch. She placed the first piece of wired holly on the side of the work bench knowing that it was the first of many she would need before the end of the day. As she ploughed through, her mind wandered. She looked around the shop at what she had achieved in a relatively short space of time. She had been accepted by the local community and the locals seemed to love the shop. New customers were arriving each week, building a good solid client base, which every shop needed. It was no good relying on the peak periods to carry her through the year. They were important but she needed customers all year round and if her start was anything to go by, she might well achieve that. She was never going to become a millionaire being a florist, but the bills were being paid and she loved her job. What more could she ask for.

Annie's thought's turned to Violet. She seemed to have settled well at college. There had been no calls from tutors wanting to know why she hadn't been in class and the end of term report was positive and almost glowing. Her work at Priory Hall was keeping her busy and allowing her to save money to go travelling when college was over. This was something Annie had known about for a long time and indeed encouraged. Annie wanted her to have the chance to see the world first hand, not wait for her friends to come back and tell her what they had experienced. It was not an option that had ever been open to Annie, but neither did she regret the path her own life had taken, Violet was her world and had been since the moment she found out she was pregnant. Annie was pleased that Violet had a plan, but she didn't know how she would manage; not seeing Violet on a daily basis, but all this was in the future, no need to worry about it now. Annie glanced across at the growing pile of wired holly, there was still nowhere near enough. She willed her fingers to work faster. Thinking about Violet made Annie's thoughts turn to Jack. She had come to terms with the fact that Jack was not a part of life or her future. In the days following Marcia's departure, Scarlett had been her informer she half expected him to turn up on her doorstep as if nothing had happened, no injuries, no hospital, no deaths door – but he didn't. There had been no sight or sound. Not even Violet had seen him when she'd been working, Annie had asked each day on her return – subtly of course. For all Annie knew, he could have left the country, except for the fact that Scarlett had given her occasional updates on his wellbeing when ordering flowers for Priory Hall. The fact that she knew he was recovering well, yet still not making contact brought out the stubborn streak in Annie. She was the one who had been sent away, so he should be the one to make the first move. She had been tempted to deliver to Priory Hall in person, hoping that she may bump into him, but each time she chickened out at the last minute and sent Pippa. If Jack wanted to see her he knew where she was. Now, some weeks later, she had given up all hope of things turning out in her favour. Some fences couldn't be mended and the longer it went on the stronger her resolve became. Work and Violet were her only priorities now. Jack? – Jack who?

The wired holly grew into a large mound, finally there was enough ready to start assembling the first of the Christmas door wreaths. Annie looked up from her work to realise that dawn was just beginning to break. She could see the faint outlines of the buildings outside. They looked different somehow. She went over to the shop window to investigate. Snow - snow was the culprit. All the buildings had been dusted with white gleaming snow. She unlocked the door and stepped out onto the street. There was silence. No cars or pedestrians. The amber street light further along the street gave it a Dickensian feel. She stood absorbing the moment and her surroundings. Annie was at peace with herself and the world - if only she didn't have holly to contend with.

Pippa arrived at eight a.m., dressed in wool from her feet to the top of her head. Gloves, hat, jumper, scarf, you name it she was wearing it. She looked as if she had just stepped out of an advert for the North Pole.

'God, it's cold out there. I love looking at snow, but it's not too good when you have to go to work in it! You've done loads of holly!' She squealed as she walked closer to Annie. I can take my gloves home intact.' She laughed pulling a pair of rubber gloves out of the pocket.

'I was awake so I made a start – but you can't wear gloves to make these – that's cheating!'

'Cheating or not you'll not catch me making them without them! Go on! Pass me a base. The sooner we start the sooner we finish!' It took them both all day, in between serving customers to get ahead with the orders. Luckily, Stan had been drafted in to make the deliveries leaving them more time to concentrate on the shop, which they desperately needed. Every time Pippa sold one of the door wreaths, Annie growled at her knowing it would have to be replaced, still it was money in the till.

The snow seemed to heighten the feeling of festive spirits in the village. Several regular customers had been in to the shop to drop off a Christmas card. She felt warmed and charmed by their generosity. They had accepted her – it was home.

The next few days were a blur of activity. Orders were still coming in left, right and centre, especially as there had been no let up with the snow. For those people who had left their shopping until the last minute, local was best. Fighting against the snow and traffic to get to Preston town centre looking for presents was not an option for many, so a trip to Violet's florist, which was close to home and in many cases walkable, became a priority. Sales of flowers, plants and ornaments far exceeded Annie's expectations, so much so that when Christmas Eve arrived Annie and Pippa were quite relieved that they had managed to make it through their first Christmas at the shop. Annie had called a halt to the holly wreath making. Their stocks of holly were diminished and there was no way Annie was going to fight against the snow and the cold to go cutting again. When it was gone it, that was it. Luckily, most of the work had been completed and they could manage to finish the rest with what they had. Christmas Eve was mainly taken up with people collecting items already ordered, it meant an early start to make sure everything was prepared, but usually towards the afternoon the pace slowed down and the long unwind to Christmas could begin. To help and encourage this process and inject a little Christmas spirit into themselves, Annie and Pippa laid out a platter of mince pies from the local baker and a tray of mulled wine to thank the people for their custom, but it made the process of serving each customer twice as long, with everyone wanting to chat and tell of their Christmas plans. Eventually Annie bribed Violet, who was 'resting' upstairs, into coming into the shop to help before she was due at Priory Hall for a shift later. Violet was quite happy to chat and keep everyone topped up with mince pies and drink including herself. Annie wondered how many dishes would be spilt in laps by Violet tonight, if she didn't slow down on the amount of hospitality she was showing to herself. Annie on the other hand needed to keep a clear head, until she was sure all the orders had been made. She was persuaded into having one glass of mulled wine with Violet and Pippa when there were no customers in, to celebrate the good team work and friendship that had been forged between them since moving to longridge. Any more would have to wait until the door was firmly closed.

It was mid-afternoon before Annie managed to persuade Pippa to go home. Annie knew how much Pippa still had to do to finalise all the last minute Christmas details for her children. It was also her first Christmas with Zach and Annie knew how important it was to Pippa that everything was perfect. If things went well between them, Annie knew that Zach was hoping Pippa would ask him to move in. Annie could see a bright and rosy future for her friends; at least things were working out for someone.

'Are you sure you and Violet don't want to come and join us for Christmas dinner?' Pippa offered, 'There's plenty to go around and we'd be glad to have you. You know the kids would be thrilled?'

'No! Honestly.' Annie declined the offer. 'Thank you, but I'm looking forward to relaxing and doing nothing. Give me a bottle of wine and the TV and you are looking at a happy woman. Now get yourself home and I'll see you after Christmas.'

'But you're not even going to see much of Violet with her working. I don't like the thought of you sitting alone and brooding over Jack, especially on Christmas Day.' Pippa tried one last time to change Annie's mind.

'Pippa you are a good friend, but I have no intention of sitting and brooding over Jack and we'll fit Christmas dinner around Violet's shifts and the thought of being alone and peaceful sounds fantastic to me!' Pippa signalled her defeat by kissing Annie on her cheek. She shouted behind her on her way out of the front door, 'You know where we are if you change your mind!'

'I won't!' Replied Annie smiling broadly, knowing peace and that bottle of wine was on the horizon.

By three o'clock all the people had been in for their collections and had taken them to their respective homes, the high street was deserted; most people had begun to head home to begin their Christmas festivities. Annie poked her head out of the front door. The snow was falling again, as if on cue to create a perfect Christmas. Annie decided she had had enough and those customers who still needed things would have to do without. Annie turned the sign on the door to 'closed' and shut up shop for Christmas to begin. She felt a great sense of pride and achievement as she turned the key in the lock. The shop had been a success; she was making enough money to keep the business afloat. After all the hard work she had put herself thought over the past few months, the thought of being able to walk away for a few days with no responsibilities made her feel giddy. She could hear the wine calling her from the fridge where it was cooling. Annie flicked off the light switches, she would clear everything away another day, even if it was Boxing Day, she didn't care, for now she simply wanted to relax. As she started to climb the stairs to the flat, she found Violet stood at the top, wrapped in all things warm, ready to go and start her shift at Priory Hall.

'I'm off mum. I don't know what time I'll be back. I think it may be a late one, but wake me in the morning for present time won't you?' Violet was knotting her scarf tightly around her neck.

"You know I will, but you can sleep in if you like. It's only me and you so there's no rush?'

'Yes there is! You know I love to see what Father Christmas has brought us!' Annie gave Violet a wry smile. Especially since the days of Christmas surprises were long gone and Violet had been to town and chosen all her presents' weeks ago, then presented them to Annie for wrapping, except of course for a couple of surprises that Annie had managed to hide from her.

'Promise me you'll wake me?' Violet kissed her mum on the cheek as she dashed past.

'What if I want a lie in?' Annie questioned.

'You! You've never had a lie in since I was born!' laughed Violet.

'I wonder why?' Annie replied with a twinkle in her eye.

'Don't wait up for me Mum! Happy Christmas!' And like a magic genie out of a lamp Violet disappeared though the door. Annie went to the fridge to pacify the wine that had been calling; she poured herself a small glass and placed the remainder back in the fridge. She took a sip. Immediately she could feel her tensions start to release. The next household item vying for her attention was the sofa. Annie hated to disappoint, she threw her gangly legs out to the furthest reaches, making herself comfortable on the sofa, resting every muscle in her tired body. It was blissful, surrounded by quietness and nothing that had to be done at this moment, as long as she didn't count preparing the meal for tomorrow and wrapping a few last little parcels for Violet's stocking. They would wait a while, everything could wait. Annie closed her eyes for a moment absorbing the relaxation. It only took two minutes for sleep to come and find her; she was dead to the world in an existence without holly and glitter.

Annie awoke with a jolt as she heard Violet shouting her name as she ran up the stairs.

'Mum! Mum, the bus hasn't come, it must be because of the snow, but I can't get to work. I'm going to be late. Can you run me there in the car?' Annie exhaled deeply, trying to bring herself back to reality from her dreams.

'Give me a minute and I'll be with you.' It was going to take time for her to muster her muscles and coax them into moving so soon after they had been promised a break.

Annie grabbed her keys, coat and hat as swiftly as she could under the circumstances. Annie didn't relish the thought of driving in the snow, but she understood how important it was for Violet to get to work on such a busy time of year for the hotel. The snow was falling fast and thick, depositing a fresh layer on top of the previous downfalls. The lack of traffic on the roads meant that the road markings were buried beneath snow, making the journey more treacherous.

'Violet, I don't think it's a good idea to drive in this. The roads around here won't have been gritted. I'll call them and tell them you can't make it.'

'No! Mum I have to go. You know how busy they are. Plus we get to have a little staff party after the customers are all served and finished - and the tips are great tonight according to Nirah. They get so drunk they don't know what they're tipping! - Please Mum? I've got all my cards to give out and a present for Nirah and Scarlett? You'll be the best mum ever? If we take it slowly we'll be fine – At least you can still tell where the road is and you are a good driver.' Annie against her better judgement fell for Violet's pleading and flattery.

'You are washing up after Christmas dinner then – and boxing day!' She demanded.

'No worry – there's not much washing up from two, Marks and Spencer's turkey dinners for one!' Giggled Violet.

'Cheeky! Be careful or next year I'll make all your dreams come true and it will be two Marks and Sparks' dinners!'

They climbed into the car, only to get out again. The weight of the snow was too much for the wipers and they had to clear the windscreen and windows by hand before they could move.

'Isn't this making you feel festive mum?' Enthused Violet.

'No!' Said Annie throwing a snow ball at Violet, who had been to slow to consider, that her mum may fire first. 'I can think of other ways to be festive and they don't involve being frozen to death in the snow outside my home!' When the screens were clear they set off. Annie moved cautiously along the road. A few cars had passed in the time it took them to make the car safe for the journey cars, leaving a path of tyre tracks in the snow to follow. Most people, excluding Annie and Violet had the sense to stay home. The snow was soft and giving, allowing the tyres to compress the snow giving a little grip to the road, at least there hadn't been a frost, so most of the roads were passable with care, but if the snow continued to fall at the same rate, that wouldn't be for long.

'Did granddad teach you how to drive this slowly or does it just come naturally?' Violet not being a driver, didn't understand the severity of the conditions.

'Wait until you drive and see what it's like. If only I had some 'L' plates you could have your first lesson now!' Annie's temper was beginning to fray.

'Do you wish you and Jack were together?' Violet knew the best time to get an honest answer out of her mum was when she was distracted.

'What? - Where did that one come from?' Annie was bewildered by Violet's train of thought. 'How did we get from driving lessons to Jack?'

'Well it's the sort of things dads do – teach their children to drive? And it made me think, do you wish you were together?'

'I don't even think about it Violet. Jack has his life and I have mine.'

'But if you were to get together…..'

'Violet! It's not going to happen so you don't need to worry! Jack and I…,' Annie corrected herself, 'There is no Jack and I.' Annie's tiredness was showing, she was losing patience. Jack was the last person she wanted to discuss whilst trying to navigate the perilous roads.

'There will be a you and Jack after Christmas.' Violet added innocently.

'What *are* you talking about? I think you had too much Mulled Wine in the shop earlier!' Violet was regretting opening her mouth, but it had gone too far for her to back down now.

'If I tell you something will you promise not to get angry with me?' Annie was becoming more and more confused and worried what Violet had been medalling in.

'Go on then – spill the beans. I can't wait to hear this!'

'I've been to see Jack…..a few times. I bumped into him at work and we got chatting.'

'You did what? Why didn't you say? How did it go and what have you told him?'

'Okay, okay calm down Mum, one question at a time. It went well……eventually. It was a little hard at first. I told him a few home truths and he did the same, but overall……I quite like him. He takes a bit of getting used to, but I can cope with him.' Annie's mouth was open wide and would be catching snowflakes if the window was open. 'I know it's not for me to say Mum, but he's still in love with you… I can tell.'

'That's simply nonsense! If he cared for me, let alone loved me at all Violet, he would have been in contact with me, but I've heard nothing since the hospital. You can't make presumptions and make it up!'

'I'm not! Please don't be cross at this bit, but there is a reason. - I asked him to let me have this last Christmas with you, before you, well you know, get together.'

'You did what!' Annie couldn't believe her ears. In her anger, she turned sharply to look at Violet, pulling the steering wheel slightly with her, but with the road conditions as they were it was enough to send the car into a skid. Annie tried to pull on the wheel in the opposite direction in an effort to correct it. She seemed to remember being told not to use her brakes, or should she use them, she couldn't remember. The car swerved back and forth through the snow as Annie tried to fight the wilful monster with four wheels and a mind of its own. In the end, her attempts were in vain, the car won, landing sideways in a hollow ditch, leaving Annie and Violet stunned and in shock. Silence followed for a few timeless seconds whilst they both assessed the situation.

'Are you alright?' Annie's concern was for Violet.

'I'm fine Mum. What about you?'

'Yes, yes I'm fine. Just kicking myself for being so stupid, but fine.' Annie didn't know if she was more shocked from the crash or the news that Violet had been meddling in her life. The car was well and truly stuck. They were going nowhere, so Annie decided to probe into Violet's meddling a little more, whilst she was pinned in a corner with nowhere to go.

'So! What exactly have you and Jack decided amongst yourselves?' Asked Annie, far from amused.

'Aren't you worried about the car?' Violet couldn't get a handle on her mum's priorities. She was usually so practical.

'No, the car is a goner. I'd like to know more of the plans you've hatched!' Violet against her better judgement gave Annie a potted version of her conversations with Jack. She was literally pinned into a corner, so the easiest way out was to spill the beans.

'So it's me that's really to blame for him staying away.' Violet hung her head in shame. She could feel the anger radiating from her mother. 'Please don't be mad Mum? I can get over the fact that you two will be together.'

'You're taking an awful lot for granted there! I suppose I don't have a say in this?'

'Of course you have a say. I just wanted you and me to share one last Christmas – is that stupid?' Annie wanted to say 'yes, it is', but she held her tongue.

'You seem to think that everything is pre-destined. I may not want to be with him. I'm perfectly happy on my own. – Anyway we have other things to sort that are far more important than my love life or lack of it!' Annie didn't want to hear anymore. 'The car's a right off and we're stuck in the middle of the countryside and it's snowing buckets and if that isn't enough, it's Christmas Eve!' Annie rested her head on the steering wheel, hoping a miracle would arrive – It didn't.

'Come on, we're going to have to get out and walk.' Said Annie pushing against her door to open it.

'Walk!!!' protested Violet.

'Yes. Priory Hall isn't too far down this road. We'll be able to get some help there and you can get to work! That was the whole point of this trip wasn't it? – and you'll have to climb across, you won't get out that way.'

'But it's snowing! We'll get cold!'

'We'll get colder if we stay here, it's getting darker and if it doesn't stop snowing we'll be snowed in - so we need to get into the warmth as soon as possible. There's no way we're going to get the car out of there today, especially as its Christmas Eve. We'll lock it up and deal with it later. Have you got everything?' Annie and Violet zipped up and wrapped up before they set off on their march in the snow. Their feet disappeared as good five inches into the snow before they hit solid ground. Violet's black work shoes were sodden in seconds, her feet frozen solid and unaware of the work her legs were making them do. Annie linked arms with Violet. Violet wasn't sure which one of them she was trying to keep upright. Annie didn't dare admit it to Violet, but she was enjoying the adventure, knowing they were both safe and unharmed from the car incident. There was something wild and freeing in walking in heavy snow in the middle of nowhere, it was almost ethereal.

'Come on, let's imagine we're on an adventure in the Arctic Circle?' Annie was trying to lift violet's spirits for the twenty minute walk, 'Make sure to watch out for polar bears!' Violet did not appreciate her mother's sense of humour and barely raised a smile. She was cold and wet and she hadn't even started work yet. Everyone would be happy enjoying Christmas Eve, it was going to be a miserable time for her. It was hard enough smiling at the customers all the time when she was in a good mood. She was going to have to fake it tonight; at least Harley didn't work there anymore, so she wouldn't have to worry about bumping in to him. Her mind wondered for a moment, it was possible there would be a fit looking new replacement to work alongside, but even if there was, the state she was in now was enough make anyone run a mile.

Chapter 28

Christmas Eve was Jack's first full day back at work. He had worked a little from home in the lead up to Christmas, mainly organising Harley's downfall. Violet had enlightened Jack on Harley's business operations on one of her visits. Jack was aghast when she told him what he was doing and how he was doing it. He knew that the ledgers in the cellars were not balanced and he had spent hours poring over the numbers trying to resolve the differences. Now, all became clear, Harley had never been an easy member of staff to manage, always truculent and surly, but never in a month of Sundays would Jack have accredited him with enough intelligence to pull off this scam on the scale he had managed. There was no time to loose in setting a trap. Everyday Harley worked at Priory Hall was a day they could potentially loose more money.

It was easy enough to rent the surveillance equipment, along with an engineer to set everything up. Jack made sure the cameras were fitted on a day when Harley was off duty and if anyone asked what the workmen were doing, the answer was 'Routine maintenance'. At first Scarlett had been shocked by Jack's news, then little instances kept coming to mind, how he had offered on many occasions to go to the cellars and collect the wines and spirit, and because he always did a good job she came to rely on him and even seek him out if she knew he was on duty. He had taken her in; she wouldn't let it happen again.

Jack had the monitors for the surveillance set up in his cottage, away from prying eyes; the last thing they wanted was for him to be tipped off. It was also the perfect remedy for Jack's boredom. Every time the cellar doors opened, Jack was watching, waiting to catch him. On the second day Jack watched with interest as Harley took some boxes out from the cellar and placed them by the bins. It was all very casual, anyone watching his movements wouldn't be suspicious. When Harley was back inside and the doors firmly closed, Jack went across to check the contents of the boxes. It didn't take much searching for Jack to find a bottle of whiskey and two bottles of champagne. Jack left them exactly where they were; now the task was to catch Harley moving the bottles from the bin area to his car. All Jack needed was a little patience and Harley delivered the much needed evidence for his own dismissal.

At first Harley denied it, when he was called to Jack's office, claiming that he knew nothing about any missing drink, he threatening to call the police for slander and defamation of character, but when he was shown the video recording of his actions, he had no option but to confess. Jack had promised Violet that he wouldn't involve the police, which was against his better judgement, but he kept his word for Violets sake. Harley's parents were informed and he was dismissed with immediate effect and made to pay back and estimation of the cost of booze stolen, which his parents were only too pleased to do in order to make sure their son didn't incur a criminal record. They had high hopes for Harley and a criminal record was not a welcome addition to his list of qualifications. Harley showed no remorse, the large chip on his shoulder still clearly visible. Jack wanted to wipe the smug look from Harley's face, but was wise enough to hold his temper; more than anything Jack was relieved that Violet had kicked him into touch. The thought of them still being together would have been too much to bear. Of course Harley implicated Violet in his bid to wriggle out of the situation and many choice words passed his lips when describing Violet and his assumption that it was she who was to blame for his capture, but Jack was determined to keep her out of the whole saga, so he fiercely denied she had told him anything and claimed that the camera's had been placed on the evidence from the cellar ledger and the shortfall of stock identified, as Jack told Harley, ' The alcohol was leaving the premises by one of the exits ,we covered each one to find out which'. Harley still didn't buy it, but Jack couldn't care less, so long as he stayed away from Violet, so for her protection, he added a caveat stating that if Harley contacted Violet in any way, the police would be called and Harley would be charged with theft. Harley's parents gave their word that their son would follow this stipulation and Harley was released into his parents care, never to darken the doorstep of Priory Hall again – Jack hoped.

That had been several days ago, now it was time to concentrate on the complexity of running Christmas in a hotel. Jack showered and dressed in his work suit, ready to start work early. The snow would bring with it a host of extra headaches, he was sure, not to mention that the hotel was fully booked for Christmas. Jack had been very pleased when Scarlett told him the news. This failing hotel had turned a corner and was making a strong comeback as the place to go. Jack was enjoying being back at the helm, within minutes he was barking orders and directing staff as if had never been away. He had missed being at the centre of all the activity. Jack always thought that he merely tolerated people, that it was just a job to be done, but after spending so much time in confinement, he realised that he did actually liked people and getting involved, making the guests stay as enjoyable as possible.

The staffing rota had been turned upside down by the snow. Scarlett had a list that filled one side of A4 paper of staff not coming in. Many of the extra casual staff had rung in to say they couldn't make it because of the snow, this was true in some cases, but Jack was aware of several, that had used the snow as an excuse to go to a Christmas party they would otherwise have to miss. Jack was stood in the reception with Scarlett, helping her to redeploy staff to areas of necessity. It was going to be tight, but if everyone pulled together, they might just get all the guests served with dinner. This task took the most amount of man power at one time, after that, as long as the bar and reception were staffed, Jack was sure they could manage. He was hoping for understanding and empathy from some of the clients to help them through, but he wasn't sure if he would get it. Scarlett was just about to put a line through Violet's name as unable to attend work when she and Annie walked into reception.

'You two looked like you've walked here!' Scarlett exclaimed. Jack looked up from his lists to see who she was speaking to. His heart skipped a beat - in a manly way of course, he tried to hide the broad grin that was independently creeping across his face. Annie and Violet looked like a pair of drowned rats, absolutely sodden and shaking with cold.

'You won't believe what happened!' Violet couldn't wait to relay the events. 'Mum's crashed the car – it's a right off. We had to climb our way out of a ditch and walk all the way here!!!' Violet's imagination was enjoying a trip out; the fact that it bared no resemblance to the truth was a mere inconvenience. Jack's mind momentarily jumped back to his own accident. He pushed the thoughts aside; he needed to check that Annie and Violet were unhurt.

'Oh my God! Are you okay?' Jack had moved swiftly from being behind the reception to the front of the desk. 'Are you injured? Is anyone else hurt?'

'It's fine, we're fine. It was a minor accident. The car slipped on the snow and we ended up in a ditch. The car will be fine it's not a right off; it just needs winching out of the ditch. The bus didn't arrive, so I was giving Violet a lift into work.' Annie was quick to ease their minds.

'I am grateful Annie, many of the staff have cried off and we are desperate, but I'm sorry you skidded.' Said Scarlett who was very pleased to see Violet.

'It was one of those things, no one's fault - an act of god.' Annie blushed conscious of Jack's gaze. 'It looks like it's going to be a hard night Violet. I hope you're up for it?' Annie was madly trying to deflect the attention away from herself.

'I think I can manage, so long as the tips are good!' She smiled. 'I'll go and start getting dried out. – Scarlett, do you know if there are and spare dry uniforms. I'm a bit too wet to serve dinner like this? – and any shoes?' Violet looked down at her poor sodden, cold toes.

'I'll come with you, I'm sure I can find something – what size shoe are you?' Said Scarlett leading Violet away, purposefully leaving Jack and Annie alone together. An awkward silence hung between them, like a physical wall. Jack took the initiative and scaled it.

'Annie I ...'

'Don't Jack, there's nothing you can say that I want to hear at this moment in time.'

'..But Annie I want to explain, it was...'

'Jack! I mean it. Violet has just informed me that you two were in cahoots together, but at this moment I don't care about that. What I do need though is to get home and warm and dry.'

'Do you want me to see if I can get the car out for you? I can grab some of the male staff and take them with me?' Jack knew he couldn't afford to let the staff go out of the Hotel, but more importantly he couldn't see Annie abandoned, especially in the bedraggled yet beautiful state she was in.

'No, no Jack. It's not on the road, so it's in no-one's way. It would be foolish to try and move it in this weather and in the dark. The damage is already done. I'll contact the relay services after Christmas and they'll sort it. Do you think you could get me a taxi to take me home?' Annie was soaked to the skin and shivering. She needed a warm bath and dry clothes as soon as possible.

'Annie, I don't know how to tell you this, but there are no Taxi's. I rang around all the local firms for a taxi for a guest, but many are off the road and those that are working have been fully booked in advance for Christmas parties. You and Violet are going to have to stay here I'm afraid – I can't even get the staff home tonight.'

'But I can't stay. I need clothes and its Christmas! Violet's presents are at home and the turkey!!' Annie was about to lose the plot.

'Your safety is more important than giving Violet her presents on Christmas Day and if by some miracle we do get you home, Violet may well be stranded here and you still won't manage to give her presents?' Jack waited for a response from her, she didn't answer, 'I'm sure Violet will understand, it's not as if she's three years old and still believes in Santa? All the other problems we can solve. You can go and have a bath at my place and, I know it's not ideal, but I'm sure there will be some clean, dry clothes in lost property that you can wear?' Annie scrunched her face up in disapproval when he mentioned lost property. She had visions of a floral twin set or a pair of leopard skin print leggings. Jack detected her look of horror.

'In a crisis you have to compromise Annie.' Jack was losing patience.

'Are you sure there's no taxi's? There must be some somewhere?'

'Have you noticed the weather out there recently??' Silence hung in the air whilst she made her decision to give in.

'Okay.' She whispered begrudgingly.

'Good! I'm glad you're thinking sensibly!' Annie wanted to slap him in the face with the arm of her sodden raincoat. Christmas couldn't be any more ruined if she'd tried to sabotage it on purpose.

'I'll go and find something for you to wear and send it over with one of the staff.' He was Just about to pass Annie the keys to his place when they were interrupted by one of the restaurant staff.

'I'm sorry to interrupt Mr Parrish, but Scarlett has asked me to come and get you, we have a situation in the kitchens.' Said the girl in hushed tones, but still hinting at a degree of urgency.

'It's okay; you can talk in front of Annie, she's not a guest.' That tells me thought Annie.

'The chef is throwing a wobbler! He's says that if he doesn't have enough staff to serve the customers his food whilst it's hot – he'll stop cooking as it's his reputation on the line!' The girls stared at Jack looking for a miracle solution.

'Tell Chef I'll be with him presently to discuss the situation.' Jack dismissed her with the wave of his hand.

'Thank you Mr Parrish.' The girl scurried down the corridor back towards the kitchens.

'Are you really that short staffed?' Asked Annie concerned. Jack nodded,

'I'm afraid so. Our chef is fantastic, but with that comes his temperamental, artistic side. Probably like you – as a flower designer.' He said without thinking. Annie raised her eyebrows to show distain for his comments.

'When have you ever known me to be a prima donna? - I was about to tell you to find me a uniform to wear and I'll help you serve dinner, as I'm stuck here, but I may reconsider now!' Jack back peddled fast.

'I would be very grateful if you would help me and obviously you have the talent without the temperament – that goes without out saying!'

'Okay I'll do it. I'd rather wear a uniform than lost property!'

It didn't take long for Annie to have a quick soak in Jack's bath to warm her bones. Jack had sorted a uniform for her before she went across to his cottage. It was a strange feeling, being in his home alone, taking a bath. She felt like an intruder. She was thankful that Jack was busy and didn't follow her to start a deep and meaningful conversation about their future – if there was one; in fact Jack did nothing to suggest that he felt anything for her other than friendship.

The more Annie thought about Violet's outburst in the car, the more she put it down to her vivid imagination. She would help Jack, because he had helped her with the wedding, all those weeks ago. She would have been in deep water had he not put himself out to help her, this was the least she could do. She dressed in the bathroom, not wanting to intrude into Jack's bedroom again. She cleared the steam from the bathroom mirror to try and see what she looked like. She had never worn a uniform, unless you count brownies? She felt quite smart, but also petrified, as she didn't have a clue what she was doing or how to serve in a restaurant. She had never had a Saturday job in a café or bar. It was going to be an interesting night. She wondered how many turkey dinners would slip off their plates and into someone's lap? There was no time to have any training. It was a case of learning as she went along.

Violet was amazed when her mother walked in wearing the same uniform and exceedingly well. 'What are you doing?' She asked in surprise.

'I'm helping out. You're short staffed and I'm stranded here, so I may as well do something useful and then I get to see you at Christmas too.'

'Does Jack know you are doing this?' Violet was amazed.

'He got the uniform for me. - Now you'll have to help me Vi, I'm warning you, I'm going to be crap at this. If you see me making any huge mistakes, please butt in and help me. I'm counting on you.'

'That'll be a first mum – you taking advice from me! – but you'll be fine mum, It'll be fun working together, just don't tell anyone you're my mother!'

There was no time to speak to anyone other than ask questions about which side you served from, did you serve all the ladies first, how do you hold more than two plates at one time, how do you work the coffee machine. Violet tried her best to explain the general lay out of the room, which door went into the kitchens and which one out, getting it wrong can cause disaster. The details were endless, but Annie took it all in her stride. It only seemed like minutes before Jack and Scarlett arrived with the first of the guests. It was the Christmas rush repeated, but this time serving food not flowers.

Jack spent his time liaising between the kitchens keeping Chef calm and the front of house running smoothly. All hands were on deck. Jack had also taken charge of going to the cellars to fetch the bottles, he didn't want a repeat of Harley's antics and they were all far too busy tonight to keep a keen eye on what was going on in there, if another member of staff went in. On the surface everything seemed to be running smoothly, at least from the perspective of the customers.

Annie to her surprise found the experience enjoyable. The novelty factor had a great part to play in it. The guest's spirits were high, everyone determined to enjoy Christmas Eve despite the snow, which was a help when minor things went wrong. Annie managed to place the wrong meal in front of one of the guests who was in fact down for a vegetarian meal, but luckily another member of staff noticed and corrected the mistake before a mouthful was taken. Most people were from out of town, choosing Priory Hall as their festive holiday destination, but a few were locals, who had booked in on the Christmas party night. Annie noticed one or two nudges between guests as the penny dropped where they had seen her before, and one lady offered her sympathy that the shop wasn't doing well enough on its own and admiring her for taking a second job to make ends meet.

Another issue to contend with was the gossip from the staff who knew about Annie and Jack's history. All eyes seemed to be watching, looking for some indication that the romance or friction had been reignited and all behind a whitewash of false, friendly smiles. Annie was too busy to care what people thought. They would draw their own conclusions, no matter what the facts were. She decided to let them get on with it.

Jack had taken the managerial decision of giving each table a complementary bottle of house wine to soften the impact of the potentially slow service. It did the trick and overall the service was a success. There were a few minor problems as you would expect, but generally people were forgiving under the circumstances and with the added dash of Christmas cheer everyone left the dining room smiling and ready for the night's entertainment in the large function room. Annie breathed a large sigh of relief when the last of the dinners left to continue their revelling elsewhere.

'Thank you ladies and gent's, the service is over.' Jack announced in the kitchens.

'Does that mean we've finished now?' Asked Annie innocently. The people surrounding her laughed. Annie didn't understand what she had said that was so amusing. 'I wish!' Shouted one of the young lads from the back of the room.

'No Annie – now we get to clean the dining room and set it up for breakfast. If you can encourage any of the stragglers to take their coffee from the bar area and into the function room, we'll be able to get organised without hindrance.' Jack's words were announced to the whole group.

Annie's bubble of elation at the prospect of finishing popped. She was dead on her feet. All the early mornings at the shop in preparation for her own Christmas rush were telling on her now. Jack could see that Annie was shattered. He called her to one side as the others went back out into the dining room.

'Annie, you have been a god send, but you've done enough. I can see you're exhausted. You've already done your own days' work. Why don't you finish now?' Annie was tempted, but her loyalty to Violet and the other people who were still working came to the surface.

'I'm okay Jack. I'll see it through. The worst is over now. I presume? You worked through the night to help me; I owe you at least the same.' Jack moved more central to Annie's line of vision.

'You owe me nothing. I helped you because I wanted to. Nothing more or less. There is no debt to repay.' Annie didn't argue, she accepted his words with a simple nod of her head.

'Now,' Said Jack, 'let me show you where we keep the shredded wheat.'

'I bet you say that to all the girls!' She replied, finding her sense of humour was still awake.

It took an hour and a half for the restaurant to be cleaned and reset for breakfast. When the final serviette was folded and silver fork polished, Jack called all the staff together.

'Thank you everyone for your help this evening. As most of you are aware, we are fully booked in the hotel this evening, so those of you who can't get home will have to either double up in the staff quarters or housekeeping have been setting up 'z' beds in some of the conference rooms. I know this situation is not ideal, but we have to make the best of it and as a thank you, in the private dining room there is some food and drink for you all as a thank you from myself and Scarlett, but remember some of you are still on duty – I don't want to see anyone drunk or there will be reprimands!' The staff cheered at the declaration of 'drink' before showing their appreciation by a wave of clapping for Jack and Scarlett. There was a mass exodus to the private dining room, leaving Jack, Violet and Annie, unsure of the next step.

'I hope you don't think I've presumed anything, but I anticipated you might both like to stay in my accommodation. I've had a couple of beds set up in there. If that's okay?' Annie was so tired she didn't know what to do. She was annoyed at his presumptions that they would sleep there, but at the same time thrilled, as the thought of trying to sleep with a group of teenagers wanting to party all night was almost intolerable, considering how tired she was. At least she would have Violet for safety and conversation. She didn't want to be alone with Jack. She was too tired to wonder if it was herself or Jack she was afraid of. Remarkably she made a decision.

'That would be fine thank you Jack. We'd be pleased to stay there.' Annie accepted. Violet's face dropped. She had planned on being with the group that partied all night.

'Mum, would you be cross, if I stayed in the hotel with my friends? It is Christmas Eve and I know as soon as you sit down you'll fall asleep and Jack, you're just as old so you probably will too! I'm young and should be out enjoying myself before I reach your age and have to stay home?' Jack and Annie laughed. Violet's eyes and body language were pleading with Annie.

'Oh go on Mum? Please?' She could understand why Violet wanted to be with people her own age and have some fun. She was the same at her age. The down side was that it would leave Annie alone with Jack, and the last thing she needed now was some big declaration of love or an in depth conversation. She was too tired for logic. Annie decided to sacrifice her sleep and stay in the hotel rather than at Jack's.

'Well, I'll stay over here with you, and then we can be together for Christmas morning.'

'Can't you take a hint? You'll be the only old one, you'll get no sleep, you'll be ratty, you'll embarrass me and everyone will end up hating me and you!'

'Don't hold back will you Violet?' Scalded Annie. 'Say what you think!'

'Sorry Mum, I'll come across as soon as I wake up. I need to be young without you looking over my shoulder! Do you really want to sleep over here when there is going to be a party on all night? Annie already knew the answer to that question.

'Jack won't try to jump your bones, will you Jack?' Violet grinned wickedly.

'Violet!' Exclaimed Annie in horror, shocked by Violet's words.

'I can assure you, your mother's virtue is completely safe with me Violet.' Jack was trying to stifle a grin as he spoke.

'Jack, it's a little too late for you to talk about my mother's virtue when you consider your previous history together! – but she's so tired it wouldn't be much fun!'

'Violet! Shut up for God's sake!' Annie was cringing; she just wanted to get away from the conversation. 'Right, alright. I'll stay at Jack's and you go to your party, but go now before I ground you when we get home!' Violet smirked; she knew her mother wouldn't be able to stand her discussing her sex life with Jack. One nil to Violet.

'Have fun but remember not to get drunk! You have to serve breakfast in a few hours.' Jack added trying to regain some authority with his daughter.

'I won't, besides Scarlett is staying to keep an eye on us. Happy Christmas!' Violet hugged her mum, planting a kiss on her cheek, and then whispering in her ear *'don't do anything I wouldn't do.'* Annie shook her head in disgust. Next she threw her arms around Jack and he in return kissed the top of her head. Annie watched in surprise. Maybe they were building bridges in the time they had spent together. Unexpectedly a warm glow ignited in Annie's heart, maybe the faint embers of family were beginning to grow.

Annie was relieved when Jack showed her to his bedroom and then began to leave. 'I still have to details to finalise for tomorrow. I'll probably be another couple of hours across at the hotel. I also need to give Scarlett a hand making sure the staff party doesn't get out of hand. Help yourself to anything you need. I'll sleep in the lounge on the 'Z' bed, so I won't disturb you when I come back.' The words were direct and to the point, at least he wasn't going to try anything – she was glad – or was she? A tiny part of her , deep in her subconscious was disappointed that she wasn't going to have to fight for her honour.

'If you need something to sleep in, you know where there they are from last time.' Annie blushed, 'Unless you want me to check lost property for a nightdress?' She slapped him on the arm in the old familiar way she used to. They both smiled in a relaxed and easy manner, something that had been missing since their teenage years.

'There is one thing before I go.' Annie froze on the spot; maybe she wasn't going to be let off and would have to fight for her honour? She'd rather do that, than have to sit through a long heartfelt discussion at this moment in time. ' I know we are both tired and now is not the time to talk, but I want to say thank you for being with me in the hospital, as you know I was out of it and had no idea what went on, until Scarlett filled me in –which was just before my mother left. You have no idea how much it meant to me, knowing you were there and caring about me – I'll let you sleep now.' Before she could reply he was gone. She wanted to shout after him, *'don't read anything into it, I'd do it for anyone! You're no one special.'* But she didn't.

A wave of familiarity swept over her, being back in Jack's room, as she was on the night of the wedding. She found a large 'T' shirt that would do just fine as night attire. She held it to her nose and inhaled. It smelt of Jack, he had always liked aftershave and body sprays. Indeed, he was one of the best smelling boys in school, things hadn't changed. Annie removed her clothes and put on the shirt. She caught sight of herself in the mirror. She looked tired and worn out. Her face was red and blotchy from tiredness or the change from working in a cool florist's to the heat of Hotel. There were bags under her eyes and she was wearing no makeup. What a mess, no wonder he ran a mile. There was nothing she could do about it, so she threw off the negative comments she was torturing herself with. Sleep was what she needed. She pulled back the covers and climbed into Jack's bed. She was asleep before you could say 'Would you like Christmas pudding or profiteroles for dessert?'

Jack paced the corridors of the hotel like an expectant father. He was checking to make sure all the guests were happy and that the staff party didn't spill over into the main hotel. Scarlett was at the party, playing a dual role, enjoying the party on one hand and making sure the staff didn't get too drunk on the other. It was after three before Jack felt it was safe to get a little sleep. The night porter had strict instructions to wake him if necessary.

He cursed the front door as it creaked when he pushed it open. There was no sign of Annie and his bedroom door was shut tight. He stood outside for a few seconds to see if he could hear any signs of life. There were none. He tip toed into the lounge heading straight for the 'Z' bed. There was no point in undressing; he would have to get up in a couple of hours to go and check on things, besides, all his clothes were in his bedroom. He pulled at his tie and released his top button, then next to be shed was his jacket and shoes. He lay on top of the small inadequate makeshift bed; the room was still warm from the fire that had been blazing all night. He was shattered, it had been a hell of a first day back, but it had also been spectacular. If you had told him this morning that Annie would be sleeping in his bed by nightfall, he would have had you certified, but she was. The only thing spoiling it was the fact that he was on the wrong side of the door. What he wouldn't give to be curled up next to Annie, holding her and telling her how much he still loved her. The frustration was almost unbearable. He tried to focus his mind on work and the tasks that needed to be divided to cover the staff that hadn't managed to make it through the snow, but every few seconds his mind and his eyes wandered towards the bedroom door. He fantasied that she was on the other side of the door waiting for him to make the first move, but he couldn't, no matter how much he wanted to – and he wanted to. If it was a wrong call, it could ruin things again and he wasn't prepared to take that risk. Jack made a mental note to take a cold shower at the first opportunity.

'Annie, Annie. It's morning; it's time to wake up.' Annie was disorientated and couldn't understand why she could hear a man's voice talking to her. She peeled

one eye open to see Jack standing at the foot of the bed with a breakfast tray in his hand.

'I thought you might be hungry. I didn't know what you'd like so I brought a little of everything. I'll set it up on the coffee table in the lounge, come out when you are ready.' Jack smiled in that old familiar way; it was a good job she was lying down as her knees went to jelly and a faint familiar feeling of longing began to emerge.

'I'll get up and help you serve breakfast for the guests. It won't take me long and I'll be with you.'

'Annie it's ten thirty. Breakfast is over, you slept through. You were out for the count, so we left you. Violet came over at six thirty to wish you a 'Happy Christmas', before she started in the dining room, but you were sleeping.'

'Why didn't she wake me?' Annie was cross with herself for missing Violet.

'She tried, but you were dead to the world. Other than shaking you awake, we stood no chance. She's coming across in a while when she has finished in the dining room. She said to save her a croissant.' Jack's eyes fell away from Annie's face and were drawn to the contours of her body through his 'T' shirt. His mind was no longer on Christmas or the hotel. He still hadn't found time for that shower, he had to get out of there before he did something he would regret, like kissing her.

'I'll see you in a few minutes.' Said Jack as he and the tray made their way carefully out of Jack's bedroom.

Annie couldn't believe that she had slept for so long, especially as she was in a strange bed. Her clothes were on the radiator, now fully dry. At least she could wear her own clothes today, even if they weren't special for Christmas day. It was better than sitting in lost property or the waitress uniform. She peeped out of the window to see if the snow had stopped. It had, but the sky was full and it wouldn't be long before it started again. Old large trees were dressed with snow, branches labouring under the weight of the fall. It was the perfect Christmas morning scene. The sort of picture you would find on cards in millions of homes. The view here was certainly better than the one at home, which overlooked the high street. When Annie was dressed she looked in the mirror again, to see if there had been any magical improvement in her appearance overnight – there hadn't. Her hair, although reasonably clean from the bath last night, was tangled and knotted. At the very least it needed a comb through it, but she had no comb or brush with her. In front of her, below the mirror there was a set of draws. She opened the top draw to see if she could find one. There, right in front of her was a brush placed neatly on top a photo frame that had been turned upside down in the draw. She recognised it immediately. It was the frame she had given Jack on the day he left Preston for Australia. She picked it up and turned it over. Annie looked down at the picture of herself. She looked young, beautiful and full of hope; although she would never have used those words to describe herself at the time. Annie wondered where that girl had gone, she didn't even remember when she went. Jack had kept it all these years and not just buried away in a box, it was close at hand. The sentimentality of her discovery threatened to send her into floods of tears. She bit the inside of her cheek to stop herself. She had to get a grip, put it into perspective. That was then, now they were completely different people, she was different, Jack was different, life had changed them and just how much she was still to find out. The girl in the picture was a stranger. They had nothing in common, except for a name - and a love of Jack.

Jack was sitting, waiting for her in the lounge. She hadn't realised when he came in to the bed room, but he was formally dressed in his suit, even on Christmas day, he was on duty. A small artificial Christmas tree sat in the corner of the room. The fibre optic's catching the light and giving the room an electric Christmas glow.

'How are you feeling?' Jack enquired 'I know you slept well, but do you feel any better for it? Sometimes when I sleep like that, it leaves me with a thick head.'

'I do actually feel better. I was ready to drop last night, after the day at the shop, then working in the restaurant, but I enjoyed it, far more than I expected.' Annie sat down on the settee opposite him.

'Tea or coffee? I remember you used to drink tea, but I didn't want to presume?'

'Tea would be lovely thank you.' Annie felt as though she should fill the silence whilst he poured the tea, 'How was Violet this morning? Did any of them get any sleep?'

'A little, I think. I had to go across and read the riot act to some of them at four A.M. as some of the boys were making too much noise, they soon settled after that. It's amazing what the threat of dismissal will do.' Annie sipped her tea and took a croissant from the plate of pastries.

'I could have helped this morning with the breakfast, if you had woken me?'

'You looked too peaceful.' Annie wondered how long he had stood watching her, whilst she was asleep. She found the prospect un-nerving. She wondered if he had found her snoring or dribbling out of the corner of her mouth, oblivious to all that was happening around her.

'- and besides breakfast is mainly self-service for the guests, we only have to bring tea, coffee and toast in the main and clear the plates. - I could however do with your help to serve Christmas lunch?' He looked at her optimistically.

'I might have known. There's no such thing as a free breakfast!'

'What can I say, you know me too well.' A moment of awkwardness lay between them. Annie jumped in to fill the empty space.

'I'll help you, as long as I get a Christmas dinner later, when all the guests have had theirs?'

'You will. I promise. - In fact I've already invited Violet to come across later. I'm afraid I'm not cooking, although maybe you should be thankful for that! But chef is cooking and we can eat Christmas dinner here, if you accept that is - or I can set you a place in the corner of the kitchens if you prefer?'

'Jack I don't want you to go to any trouble on our behalf. we can easily sit with the other staff to eat. We've just descended on you and….'

'Annie, every year I eat Christmas dinner with my work colleagues. This year I have been given the opportunity to eat with some people I actually want to be with. Please allow me to do this for you and Violet. It would mean a lot to me? He was looking deeply in to her eyes, silently pleading with her.

'If I stand still or sit in that kitchen to eat, Chef will have me working again, so I think here is safer – thank you. I, we accept your kind offer.' The look on Jack's face said it all. She had just delivered him the best Christmas present ever.

Christmas day service in the restaurant was every bit as hectic as the evening before. Annie had managed a few minute with Violet to wish her a 'Happy Christmas' and make sure she didn't have a problem with eating Christmas dinner at Jack's.

'I don't mind. As long as he doesn't make me serve it! I don't care where I eat it!' Violet gave her mum a hug and a kiss. 'Happy Christmas Mum. I hope Santa brings you everything you desire.' Violet winked, before picking up some starters ready for delivery to the tables.

'Get away with you, go and do some work!' Annie slapped Violet's bum as she passed. Annie didn't know if she could stand to eat any turkey after she and the other staff had despatched one hundred and twenty five portions to the guests. Annie found herself looking forward to serving someone with the vegetarian option, simply to carry a plate that looked different. All the staff had been ordered to wear a Christmas hat, to help with the Christmas spirit. Christmas carols were playing in the background, reminding Annie of childhood Christmases when they went to church every week and especially looked forward to the carol service on Christmas Eve. She and Jack had both been in the school choir and subsequently loaned out to every event taking place in their parish before

Christmas and their only payment, a mince pie and orange squash— if they were lucky.

It was five pm before the dining room was set up ready for the evening buffet. At least this didn't need as many staff as the lunch time sit down meal. Jack had squared it with Scarlett for Violet to have some time off. A few staff that should be on shift the day before had managed to make it through the snow, mainly those whose families were farmers and had tractors to bring them in. The roads around the Priory were too insignificant to be treated with salt by the council. To all other intense and purposes the hotel and the surrounding area was in lock down. There was still no chance of getting back to town; they were going to have to hunker down for yet another night at Priory Hall.

When Annie and Violet finally returned to Jack's cottage, they found him lighting some candles on a table that had appeared from nowhere and now took position in the centre of the lounge.

'Ah, you both made it. Come in and sit down. Can I get you ladies a glass of champagne?'

Annie and Violet threw glances at each other, showing their surprise at his hospitality.

'I hope you didn't steal it from a table in the garden? And are you sure I'm off duty and can drink it?' Remarked Violet, who was never going to forget the champagne incident.

'Are you ever going to get over yourself - or are you going to remind me of that forever?'

'Probably forever.' Admitted Violet nodding in agreement. Jack poured them all a glass of champagne.

'Now come and sit down and take the weight off your feet. The food will be here soon, but before it comes I have a little surprise. A gift for you both. It's nothing major, just a simple token of thanks. I wasn't sure if I'd get the chance to deliver them, but fate has dealt me a kind hand this Christmas.' Annie and Violet looked at each other in surprise. Violet was delighted at the thought of presents, Annie was mortally embarrassed.

'We haven't got anything for you – we didn't think........' Annie tried to apologise.

'I'm not expecting or wanting any gifts in return – it's just a little something. It's nothing to get too over excited about. It's really a little thank you for the time you spent being with me at the hospital. I can't tell you how much I appreciate the fact that I wasn't alone, even though I knew nothing about it at the time, although I did have some weird dreams involving you two – very strange.` Annie and Violet both shuffled uneasily in their seats, afraid he was about to quote their private conversations with him. 'So this is for you Violet.' Jack passed her an envelope. It contained a cheque. 'I don't know you well enough to choose something I could be sure you would like, so this way you can choose to do with it as you will, but I do hope one day you'll let me be close enough to you to know what you would like?' Violet opened the envelope. The cheque was for one hundred pounds.

'Jack this is loads! It's not just a little gift.' She looked at Annie for a sign to help her decide if she should keep or return the cheque. Annie nodded, if Jack wanted to treat his daughter and make up for lost time it was fine with Annie. Violet had had a rough few years, it was time she felt spoilt again. This was the sort of impromptu gesture Nick would have done; maybe they weren't so different after all. Violet rose to her feet and hugged Jack, kissing him shyly on the cheek.

'Thank you Jack, but it was Mum who was there most of the time.' Annie bowed her head trying to hide her scarlet cheeks. 'I was too cross at you both at first to come and sit with you, but eventually after talking to mum, I began to understand why things happened the way they did - and for future reference' quipped violet 'Mum knows what I like on the present front, so you can always check with her.'

'I'll remember that Violet.' Said Jack returning the gesture of kissing her on the cheek, ' – Now for Annie. I have a small parcel for you.' He passed her the package, beautifully wrapped in silver paper with purple ribbons.

'Jack you don't need to buy me presents. I did what anyone would have done for you.' Jack stared deeply into her eyes. 'Now you and I both know that isn't true?' she decided not to challenge him and busied herself with opening the present.

'Come on mum, faster! I want to know what it is.' Encouraged Violet, who seemed more excited about Annie's present than her own.

Annie tore at the paper to reveal a CD of 'Wham's greatest hits' and a bottle of 'Charlie' perfume. Violet's face sank; she had enough manners not to comment of what a lousy present he had chosen, but god, mum must be disappointed. If he was going to buy her perfume, he could at least have bought something decent and 'Wham', they were a really old group that hadn't made records for decades. Violet was too wrapped up in her own reaction to notice that Annie had moved from her seat and was staring out of the window. Jack watched her, wanting to go and put his arms around her, but not sure if he would be welcomed. As if on cue the doorbell rang.

'That will be our Christmas dinner!' Enthused Jack trying to lighten the sombre atmosphere that had descended upon the room.

'I'll go and get it.' Volunteered Violet, rushing out of the room leaving Jack and Annie alone. 'I'm sorry if I've upset you.' He began. 'I didn't have a clue what to get for you, and then I remembered the college ball and you making me dance to Wham and the smell of your perfume. I still recognise it if someone is wearing it.....' He moved towards her and turned her to face him. She was crying and trying desperately to stop.

'Annie - I am so sorry. It was never my intention to make you cry. They were just things that I remember about you as a girl and I wanted you to know that I had never forgotten those moments, in all these years.'

'But Jack I'm not a girl now, I'm a woman, racing towards my forties. That girl doesn't exist anymore.'

'She does in your heart Annie and in mine. If it's the outside you want to focus on, then she's been replaced by a beautiful woman whose been through things no one should ever have to endure, but in your heart, you're still the same person and I'll tell you Annie when you were a girl I fell in love with you, and now as an independent woman, I still love you, maybe even more so.' Jack stopped speaking; they didn't need any more words. She wanted to believe him. She reached up and touched his face, he was just about to lean in and kiss her, when Violet barged back into the room with the finesse of a hippopotamus. Jack and Annie swiftly moved apart, hoping she hadn't noticed their close proximity to each other.

'You should see what Chef has sent! There is a full Christmas dinner, a Cray fish and rocket starter and a platter of desserts to die for. I'm almost drooling at the thought! They look even better than the food served in the dining room! Can we eat soon?' The question was directed to their host.

'We can eat right now. Let's all go and see what we have.' Said Jack leading the way into the kitchen.

Annie wasn't sure if she was glad or disappointed that they hadn't kissed. It had felt the right thing to do at the time, but now only a few minutes later, she realised that she needed to come back to earth. She realised that she was in love with a memory, the memory of what Jack used to be and only time would tell, if he was still worth loving or if he had changed beyond recognition. They weren't love sick teenagers anymore. Whatever actions they took or didn't take, had repercussions on those around them, especially Violet, and Jack was only here temporarily, what would happen when he moved away, which would happen eventually, but all of these factors put together didn't match her main problem, which was that she could no longer deny she had strong feelings for him. She didn't know if they were created out of a sense of nostalgia or if they were for the man about to sit opposite her now, because of the way he was now. One thing was for sure, she was going to have out find out. Jack and Violet came rushing back into the lounge carrying the starters and a bread basket.

'I hope you're starving mum, there's lots of food out there. Jack are you sure you didn't tell chef you were feeding fifteen?'

'Well I might have told him a few more than three. I can't quite remember! Annie Do you like Cray fish?'

'What, oh – yes.' Annie had been lost in the easy way Jack and Violet of speaking to each other; it reminded her of how she was with Nick. Annie could tell that Violet's barriers were down as far as Jack was concerned, she hoped he wouldn't ever abuse her trust.

'Come and take a seat Annie! It's time for the festivities to begin!' Jack held out a chair for her. She dutifully sat in it as requested. He helped to push her chair and lay out her napkin on her lap. He couldn't resist a gentle squeeze of her neck as he passed her. His soft touch against her skin made all the hairs on her back stand on end. Now it was her mind that wasn't on Christmas dinner.

The meal was a great success. The food and wine were delicious and the conversation flowed as fast as the wine. There were no awkward moments, where tumble weed crossed the table between them. Jack and Violet seemed to be forging the start of a relationship. He was keen to know her likes and dislikes, her views on the world and what path she wanted to take for her career. In turn Violet asked Jack numerous questions about his life in Australia and the hotels he had worked in. She didn't however mention Marcia or his father. The little she already knew was enough.

'Tell me about the first time you two met?' Violet was asking Jack.

'It's so long ago, it's hard to remember. It was at primary school and I think it was our first day?' Jack looked at Annie for confirmation. She nodded in agreement. 'And the teacher sat us together because your mother was not paying attention.'

'Somehow I think it may be the other way around Jack?' Violet was no fool.

'Jack was too busy trying to swap football cards and not paying attention, that's why the teacher moved him and I was the unfortunate that had to put up with him for the rest of my school days!'

'Maybe I did it on purpose. By miss-behaving I made the teacher move me and I got to sit next to the most beautiful and intelligent girl in the class – so who's the fool? I never liked football cards, it was just an excuse!'

'God mum, was he always this smooth? No wonder all the girls chased him like you said!' Jack raised his eyebrows and threw Annie a glance which conveyed his surprise at being discussed.

'Oh he had a line or two, but he didn't use them on me! He saved them for the lipstick posse.'

'I didn't need to use them on you Annie. You knew me better than anyone. Half the time I didn't even need to speak and you knew what I was thinking. You were my best friend – I wish you still were?' Annie blushed and blamed it on the wine.

'That was a long time ago. It doesn't work like that now.' She stood up to clear the plates. 'Things have changed, we've both changed. – Now who wants coffee!'

A little while later, when they were all stuffed to the gills and sitting on the sofas, trying to stay awake, the TV was on and the proverbial bond movie was over half way through. Annie could tell that Violet was starting to get fidgety.

'Jack do you think the roads will be passable tonight?' Annie was asking thinking that the best thing she could do was to take Violet home.

'I'm not sure. You still have no car and I'm sorry I'm over the limit for driving -I assumed you would be staying another day, till we could sort the car tomorrow?'

'You've been great as it is, we can't stay another night. It's too much of an imposition.'

'Nonsense! I insist. I promise we'll call the breakdown services out tomorrow and if they can't repair the car for driving, I'll drive you home personally and if I can't do that I'll mug a farmer and pinch his tractor.'

'Oh go on Mum! We had a great time last night and I know there's going to be another party tonight – ooops – I shouldn't have told you should I?' She was looking at Jack.

'I heard nothing.' He said pretending to look the other way, 'but if there's trouble you're sacked!' Violet could tell now that he was joking.

'I was going to ask if you two minded, if I went across to the hotel. I can help my friends finish off their work and then we can get to the party that bit sooner?' Violet looked at both of them in turn, searching for approval.

'I don't mind?' Said Jack, 'It can't be that much fun sitting with the old people on Christmas day!' Annie threw Jack a cursory glance.

'You speak for yourself Jack. I still consider myself young – ish.' Violet mouthed the word 'delusional' to Jack.

'Go on mum, let me go?'

'Make sure you're not too noisy and don't disturb the guests! – And don't get too drunk!'

'I won't and I'm on duty for breakfast tomorrow, so I'll come across after breakfast and find you.'

'But you'll be coming back after the party to sleep?' Annie needed clarification.

'No. I'll stay over in the conference rooms like I did last night. It was so much fun. I haven't laughed like that in ages. Night Mum, Night Jack.'

Annie was in shock at the realization that she was going to be left with Jack for the whole evening, with no work to distract them and no one else to converse with – what had she done! The easiest remedy was to drink herself into oblivion, that way she would pass out and wouldn't have to talk to him. She picked up her glass of wine and downed it in one.

'Would you like a refill?' Jack already had the bottle in his hands. Annie wondered if it was his plan too.

'Yes please. A large one.' She held out her glass towards him.

'You wouldn't be trying to get drunk to avoid a conversation would you?' He knew her too well.

'I'm just having a glass of wine. It is Christmas Day?' He poured the wine without another word. They both sat pretending to watch the bond film. In truth Annie hated them, but it was a better choice than conversation. All too soon it finished and the credits rolled. There were no more excuses to avoid conversation. Annie had refilled her glass three times before the end of the film, but it didn't feel like

it was having any effect, she was still stone cold sober.

'There's nothing much on now. I looked through the paper earlier.' Jack flicked the switch on the remote turning off the TV.

'Why don't we listen to some music?' He suggested. 'I know what would be ideal, your new CD?' He picked it up from the table and placed it on the CD player. Last Christmas came booming out from the speakers. Annie couldn't help herself, she started to laugh.

'Does it still stand up for you as a great pop song?' He asked teasing her.

'I listen whenever I can.' She lied. He moved across and sat on the sofa next to her. This was it, she knew it. There was no escape now; she was going to have to talk. He took her hand in his. The fit was perfect as it always had been. The same fizz of electricity charged between them as it had all those years ago. As much as Annie wanted to pull her hand away and run, she couldn't.

'Annie, I know we have so much to talk about and say to each other. We have had nearly twenty years apart and each a life of our own. We both know it's impossible to learn and know everything about those years. I can't claim to be the same man I was back then, nor you the same woman, but for both of us some of that person still remains. Annie, I want to know if you are willing to spend some time with me, so that we can get to know each other again - I can't deny I still have very strong feelings for you.' He was hoping he wasn't scaring her. At least she wasn't running from the room, but then he was holding on to her hand.

'I have to ask you Annie, do you still have any feelings for me?' Annie didn't speak. Jack was pouring his hearty out, but he was getting no response from her. She didn't know how she felt. She wanted to tell him she loved him, but she didn't know if her feelings were real. She freed her hand and poured another glass of wine instead.

'Annie, you have to let me know if you don't feel the same, because I'm going crazy here. I want you – I – I still love you. – I have never stopped loving you.' Silence filled the room.

'For god's sake Annie stop avoiding the issue and tell me how you feel! Even if it's to tell me to go away! Just let me in!'

Annie stared him in the eye. 'Why didn't you come to see me when you came out of hospital? I even suffered the wrath of your mother for a second time coming to see you but you didn't even phone?' Annie wanted some answers to try and help her sort out her feelings.

'I know I was wrong and for that I apologise, but at first, my mother told me you hadn't been to see me in the hospital - ever. I was angry at you, that you didn't even care enough to come and see me – even as an old friend. Then, when I learned the truth after I had sent my mother packing, I didn't want you to think I was looking for a baby sitter. At that point I still needed a lot of help. I wanted to be able to come to you as an equal, not an invalid who needed a nurse. Then when I reached the point of being almost back to normal I bumped into Violet and she agreed to speak with me. We did a lot of plain speaking, clearing the air and it did us both good. She asked me to let you and her have one last Christmas together. It was the only thing that she has ever asked of me. I couldn't refuse her and I knew if I came to see you at the shop, I wouldn't be able to keep my word to Violet and stay away from you.' Annie thought carefully about his words. The story corresponded exactly with Violet's. He had put her first and that's what a dad should do. How could she be cross at him for being a father?

She knew then it was a losing battle. Her feelings for him would not be denied. They had survived a happy marriage to someone else and twenty years apart. The only thing standing in her way now - was herself. She remembered the times she longed for him to notice her as a woman in their school and college days and now he was here again wanting her, needing her and wanting to be a part of Violet's life. She wasn't sure if she was brave enough to grab the one thing she had wanted all of her life, but ignoring it wasn't going to work either.

'I found the photograph I gave to you when you left for Australia– in your draw yesterday; I was looking for a brush. Why did you keep it?'

'Because I never stopped loving you – and it's in the draw because my mother put it there. It travels with me everywhere and is out on display - normally – and in truth, it hurts to look at it at the moment. It's a symbol of everything I want from life, but it's still just out of reach.' Annie leaned forward and placed her glass onto the small table in front of them.

'It's not out of reach Jack. I'm not out of reach.' Then she kissed him, but this time it was with the warmth and passion of a woman rather than a young girl. Her directness took his breath away. He pulled away from her.

'Annie – I need to know this is really what you want, because if we start this, I don't think I'll be able to stop. We can't just keep it at friends.' He could feel her breasts pushing against his body, her nipples already hard.

'Can't you tell that I want you?' She asked before kissing him again. He returned her kiss wholeheartedly. It was a moment he had never been brave enough to hope for, that he would hold her in his arms again. His whole being ached for her, she was a drug he had been addicted to for all of his life and he couldn't ever get enough. He had been clean for many years, but tonight he was going to feed his addiction. He pulled her even closer towards him until there was no space between them. She was yielding and responsive in his arms. He kissed her again and again, building the passion between them. Annie thought she would explode if he didn't take her soon. He ran his hands along her body, remembering every curve and angle. He couldn't wait any longer. He pulled her to her feet, and then swept her up in his arms.

'Jack! You're no spring chicken. Don't put your back out before we get to the bedroom!' She laughed through the kisses.

'Don't worry. I have no intention of putting my back out. I've waited a bloody long time for this moment and nothing or no one is going to stop me!'

It was a miracle that they made it through to the bedroom without injury, with chairs and tables in the way, not to mention narrow door frames. Once they were in the bedroom he placed her gently on the bed. He stood looking at her smiling. She was even more beautiful now than when she was a girl. Her hair still wild and temperamental, her breasts were larger, her figure had filled out to that of a curvaceous woman. He was happy beyond belief.

'What?' She asked, feeling self-conscious.

'I want to remember this moment, because if it all goes wrong tomorrow, I'll still have now and I want to remember how beautiful you are and how lucky I am to have this second chance and I promise that I'll do everything in my power to show exactly how much I love you.' Annie pulled him on to the bed next to her and kissed him hard. It was unlike any kiss she had ever had before. Twenty years of longing and bottled passion exploded between them.

'Jack I spent so long hating you for leaving me, that I couldn't see what was in front of my eyes. I do have feelings for you and believe me I'm feeling them right now!' She placed her hand on his chest, then gently ran her fingers down towards his groin. He slipped his hand under her blouse, cupping her breasts. She whispered in his ear, words of love he had waited to hear since leaving for Australia. Within no time they were both naked, but under the covers for warmth. There was no strangeness or awkwardness between them; it felt like the most natural thing in the world to be in each other's arms again. He was on top of her now; she could feel the full power of his appetite. He touched her in ways she had never been touched before, bringing her to orgasm effortlessly. They were completely absorbed by the moment and each other; finally all the distractions and setbacks that had kept them apart for so long were gone. It truly was magical.

Sometime later Annie laid in Jacks arms. Relaxation and tiredness took hold of her, not to mention the drink. She was moments away from sleep. Annie kissed his chest.

'Good night Jack. Happy Christmas – I love you. I've always loved you.' Jack smiled. He had no intention of sleeping. Last night he had slept on the wrong side of the door. Tonight, he was on the right side, he wanted to stay awake and savour very moment of being with Annie. He was still afraid that someone or something would come and snatch their happiness away – Jack could already see a great big problem looming on the horizon and it wasn't going to go away easily and very soon, he was going to have to tell Annie.

Chapter 29

It was only when Annie tried to focus on the view in front of her, that she realised how much she had drunk the night before. Her head was pounding and her mouth felt as if she had chewed sawdust in her sleep. She turned her head to see if the other side of the bed was still occupied. It wasn't. Jack was on duty, she had a vague recollection of him telling her he was leaving, but it was all a blur. She sunk into the pillow next to her, his fragrance still fresh. The memory of last night returned, she blushed at the thought of what they did. It was a far cry from their first liaison, when Annie was scared and didn't have much of a clue, being a good Catholic girl as she was then.

Last night was sublime, but in the cold light of day she felt ashamed. When she and Nick had made love for the first time, she felt as if she were cheating on Jack. Now after all these years of being with Nick and then a widow, she felt as if she was cheating on Nick. She knew it didn't make any sense, but that was how she felt, disloyal, as if she had thrown Nick and his memory out of their life.

Annie was desperate to leave, she panicked unsure of what it was she wanted from life or from Jack. The snow had stopped falling, and the outside temperature had raised a little, allowing some of the less compacted snow to start melting. Annie pulled her clothes on and made her way into the lounge looking for her handbag and her mobile phone.

It only took one short phone call and the emergency breakdown team were organised to be with her within the hour. There was no time to loose, if she wanted to leave without bumping into Jack. She made a quick cup of coffee, if only to take away the taste of the sawdust and two paracetamol to try and tame the headache. She found an extra jumper of Jack's to borrow for extra warmth. It would only take her fifteen minutes to walk to the car, but she wanted to make sure she was there in plenty of time.

Annie pulled the door to Jack's cottage fast shut as she left. Her first instinct was to bolt for the exit and the breakdown man, but she couldn't leave until she had spoken to Violet. There was nothing for it, she was going to have to go into the hotel and look for her. She knew her way around the back corridors with ease after her stint as a member of staff. If she went via the kitchens and cut out the reception, there was a greater chance she would avoid Jack, so that's exactly what she did. Annie made small talk with the chef whilst waiting for Violet to return to the kitchens for the next round of tea coffee or toast for a guest. She didn't have to wait long.

'Hi Mum. You're all wrapped up. Where are you off too? Are you going for a walk?'

'No. I'm meeting the breakdown man, but I'll be back for you later. What time do you finish work?'

'About eleven today…..How was Christmas day Night?' Violet asked innocently.

'What….What do you mean?' Fired back Annie who was afraid her sins were showing all over her face.

'Chill Mum! I was just asking if you two managed to have a good chat and get through the evening without arguing.' Annie's over defensiveness nearly gave the game away.

''Yes, it was fine. We did chat.' The shame she felt kept her from elaborating on the subject.

'I'm glad you two managed to clear the air. I thought you might have worked things out, Jack looked very happy this morning.' Violet was still fishing for more information, she didn't realise just how close to the truth she came.

'It's probably the thought of getting his home back to himself.' Said Annie who was desperate to get out of there before she said something she would regret. 'Keep your phone turned on when you finish. I'll call you to let you know what's happening.' Annie could have won an Olympic medal at exiting if such a category existed. She hadn't however expected to bump into Scarlett.

'Annie, good to see you. I hope we made you feel comfortable here? I know it wasn't your first choice for a Christmas destination and you had no idea you would get snowed in, but did you manage to make the best of it?' Why was Annie suspicious of every comment spoken to her. She was her own worst enemy she may as well slap it on a 'T' shirt, *'yes I slept with Jack – again!'* and have done with it.

'Eh, yes, it was good of Jack to put us up.' Annie was looking for the shortest conversation possible without being rude. It wasn't Scarlett's fault she was trying to avoid Jack.

'I'm so sorry, I have to go Scarlett. The breakdown man is on his way to the car and I don't want to miss him.'

'I'm sure we can spare Jack to go with you in case you need some help?' offered Scarlett.

'No! – no, I'll be fine on my own, but thank you.' Annie started to leave.

'It's a shame about his news isn't it?' Scarlett called after her.

'His news?' Annie questioned.

'He's done such a good job in turning the hotel around, that they are moving him on. I think he said it was a hotel in Italy didn't he. We're going to miss him greatly and so will you I imagine?'

'Surely they didn't ring him today, Boxing Day to tell him the news?' Annie was aghast at their callousness.

'Oh, no they rang on Christmas Eve morning. He was very surprised I can tell you. I think he thought he would be with us for a while, but that's what happens when you're good at your job!' Annie was fuming. He had seduced her knowing full well that he was going away again. How could he be so cruel and heartless? He should have told her. He had no right keeping something as important as this from her. Annie's need to leave was now more urgent than ever. Scarlett was still talking, but Annie had stopped listening.

'Scarlett I have to go.' Annie didn't wait for a response; her mind was already out of the door, followed swiftly by her body.

The breakdown man was true to his word, arriving before the hour was up. Releasing the car from the ditch was an easier process than Annie had expected. A large winch hooked under the chassis and a great deal of horse power was all it took and the car was free. The damp had got into the engine, from sitting in the deep snow for the past two days, but the very nice man managed to jump start it with his trusty kit. On closer inspection, there were a few small scratches and dints from the impact, but nothing that would stop Annie from driving it home. Freedom and independence at last, she couldn't wait to get home or more to the point away from Jack.

Several hours later Annie sat on the sofa looking at the long list of missed calls and text's on her phone. One name was repeated constantly – Jack. She starred at it wondering what he could possibly have to say to justify his lies. Last night had been wonderful, but it had all been a hollow sham. She was just one last fling for old times' sake – 'Wham bam I'm off to Italy mam'. He couldn't love her to do what he did. He knew she was cautious about getting involved, especially with the repercussions it could have on Violet, but still he ploughed on satisfying his own needs, sod everyone else who would be left to pick up the pieces after he had gone. Annie had no intention of reading his messages. There was nothing he could say that she wanted to hear. The implications of Jack leaving would be even more devastating for Violet. All the time and effort that had been put into building bridges would go to waste, the moment he abandoned her and moved away. Annie knew that Violet would be distraught by the news. Violet had forgiven him for not being there for her as a child, as he was oblivious to her existence, but for him to choose to walk away at such an early stage would be suicide as far as their relationship was concerned and it would be Annie yet again clearing up Jack's mess. For a moment she wished she had never met Jack, and then she took it back, because no Jack - means no Violet.

Annie had returned to Priory Hall and collected Violet after her shift. Annie made her come out to the car park, there was no way on earth she was setting foot inside there again today. Now Annie had Violet back safely at home in their own world. They didn't need interference from Jack or anyone else. They were fine as they were. After a belated exchange of present's Violet took herself off to her bedroom, she needed to catch up on all the sleep she had missed over the last couple of days. The flat was quiet - too quiet. The only sound Annie could hear was her mind whirring and churning over the events of the past few days. She flicked on the TV to try and deflect her line of thought. The song 'climb every mountain' from the sound of music echoed around the room. She turned it over, it was another tale of unrequited love she didn't need today. Next on offer she found Top of the pops 2 showing old hits from its archives. The year happened to be the year they left college. Every song stirred a moment in their history. Two songs in she switched it off, she didn't need any emotional triggers to set her off crying, she was doing a perfectly good job on her own. She had to find something to do. Sitting and waiting for the shop to open and normal life to begin was driving her mad. The turkey was still sat in the fridge uncooked. She decided to make some stuffing and cook it. She had no intention of cooking a full Christmas dinner at this late stage, but it was a sin to waste it. She could always freeze some of it, but she knew she wouldn't. Annie pulled the onions out from the bottom of the fridge and began to peel them. She had only stripped the outer layer of one onion and the tears began to fall. She looked at the label on the packet – Spanish – they were always the strongest and always made her cry. Her thought strayed to work, she could hardly believe that Christmas was over and the shop would re-open tomorrow. – Some break! – But normality was good it was what she needed.

She started to make a mental list of the flowers she would need to get from market in the morning, when her train of thought was rudely interrupted by someone banging loudly on the front door of the shop. Annie ran to the front window to see who it was. It was Jack, she darted back behind the curtain, not wanting him to see her, but it was too late, he had looked up, just at the moment she appeared at the window. Annie could hear him shouting from the street.

'Annie! Come down here and open this door!' She ignored him and went to sit on the sofa, holding on to a cushion for protection. She wasn't going to take orders from him. She was no longer Priory Hall staff! Moments later Violet came rushing in from her bedroom to see what all the commotion was about.

'What's happening? Who's banging?' she asked looking at her mum for answers.

'It's no one. Go back to bed and get some sleep.' Replied Annie curtly. Violet ignored her mother and went to look out of the window. Jack was standing across the road looking up at the flat. Violet smiled and waved at him. He waved back, but his face was like thunder.

'Mum, its Jack, why haven't you let him in?'

'Because I don't want to speak to him! He can rot in hell for all I care! The self-centred, two faced, lying, cheating, complicated little shit!' Violet marvelled at her mother's outburst, it was a new experience for her.

'Mum! – You don't mean that? I'm going to let him in. You can't leave him out there in the snow!'

'I've told you - I don't want to see him Violet!'

'Well, I do want to see him so you're going to have to get over it! You can't keep changing your mind like this. Remember he's my father now! I'm letting him in.' Violet signalled to Jack that she was coming down in a minute to let him in.

'Mum, please what can have happened that could be so bad?' Annie didn't answer; she buried her head in the cushion. There was no escape for Annie. The front door was the only entrance and exit to the property – she was trapped. Violet went down and opened the front door. Jack strode past her, barely acknowledging her, leaping up the stairs to the flat two by two.

He found Annie stood with her back to the wall, still cradling the cushion in her arms.

'Annie, what on earth is the matter? Where did you go? Why won't you answer my calls? –And why wouldn't you let me in!' He was angry. Annie had only ever once seen him this angry; when his parents told him he had to go to Australia.

'I'm waiting! He was stood a few inches from her face, his eyes full of animosity and hurt. He didn't know whether to shake her to her senses or kiss her. Annie didn't speak to him or acknowledge him. She turned her attentions to Violet.

'Please can you give me and Jack some space Violet? I need to talk to him alone.' Violet nodded; she was upset and confused by her mother's reactions. She had never seen her behave like this – ever. Annie waited until Violet's bedroom door clicked shut. Annie starred back at Jack, showing no intimidation from his exhibition of anger. He was still standing extremely close to her, she inhaled his scent unwillingly, her mind flashed back to the night before and the passion that had united them.

'Well?' He demanded.

'When were you going to tell me that you are moving to Italy?' Jack's solid gaze melted.

'It's not what you think Annie...'

'It sounds pretty clear to me. I have to say, I have the strongest feeling of de ja vous! Ring any bells with you?'

'There's a reason I didn't tell you, if you let me explain?'

'Explain what. That we let you in to our lives again, against my better judgement and how can you turn your back on Violet when you've just found her. What sort of devastation is that going to cause her? She's already lost one dad. I don't think she's strong enough to go through that again. You are so selfish Jack. You think of no one but yourself. If your career is more important to you than Violet then she's probably better off without you. I know I am!' Annie lowered her voice for the next part of the dressing down, she was adamant that Violet wouldn't hear. 'And my only excuse for – for what happened between us was drink! I was drunk or I would never have done what we did and to think I trusted you and let you into my bed,'

'Actually it was my bed and I don't remember having to drag you there!' He retorted.

'It doesn't matter whose bed it was and I was drunk - what matters is that all the time you were telling me how much you loved me you were planning your escape! How could you!!' Annie had run out of words.

'Is that what you really think and feel Annie? – and you had to be drunk to want me?' He was choking on the words. Trying his best not to breakdown in front of her.

'Yes!' Confirmed Annie knowing full well that her words were destroying him,

'Yes because if I'd been sober, I'd have known you weren't sincere. You just wanted your leg over for old time's sake! I wish I'd never met you Jack Parrish. I'm not going to let you ruin my life for a second time!'

'Then there's no more to say.' All his anger had dissipated, replaced by submission. If her mind was already made up, he's wasting his time trying to change it. He wanted to be with her, but he wasn't going to beg her. The mood she was in, it was impossible to reason with her. He turned away and left the flat without speaking another word.

Violet heard Jack's footsteps on the stairs and came running out of her room.

'Where is he going? Why didn't you listen to him?' She had heard everything, even the hushed conversation. The walls were paper thin, she had no choice.

'Violet, you are too young to understand….'

'I'm not too young to know you two should be together and I know you're just running scarred! Admit it you love him. Stop running away from life Mum! You are allowed to be happy again! – and If you push him away from us I'll never forgive you!' Violet started to run down the stairs after Jack.

'Violet come back!' Annie demanded in vain.

Jack was in his car, about to shut the door by the time Violet caught up with him. She ran to the front of his car, stretching her arms out in an effort to stop him driving off. He gestured for her to get into the car.

'Violet it's freezing out here! You have no coat. You need to get back inside where it's warm!'

'Spoken like a true father!' said Violet trying to lighten his mood. 'Why are you two rowing?' Violet climbed into the front seat next to Jack.

'I'm not altogether sure Violet. One reason is that your mother feels I have lied to her, which I haven't, but … well….You're going to find out soon enough. I've been posted to another hotel in another country.'

'You've what?' Violet thought she was going to cry, which was stupid because she hardly knew him.

'To be more exact they want me to move to Italy. I didn't tell your mother because I'm trying to get it changed – I don't want to go and leave you or your mother when I've just found you both, but the man who makes all the decisions is still away on Christmas holidays. Your mum is too cross to listen to me after yesterday and…'

'Why? What happened yesterday?' Jack was on the verge of blushing. It had never been his intention to discuss his sex life with his daughter, especially as it involved her mother!

'Let's just say we were making progress at understanding each other and letting barriers down.' He hoped that was enough for her.

'You mean you kissed her?' Thank god for the minds of the innocents he thought. 'Something like that.' He tried to play it down.

'But she loves you. I can tell she does.' Jack was surprised by Violets' words. 'The problem is she's spent so long thinking about other people Jack, she's forgotten how to recognise what it is she wants for herself. Her feelings are all mixed up, her feelings for you, for me and for Nick. Give her a little time, time to calm down and decide what she wants. I'm sure she'll realise. It's hard for her when she's had to be so self-reliant, she had to be after dad died and the moment she start to melt, she finds out you have to go away, look at it from her side?'

'When did you get so wise?' He complimented her.

'I hope I get it from my parents?' She crossed her fingers in front of him.

'I need to speak to her Violet, but she won't listen. Please explain to her that I haven't agreed to go to Italy – yet. My answer depends on what your mum wants. Make sure she knows that!' He stressed the point, 'I never want to be parted from you Violet or your mother, as far as Annie goes, it's her choice, but I will never stop being here for you whatever happens. You are my daughter and no amount of distance will change that. I will do my best to stay close to you.' The little flicker of warmth in her heart for Jack was growing stronger. Her defences were tumbling. At first she didn't want to think about anyone other than Nick being her father, but history had been made and couldn't be changed. She loved Nick and always would, but her heart was big enough to find space in it for Jack. He was starting to creep in to the corners and a little beyond. Violet was starting to visibly shiver.

'Go on, get yourself inside where it's warm young lady!' Jack insisted. 'I'll see you at work tomorrow.'

Annie was watching them both through the upstairs window. What could they possibly be saying without her? She was tempted to run down demanding to know, but it would be futile. Her emotions were so out of control, she didn't trust herself to be civil. She would have to wait it out. It was only a matter of minutes before Violet was out of the car and making her way back up the stairs. Violet went to sit next to sit next to Annie on the sofa. Cold radiated from her. Annie put her arm around her, extending the cardigan she was wearing around Violet's shoulders trying to transfer some warmth.

'You're freezing! You should be careful or you'll be ill, going out like that!' Violet snuggled into her mother, extricating as much warmth as possible from her. 'Well? Are you going to tell me what he said or do I have to beat it out of you?'

Annie was only half joking.

'He needs to speak to you. He hasn't told them that he'll go to Italy, but he wants to discuss things with you. I can tell he wants to stay, but if there's no future with you – I think he might go? Don't blow it Mum. I know you love him. Now isn't the time to stand on your soap box or your pride. I need Jack in my life mum, and I think you do to.' Annie's face was shocked.

'Come on Mum, you wouldn't get upset if you didn't care about him?' The very least you owe him is to hear him out without shouting him down?'

'Owe him? I don't owe him anything!' Annie shouted indignantly.

'You owe him my life. Something good did come out of your relationship and if you can't do it for him – then please do it for me. If the roads are clearer tomorrow, will you drive over to see him?' Annie's first instinct was to shout 'NO, I bloody well won't', but she could tell this friction was hurting Violet. Annie didn't want Violet to feel as if she had to take sides, there was no guarantee which side she would take. After a few moments hesitation Annie answered.

'Okay, I'll do it for you, but I'm making no promises and I'm not going tomorrow, I need a few days to think about things – but I will go.'

'I don't need promises; I just need you to hear him out.'

Most of the snow had melted away by the time Annie had finished her first day back at work after the Christmas break. Everything seemed inappropriately covered in glitter in the shop. Annie had an urge to hoover everything until it had all vanished, but she knew only too well that she would still be finding glitter splattered on her body and face as late in the year as Easter. Customers were thin on the ground, many still away on holiday, others sick of all the pre-Christmas shopping and staying well clear, consequently the day dragged, every hour feeling like two. Pippa wasn't due in work, but she popped in to see how Annie's Christmas was and to give her an update on the situation with Zach.

'Well?' Asked Annie anxious to find out how Christmas had panned out with everyone together.

'It was good.' Admitted Pippa in her own understated way.

'So by my standards it was fantastic!'

'Okay it was fantastic! The kids loved having him around. He played every new game that arrived in the house. He took them out building snowmen whilst I prepared the Christmas dinner, then he washed up and made me sit down. He's been wonderful, truly!'

'And did you ask him to move in?' This was the part Annie was most interested in hearing about.

'No I didn't.'

'Oh Pippa, I thought you were going to bite the bullet and ask him, you said yourself 'he's wonderful'?' Annie wanted to inject Pippa with courage to be bold and ask.

'I didn't have to ask him to move in, because the kids did it for me. On Boxing Day when Zach was packing a few things to take home with him the children asked him why he didn't live with us all the time, because they were sad he was leaving. Zach told them it was Mummy's decision if he should move in or not. So they asked me if he could and I said - yes, if he wanted to we'd love to have him live with us and he said – Yes!' Annie and Pippa hugged and danced making whooping noises as they celebrated.

'So what about you?' Pippa asked when they had both calmed down, 'How was your Christmas?' Annie gave Pippa a look conveying an eventful time.

'What? Have you seen Jack?' Annie couldn't look Pippa in the eye.

'No! – You've slept with him haven't you?' Pippa as Annie knew was good at reading people.

'Okay I'm putting the kettle on and I want to know everything!'

Annie spent the next hour telling Pippa of all the events that had taken place over the holiday period – leaving nothing out, well almost.

'So he wants to see me and speak to me, but I'm not falling for his lies again. I can't do it Pippa. I'm not strong enough to let him in and then loose him again.

'You don't know that's going to happen Annie. Violet is right. The only way to know for sure is to speak to him, face to face. You've had a lifetime of other people interfering in your relationship, it's time to sort it out on your own – communicate with him, what are you waiting for? The longer you leave it the harder it will be. Ring him and set up a meeting. Do it now.' Pippa was what Annie needed – a kick up the bum.

'I'll text him and see if he can meet later.' Within five minutes Annie had her reply. He was willing to meet her later.

'Oh Pippa – what have you made me do?' Annie didn't want to take responsibility for the decision.

'Don't look at me like that! You know it's what you had to do, but never mind that – you didn't tell me what it was like? Being with Jack again?'

'Pippa! I can't discuss that!' Pippa raised her eyebrows, not believing Annie had nothing to say on the subject, 'No. Really – I can't remember – I was drunk!' They both burst into fits of giggles. It was just what Annie needed to release some of the anxiety she was feeling about her pending meeting with Jack. In truth Annie remembered every kiss, every touch, but it was comitted to her memory and not to be shared.

The meeting had been arranged for six p.m. at the cottage. She had felt sick since the moment he had confirmed their meeting and her stomach was jumping summersaults. She kept telling herself that it was better to face what was happening instead of running away and to focus on the fact that she was doing it for Violet. The tyres crunched on the frozen gravel announcing her arrival. Jack peered through the window; he was already waiting for her. The front door was opened for her to go in, but Jack had gone back into the lounge. Annie closed the door behind her, sealing her commitment to talk.

Jack was sitting in the arm chair by the fire. The flames licked the logs enthusiastically, generating light and warmth. A half empty bottle of wine was sat on the table in front of him. One glass placed furthest away from him was full, Jack had already started drinking from the other. She sat down opposite him, like two strangers in a railway carriage, forced together by circumstance. Jack was calm, cool and emotionally despatched, or at least those were the vibes he was emitting. Annie took a sip of the wine; she had no intention of repeating the outcome of their last meeting. She needed to stay sober. As Jack was playing bad cop, Annie decided to set the ball rolling.

'Jack I'm here because Violet asked me to come and speak to you. I am sorry that I wouldn't hear you out the other day. I'm here now and I'm listening.' She could see Jack shift in his chair relaxing slightly.

'Are you only here because Violet asked you to come? What about for your sake, for our sake, don't you care what I have to say?' Annie changed her gaze from the wine glass to Jack's face. He wasn't going to make this easy for her.

'Yes, I care, that's why I'm here.' Her gaze was fixed and sure.

'I'm sorry you found out about the change in job from Scarlett, but there were good reasons why I didn't tell you straight away. Firstly, I didn't know what was going to happen between us. I didn't know you were going to seduce me on

Christmas day.' Annie opened her mouth to object, then closed it again just in time, realising that he still had the ability to wind her up effortlessly. 'I wanted what ever happened if anything, to be about us, and what we wanted, not ruled by the circumstances around us. Secondly, and most importantly, you and Violet mean more to me than any job. If it was necessary I would quit my job for you and find something else, some other line of work, but I need to know what you want before I can make those decisions.'

'Jack I don't want you to give up your career for me and Violet. All your life, it seems to me you have been put into the position of doing things for the sake of other people not for yourself. The last thing I want is to hold you back and have you resenting us both in the years ahead. You are obviously talented at what you do.'

'Annie, I never would resent changing my life for you. My only regret is that you slipped through my fingers twice before and I'm not prepared to let that happen again.'

'Twice?' Questioned Annie.

'When I went to Australia - and when I found you with Nick.' Annie nodded.

'You must know how much I wanted to grab you and run away with you that night. It almost killed me to have to walk away and leave you with Nick.' Annie could feel a lump rising in her throat, she decided to trust him with the truth.

'God forgive me Jack, but on that night – if you had of asked me to go with you, I probably would. It was one of the hardest moments in my life, letting you walk away and not running after you shouting at the top of my voice that Violet was your daughter.' Annie was shaking, trying to speak without losing control of her emotions and breaking down. She reached for the wine and took a large gulp. Jack sat forward in his chair now interested in what she was saying, no longer uninvolved.

'Why didn't you? Our lives would have been so different if you had?'

'I couldn't bring myself to hurt Nick so badly. He was a good kind loving person Jack, who brought up your daughter without ever making her feel second best and no matter how you might like to think I've been miserable waiting for you all my life – that wasn't the case. We were very happy and still would be if it wasn't for the crash.'

'What happened? Or do you prefer not to speak about it?' Jack was sensitive enough to realise that it may be too traumatic to go through.

'No, I think you should know, and then you'll know what Violet had to go through. It was a juggernaut on the motorway that didn't see him. It side swiped him into the central reservation. He was in hospital for two weeks, fighting for his life, just as you did - only he didn't make it.'

'So being with me was a reminder? It must have been hard coming back to spend time in the hospital.'

'Parts were like living it again - but thankfully there was a happier outcome.'

'That makes me even more grateful that you stuck around. It must have been hard to do.'

'I've been in easier situation.' Annie started to fidget; the conversation was making her feel uncomfortable. She didn't want to hit melt down.

'I know it's a hard thing to ask you, but what do you actually want Annie? Do you want me in your life, to see if we can make this work together?' Annie was thrown, she didn't know she had to make a decision right away. She came here to talk, not map out her life plan.

'I have to be honest with you.' He continued when she didn't contribute. 'I can't stay around here watching you and Violet getting on with your lives, if I'm not involved in them. I'm not giving you an ultimatum; I'm just being honest, because I've spent too long wanting you and not having the power or sense to do anything about it. I can't lose you again and see you every week around the village. I'll have to take the job in Italy.' Annie crumbled, she didn't want him to go, but for some reason she couldn't let the words pass her lips, she didn't know if it was pride or loyalty to Nick. She wanted to scream – instead she just cried. Jack moved across to the settee Annie was perched on. He pulled her into his arms and just held her. He didn't speak or tell her to stop; he simply made sure she felt safe. Once Annie had started to cry, she couldn't stop. So many feeling suppressed for so many years that had been bubbling under the surface had now exploded. Part of it, Annie was certain, was grief, held in as a consequent of trying to be strong for Violet. When Nick had died, she had never fully let go of her feelings in case, as she suspected, when she started, she couldn't stop.

Jack was no expert on women, but he used to be an expert on Annie, even if it was nearly twenty years ago. He purely waited, waited until the tears subsided and she wanted to talk. When he felt the worst of the drenching was over he began to speak again.

'Annie – I love you – I always have and always will. I want to be with you.' Her heart stopped beating for a moment, sending her heart rhythms haywire. They were words she never thought she would hear again after her behaviour on

Boxing day. She had almost ruined everything with her pride and judgemental attitude. She placed her arms around his neck and hugged him for dear life.

'I don't want to go to Italy Annie or anywhere that you are not. One of the reasons I didn't tell you the news was because I had an idea about setting up Priory Hall as a training centre for all new management in the hotels across the chain. That way, I could stay here and run it. It's something I would enjoy doing and I would be good at it. The building is perfect for it; we could make it a centre of excellence, but the person with the power to say yes is away for the Christmas break, so I didn't want to raise your hopes until I was sure. I've been summoned to London at the end of January to give them a full outline of my proposals, so they are at least thinking about it. If they happen to say 'no' – there is plenty of hotel work around. I'm sure I could get something local –maybe even seek out our own small hotel to run? Or maybe I could come and work for you?' Annie laughed.

'Over my dead body!'

'Okay we cans skip that idea, but there are lots of things I can do and I'd look forward to the challenge.' Annie could see a glimmer of hope on the horizon. She could tell he had thought it through in detail; it wasn't some half-baked idea to make her feel he was trying – he really was. Finally she was ready to admit to her feelings.

'Jack, I love you too. I do want to be with you. I'm just stubborn and find it hard to tell you. I've spent so many years denying my feelings for you – I guess I just got very good at it.' She kissed him and he kissed her back. It wasn't passionate, it was loving, intimate, warm and homely, at that moment in time, it was what they both needed.

'How do you think Violet will feel about us being a couple?' Asked Jack, it was a subject that was constantly on his mind. Annie giggled, she tried to stop herself and sound serious, but it wasn't working.

'What?' He asked.

'No – it sounds strange – being a 'couple' – Nice, but strange. Violet will be thrilled that we have sorted our differences. If she had a problem with us, I'm sure we would have known by now.'

They both sat on the sofa for hours chatting and catching up on years of history. The main topic was Violet's childhood. What she had been like as a child, if she was an early walker, when she said her first words. Many times she found herself quoting Nick and apologising. Jack stopped her to put her straight, 'I know there were things you shared with Nick and I'm so glad he was good to you and Violet, so it's okay to use him as a reference point. I'm never going to get into a jealous rage. He was there for you when I couldn't be. I have a lot to thank him for – So tell me more about Violet's childhood?' There were thousands of moment that Jack missed; Annie vowed to herself that in time he would know everything. It was beginning to feel natural to be with him again, the damage of years lived separately was slowly dissolving. She could see a flicker of Jack the student creeping in; maybe she was re-tuning to his wavelength. The decision had been made by the time Annie was ready to leave. They would give their relationship a go. Even if Jack was forced to change jobs or temporarily move away, they were going to try their hardest to make it work. All that was left to do now was to tell Violet – and Jack's mother.

Chapter 30

On the day after Valentine's Day, Scarlett escorted Annie up to the grandest suite in the hotel. A large four poster bed dominated the centre of the room as they entered, it was impossible to miss; it should have had a sign on it reading *'Please use me for wild passionate sex'*. Also in the suite was a small sitting room with a table and chairs, a settee and the largest TV she had seen in a hotel. The décor was vintage, lush creams, caramel and gold tones flowed through the entire suite. She felt as if she were stepping into a page from a magazine. She recognised the vase of fresh flowers on the console table as being from her shop, but she still enjoyed the extra detail and effort that had been made on her behalf, Jack must have ordered it with Pippa. Two dressing gowns and two pairs of slippers were arranged neatly at the bottom of the bed.

'Over here are your bathroom and a small dressing area. I love this room.' Enthused Scarlett, Annie set her case down on the luggage rack and followed Scarlett in to investigate.

'Now your spa appointments are booked to begin in about an hour and the hairdresser will be here to work her magic after that. Jack has ordered lunch to be brought for you in the spa and your morning coffee will be arriving shortly – God, I think I'm more excited than you Annie!' laughed Scarlett, who was watching Annie struggle to hide her lethargy.

'No Scarlett, I am excited, I'm just shattered! Yesterday and all this week, it's been mad busy for Valentine's Day. I can't count how many hours sleep I've missed and now it's over my body is rebelling and has gone into melt down. My body is here, but my brain is still on last Thursday! - I'm looking forward to going to the spa and being pampered, it's what I need, but I guarantee I'll fall asleep! They could dye my hair purple and tattoo me from head to foot and I doubt I'd wake up.'

'You won't be the first to do that!' laughed Scarlett.

'Do you think they'll wake me if I start snoring?' Asked Annie, who was truly concerned.

'If they don't I will.' Promised Scarlett, 'Is your dress in your case? I can't wait to see it?' Scarlett was as enthusiastic as a small puppy on its way to the park. Annie nodded.

'Do you want to see it? I hope it doesn't make me look like a dog's dinner? Said Annie with caution. Violet was very insistent that it was the right one, in the end I gave in for a quiet life – but I'm not sure?' Annie opened the case and pulled out the dress which had been carefully laid on top to minimise creasing.

'I know you'll look fabulous in that Annie. Violet has a good eye for clothes' Assured Scarlett. '– What time do you expect Jack back from London?'

'He said he would ring when the meeting was over. I just hope he doesn't get stuck in traffic on his way back or I'm going to look very silly on my own later!'

'He won't let you down Annie. I've already read him the riot act about making sure he gets away on time – if not early! I'll leave you to relax Annie. Maybe you can cram in a short snooze before your first spa treatment? Call my extension if you need anything.' Scarlett was almost skipping with excitement as she left the room to sort the seating plan for the evening ahead.

Annie flopped into the cream and gold velvet winged chair in the corner of the room and surveyed her surroundings. It had been a complete surprise to her when Violet passed her an envelope on Jack's instructions the day before in the middle of making a wave of rose bouquets for Valentine's day.

'What's this?' Demanded Annie who was in the middle of an order and didn't want to be forced to put it down and have to start again – time was too precious. Violet and Pippa who was also in the workroom exchanged a knowing glance.

'Here.' Said Pippa. 'Pass that bouquet to me.' Violet placed the letter into Annie's hands.

'It's from Jack. Open it and see?' Annie could tell that it wasn't bad news as Violet's smile was so wide it could be seen from space. Annie opened the envelope. Inside was a beautiful Valentine's Day card from Jack and a ticket to the Valentines Ball at Priory Hall. A quizzical expression invaded Annie's face. Inside the card he had written –

To my darling Annie,

'Happy Valentine's Day'.

I would be honoured if you would come to the Valentine's Ball with me tomorrow. Everything is arranged, including a day of pampering to relax you after working hard all week, making everyone else's Valentine's Day special. I'll be back from my meeting in London as soon as possible tomorrow and can't wait to see you. Violet knows everything- if you have any questions ask her.

All my love - Always

Your valentine, Jack xx

'What does he mean about going to the Valentines Ball tomorrow?' Asked Annie.' I can't go. There's work to see to and I have nothing to wear!'

'Don't worry it's all taken care of.' Interrupted Pippa, trying to keep Annie calm. 'I'm coming in to look after the shop and Violet will help me if I need her. Most people will have bought their flowers today for Valentine's, there'll only be a few who weren't going to bother, but got in so much trouble they changed their minds! We'll have spare made up, so there is no problem there, besides if there so desperate they'll take anything – Next problem?'

'I have nothing to wear! I can't go to a fancy Ball in my jeans and trainers! Ball gowns are not a stock, standard item I have in my wardrobe and I haven't got time today to go to town to find a dress. It's impossible!' Violet stepped forwards to catch Annie's attention.

'Ah, well that's sorted too – Ingrid from the dress agency at the other end of the high street has a large selection of Ball gowns upstairs and she's expecting you to go after work and choose one. I went to see what she had last week, to make sure there was something I thought you'd like and we've put some dresses aside for you to try on and I'm coming with you to make sure you don't chose the frumpiest, old woman gown they have!' All three of them laughed. Annie exhaled in exasperation.

'It seems like you have it all covered and I've no choice in the matter?'

'No!' Chorused Violet and Pippa.

'You deserve it mum. It's about time someone spoilt you for a change!' Violet kissed her on the cheek, 'now come on you've work to do if you want a day off tomorrow!'

Annie was brought back to the present by a knock on the bedroom door. It was Violet with a tray of coffee and pastries.

'What a surprise! I can honestly say that this is a first – you waiting on me. Be careful or I may get used to it!'

'Enjoy it mother. It's back to normal tomorrow and I'll be expecting the same!' Violet sat the tray on the coffee table.'

'Can they spare you for a while to join me?' Offered Annie.

'I wish, but there's too much to do for the Ball tonight. I'll have something to keep my energy levels up though.' Violet reached for the largest pastry on the plate. 'I'm saving you really, if you ate this you wouldn't get into your dress!' Annie tried to cuff Violet on the back of her neck, but Violet was too fast. 'Isn't this room sick Mum? Jack and I came for a look around the hotel to see which suite we thought you'd like. I said this one because it had the largest TV. Jack agreed with my room choice, but I feel it wasn't the TV that swayed him?' Said Violet who was well aware that she was embarrassing her mother.

After she had gone Annie enjoyed her coffee at a leisurely pace. It was the first hot drink she had managed for days, as soon as a cuppa was made at work; a string of customers always seemed to file through the door, only leaving when the drinks were cold. This was a regular occurrence, some florist's get used to drinking cold tea, but Annie never could, she liked hers piping hot, so the drinks would end up being wasted. This hot coffee was an extra shot of luxury. Annie closed her eyes when she had finished the coffee. Her body ached from head to toe. Maybe she was getting too old to be a florist. Ever since the New year she had been constantly tired, falling asleep every time she sat on a comfy chair in the evenings. It was probably a result of trying to make time for Violet and Jack as well as run the shop. The sickness bug she caught a couple of weeks ago didn't help either. All the running around was doing her waist line good though, she was so tired most days, she had lost her appetite, some days to the point of Pippa's take away hot curry lunch from the sandwich shop making her heave. Jack couldn't have chosen a more perfect present for her than to have a day of pampering. The ball was the icing on the cake.

The phone rang a little while later requesting Annie's attendance at the spa for her treatments to begin. Jack had booked her in for every treatment possible in the time limit. She hoped he wasn't expecting miracle work to take place on her appearance - that would take months, not the few hours they had. She started off with a full body wrap and massage to relax her tired muscles. It was bliss. Annie was not the sort of woman who spent hours each week at the beauty salon, which made it feel even mode special and delicious. Next her feet were pedicured and preened to perfection, followed by a hand wax and manicure and slowly, inch by inch every muscle in her body was helped to recover from the stresses of Valentine's Day.

Lunch was brought to Annie on a silver platter by the side of the pool, pan-fried salmon on a bed of wilted spinach, washed down with sparkling apple juice. She was offered champagne, but decided to keep a clear head for the evening. It was pure luxury. After lunch it was the turn of the hairdresser, to turn her unsightly mop of split ends into something more suited for a ball. By the end of the afternoon, she had been preened and pampered to within an inch of her life - and it was fantastic! She felt like a new woman, her body and spirit revitalized and looking forward to the evening ahead – as long as Jack made it back in time.

Annie returned to the suite there was still no sign of Jack. Her dress was still waiting for her where she had hung it. She picked it up and held it in front of her, looking into the mirror. Annie had been persuaded to let the girls in the salon do her make up for her, again this was a new experience for Annie, who managed on limited face paint – usually zero, unless it was a special occasion, when she occasionally went wild with a little eye shadow and lipstick. She felt like a painted doll, but had been persuaded not to change anything until she witnessed the full effect whilst wearing the gown. She had promised them, but she was unconvinced. She looked at her reflection – it wasn't her usual look, but that was the point of a Ball – to go and look very different than you would normally. She decided to leave the final decision until the dress was on.

Next Annie checked her phone messages to see if Jack had rung .There was a text from him to say he was running late due to traffic on the M6 and that he would go straight to the cottage to shower and dress to save time and then he would be with her. She had to admit that she couldn't wait to see him. He had only been away for a few days, but it made her realise how integrated their lives had already become. Since Christmas they had become inseparable, spending every spare moment together, which on some weeks, due to work commitments on both sides, were few and far between. Most of their time was taken up by talking, rebuilding their relationship, reminiscing about school days and the years in-between. There was so much to find out – on both sides. It had been an easier transition than expected, becoming a couple. Jack and Violet's relationship was also blooming. Jack had the sense not to rush in and be too overpowering with her, leaving Violet to lead the way. Everything in the garden was rosy, well it would be if Jack came back with a positive answer on the management programme.

Jack had been in London for three days in total, with meetings morning, noon and night, giving numerous presentations and trying to persuade the bosses that changing priory Hall into a training centre. He had casually added that if the decision was against his proposal, then he would be forced to leave the company. He in no wanted to blackmail the company, but he wanted to leave them in no doubt how important this proposal was to him. Luckily for Jack he was well liked and known within the company and the bosses took this news in the spirit it was intended, but they also assured Jack that they would not tolerate the proposal unless it made good business sense for the company. Jack understood this and had spent weeks working on figures and targets to support his proposal. The final decision was imminent, but he had no time to wait around at the end of his final presentation, he needed to make sure he was back in time for the ball. He was assured that a phone call would follow later. Jack had promised Annie that whatever the outcome, he wouldn't be leaving her or Violet.

Annie's text bleeped again, it was Jack announcing that he was back on home ground and would be with her in fifteen minutes. She texted him back a line of kisses followed by a smiley face winking. Annie slipped into her dress, it wasn't dis-similar to the colour of the dress she wore on the night of the leaver's ball all those years ago, Violet had insisted that it was the most flattering colour for her to wear and that she looked stunning in it. The purchase had been agreed before Annie had time to object. It was more sophisticated than her previous dress, the top of the gown created a wonderful cleavage, which Annie didn't even know she had, her boobs seemed considerably bigger. The gown was elegant, but simple, showing off her figure without looking like mutton dressed as lamb. It touched in all the right places and covered the lumps and bumps she disliked. She observed the finished product in the full length mirror. For a moment she was transported back to the night of the leaver's ball and the anticipation it held. The butterflies were released and wreaking havoc inside her. She felt slightly sick. What if Jack thought she was trying too much to be the girl all those years ago? He might hate how she looked. Her answer would come soon enough as Jack was due to arrive. The girls in the salon were right, the shades of make-up became more subtle and blended with the gown, and she didn't look like a painted marionette any longer.

She had just managed to get her strappy shoes on without plucking the gown when there was a knock at the door. Her heart jumped, she knew it was Jack.

He was dressed in his dinner suit, looking every inch the part. The suit was handmade and fitted him like a glove; unlike the borrowed suit that he wore for their last ball. The lost years had made him even more handsome, his edge of experience shining through.

'Wow!' He exclaimed as he feasted his eyes on her. 'You look absolutely magnificent!' she smiled taking pleasure in the complement. She was about to complement him on how smart he was looking, but before she could speak he had swept her into his arms and was kissing her fervently, undaunted by the possibility of lipstick smeared across his face.

'Wow!' Copied Annie a little time later 'What a greeting! I bet my lipstick is up to my ears now!'

'If it's not now, it will be later!' He promised. 'Have you enjoyed your day? Did they look after you?' He asked at the same time as wiping lipstick from his face.

'It's been fantastic Jack. I've had the best time, but you realise I'll expect this every year!' He smiled at the thought of being with her for year upon year. 'Any way – how did you get on?' She asked him, the suspense of not knowing their fate was killing her.

'It seemed to go well; there were one or two issues that needed to be ironed out. They haven't given me an answer yet, but the chief promised to let me know in a day or two, so tonight we're going to forget all about it and I'm going to escort you to the ball!'

'Do we have to pick anyone else up on the way?' She mocked, remembering how he allowed her the honour of tagging along to the last ball all those years ago, 'No Shelley this time?'

'No.' He replied feigning a wounded expression. 'I'm exclusively yours.' He kissed her again. 'But before we go downstairs I have something for you.' Out of his breast pocket he pulled an oblong jewellery case and handed it to Annie. 'I thought this might look nice with your dress?' Annie opened the box to find a very beautiful necklace set with a cluster of small diamonds. 'I thought diamonds are neutral so they'll go with anything?'

'I've never heard diamonds called neutral before? They are beautiful, but I can't.....' He stopped her.

'Yes you can and you have to. It would be rude to refuse and if you add up all the birthdays and Christmases I've missed buying you things, the cost still doesn't come anywhere near what you deserve and most of all it makes me happy.' Annie dabbed a tear that was threatening to ruin her face paint.

'Will you help me put it on?' She asked. He lifted her hair and fastened the necklace with ease, kissing the nape of her neck before replacing her hair.

'Thank you.' She enthused. 'It's beautiful.'

'Now are we going to this ball or should I keep you here and have my wicked way with you instead?'

'The Ball definitely! I've not gone to all this trouble all day for no one to see me and besides, I have to show off my diamonds!'

Jack and Annie made a striking couple and they didn't go un-noticed when they walked into the main room. Annie observed many of the women turning to look at Jack, in a fashion that was far from discrete. For a moment she understood how Michelle must have felt on the night of the leaver's ball, proud to be stood next to one of the best looking men in the room. No wonder she kicked up such a fuss when Annie tried to tag along all those years ago.

'You're causing a stir Mr Parrish. You're going to be in demand tonight!' He was so easy to tease.

'As long as I'm in demand with you, that's all that matters to me.' Said Jack kissing her on the cheek and sending a subliminal message to the women that he was not available and to the men that neither was Annie.

'Anyway they're not looking at me Annie. There're looking at you. You're putting them all to shame. You look stunning!' Annie noticed that Scarlett and Violet had been watching their entrance and had seen them kiss, Annie blushed. Jack was a perfect escort. They had been seated on a table which included the organisers of the Charity Ball. Jack introduced her and made sure she felt at home in their company. He was humorous, attentive and amicable. During the meal Violet and Scarlett came up to Annie on separate occasions to complement her on looking so beautiful.

'What's that around your neck Mum?' Asked Violet, noticing the moment she came close enough. 'You look like Julia Roberts in pretty woman with those rocks around your neck!'

'I feel like her Violet. I've had such a wonderful day and Jack has totally spoilt me with this necklace, it's wonderful!'

'I know.' Slipped violet, 'I thought that when he showed it to me last week. I'm getting good at keeping secrets aren't I?'

After the meal a live band took to the stage. The musicians were good, but the number of couples on the floor dancing was minimal. The lead singer was almost standing on his head trying to encourage the guests to get up and Join in, but nothing he did seemed to be working. The men were waiting to be served at the bar and happy to chat, and in no hurry to return to their partners in case they were dragged on to the dance floor, Annie concluded that they were waiting for the alcohol to take effect, then maybe they would be tempted. The women were no better either, none of them were dancing around their handbags in the traditional manner and to make matters worse, there were two couples who hadn't rested since the band began, both fighting it out for the title of best ballroom couple – not that there was such a prize on offer. Each dance brought a new set of complicated moves to thrill and keep the on-lookers in their seats. Finally Jack had had enough of their domination of the dance floor, he could tell by the expression on his sponsors faces that they were hoping for an event with more atmosphere.

'I think we need to stop this.' He whispered in Annie's ear. 'This Strictly come dancing set are never going to get off the dance floor whilst they have a captive audience. We need to intervene.' Jack leaned across the table to speak to the organiser of the ball Philip Cartwright and his business partner, Simon Chandler. Annie couldn't tell what was being said, but the conversation was animated with lots of gesticulating and pointing around the room. Moments later Jack, Simon and Philip were on their feet commanding a dance from their partners. Annie shrieked, luckily no one heard over the noise of the music.

'I can't dance like that! She yelled trying not to point at the middle aged couple closest to her on the dance floor.

'It doesn't matter! Neither can I, but if we don't get this lot off the floor, the ball isn't going to be a success. Think of it as work. You have to do it to help me?'

'But I'm useless at dancing!'

'Good – that will make two of us……You only have to sway a little. Please if you love me?' She couldn't refuse and he knew it. Annie gritted her teeth and let him lead her on to the dance floor. Philip, Simon and their wives were all equally as embarrassed. Annie decided to try and cling to the side of the dance floor where not everyone could see them, but Jack had a different idea twirling and spinning Annie until she had lost all inhibitions because she was laughing too much. The dancing was atrocious from all three couples, but the most entertaining thing the guests had seen all evening, by the second song people were starting to fill the floor, not bothered I if they could dance of not.

'See!' Said Jack smugly 'It's worked. It won't be a dull night after all.' He made her dance for two more dances before he would accept the fact that she needed a rest and a top up of alcohol. Jack picked up the wine bottle to refill their glasses when he noticed that Annie hadn't touched hers.

'Not drinking?' He asked

'If I do I'll fall asleep in five minutes with all the sleep I've missed over the past week. I'll be more fun sober!'

'Is that a promise?' He enquired.

'Yes. If you're a good boy!' She agreed.

Jack was just about to sit down when he felt his phone vibrate in his pocket, he checked the number. It was the chairman of the hotel chain.

'Sorry Annie I need to take this.' Jack excused himself and left the room. Annie turned her chair slightly to face the dancers, enjoying a moment to absorb the full atmosphere. It was a long time since she had felt this contented. In some ways she felt as if she had come full circle, back to the beginning. There were still times when she felt the guilt of enjoying herself without Nick, lurking like a large shadow in the background, but Annie being on her own wouldn't bring Nick back. Still, she didn't dare imagine what he would think, if given the chance to tell her. She decided it was best not to think about it at all. The only persons approval she needed was Violet's – and she had that.

At the far side of the room Annie spotted Zach and Pippa making their way towards her, sporting large smiles. She knew instinctively that they were going to make her life a misery regarding the dancing. He was dressed impeccably, looking very dashing and brutally young and Pippa who had youth on her side was dress in a simple yet elegant black gown. They looked every bit as splendid as she and Jack.

'Very nice moves!' Zach complemented, offering Pippa the seat next to Annie and standing behind them. 'I would have asked for payment in dancing lessons had I known!'

'Don't!' she said pointing her finger at him firmly. 'There is more work to be done on the flat and I don't want to make you pay for your comments by giving the job to someone else! – Anyway, how come you didn't tell me you were coming tonight, we could have sat together?'

'Well maybe Jack and Zach are more similar than we realise. I was given the ticket as part of my valentine's present when I got home, so the last time I saw you I didn't know I was coming to the ball either!'

'Well you look sensational on such short notice!'

'Thanks! Piped up Zach before Pippa had time to answer. Annie shook her head in exasperation at him.

'Okay, okay, you look handsome as well; you didn't give me chance to get to you!'

'I always look handsome, but you know that!' The two girls rolled their eyes at his deluded self-worth; they both knew him well enough to know he was joking. 'I've come to ask you to dance Annie?' He said offering her his hand.

'And what about dancing with your girlfriend?' Annie gestured to Pippa.

'She won't mind. I have the rest of the night to dance with her and when Jack comes back you'll be lost to him forever, besides, I told her you were too old for me anyway and she agreed with me' Annie and Pippa shook their heads with disbelief at his string of insults. Annie was enjoying the banter. It was clear to see that they were good together, Zach had never been this much fun when they were working. Pippa was obviously bringing out his fun side. Annie had high hopes for their future together.

'As my age is much greater than yours, you'll be able to understand that my feeble body is out of puff and I won't be able to dance with you, but thank you for the offer'

'My heart breaks Annie!' he said holding his chest 'but I'm not giving up yet.' He took her hand and kissed the back of it.'

'Are you deliberately trying to get me in trouble with Pippa?' Annie suggested.

'No, but it'll keep her on her toes, knowing that I'm the most sought after man in the room, with all my wit and charm.' Pippa and Annie laughed loudly, sparing no thought for his feelings.

'Does this tactic usually work?' Asked Pippa trying to stop laughing.

'Always!' He admitted touching Pippa's cheek. Annie laughed in dis-belief.

'Away with you! Go and take Pippa to dance. That's where you should be!' She shooed them both away.

'I told you she wouldn't dance with me because she was intimidated by my beauty!' He said purposefully in ear shot. Pippa cuffed him on the arm. He blew Annie a kiss, then escorted Pippa on to the dance floor. At the same time, from the other direction, Jack returned, beaming broadly.

'Good news!' He declared kissing Annie on the cheek before he sat down. 'They have agreed that I can stay here and set up the trainee manager's programme. He was trying to shout above the music. Annie was delighted.

'That's wonderful news! – But are you sure it's what you want? You're giving up a lot to stay here?'

'What? - Living on my own in a hotel for a few months, then being transferred and doing the same thing over and over again. It's not what I want and Annie – you know what I want. I want you.' He squeezed the top of her thigh under the table. She playfully pushed him away, aware that people may see.

The band slowed down the tempo of the music. Jack took Annie's hand and squeezed it.

'Dance with me?' He mouthed. She laughed.

'You know where that got us last time don't you?' she questioned.

'I do and I'm hoping for the same response later!' He boasted. She didn't say anything, but the same idea had crossed her mind.

Jack escorted her on to the dance floor. The feel of his body against hers had become a familiar feeling over the past weeks. They moulded together naturally. He pulled her close, dancing with her cheek to cheek He could smell her perfume.

It wasn't the fragrance of the young girl as she had been all those years ago. She was a woman and smelt like one. He was lost in the moment, in her fragrance and her arms. He couldn't help himself from murmuring in her ear.

'Annie, I love you.' She pulled away slightly so she could kiss him on his lips. The spark between them, had always been there, but now it was much stronger.

'I love you to Jack. I wasn't sure at first if we could work through all the years we spent apart, you can't always turn back the clock, but I'm sure now. I know we did the right thing, giving us another go.' He stopped dancing and stared into her eyes. Everyone around them on the dance floor was still moving.

'Jack? What's the matter?' Annie asked confused by his response. Jack didn't answer; he got down on one knee in the middle of the dance floor and pulled a small box out of his pocket. The band leader noticed the commotion around them and stopped the music. It was the second time in the evening Annie was dying from embarrassment. The room was hushed waiting for him to ask the question. Violet, who was privy to the choosing of the ring and had been expecting this moment all evening was standing at the side of the dance floor next to Scarlett.

'Annie. I have loved you my whole life and even though circumstance and sometimes because of people we couldn't be together, I always hoped that one day we would find each other and now that we have, I have no intentions of ever letting you disappear from my life again – So Annie – Please will you marry me?' The whole room was till waiting for her answer. Annie searched the crowd looking for Violet; she was standing close by waiting and watching with everyone else. Violet was smiling proudly, she nodded giving Annie her seal of approval.

'Yes. Yes I will!' Annie threw her arms around Jack, knocking him off balance, they both ended up in a heap on the floor. The crowd around them erupted into a cheer. Once back on their feet Jack placed the diamond square cut diamond ring on to her finger.

'I'm glad it's a diamond.' She smiled, 'they're neutral and go with everything!' Then she kissed him hard and long, oblivious to the world around them. They heard a cough behind them, bringing them back from bliss to the present. It was Violet.

'Well? What do you think?' Annie asked her.

'I think it's about time my mother and father finally married. I'm happy for all of us!' Violet hugged and kissed them both.

'Come on, there should be champagne waiting on our table for us, you too Violet!' When they reached their table Scarlett was waiting with the champagne already opened.

'Jack I am on duty! It's a stackable offence to drink one of the guest's glasses of champagne!'

'You're right!' He said, Violet's face dropped, thinking she was about to miss out on the celebrations. 'But if I suspend you temporarily, then that covers the legalities – Violet you are suspended for the rest of the evening!'

'Yes!' Exclaimed Violet punching the air.

'Annie, Champagne?' Jack passed her a glass, then one to Violet and Scarlett.

'To my fiancé and a short engagement!' Toasted Jack. Annie took the champagne and barely let it touch her lips, no one noticed.

'And thanks for your help Violet.' Jack whispered into her ear. They would tell Annie later that it was all planned and Jack had already asked Violets permission to propose beforehand.

'I do expect to be bridesmaid.' She insisted to seal the deal.

They spent the next hour being congratulated by friends and strangers alike. Annie wanted to speak to Jack on his own, but the task was impossible. She would have to wait to tell him her news. She didn't want to share her secret until the subject concerning his staying or leaving had been settled.

Eventually, the band finished playing and people started to leave. Annie was shattered, completely elated, but shattered. When they knew they wouldn't be missed, Jack and Annie walked slowly up the corridors to their room. Annie was barefoot carrying her shoes in her hand. Jack had undone his tie and was carrying his jacket over his shoulder. Exhaustion was creeping up on Annie, together with a knot in her stomach from anxiety over what she was about to tell him.

'So Annie, when do you want to get married? We'll need a few months to get thing sorted I suppose. Violet has already made me promise she can be bridesmaid. How about an autumn wedding? What about September?' Annie knew that there would be no wedding in September, they would be too busy with another project, but she had never seen Jack so excited. He was the kid in the proverbial toy shop, but she needed him to calm down, she had things to say.

'Why tonight?' she asked him 'why did you ask me to marry you tonight?' she asked him once they were back in their suite.

'I needed you to know that I had planned on staying no matter what the outcome of the board's vote. I figured, if it went our way, it would be a good way to celebrate and if not, then you would know I was serious, it had all been organised before I went to the meeting, whatever the outcome, I had planned to propose to you tonight. I want to be with you and Violet for the rest of our lives.'

'I think Violet may move out one day!' he wanted to let him down gently. He smiled at her sarcasm.

'At least I can enjoy being a 'hands on dad' while it lasts, the eternal bank and taxi? we may get a couple of years before she goes, if we're lucky, at least it'll give me some idea of what you went through with her for all those years.' His words were too close to home.

'Are you sad that you didn't get to be a 'hands on dad' for Violet, when she was growing up?'

'In honesty, yes I am, but there's no point letting the past eat me up, what's done is done, we can't turn the clock back? We have to live with how things turned out and make the future batter for us all.' Annie could feel the palms of her hands perspiring. Maybe now was the time to tell Jack her news. He was going to have to know sooner rather than later.

'Do you think you would ever want to go down the road of nappies and sleepless nights? – Maybe experience it first hand?' She was watching him closely to gauge his true response.

'Are you asking me how I feel about the possibility of having another child - with you?' Jack's face lit up with delight. 'I didn't dare think you'd want to go through it again, especially as, well, we're no spring chickens, but if it happens, well - it would be fantastic news! The best news ever!'

'And if it's already happened?' Annie was shaking with apprehension at his reaction.

'Are you trying to tell me you're pregnant?' Annie nodded.

'Yes Jack I think I am.' Jack folded his arms around her, like he was never going to let her go.

'So there can't be an autumn wedding as we'll be busy with the birth.'

'Well we'll just have to make it sooner! How do you feel about an early spring wedding?' He asked hopefully.

'Perfect!' she agreed, 'As long as it's after Mother's day!' she said guiding him to the large four poster bed behind her.

Printed in Great Britain
by Amazon.co.uk, Ltd.,
Marston Gate.